THE ILLUSTRATED ENCYCLOPEDIA

THE

ILLUSTRATED

ENCYCLOPEDIA

p

CONTENTS

Authors
Francesca Baines, Jack Challoner, Fiona Macdonald and Steve Parker

Designers
Diane Clouting and Phil Kay

Editor
Linda Sonntag

Project Management
Raje Airey and Liz Dalby

Artwork Commissioning
Susanne Grant

Picture Research
Janice Bracken and Kate Miles

Additional editorial help from
Lesley Cartlidge, Jenni Cozens, Libbe Mella and Ian Paulyn

Editorial Director
Paula Borton

Art Director
Clare Sleven

Director
Jim Miles

This is a Parragon Book
This edition published in 2000
Parragon, Queen Street House, 4 Queen Street, Bath, England BA1 1HE, UK

Produced by Miles Kelly Publishing Ltd
Bardfield Centre, Great Bardfield, Essex, England CM7 4SL

ISBN 0-75254-346-6

Printed in Spain

HOW TO USE THIS BOOK

THE ENCYCLOPEDIA is divided into seven sections: Earth and Space, The Living World, Human Body, The Way We Live, Science and Technology, and History. At the back of the book is an Atlas section.

The first six sections contain fifteen different topics, each covered by a double page spread.

On every spread you can find some or all of the following:

- Main text introducing the topic
- The main illustration, designed to inform about an important aspect of the topic
- Smaller illustrations with captions, to describe aspects of the topic in detail
- Photographs of unusual or specialized subjects
- Fact boxes or charts, containing interesting nuggets of information
- Biography boxes about the people who have changed our understanding of the world
- Projects and activities

The different sections are identified by a coloured strip along the top of the page and a specially-designed icon at the top corner. At the end of each section is a page of Questions and Answers relating to the topics covered...
How many will you get right?

EARTH AND SPACE

THE UNIVERSE

WHEN YOU LOOK UP at the sky on a clear night, you are looking out into the Universe. Most of the Universe is just a vast ocean of empty space. But there are islands in the ocean, called galaxies. A galaxy is a huge group of stars, millions of millions of kilometres across. Each star is a huge ball of hot glowing gas like our Sun, only much farther away. Each star that we can see from Earth is in our galaxy, which is called the Milky Way. The Universe contains thousands of millions of galaxies. You may have wondered where the Universe came from. Most astronomers are convinced that it all started as a tiny, very hot ball about 15,000 million years ago. Astronomers believe that in a kind of explosion called the Big Bang, the ball expanded (grew) rapidly, like a balloon being blown up.

In the beginning...

If the Universe really did begin with a Big Bang, then the galaxies in space should still be moving away from each other, like debris thrown out in all directions from an explosion. And this is what astronomers have found – that every galaxy, in every direction, is moving away from us.

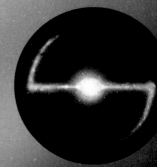

Barred spiral galaxy

Elliptical galaxy

Galaxy shapes

Maybe one day humans will travel out of our galaxy and look back at it. If they do, they will see a huge, slowly spinning white spiral-shaped disc. Many galaxies are spirals like this, but others are egg-shaped (elliptical). A third type of galaxy, irregular, has no regular shape at all.

Spiral galaxy

You are here!

Our nearest star is the Sun. Our planet, Earth, travels around the Sun at a distance of about 150 million kilometres. The next nearest star, Proxima Centauri, lies at a distance of about 40 million million kilometres – nearly 300,000 times as far. Light that reaches Earth from Proxima Centauri has travelled for four years. An astronomer would say that Proxima Centauri is four light years away. The Sun and Proxima Centauri are both part of our galaxy, the Milky Way. It is about 100,000 light years across. The distance to the next galaxy is about two million light years. Light from the most distant galaxies, at the edge of the known Universe, takes about 10,000 million years to reach us.

The nine planets of the solar system orbit the Sun (above, right). Nearest to the Sun is Mercury, followed by Venus, Earth, Mars, Jupiter, Saturn, Uranus, Neptune and Pluto

A star is born

Stars form in huge clouds of gas and dust inside galaxies. These clouds are called nebulae (singular 'nebula'), from the Greek word 'nephos', which means 'cloud'.

What is a star?

The Milky Way galaxy contains about 100,000 million of them. A star is a huge ball of hot gas – the Sun is more than a million kilometres across, for example – more than a hundred times the size of the Earth. Its high temperature means that it glows, just as the element of an electric toaster glows when it is hot, although the Sun is much hotter than a toaster. When a star comes to the end of its life, it may just cool down and stop shining. Some stars explode at the end of their lives in spectacular explosions called supernovae. The largest stars shrink at the end of their lives to become very dense objects called black holes, which can swallow whole stars without growing in size.

Young hot stars

This photograph, which was taken through a telescope, shows a group, or cluster, of stars. They are all hot young stars that have formed from the same nebula, which looks like a blue and pink cloud. Some nebulae are visible to the naked eye as small fuzzy patches of light.

LOOKING AT THE STARS

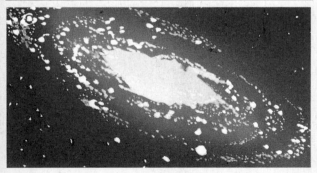

On a dark, clear winter's night, you can see the heart of our galaxy with the naked eye. It is a hazy white band across the sky, which is why it is called the Milky Way. Now find the constellation of Andromeda using a star map. On a clear dark night, it appears as a hazy patch of light. At more than two million light years away, it is the most distant object visible to the naked eye. If you live in the southern hemisphere, try to see the Large and Small Magellanic Clouds: they are 'small' nearby galaxies. All these things look much more spectacular through binoculars. See if you can borrow some.

Holes in space

Some stars become bizarre objects called black holes when they reach the end of their lifetimes. Objects – and even light – anywhere near a black hole are pulled into the hole by a strong gravitational force. Once inside, any material object is stretched and squashed out of existence. Time runs more slowly near a black hole, and stops altogether inside it.

ASTRONOMY

ASTRONOMY IS THE STUDY of the stars, planets and other objects in space. You can see stars, the Moon, some of the planets and the Sun using just your eyes, but a telescope gives a much better view. The telescope was invented about 400 years ago, but astronomy is much older than this. Ancient astronomers in China and Greece could predict when certain events such as eclipses would take place. The ancient astronomers identified patterns in the stars, which they called constellations. They thought that the patterns were pictures of characters from their myths and legends, so they have names like 'Taurus, the Bull' and 'Ursa Major, the Great Bear'. Modern astronomers still think of the stars in constellations, but only for the purpose of identifying stars. Today's astronomers use telescopes that detect radio waves and other rays, as well as light, coming from outer space. They can even study stars and planets using remote-controlled telescopes in space.

A map of the sky

Looking up at the night sky, the stars appear to be painted on a great dome. These two sky-maps show a flattened-out version of the night sky as seen in the southern and northern hemispheres. Which stars you see on a certain night depends on your latitude, the time of year, the time of night and, of course, the weather. At the centre of the northern sky is Polaris, the North Star, which appears to remain above the North Pole.

Astrolabe

The ancient astronomers used complicated devices like this astrolabe to follow the motions of the stars, the planets, the Moon and the Sun across the sky. Today, astronomers track the stars using sophisticated computers and extremely powerful telescopes.

GALILEO

Italian scientist Galileo Galilei was born in Pisa in 1464. He first looked at the night sky through a telescope in 1609, and described the craters on the Moon, the moons of Jupiter and the millions of stars in the Milky Way. He was put in jail by the Catholic Church for suggesting that the Earth orbits the Sun.

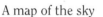

MAKE A TELESCOPE

You can see how a telescope works, using a magnifying glass and a spectacle lens. Hold the magnifying glass at arm's length and hold the other lens about 5cm in front of your eyes. Move both lenses nearer or farther from your eyes until you can see a clear image. The object will not look much closer than you see it with your eyes. The specially designed lenses in a refracting telescope can make things look much closer than the lenses you have used.

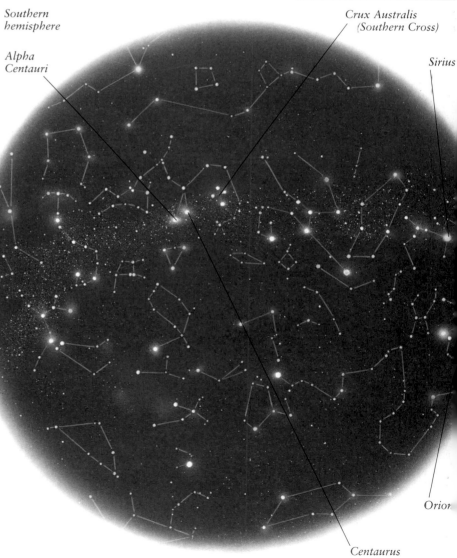

Southern hemisphere

Alpha Centauri

Crux Australis (Southern Cross)

Sirius

Orion

Centaurus

Telescopes

Most telescopes contain lenses and mirrors that allow astronomers to see objects in space much larger and brighter than they appear to the naked eye. You may have looked through a pair of binoculars, which work in the same way. Light from a distant object passes through a lens, or reflects off a mirror and is focused by a lens, to form an image of the object in your eye. The larger the lens or the mirror, the more light the telescope collects and the brighter the image will be. Not all telescopes use light to form images, however. A radio telescope, for example, produces pictures of distant stars and galaxies from the radio waves they give out. There are also telescopes that can form images by detecting infrared, ultraviolet and X-rays.

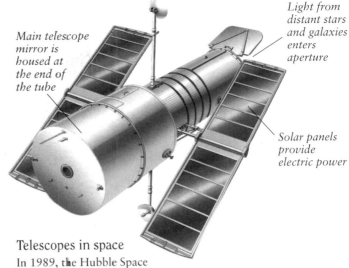

Main telescope mirror is housed at the end of the tube

Light from distant stars and galaxies enters aperture

Solar panels provide electric power

The southern hemisphere

The constellations of the southern skies were given names by the European explorers of the 17th and 18th centuries. Among them are Centaurus, the centaur, a beast that is half-man and half-horse. This contains the nearest star system in the sky, Alpha Centauri, 4.3 light years away. Below Centaurus are the spectacular stars of the Southern Cross, which guided the navigators of the past.

Telescopes in space

In 1989, the Hubble Space Telescope was launched by the Space Shuttle. Because the telescope is above the Earth's atmosphere, it can get a better view of the stars than a telescope on the ground. There are telescopes in space that detect infrared and X-ray radiation as well as light.

Astronomers at work

Most modern astronomers work in buildings called observatories. The domed roof of this observatory slides open, so that the telescope can be directed to any point in the night sky.

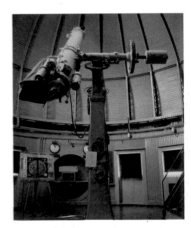

Northern Hemisphere

Polaris

Ground-based observatory (above) and photograph taken by space telescope (below).

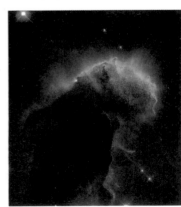

Come closer...

A telescope can make things look closer than they are. You can see craters and mountains on our Moon, and the moons of planet Jupiter, for example. Telescopes with only lenses are called refracting telescopes, while those that use mirrors are called reflecting telescopes. This photograph of the birth of a star was taken by the Hubble Space Telescope.

THE SOLAR SYSTEM

YOU ARE LIVING ON one of nine planets that together with their moons, the Sun, and millions of chunks of rock and ice make up what is known as the Solar System. The chunks of rock and ice are called comets, asteroids and meteoroids. Comets have been described as 'dirty snowballs', which is accurate, except that they are probably made of rock at the centre. There are millions of asteroids, the largest of which is about 1,000 kilometres in diameter. Meteoroids are small pieces of debris left over from the formation of the Solar System some 4,500 million years ago. Every day, tonnes of meteoroids enter the Earth's atmosphere at high speed. Friction with the air heats the meteoroids to white hot, and most vaporize completely in an eye-catching display known as a meteor, or shooting star. The Sun sits at the centre of the Solar System. The other objects, including our own planet, Earth, move around the Sun in paths called orbits.

The Sun and planets

Each of the inner planets, including Earth, is made mainly of solid rock, and has a molten core. The outer planets, except Pluto, are called 'gas giants', because they consist almost entirely of gas. If you could weigh the objects of the Solar System, you would find that the Sun would weigh more than everything else put together.

Orbits

The closer a planet is to the Sun, the less time it takes to complete each orbit. So, while the Earth takes one year, Venus, which is closer to the Sun, takes less than five months. Orbits are shaped like slightly flattened circles called ellipses. All the bodies of the Solar System are held in orbit around the Sun by the force of gravity. Gravitational attraction between the Sun and the Earth is what stops the Earth moving off in a straight line, out of the Solar System. Just as the Earth orbits the Sun, the Moon orbits the Earth, and there are moons orbiting most of the other planets.

Jupiter is by far the largest of the planets. A large red spot on its surface is a huge storm, bigger than the whole of the Earth

Mars is known as the red planet. This is because of the abundance of a chemical compound called iron oxide in its rocks and soil

Earth is the only planet we know to have life. Its atmosphere is rich in oxygen, and there is plenty of liquid water on its surface

Venus is about the same size as Earth. Its thick atmosphere traps the Sun's heat, so the planet is very hot

Mercury is the closest planet to the Sun. It is too hot and too small to have an atmosphere

Sun

Our star

At the centre of the Solar System is our star, the Sun, a huge ball of very hot gas that has more than 100 times the diameter of the Earth. The temperature at its centre is around 15 million degrees Celsius, and heat flows outwards in all directions to the surface.

Inner planets

The four rocky innermost planets and their moons have marks on their surfaces called craters. These are the result of millions of years of bombardment by meteoroids. On Earth and Venus, many of these craters are covered over by molten rock that escapes from beneath the surface.

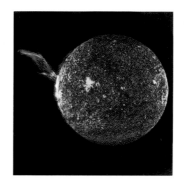

Infrared

This photograph of the Sun (left), taken using a camera sensitive to infrared radiation, shows how active the surface of the Sun is. You can clearly see a solar prominence, a gigantic plume of gas shooting up from the surface.

Gas giants

The planets Jupiter, Saturn, Uranus and Neptune are made mainly of gases, though their cores are liquid and in some cases probably solid. High-speed winds swirl different coloured bands of gas around these planets, making them look like polished marbles.

Uranus and Neptune orbit at huge distances from the Sun. They are cold, lifeless gas giants

Pluto, with its moon, Charon

Saturn is famous for its beautiful set of rings, by far the most impressive in the solar system

Neptune

Odd one out

Planet Pluto is unlike the other outer planets. It is made of rock, unlike the gas giants, and is much smaller than they are. It has an unusual orbit, which for some of the time brings it closer to the Sun than Neptune. Pluto is orbited by its own moon, Charon.

Long-tailed visitor

Comets spend most of their time very far from the Sun. When a comet comes close to the Sun (within a few hundred million kilometres), clouds of gas, ice and dust are thrown off it, forming long tails that can be seen from the Earth.

Shooting stars

Most meteoroids are very small – the size of a speck of dust. Even they can produce a spectacular display when they hit the Earth's atmosphere. Larger meteoroids survive the journey to Earth and once they land they are called meteorites. Only about 3,000 meteorites have ever been found.

GLOSSARY

● Degree Celsius (°C) – a unit of temperature. Normal human body temperature is about 37°C, and water normally boils at 100°C.

● Gravitational attraction – a force between any two objects that pulls them together.

● Molten – another word for liquid, most often used when describing a substance that is normally solid, such as rock or metal.

● White hot – hot enough to glow with a bright white light. The filament of an incandescent light bulb glows white hot.

● Infrared – a type of radiation like light that is invisible to human eyes, though some animals and some camera films are capable of detecting it.

Potatoes in space

We can see asteroids from Earth because they are lit by the Sun. However, they are not bright enough to be seen with the naked eye. Through a powerful telescope, you can see that they are shaped like potatoes. Most asteroids orbit the Sun between the orbits of Mars and Jupiter.

SPACE EXPLORATION

WHEN YOU LET GO of an inflated balloon, air rushes out of the nozzle and pushes the balloon in the opposite direction. Huge rockets that take satellites, space probes and even people into space work in a similar way, except that it is hot exhaust gases, and not air, that escapes. Rockets have taken astronauts into orbit around the Earth, and to the Moon. Satellites that give us a good view of the weather, or enable people to talk to each other across the world, are also launched into orbit by rockets. Rockets were invented nearly 1,000 years ago in China, where they were used as fireworks and weapons. However, it is only in the past hundred years or so that people have thought seriously about the role of rockets in space travel. Only as recently as 1958 was the first satellite launched, and a person first walked on the Moon as recently as 1969. What might space exploration bring us in the next hundred years?

Reaching out
The first ever object that humans put into space was a satellite called Sputnik. It was launched on 4 October 1958, and it orbited the Earth for 92 days, and then burned up as it re-entered the atmosphere.

Up and away
A powerful engine lifts the rocket and its payload, and speeds it up to make it reach escape velocity (see above, right). The payload may be a satellite, a space probe or a spacecraft with people aboard. This picture shows the US Space Shuttle, a 're-usable' space vehicle.

One small step...
In July 1969, American astronaut Neil Armstrong became the first person ever to stand on the Moon. As he stepped down from the spacecraft, Armstrong spoke the now famous words: 'That's one small step for a man, one giant leap for mankind.'

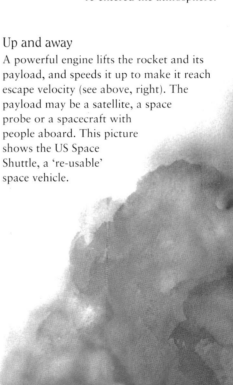

SPACE FACTS

- The first telecommunications satellite relaying telephone and television signals was Telstar, launched in 1962.
- The Space Shuttle was launched in 1982 and there have been more than 70 missions since then.
- Some experts believe that a person will walk on the planet Mars by 2010.

Rocket engines

Inside the engines of most rockets, liquid fuel burns with liquid oxygen, producing huge amounts of hot gas. The gas can escape only through the nozzle at the bottom of the engine, so it is forced downwards. This pushes the rocket in the opposite direction – upwards – with a great force, or thrust. In order to escape the Earth's gravitational pull and not to crash back to Earth, a rocket must reach a speed of about 39,000 kilometres per hour. This is called escape velocity. At this speed, the rocket travels more than 10 kilometres every second! The job of rocket engines does not end when a spacecraft clears the Earth's upper atmosphere. Smaller rocket engines, or retro rockets, are used to steer craft as they move through space.

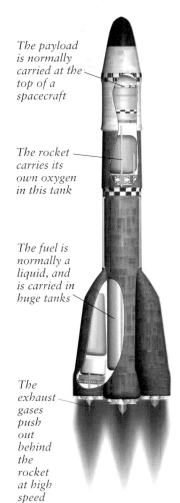

The payload is normally carried at the top of a spacecraft

The rocket carries its own oxygen in this tank

The fuel is normally a liquid, and is carried in huge tanks

The exhaust gases push out behind the rocket at high speed

Into the future

Travelling to the nearest star will take hundreds or even thousands of years. To get there as quickly as possible, future spacecraft may have engines powered by nuclear fusion. These would be able to reach much higher speeds than today's spacecraft.

Probing space

We have explored distant planets, their moons, and also the Sun, comets and asteroids – without ever visiting them. Unmanned spacecraft called probes carry cameras and other equipment, and send back pictures and other data to Earth as radio signals. The Cassini-Huygens probe (right) is in orbit around Saturn.

Looking down

Satellites orbit the Earth. Some of them help us to learn more about our world. From their position high above ground, they produce photographs and make measurements that would be impossible to make from the ground. Other satellites help with weather forecasting (above left) and relay telephone and television signals (above right) around the world.

Is anybody there?

The first object made by people to leave the Solar System was the space probe Pioneer 10. Launched in 1972, it flew past the planets Jupiter and Saturn, and passed outside Pluto's orbit some 17 years later. Aboard is this plaque carrying information about our world.

MAKE A BALLOON ROCKET

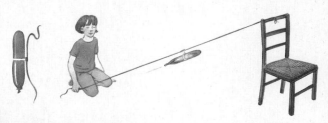

You can make a balloon rocket go in a straight line using string, sticky tape and a drinking straw. Blow up a long straight balloon, and clip the nozzle closed with a hair clip or a bulldog clip. Cut a piece of straw about 2 cm long and tape it to the balloon. Feed a long piece of string through the straw and attach one end to a chair. Now, hold the balloon at the other end of the string, near to the ground, and release the clip. The balloon will shoot up the string towards the chair.

EARTH IN SPACE

IMAGINE HOLDING A BALL in a dark room and shining a torch at it. Half of the ball would be lit up and half would be in darkness. In the same way, the Sun lights up only half the Earth – when you are in daylight, it is night for the people on the opposite side of the Earth. The Earth spins as it moves through space, once every 24 hours, and this explains why we have day and night. Other measurements of time are also determined by the Earth's position in space. For example, a year is the length of time it takes for the Earth to complete each lap of its orbit around the Sun. Similarly, the Moon travels around the Earth, taking about a month on each circuit. During that time, the shape of the Moon varies from a thin crescent to a full circle. Sometimes, the Moon moves between the Sun and the Earth, blocking our view of the Sun. This is a solar eclipse.

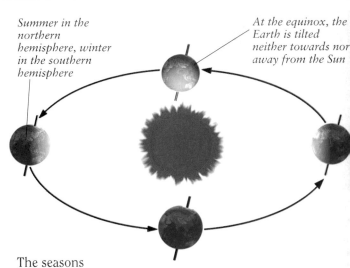

Summer in the northern hemisphere, winter in the southern hemisphere

At the equinox, the Earth is tilted neither towards nor away from the Sun

The seasons

As you can see from the picture, the Earth is tilted slightly in space. This causes the seasons. In June, for example, the North Pole points towards the Sun, so it is warmer in the northern hemisphere than in the southern hemisphere. In December, it is winter in the northern hemisphere and summer in the southern hemisphere. During summer, daytime is longer than night-time. During winter, it is the other way around. There are two times in the year – called equinoxes – when daytime and night-time are of equal lengths, all round the world.

Moon blocks the Sun during a solar eclipse

Day and night

You may find the view of Earth from space surprising. In this photograph, there is a line dividing the parts of the world where it is day and those where it is night. As the Earth spins, the people in the dark move into the light, and those in the light move into the dark. The Moon is in the foreground. It is also in half-shadow, and it too has daytime and night-time. One 'Moon day' lasts more than 20 'Earth days'.

Blocking the Sun

In a total solar eclipse, the Moon passes in front of the Sun, blocking it completely for a few minutes, and darkness falls. A partial eclipse is when the Moon passes in front of the Sun but covers only part of it.

MAKE A SUNDIAL

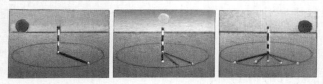

It is easy to track the Sun's movement across the sky by recording the shadow of a stick at various times during the day. On a sunny day, push a long (1 m) stick into the ground. Choose somewhere that will not be in shadow at all during the day. The stick casts a shadow, forming a dark line on the ground opposite the Sun. Place a small stone at the end of the shadow. Do the same each hour for a few hours, and you will have a record of how the Sun has moved. The next day, the shadows will move in the same way. Can you tell the time from where the shadow falls at any time of the day?

Our changing Moon

As the Moon moves around the Earth, different amounts of its lit half are visible to us. The different views of the half-lit Moon that we get during its path around us are the Moon's phases. You can see how this works in the diagram (above).

Moon shapes

When people are asked to draw a picture of the Moon, they most often draw it as a crescent shape. But the crescent is just one of the Moon's shapes, or phases. We only see the Moon at all because the Sun lights it up. Just like the Earth, only half of the Moon is lit up. As the Moon moves around the Earth, we see different amounts of the lit half. At one point of the Moon's orbit we can see none of its lit side. This is called new moon. At a different point of the orbit we can see the whole of the lit side. This is full moon. In between are the other phases of the Moon.

The shadow of the Earth

Occasionally, the Moon seems to disappear from the sky. It doesn't really disappear: the Earth blocks light from the Sun, so we can't see it. These occasions, when the shadow of the Earth falls on the Moon, are called lunar eclipses.

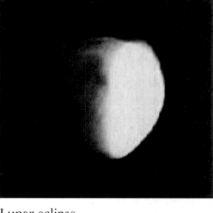

Lunar eclipse
During a lunar eclipse, the size of the shadow on the moon constantly changes, as the Earth moves.

KEY FACTS
● The Earth spins around once every 24 hours.
● The Earth takes one year to orbit the Sun.
● The Moon takes one month to orbit the Earth.
● The different shapes that the Moon has are called its phases.
● During a solar eclipse, the Moon passes in front of the Sun.
● The Sun lights up half the Earth.
● The seasons occur because the Earth is tilted.
● Other planets besides the Earth have moons.

EARTH AND CONTINENTS

OUR PLANET IS NOT AS SOLID as you might think. The ground beneath your feet seems static and stationary, but the Earth's surface actually consists of about ten sections, or plates, that are moving very slowly. These 'tectonic plates' are a little like pieces of a cracked egg shell. The Earth's solid outer layer is called the crust, and it contains a wide variety of materials that people, plants and animals need. The layer beneath the crust is called the mantle, and is made up of rock that is so incredibly hot that it is partly molten (liquid). The movement of this liquid rock shifts the tectonic plates of the crust, a bit like groceries on a conveyer belt at a supermarket checkout. As the plates collide and the crust crumples up under the enormous pressure, mountains form over millions of years. The rocks of the crust contain hidden secrets of Earth's history. Geologists – people who study rocks and minerals – have discovered some of these secrets, and have worked out that Earth was formed around 4,500 million years ago.

EARTH FACTS
● The Earth is 12,756 kilometres in diameter at the equator.
● The diameter at the poles is 12,108 kilometres.
● The average depth of the crust is 35 kilometres.
● The inner core is about 2,400 kilometres in diameter.
● Electric currents in the metallic core produce the Earth's magnetic field.

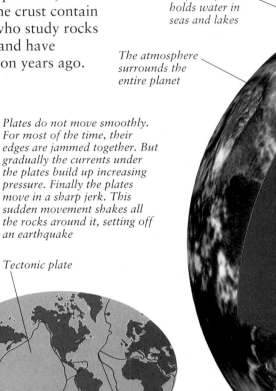

Surface of Earth holds water in seas and lakes

The atmosphere surrounds the entire planet

Down to the core

There is no easy way to take samples from the centre of the Earth, some 6,000 kilometres beneath you. Instead, geologists study how sounds travel through the Earth – from one side of the planet to the other – to try and work out the kind of materials that exist there. They need to use their imagination as well as their surveys to build up a picture of what has never been seen. The centre of the Earth is called the core, and it is a ball made up of two different parts. The outer core consists of melted metals so it is obviously very hot. Surprisingly, the inner core stays solid despite being even hotter. It is, in fact, the hottest part of the entire planet, but is prevented from becoming liquid because of the great pressure.

Plates do not move smoothly. For most of the time, their edges are jammed together. But gradually the currents under the plates build up increasing pressure. Finally the plates move in a sharp jerk. This sudden movement shakes all the rocks around it, setting off an earthquake

Tectonic plate

What's inside?

The Earth is a huge ball, but unlike a tennis ball it is not filled with air. Its core is made mainly of liquid and solid metals, and is surrounded by the mantle, which consists of semi-liquid rock. The solid crust of the Earth is like the skin that forms when a hot bowl of porridge begins to cool. The Earth is more than 12,000 kilometres across, but the crust is no more than 35 kilometres thick. This relatively thin outer coating is made up of plates, as you can see from the map, right.

Mid-Atlantic Ridge

Plate boundary

Where plates part company...

In some parts of the Earth's crust, two neighbouring plates are moving apart. Ridges of rock form between the plates, and some of these can be seen from space. The satellite photo (left) shows the Mid-Atlantic ridge that runs for thousands of kilometres along the floor of the Atlantic Ocean.

Breaking apart

A solid part of the crust can fa into the gap between two plate that are moving apart. That ca happen on land and under the sea. It has happened in Africa, to form the Great Rift Valley (left), which is hundreds of kilometres long. The floor of the valley is very flat, and lies about 1 kilometre below the surrounding land.

Finding your way

For hundreds of years, people have used magnetic compasses to find their way around. The compass needle is a small magnet that lines up with the Earth's magnetic field, which is aligned north–south wherever you are on Earth. The Earth's magnetic field is produced by strong electric currents within the core.

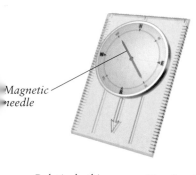

Magnetic needle

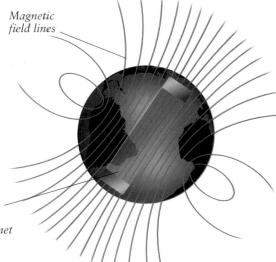

Magnetic field lines

Earth behaves as if it has a huge bar magnet at its centre

Relatively thin, solid crust

Mantle of molten rock

Hot outer core of molten iron, nickel and other minerals

Inner core of hot but solid iron

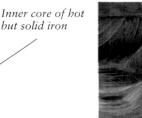

Folding up

The different layers in these sandstone formations were once flat, laid down one on top of the other. They have been folded by the enormous force of two tectonic plates being pushed together. Geologists can tell much about the Earth by studying these folds, called synclines and anticlines.

A moving experience

As the tectonic plates of the Earth's crust slowly move around on the mantle, they carry the continents with them. Geologists have worked out how the continents looked millions of years ago and made a world map of the ancient past.

280 million years ago

180 million years ago

65 million years ago

Where plates collide...

There are two types of crust: oceanic crust, which forms the floor of the deep ocean, and continental crust, which forms the land. When a plate of oceanic crust collides with one made of continental crust, the oceanic crust is always forced downwards. This is called a subduction zone.

Magma pushes through crust

Plates move apart

Subduction zone

Plume of smoke accompanies an erupting volcano

The cone grows each time the volcano erupts, as more lava solidifies

EARTHQUAKES AND VOLCANOES

THE FIREWORKS OF A VOLCANO and the trembling of the earth during an earthquake are two of the most dramatic and terrifying happenings on our planet. They are both caused by the slow movement of the plates of the Earth's crust. A volcano is a place where molten rock, called magma comes to the surface. On land, volcanoes form where rocks have been melted underground as two plates are forced together. When such a volcano erupts, magma is pushed out of it, together with tonnes of ash. Once it is above ground, magma is called lava. It flows down the side of the volcano, devastating the land. Earthquakes are powerful vibrations caused by sudden movements in the Earth's crust. Most tremors are too slight to feel, but a large earthquake can destroy a city.

Submarine volcanoes

Volcanoes are found on the ocean floor as well as on land. They are called submarine volcanoes. When a submarine volcano erupts, it disturbs the ocean, and a huge tidal wave may be produced. Some tidal waves are taller than a house, and very destructive. Most submarine volcanoes are found along ocean ridges – places where two plates are being pulled apart, which makes the crust thinner, allowing magma through. The molten magma solidifies as it meets the cold water of the sea, and the sea water boils. You can imagine what happens to the fish.

Inside a volcano

Most of the time, magma is held safely inside a volcano. A volcano erupts when the magma is pushed out. In a very violent eruption, magma is forced out under great pressure, and the molten rock is shot high in the air in a series of explosions.

Earthquake!

The tectonic plates of the Earth's crust move slowly (a few centimetres per year), but where they collide or rub against each other, they do so with enormous force. When one plate is forced against another, vibrations are set up (imagine the noise of rubbing two heavy stones together). These massive vibrations are earthquakes and can cause great damage.

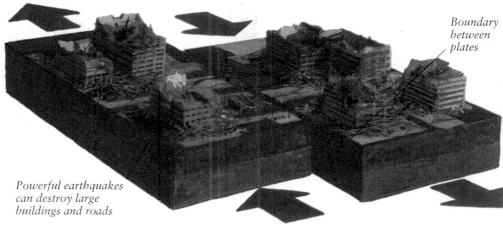

Powerful earthquakes can destroy large buildings and roads

Boundary
between
plates

Danger zones

Volcanoes and earthquakes occur most often along the boundary between two of the Earth's tectonic plates. Cities built near these plate boundaries are most likely to have volcanoes and earthquakes. Children who go to school in these zones have to practise earthquake drills as well as fire drills.

Some earthquake zones are in the middle of oceans, others are on land, where people live

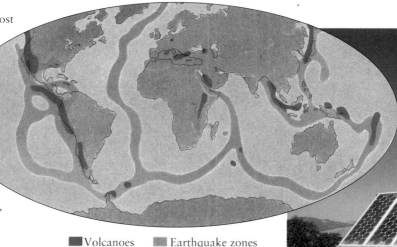

■ Volcanoes   ▨ Earthquake zones

Measuring the quake

Devices called seismographs record the vibrations of the Earth, including those during earthquakes. The seismograph in this photograph is buried under the ground. The readings are sent as radio waves by a radio transmitter, which is powered by a solar panel.

Black smoker

An underwater volcano (left) is sometimes called a black smoker, because huge plumes of black underwater smoke form where magma leaks out through the sea floor. This can kill some living creatures, while others thrive on it.

Mountain of fire

Lava does not erupt from a volcano all the time. Instead, eruptions may happen every few years or perhaps every few hundred years. As lava pours out of the top, or cone, of a volcano, it solidifies – just as hot sauce hardens as you pour it over ice cream. The volcano grows each time it erupts, as more and more lava solidifies on its sides.

MAKE A SEISMOGRAPH

Inside a modern seismograph is a pendulum. You can see how this can monitor the vibrations of the Earth for yourself. Hang a weight from one end of a string, to form your pendulum's bob, and tie the other end of the string to a chair. Now, gently rock the chair to and fro, to mimic the vibrations of the Earth. The pendulum stays motionless as the chair moves. If you attach a felt-tipped pen to the bob, and place some paper beneath it, you can create a record of the vibrations.

ROCKS AND MINERALS

THE SURFACE OF THE EARTH is made up of rocks, although most of them are covered by oceans, forests, cities, rivers and hills. All rocks are made of mixtures of minerals. Different rocks have different recipes, which is why they don't look the same, and some are harder than others. Geologists can identify rocks by the minerals from which they are made. Minerals are chemicals that occur naturally, and they can be different colours such as green, brown, white and red. Minerals are used for many purposes including cement, paint and fuel. Some minerals are called ores and these contain metals like copper, iron, lead and tin. Some are pure metals, such as gold and silver. Rocks are classified into three main types – igneous, sedimentary and metamorphic – depending on the way they were formed. Most rocks consist of crystals with regular shapes and smooth faces that grow in a symmetrical way.

Beautiful minerals

Minerals sought after for their beauty are called gemstones. Many of them are used in jewellery. Some, such as diamonds, are prized for their sparkle, or 'fire'. Others, such as rubies and emeralds, are beautifully coloured. Shown above is Chilean rhodochrozite.

Rock concert

You can often see sand or shells in sedimentary rocks. The mineral grains in igneous rocks are large if the rock is formed slowly. Metamorphic rocks, such as shale, are often flaky and brittle.

Igneous rock

Sedimentary rock

Metamorphic rock

Types of rock

Igneous rock, sometimes called fiery rock, is made from lava that has become solid either above or below the Earth's surface. Most of the Earth's crust is made of this type of rock. Sedimentary rock often covers igneous rock. It is formed by layer upon layer of soil, sand or other small particles deposited by wind or water. These layers are squashed over millions of years and become rock. This type of rock often contains fossils and geologists use these to work out when the layers of sedimentary rock were laid down. The third rock type is called metamorphic. Its name comes from the word metamorphosis which means transforming, or changing. This is a good name because it describes exactly what happens to the rock. The rock is changed by being heated by melted magma or by being forced together by moving plates.

A synthetic diamond made in a laboratory has the same properties as a natural diamond

Unnatural minerals

Certain useful minerals that are very rare are made, or synthesized, in laboratories. The properties of the minerals can be carefully controlled by 'cooking' them at the correct temperature and pressure. These synthetic diamonds will be as hard as natural diamonds, and may be used in a drill or a cutting machine.

Under the microscope, the smallest mineral grains can be observed

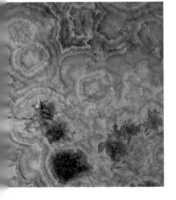

In the field

Geologists are scientists who study the rocks and minerals of the Earth. Much of their work is carried out 'in the field', collecting and classifying rock samples that they study later in their laboratories.

A geologist working in the field collects rock samples by chipping away at a rock face

Rocks to order

Concrete is made with cement, which is produced by heating a rock called limestone. Once mixed with water, the concrete can be poured into moulds and will set hard like a rock, to form strong, long-lasting structures such as bridges.

Out of the ground

Many rocks and minerals are obtained from deep underground, in mines like this one. A lift takes people down to the mine and carries the rocks to the surface. Some rocks are obtained from quarries, that are at ground level. In each case, explosives may be used to break the hard rocks apart.

Grainy rock

Nearly all rocks are made of countless tiny crystals, each called a grain. This close-up of a sample of the igneous rock granite shows the grains. There are three different minerals in this sample, and this explains why the grains are different colours.

New rocks from old

Can you see how rocks are recycled in the Earth's crust? Igneous rocks are made from molten rock called magma, formed from rocks that have melted. Sedimentary rocks are made from bits that are worn away from other rocks. Metamorphic rocks are made from rocks that are at high temperature or under great pressure.

The large wheel drives the lift that carries people deep underneath the ground

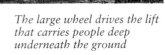

Mineral fuels

Oil and coal are burned as fuel, and are used to generate electrical power, to drive cars and lorries, or to heat our homes. They were made naturally from plants and animals that died millions of years ago, and they have been trapped in rocks ever since.

MINERAL FACTS

- Diamond is the hardest natural substance.

- The word 'mineral' comes from the word 'mine'.

- The colours of precious stones come from 'impurities', normally metal atoms.

- Quartz, used in digital watches, is the most common mineral.

ATMOSPHERE AND OCEANS

WE ARE LIVING IN A KIND OF BUBBLE: the Earth is surrounded by a mixture of gases that make up what is called the atmosphere. Beyond it is space, a hostile environment where there is no air. Life on Earth could not survive without the atmosphere. It provides us with rain and winds, and it protects us from being burnt up by the Sun. The two main gases of the atmosphere are nitrogen and oxygen, but there are other gases too. The atmosphere is divided into several layers, and we live in the layer called the troposphere. This is heated by the Sun. The heat mixes the gases, dust and water in the environment, giving us weather. The oceans are in constant movement. They are affected by the Moon and the winds. Tides are caused by the gravitational pull of the Moon, which makes the sea's level rise and fall, while waves are formed by the blowing of winds across the surface of the oceans.

Journey under the sea

About two-thirds of the Earth's surface is covered by oceans. Imagine a journey from one continent to another along the ocean floor. You submerge beneath the waves at the coastline, and sink gradually deeper as you move along a gentle slope called the continental shelf. Suddenly, the water becomes much deeper as you meet an underwater cliff about 200 metres into your journey. The cliff is huge – perhaps five or six kilometres, and you drop down to the deep ocean floor. Much of this floor is fairly flat, but in some places there are underwater mountains and volcanoes, some high enough to reach to the top of the ocean. When you are near to the other continent, the ocean floor slopes steeply upwards, and you find yourself on another gently sloping continental shelf, before you finally reach the coastline.

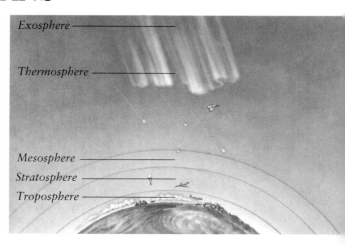

Exosphere

Thermosphere

Mesosphere

Stratosphere

Troposphere

Layers of air

At ground level, you are at the bottom of the sea of air that is the atmosphere. The atmosphere has several levels. The bottom layer, about 20 kilometres thick, is the troposphere. This is where nearly all our weather happens, including the clouds. The uppermost layer is the exosphere, where the air is very thin, or 'rarefied'. The air in the exosphere becomes more rarefied the further up you go, until you reach space, where there is no air at all.

Wave patterns

If you blow across the top of a bowl full of water, ripples appear on the water's surface. In the same way, winds that blow across the ocean's surface disturb the water, producing waves. The waves can travel great distances across the surface. They 'break' when they approach the shore, where the sea is more shallow.

Ocean ridge

Blue skies

Light from the Sun is white, a mixture of all colours. When it passes through the Earth's atmosphere, some of the blue light is sent in all directions. This is why a cloudless sky appears blue in whatever direction you look. The sky is always black on the Moon, because there is no atmosphere.

Have you wondered why sky without clouds is always blue?

Exploring the depths

There is no better way to find out about the bottom of the ocean than to pay it a visit. Submarines called submersibles explore the depths of the ocean. They are normally controlled from a ship at the surface.

The powerful sea

The gravitational pull of the Moon and the Sun cause the sea level to rise and fall twice every day. The rising and falling of the sea level are called tides. There is a huge amount of energy in the tides, and this can be harnessed by a tidal power station, like this one in France. The moving water works machines that generate hydroelectricity.

Air pressure

Air has weight. The weight of the air above you pushes you in all directions. This push is called pressure, and can be measured using an instrument called a barometer. One type, called an aneroid barometer, consists of a metal can attached to a needle. As the pressure increases, the can crushes more, and the needle moves up a dial.

An aneroid barometer measures atmospheric pressure

Where land meets sea

The waves that beat on the shore gradually wear away, or erode, the rocks of the shore. This erosion creates the interesting shapes of coastlines. Huge chunks of coastline may erode, leaving a rock 'stack' out in the sea. Waves break up rock into smaller and smaller pieces. Sand itself is made from tiny pieces of rock that have been ground down by the waves.

The sea floor

It is a strange, dark world at the bottom of the oceans. Underwater mountains called sea mounts rise from the flat ocean floor, and in some places run long cracks in the Earth's crust called ridges. In these ridges, molten rock leaks out from the Earth's mantle and solidifies to form new rock.

JACQUES COUSTEAU

Underwater explorer Jacques Cousteau invented the aqualung, which allows divers to breathe under water, and made many scientific discoveries in the oceans. Cousteau became well known during the 1960s and '70s, when he made popular television programmes that brought the magic of the oceans to millions of people.

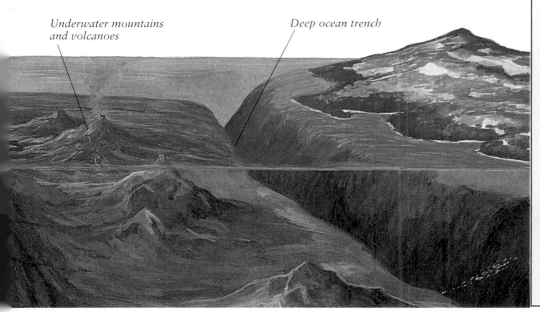

Underwater mountains and volcanoes

Deep ocean trench

WEATHER AND CLIMATES

THE EARTH HAS A HUGE VARIETY of
weather. The weather affects our way of
life: where we live, how we dress, what crops
we grow and what we eat. People who live in
hot dry areas live very differently from those who
live in cold and wet conditions, for example. Some
areas have weather that stays quite similar all year, while
other areas experience enormous changes from season to
season. Meteorologists – scientists who study weather – work
out the average weather over many years and these conditions
are called climates. There are three main climates: cold, warm
and temperate, and they are all patterns of heat, water and
moving air. The Sun's heat evaporates water from oceans, making
clouds. These are blown by the wind and eventually they drop
rain on warm areas and snow on cold areas. The position of the
Earth in relation to the Sun also affects the weather. At the South
and North Poles, the Sun is always low in the sky, making it dark
and very cold for much of each year.

WEATHER FACTS

- Weather forecasters use a kind of
radar to chart rainfall.

- Low atmospheric pressure generally
means that bad weather is on its way.

- Wind speed and strength is
sometimes measured according to the
Beaufort Scale, which classifies winds
with numbers from 0 (calm air) to
17 (destructive hurricane).

Twister
A tornado can be devastating.
Its swirling winds travel at up to
800 kilometres per hour. At the
centre of a tornado, the air shoots
upwards, and this can uproot trees
and hurl cars into the air. The air
inside the tornado is very cold,
and mist forms. This is why a
tornado looks like a rapidly
rotating cloud.

Telling the future?
Weather watchers across the world make
millions of measurements every day to keep
track of temperatures and rainfall. These
include information from
weather satellites. If you
know how the weather is one
day, you can work out what
it might do the next.

How air moves

If you have ever held your hand above a hot radiator, you will probably know that hot air rises. Cooler air moves into the space left behind by the warm air, and this creates a slight breeze. This circulation of air above a radiator is called a convection current, and winds are caused by convection currents. For example, during the morning, air above beaches rises. Cooler air from above the sea moves into its place, creating a gentle sea breeze. Winds do not blow in straight lines. The Earth's spin makes winds twist around in a spiral. If this spiral becomes very tight, the twisting winds blow at enormous speeds. This is a tornado. Our planet's winds mix warm and cold air together, and help to move clouds around.

Global weather

The world's weather is like a huge machine. Convection currents move air like gigantic conveyor belts around the planet. These are driven by the Sun heating up some parts of Earth more than others. Warm air picks up water from the oceans, which drops as rain or snow when warm and cold air mix.

On a global scale, wind directions are determined by the spin of the Earth. Around the equator, for example, winds blow from east to west

Sea breezes

Land warms more quickly in the morning sun than water does. This is why the air above a beach becomes warmer than the air above the sea. Air from the sea moves on to the land as the warm air rises. In the evening, after the Sun goes down, the land cools more quickly than the sea, and the breeze is in the opposite direction.

Sea breezes in the morning (above) and evening (below)

What's that cloud?

Meteorologists identify clouds based on their height and appearance. Cirrus clouds are wispy and high up; stratus clouds are lower down and look like blankets of cloud. There are 10 main types of cloud.

Nimbocumulus clouds are fluffy and low, and can bring thunderstorms

Cirrocumulus are wispy and high up and are generally seen during fine weather

Where in the world?

The climate of a place depends on where it is in the world. A place near the equator is normally hot, because the Sun is always high in the sky there. Climate depends on other factors too, including whether it is inland or on the coast, and its altitude.

Frozen water

When the temperature drops below 0°C, water freezes. Many clouds are made of crystals of ice, not drops of water. The ice crystals melt as they fall, to give rain. If it is below freezing at ground level, the crystals do not melt, but fall as snow.

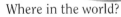

Cumulus clouds are fluffy clouds that can bring light rain

EARTH'S BIOSPHERE

THE PART OF THE EARTH WHERE life exists is called the biosphere. It stretches from the lower layers of the atmosphere down to the very bottom of the deepest ocean and even a few metres under the ground. The biosphere contains the complete collection of all living things, from plants and animals to fish and human beings. All of these elements are dependent upon one another and they are connected together in intricate patterns. If one part of the chain is damaged in some way, all of the other parts will be affected. Along with plants and animals, gases and water in the atmosphere itself, as well as rocks and soil, are involved in sustaining the biosphere. Plants, for example, take water and nitrogen from the soil, energy from the Sun and carbon dioxide from the air. They give water and oxygen to the air. Animals also use the soil and the plants themselves and these cycles are vital to sustaining life.

Living together

Different regions of the world have their own tailor-made patterns of interconnected life. These are groups of living things that are specially designed for their specific environment. The groups can be enormous. Imagine the rich variety of plants, insects, birds and animals that inhabit a rainforest. These living things would not survive in a desert, on a mountain or in an ocean. Each of these areas has its own set of patterns and collections of living things and they are known as biomes. In each of these biome systems, there are different ecosystems – particular groups of living things that depend upon each other for their survival. Humans are also part of ecosystems and biomes.

Where in the world?

The distribution of the world's biomes is closely related to the locations of different climates. Some – such as deserts and rainforests – even have the same name. Most plants and animals that live in a particular biome would not survive long in any other biome.

- temperate deciduous forest
- savannah
- grassland
- tundra
- rainforest
- coniferous forest
- chaparral (scrubby land)
- desert

Cycles in the biosphere

All animals depend upon oxygen. They take it in, and breathe out carbon dioxide. During the day, plants take in carbon dioxide and give out oxygen. If they did not, all the oxygen in the biosphere would soon be used up, and all the animals would then die.

Emerald forest

Rainforests are found in hot, wet parts of the world, around the equator. Living things need heat and water, so the rainforest biome is home to millions of different species of plant and animal. Plants grow very quickly in the humid warmth. Trees fight for sunlight, which they need to grow. The dense layer of leaves formed by rainforest trees is called the canopy. There are many different ecosystems existing side by side in a typical rainforest.

Life in danger

Animals eat plants or other animals to survive and grow. Gorillas and orang-utans (shown above) depend on the rainforest for their survival, and they have been lost in many areas where people have cut down the forest. Animals can also be hunted to extinction; the numbers of white tigers have dropped dramatically through hunting, and the animal may soon become extinct.

The mists of the forest

Water evaporates, forming water vapour, in warm weather. So, the air in a rainforest is a 'saturated vapour', which means that it carries as much water as it can. This is why millions of tiny droplets of liquid water form in the air, creating the fine, wet mist that you can see.

The rainforests contain more than half of the world's living species. Many of them are now threatened with extinction. Huge forest fires in 1997 and 1998 destroyed large areas of rainforest

UNDER THREAT

● Millions of rainforest trees are cut down every day, to make paper or to clear land for building or farming. This affects millions of animals.

● Ocean ecosystems are also affected by the activities of people. The numbers of fish in the ocean has been severely reduced by over-fishing.

● In the 1950s, large amounts of mercury found their way into a lake in Japan. People living in a nearby village suffered from mercury poisoning when they ate the fish.

● The animals most in danger from the activities of people are the predators, which are at the top of the food chain, because they eat other animals.

New situations

Plants and animals are adapted to living in their particular ecosystems. Human activity on our planet can create new ecosystems to which animals and plants adapt. In many parts of the world, foxes have come to rely on large cities for their supply of food.

Small world

An ecosystem can be as small as a drop of water. Several types of bacteria (micro-organisms) live in this drop of water (left). They depend upon nutrients dissolved in the water. An ecosystem may be much larger, perhaps as big as a large forest or a whole desert.

EARTH IN DANGER

THE EARTH'S SIX BILLION PEOPLE are all using the planet's resources of materials and energy. As we use up these resources, we produce vast quantities of waste. These actions can disrupt the natural patterns of the biosphere, and upset the fine balances in the natural world. For example, changes to the cycles of gases in the biosphere can have far-reaching effects that people sometimes do not notice until it is too late. Scientists argue about the importance of these effects, some saying that they are terrible and others that they are really quite unimportant. But most scientists agree that humans are pumping too much carbon dioxide into the atmosphere by running cars and by polluting with factories and heavy industry. The extra carbon dioxide seems to be causing a rise of temperatures all around the world known as the enhanced greenhouse effect. This, in turn, seems to be causing sea levels to rise as the polar ice caps melt, affecting the world's climate and weather patterns.

A load of rubbish
The wrapping from the sandwich someone ate last week might be among the rubbish in this landfill site. Once the site is full, topsoil is piled on top of the rubbish. Think how much material is produced each year by the inhabitants of just one town. How much of the rubbish could have been reused or recycled?

Greenhouse effect

Burning fossil fuels, such as oil, coal and natural gas, releases carbon dioxide into the atmosphere. Carbon dioxide is called a greenhouse gas, because it collects high in the atmosphere and traps some of the Sun's energy underneath it, like a greenhouse. This 'greenhouse effect' is natural, and controls the Earth's temperature. But too much carbon dioxide in the atmosphere could lead to the Earth warming up too much. This could cause the polar ice caps to melt. Sea levels would then rise, flooding many cities. We need to use less electricity and to share public transport to reduce the discharge of polluting gases.

Greenhouse gases

Up in smoke
Smoke and a variety of gases rise up through large factory chimneys like this one. Some of these gases can mix with water in the air and produce 'acid rain', which can damage trees and other plants. Large enough amounts of gases can change the atmosphere forever.

A river of change

We throw huge quantities of bleach, shampoo, washing powders and other substances down into the sewers every day. Some of these chemicals eventually find their way into rivers and seas, where they kill fish and other living things.

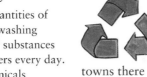

Save the planet!

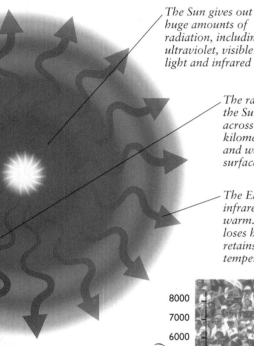

It is not all bad news, though. There are ways to stop the problem getting any worse and to slow down the destruction. In most towns there are large bins where people can put their household waste for recycling. Glass, paper, fabrics, tin cans and plastic can all be crushed, washed or melted and then used again. Most modern engineers try to design cars, household appliances and other machines that are kinder to the environment, while manufacturers and supermarkets are under pressure to cut down on wasteful packaging. You can be an environmental activist and help to protect the Earth's resources, by being energy-efficient and by reusing or recycling things in your home and at school. You will also be doing a great job if you can tell your family and friends about ways in which they can help too.

The Sun gives out huge amounts of radiation, including ultraviolet, visible light and infrared

The radiation from the Sun travels across 150 million kilometres of space, and warms the surface of the Earth

The Earth gives out infrared because it is warm. This is how it loses heat, and retains a proper temperature balance

Extra amounts of greenhouse gases such as carbon dioxide prevent some infrared from leaving the planet, making it warmer than it should be

Secondhand goods

Used glass bottles can be melted down and made into new glass. This is recycling, and many other materials can be recycled in this way. The picture shows crushed cans, newspapers and plastic bottles packed ready to be taken to the local recycling bank. Is there a recycling bank near you?

The Earth's lungs

The Earth's tropical rainforests are rich in plant and animal life. The trees produce millions of cubic metres of oxygen every day, which animals, including humans, need to survive. But humans are destroying over 30,000 square kilometres of rainforest every day. The wood is used for furniture and paper, while the cleared land is used for farming.

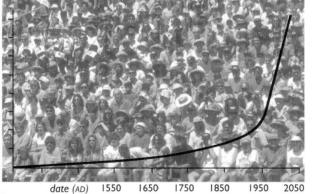

people (millions) — 8000, 7000, 6000, 5000, 4000, 3000, 2000, 1000

date (AD) 1550 1650 1750 1850 1950 2050

ECO FACTS

1 The population of the world has doubled, from three billion to six billion, in the last 30 years.

1 An apple core normally takes about a week to decay, while a plastic bag may take hundreds of years.

1 Ozone – a naturally occurring gas in the atmosphere – protects life on Earth from the harmful effects of ultraviolet radiation. Some gases produced in factories reduce or 'deplete' the amount of ozone in the atmosphere.

On the increase

The world's human population reached its first billion only 200 years ago. It now stands at around six billion, and is rising steadily. Each person needs energy and materials to live, but can the Earth cope?

Bulldozers clear many trees each day

EVOLUTION

FOR AS LONG AS THERE have been people on Earth, there have been questions about how and why life exists as it does. Many different ideas and explanations have been suggested over the years. Scientists have shown that the idea known as evolution is the best explanation. They have proved that the idea works by looking at fossils and by studying the way in which animals and plants adapt themselves to changes in their environments. Animals and plants that are well suited to their environment will survive best and pass on their characteristics to the following generations. Groups of plants or animals that share similar features are a kind of family, known as a species. Scientists can look backwards into history and show that all species come from the same ancient parents. Each living thing is a blend of older and newer features, and each species is always developing and adapting, and this branching out looks rather like an enormous and complicated family tree.

Looking back

Older sedimentary rocks are lower than the later ones, because they were laid down first, and so digging down into the rocks is like looking back through geological history. Most plant and animal remains are lost forever when they die, because their bodies decay, but some are preserved in sedimentary rocks. By studying these fossils of animals and plants, scientists have been able to trace the evolution of many species.

The woolly mammoth, shown here, became extinct at the end of the last ice age, about 10,000 years ago

Natural selection

The peppered moth spends much of its time on tree trunks. Its wings are light grey and look like small pieces of the trees' bark. This hides them from predators such as birds. In industrial areas during the 19th century, the bark of trees became darker with smoke and other pollution. This made the moths stand out against the bark, and many more were eaten by the birds. A small proportion of the moths were darker grey, so they were safer resting on the polluted tree bark. More of these moths survived, passing their darker colouring on to the next generations. Gradually the whole species has changed to have darker colouring. This process is called natural selection, and it is one of the main ideas in the theory of evolution.

CHARLES DARWIN

The English naturalist Charles Darwin (1809–82) developed his ideas about evolution into a proper scientific theory. His book 'The Origin of Species', published in 1859, explained the principle of natural selection.

Hairs kept the mammoth warm in the cold conditions in which it lived

Reaching up and down

People have long wondered how the giraffe got its long neck. Fossils show that ancient ancestors of the giraffe had much shorter necks and shorter legs. Over millions of years, giraffes' legs grew longer, so that they could reach leaves higher in the trees. People think that the neck grew longer too, so that giraffes could still reach down to drink water.

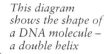

Genetics

Once the idea of evolution was accepted, scientists began to wonder how characteristics of animals, such as their colouring, could be passed from generation to generation. This is called inheritance. The rules of inheritance were worked out, and were named 'genetics'. The key to genetics lies in a chemical called DNA (deoxyribonucleic acid), found in all living things. Your DNA is like a blueprint for your body, and is unique to you. When a man and a woman have a baby, the baby's DNA comes from the mother and the father, and this is how characteristics such as eye colour and hair colour are passed on. Members of a species that are successful and produce offspring pass on their DNA, and so their characteristics, to the next generation.

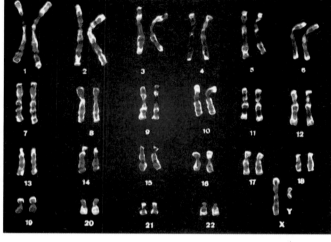

This diagram shows the shape of a DNA molecule – a double helix

DNA is found in the nucleus of every cell in your body

Information is carried along the length of DNA

Dead and gone

As plant and animal species evolve, they develop. This change means that each year some species become extinct, and most fossils are of plants and animals that have already been extinct for millions of years.

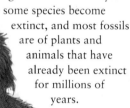

Chromosomes

The DNA inside cells of a living thing is found in lengths called chromosomes. Every human being has 46 chromosomes, in 23 pairs. One member of each pair comes from each parent. Chromosomes can be photographed under a microscope, and the photograph manipulated to show the chromosomes in a standard arrangement called a karyotype. This karyotype is of a male human being.

EVOLUTION FACTS

1 Identical twins have exactly the same information in their DNA.

1 The 'human genome project', begun in 1990, is an international effort to decode the information in human DNA. It will be finished in 2005.

1 Mistakes in the copying of DNA from one generation to the next are called mutations.

1 Life on Earth seems to have begun around 3,500 million years ago, as simple one-celled organisms in the sea.

1 Human beings evolved from apes, about three million years ago.

FOSSILS AND DINOSAURS

Head at a height of about 12 metres

FOSSILS ARE PRODUCED over millions of years as sedimentary rocks form in layers around dead animals, plants and insects. The layers help paleontologists – people who study fossils – to work out when the plant or animal lived. In some cases, bones are preserved in a fossil, but mostly, minerals from the rocks filled the gaps that the plant or animal made when it decayed. Either way, a solid imprint forms in the rocks, and that is a fossil. Plants can become fossils only if they were buried in soil and flattened quickly, otherwise they decay before a fossil imprint can be made. Among the best fossils are those of shellfish. Because they lived and died under water, they were fossilized before they had a chance to decay.

Great collectors

Paleontologists are always hunting for ever more fossils. Some do this just for fun, or to make collections, but others study fossils hoping to discover how long-extinct animals lived, or what ancient species of plants looked like. Most fossil collections contain ammonites. These were creatures that lived between 408 and 66 million years ago. Fossils of these animals are commonly found in sedimentary rock that formed at the sea bed. A modern animal, the pearly nautilus, is a direct descendant of the ammonite.

Brachiosaurus lived in Africa, North America and Europe

Terrible lizards

Dinosaurs – the word means 'terrible lizards' – were one of the most successful species ever to have lived on Earth. We know about their lives through their fossilized remains. They were reptiles, the first animals that could survive well on land. By matching dinosaur fossils with the calendar of the Earth's history that the layers of rock have given us, paleontologists have decided that dinosaurs were wiped out in a mass extinction around 65 million years ago.

DINOSAUR FACTS

There are two orders of dinosaurs: Ornithischia and Saurischia.

● Ornithischia all evolved from a single species.

● Saurischia do not come from a common ancestor.

Stegosaurus, like other dinosaurs, had dry, scaly skin

Why did dinosaurs become extinct?

Many paleontologists believe that around 65 million years ago a large meteorite hit the Earth. The impact is thought to have caused climate changes that killed vegetation and destroyed much of the dinosaurs' food. With such a shock to the environment the dinosaurs could no longer survive.

Jurassic Park

Some small animals have been preserved in fossilized tree sap, called amber. This insect may have fed off a dinosaur's blood.

Animal dies

Soft parts rot

How fossils are formed

When an animal or plant dies, it falls on to the sand under the sea or into mud or sand on the land. The soft parts rot, but hard parts such as bones and teeth do not. Sedimentary rocks form from sediment around the remains of the animal or plant. The hard parts of the skeleton are gradually replaced over millions of years by minerals from the rock-forming sediment.

Minerals fill the space of the soft body parts

Fossil

The dimetrodon was like a modern lizard, but could grow to be 3.5 metres long.

Large lizard

The Dimetrodon was a large reptile with a distinctive smile, which lived before the dinosaurs, around 250 million years ago. The sharp teeth show that it was a predator, and the sail on its back may have been used to control the body temperature, in the same way that an elephant uses its ears today.

Feathers like modern birds

Shape like a small dinosaur

Early bird

A peculiar dinosaur was archaeoptderix. This artist's impression was worked out from fossils of the species. Some people think it is a 'missing link' in evolution, between dinosaurs and birds. Archaeopterix lived between about 160 and 140 million years ago, and was typically the size of a large chicken. Studies of the arrangement of its feathers indicate that it could probably fly.

Strong legs supported the weight of the brachiosaurus, which probably spent most of its time in water

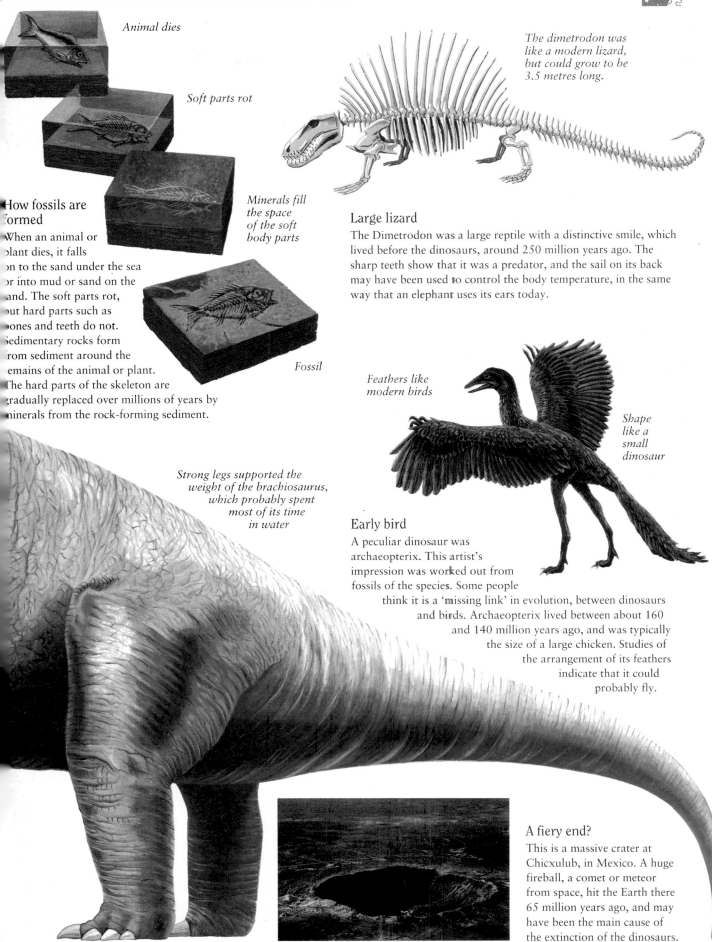

A fiery end?

This is a massive crater at Chicxulub, in Mexico. A huge fireball, a comet or meteor from space, hit the Earth there 65 million years ago, and may have been the main cause of the extinction of the dinosaurs.

THE FIRST HUMANS

HUMAN BEINGS HAVE BEEN LIVING on Earth for millions of years, and like all other living things our development has been affected by the process of evolution. Paleontologists have used fossil evidence to discover information about our ancestors. The earliest fossils have mainly been found in Africa and show how we have evolved from apes. The family that includes humans and some apes is called Hominids and first appeared on Earth around three million years ago. Modern humans – a species called Homo sapiens – are descended from these early Hominids. As they developed, their brain size increased, the skull became higher and the face flatter. Earlier Homo sapiens had a similar appearance to us, but with a prominent forehead and a sloping skull. In recent years, scientists have been able to use new technologies to show that human DNA is almost identical to other creatures in the Hominid family. Gradually, over the past 500,000 years, humans have learned to make and use fire, farm the land, and eventually to live in permanent settlements.

Home sweet home

Olduvai Gorge in northern Tanzania, Africa, is one of the richest sites of for fossils of early Hominids. As many as 50 Hominid specimens, dating as far back as four million years, have been found here, along with evidence of primitive tools and shelters.

Hunter-gatherers

Early humans wandered from place to place, gathering fruits and berries, and hunting animals to eat. It was not until about 10,000 years ago that humans started to settle and farm their food. This artist's impression shows a group of European hunter-gatherers. They have made their own shelters and are using fire to cook and keep warm. The first real city was still a long way off. It was not built until about 8,000 years ago.

A direct link?

The jaws and teeth of Ramapithicus, that lived between eight and 15 million years ago, are more similar to those of modern humans than to apes. This has led experts to suggest that Ramapithicus is a missing link in the evolution of apes to humans.

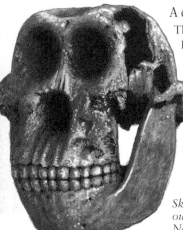

Skull of Ramapithicus, our ancient ancestor. Note the heavy ape-like jaw

Family tree

Some of the earliest humans were called Homo habilis and there is evidence that they used tools and hunted. They made hand axes and other tools from stone and these have been found in Africa, along with fossil evidence of the species. Fossils of a more recent ancestor, Homo erectus, have been found in Southeast Asia as well as in Africa, suggesting population growth. One form of Homo sapiens was called Neanderthal Man and looked very similar to modern day humans. This branch of the family is thought to have existed about 200,000 years ago. It is possible that the species died out completely, or that the Neanderthal people bred with another form of Homo sapiens. These early humans showed signs of social organization. It has been shown, for example, that they had special places where they buried people.

First light

Humans have been around for several million years, but it was only about half a million years ago – when they lived in caves to shelter from the weather and wild animals – that they discovered how to make fires and use them for heating and lighting. More recently, people used fires for cooking, and – as recently as 4,000 years ago – for smelting metals from ores.

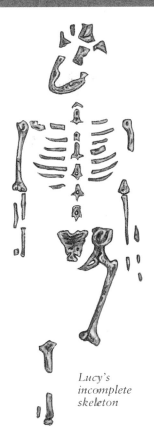

Lucy's incomplete skeleton

The right tools

Homo sapiens is among very few animal species that make and use tools. Early humans made tools from a hard mineral called flint. They chipped away at pieces of flint to make a sharp edge, which could be used as a knife, an arrowhead, or attached to a piece of wood as an axe.

Old woman

In the 1970s and '80s, many fossils of early humans were discovered in a small region of Ethiopia, Africa. One of the fossils was given the official name AL 288–1, but she was affectionately called 'Lucy'. The fossilized bones are about four million years old.

Old man

More and more skeletons of early humans are found every year, and together they help to piece together the story of evolution from apes to humans.

The first Hominids to walk upright were Homo erectus. This is a computer-generated picture showing what Homo erectus looked like.

Homo erectus lived around 800,000 years ago

HOMINID FACTS

● The oldest known Hominid species is Ardipithicus ramidus. It is dated at 4.4 million years.

● Homo habilis was probably the first Hominid with the ability to speak. Its skull has a bulge in the brain in a position related to our ability to talk.

● The name for modern humans is Homo sapiens sapiens. Our species, Homo sapiens, appeared over 100,000 years ago.

Big heads

These pictures show how the shape and size of the skull changed as humans evolved from apes. The ape's skull is smaller, and with a flatter forehead. The modern human has a much larger space for his or her brain.

EARTH AND SPACE: QUESTIONS AND ANSWERS

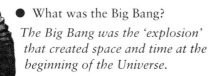

● What was the Big Bang?

The Big Bang was the 'explosion' that created space and time at the beginning of the Universe.

● What is a star made of?

Stars begin as clumps of mainly hydrogen gas. The hydrogen gradually converts to helium, as well as small amounts of some other elements, during nuclear reactions. The energy released by the reactions makes the stars shine.

● The Hubble Space Telescope is in orbit around the Earth. What is the main advantage of putting a telescope into orbit?

A telescope that is in orbit observes the sky from above the atmosphere. This gives a much clearer view.

● Why are comets called dirty snowballs, and why is this name not quite right?

A comet is mostly ice and dust, a bit like a dirty snowball, but there is rock at its centre.

● Pluto orbits the Sun, just like the other planets, and even has a moon. So why do some astronomers not consider it as a planet?

Unlike other planets, Pluto's orbit is very eccentric (far from circular), and it is not a gas giant like the outer planets are. Pluto is probably more like an asteroid.

● Which units of time are based on the following?
(i) the Earth orbiting the Sun once.
(ii) the Earth spinning around once.
(iii) the complete cycle of the phases of the Moon.

(i) A year.
(ii) A day.
(iii) A month.

● What blocks the light from the Sun during (i) a solar eclipse and (ii) a lunar eclipse?

(i) During a solar eclipse, the Moon blocks light from the Sun, casting a shadow on the Earth.
(ii) During a lunar eclipse, the Earth blocks sunlight that would have fallen on the Moon, and the full Moon becomes dark for a few minutes.

● Planet Earth's solid outer layer is called the crust. What are the names of the two types of crust?

The two types of crust are called continental and oceanic crust.

● How do rift valleys form?

A rift valley forms when two tectonic plates are moving apart, and a piece of land falls down between them. The sides of a rift valley are straighter than the sides of a normal valley.

● What are the three types of rock?

The three types of rock are igneous (formed as molten rock solidifies), sedimentary (formed as sediment such as mud or sand is compacted), and metamorphic (formed as rocks of one of the other types are changed by heat or pressure).

● Why are coal and oil called fossil fuels?

The fossil fuels are so called because they formed from plants and animals that lived millions of years ago.

● What are the two most abundant (most common) gases in Earth's atmosphere?

The most abundant atmospheric gases are nitrogen and oxygen.

● Why is the sky blue?

Light from the Sun is white, because it includes light of all different colours. When sunlight passes through Earth's atmosphere, it bounces off gas molecules in the air, and is scattered in all directions. The blue light is scattered much more than other colours, and so you see blue wherever you look in the sky.

● Most winds are caused by convection currents. How do convection currents form?

Warm air rises, and cold air moves in to take its place. If there is a source of heat where the warm air was, then the cold air will be warmed, and that, too, will rise.

● Why is recycling a good idea?

It requires less energy to manufacture recycled materials than to make them from scratch. Also, recycling uses less of Earth's precious resources.

THE LIVING WORLD

THE VARIETY OF LIVING THINGS

THERE ARE MANY different kinds of living things. Look around yourself and you may see grass, trees, flowers and other plants. Also insects, spiders, birds and other animals. (And, of course, people.) But in an unfamiliar place, like a mountain-top or seashore pool, it could be difficult to identify living things, or even tell them apart from non-living ones. A mountain 'pebble' could be a stone-plant. A seashore 'pebble' could be a mussel or oyster. What makes something alive, compared to non-living things like water, diamonds, sand and clouds? Living things have three main features. First, they take in some form of energy and use it for life processes. Second, they take in raw materials and use them to grow. Third, they reproduce or breed – make more of their kind.

The five kingdoms

Many years ago, people thought there were two kingdoms of living things – plants and animals. Fungi such as mushrooms were regarded as strange types of plants. However, most biologists now agree there are five kingdoms – monerans, protists, fungi, plants and animals. Differences between kingdoms include their types of microscopic cells (see Smallest units of life) and how they get their energy. Each moneran or protist is only one cell. Each plant or animal has many cells. Some fungi are one cell, others many. However, there are other schemes for grouping or classifying living things into kingdoms. Some of these schemes are made up of more than 20 kingdoms.

WHO NEEDS TO KNOW?

The study of life and living things is called biology. Why learn about it? There are many reasons:

● To improve farming methods, for more and healthier foods.

● To care properly for our pets, farm animals and other creatures.

● To fight harmful living things, such as germs and parasites, that cause disease.

● To understand about wild plants and creatures, conserve nature, reduce the effects of pollution and improve our environment.

● To understand how our own bodies work, and to improve our health and medical care.

Life all around us

A countryside scene may seem quiet and peaceful. But living things are growing, thriving, feeding and breeding. In this type of landscape, most of the living things are there because people want them. Large animals like cows and horses munch the grass, and the grass itself is grown to feed them. The plants of the hedgerow are trimmed and help to keep these livestock animals in their fields. But more natural or 'wild' living things can still occur. Poppies brighten the roadside verges, and rabbits hide in the long grass. Some people may regard these as pests. However, other people say that pests are simply living things existing where they are not wanted.

Petals of poppy flower

Ripe poppy seed-head

Monerans

The three kinds of monerans are viruses, bacteria and blue-green algae. Their unique feature is that inside the cell, the genetic material (DNA) is not contained in a bag-like nucleus (see Smallest units of life).

- Billions of bacteria live almost everywhere. Helpful bacteria make dead things rot away for natural recycling. Harmful bacteria cause diseases such as typhoid.

- Blue-green algae (cyanobacteria) live mainly in fresh water and form 'scum' on ponds.

- Viruses are the tiniest, simplest life-forms. They can only live by taking over another cell, destroying it in the process. They cause many diseases, such as measles, common cold and influenza (flu).

Viruses can be dried out as crystals, yet still come back to 'life'

Fungi

Mushrooms, toadstools, brackets, moulds, microscopic single-celled yeasts, rusts and mildews are all fungi. They make digestive juices which soak into a dying or dead living thing, and break it into simpler substances. The fungus then absorbs these simple substances through its outer covering. Fungi make once-living things decay and rot away, as part of nature's recycling processes. Some are harmful, causing diseases such as athlete's foot. Rusts attack farm crops and dry rot fungus makes wood weaken and decay, causing great damage to buildings and timber structures. However, other fungi are useful – yeasts make bread, beer and wine.

Protists

Each protist is a single cell, with its genetic material inside a bag-like nucleus. A drop of pond water or sea water contains thousands of protists. They include amoebas, euglenas, parameciums, diatoms and foraminiferans. Some are like tiny animals, 'eating' microscopic food particles. Others are like tiny plants, soaking up energy from sunlight. A few protists are harmful, such as plasmodium, which causes the tropical disease malaria.

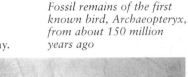

Amoeba, a protist

Nucleus

Smallest units of life

All living things are made of microscopic building blocks or single units called cells. Inside a cell (except a moneran) is a control centre, or nucleus. This contains the genetic material, DNA. The nucleus floats in jelly-like cytoplasm. The whole cell has a covering, the cell membrane. There are many other structures or organelles inside the cell, mostly made of folded sheet-like membranes. Most cells are about one-tenth to one-hundredth of a millimetre across.

Nucleus

Cytoplasm

Cell membrane

Evolution of life

Life began on Earth more than 3,000 million years ago, in the seas. The first living things were probably microscopic jelly-like blobs, similar to monerans today.

Over time, many kinds of bigger, more complicated living things appeared, thrived, but then died out. This gradual change of living things through time is called evolution. The main evidence for it is fossils – remains of once-living things, which were slowly turned to stone and preserved in the rocks.

Fossil remains of the first known bird, Archaeopteryx, from about 150 million years ago

THE PLANT KINGDOM

PLANTS MAKE UP the second biggest kingdom of
living things, after animals. They include familiar
garden, countryside and farm plants such as
grasses, flowers, herbs, bushes and trees. There are
also less familiar kinds of plants such as liverworts,
mosses, ferns and algae. Many plants grow flowers
– but not all. Many have roots in the ground – but
not all. The key feature of all plants is that they
soak up or trap light energy from the Sun, using it
to live and grow. They do this with a green
substance known as chlorophyll. So most plants
are green, or have green parts, like leaves.
However some plants have other coloured
substances, so they may be a different colour, like
red seaweeds. Plants are grouped according to their
bodily features, as shown opposite.

Why plants differ

Each kind of plant has a special
shape and features, to survive in
its habitat. For example, a desert
cactus has spines to stop
animals nibbling it, and a
stretchy barrel-shaped stem to
store precious water. The small
grey-brown flower called edelweiss
lives on high mountains and has furry
leaves to keep out the cold. Most plants take in nutrients
from the soil, so they cannot grow where soil lacks
nutrients. But the venus flytrap can. Its spiked leaves close
quickly around a fly or other insect, like grasping hands, and
absorb the nutrient-packed juices from the insect's body.

Seaweeds (algae)

Algae are the simplest plants. They include seaweeds such as
wracks, oarweeds and kelps, and some kinds of pond and river
waterweeds. They are 'simple' because they do not have many
specialized parts, such as roots to take in water. Algae soak up
nutrients from the water all around them.

Mosses and liverworts

Mosses have small, low-
growing stems with leaf-like
parts called scales. Liverworts
have flat lobes that look like
soft, fleshy leaves. Both lack
true roots, to take up water
from the soil. So they must
soak up moisture from their
surroundings, which is why
they grow only in damp,
shady places.

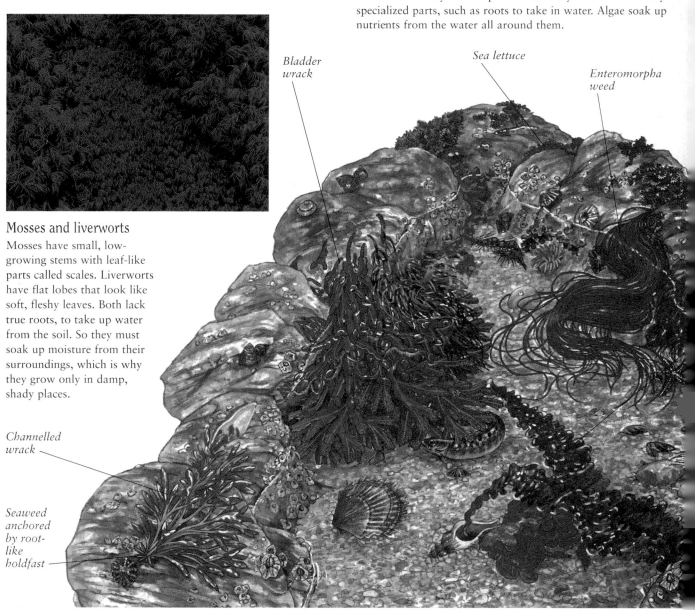

*Bladder
wrack*

Sea lettuce

*Enteromorpha
weed*

*Channelled
wrack*

*Seaweed
anchored
by root-
like
holdfast*

PLANT EVOLUTION

● Fossils show that the first plants appeared on Earth more than 1,000 million years ago. They lived in the sea and probably looked like small lumps of green slime.

● Gradually these earliest plants developed into larger algae, or seaweeds.

● About 400 million years ago, small moss-like plants spread slowly on to the rocky, empty land.

● By 300 million years ago, ferns grew as big as trees, forming steamy, swampy prehistoric forests.

● Some 200 million years ago, forests of conifer trees spread across land, as the first dinosaurs roamed among them.

● Flowering plants appeared about 130 million years ago, bringing bright colours to the landscape.

Ferns and horsetails

A fern has roots anchored in soil, to absorb water and nutrients. It also has specialized tubes inside its body, to carry water and nutrient-rich sap to all its parts. Its leaf-like fronds, held up on a strong, stiff stem, capture sunlight energy. Horsetails are similar but have a stem that looks like a pile of upturned, spiky umbrellas.

Flowering plants

This is by far the largest plant group, with more than a quarter of a million different kinds, or species. It includes flowers, grasses, rushes, reeds, herbs, the fruits and vegetables we eat, and bushes and trees (apart from conifers). Only flowering plants have true flowers (blooms), which are often very colourful, sweet-smelling and beautiful, as shown on the next page.

Conifers

Conifers are plants with cones – hard, woody parts where the seeds develop. Most conifers grow as bushes or trees, with a strong stem, the trunk. Their leaves are like long, thin needles or hard, rounded scales. Their wood is called softwood. Conifers include pines, firs, spruces and larches. Most conifers shed their leaves slowly and continually and are known as evergreens.

Sugar kelp (sea belt)

Orange sea lichen

Lichens

A lichen looks like a small, crusty plant, but it is not a single living thing. It is a combination of a fungus and an algal plant. The fungus part gives strength and support, and the plant part provides food using sunlight. This type of helpful partnership between different living things is called symbiosis. Lichens survive in harsh conditions where plants could not, such as frozen soil or dry rocks. They grow very slowly and are easily damaged by polluted air.

MAIN PLANT GROUPS		
SCIENTIFIC GROUP NAME	ORDINARY NAME	NUMBER OF DIFFERENT KINDS, OR SPECIES
Algae	Seaweeds	6,000
Bryophytes	Mosses	10,000
	Liverworts	14,000
Pteridophytes	Ferns	12,000
	Horsetails	30
	Clubmosses	400
Gymnosperms	Conifers	600
Angiosperms	Flowering plants	250,000-plus

HOW PLANTS WORK

A TYPICAL FLOWERING PLANT has four main body parts. The finger-like roots grow into the soil, anchor the plant firmly and soak up water, minerals and nutrients. The tall, stiff stem holds the leaves and flowers away from the ground, to avoid nibbling animals and dampness. The stem also has tiny pipe-like tubes inside which carry water, minerals and a sweet, sticky fluid called sap, full of minerals and nutrients, around the plant. The leaves soak up energy from sunlight. The flowers make new plants, as shown below.

Food from sunshine

Plants make their food by photosynthesis. This happens mainly in the leaves, which are green because they contain a green substance, chlorophyll. The chlorophyll soaks up or traps energy from sunlight. Meanwhile a gas in air, carbon dioxide, passes through tiny holes, stomata, into the interior of the leaf. And water from the soil soaks through the roots and up the stem, into the leaf. Inside the leaf cells, sunlight energy from chlorophyll joins the carbon dioxide to the water, to make a sweet, energy-rich food called glucose or sugar. This dissolves in the sap and flows to all parts of the plant, providing energy for life.

Leaf cells

Male parts
Each male cell is in a tiny pollen grain. The grains are inside a bag-like anther, on a tall stalk, the filament. Anther and filament make up the stamen.

Female parts
The female cells, or ovules, are usually inside a fleshy part, the ovary, at the flower's base.

Pollen grains under the microscope

Refreshing the air

Photosynthesis produces a gas, oxygen, which passes out of the leaves, into the air. Oxygen is vital because animals, including ourselves, need to breathe it. It helps to break down foods to release the energy in them for life processes. Plants, fungi and other living things also need oxygen, for exactly the same reason. So plant photosynthesis refreshes the air all around the world, replacing the oxygen that all living things use up.

Stigma
Anther
Peta[l]
Stalk
Sepal
Ovary
Style
Ovules

Making new plants

A plant's flowers are for reproduction. In most cases, a flower has male and female parts, called stamens and carpels. The stamen makes tiny powder-like pollen grains, each containing a microscopic male cell. The carpel contains ovules, or female cells. The male cell from one flower reaches the female part of another flower of the same kind, by pollination (see right). When male and female cells join, this is fertilization. The fertilized cell begins to develop into a new plant, inside a hard case, and is known as a seed.

Pollination and fertilization

A pollen grain lands on the carpel's top part, the stigma. A tiny pollen tube grows from the grain, down the carpel's stalk or style, to the ovary. The male cell moves along the pollen tube, down into the ovary. It joins with or fertilizes a female cell, and a new plant begins to develop.

Types of pollination

Pollen grains get from male to female flower parts in various ways. A flower with strong scent, brightly coloured petals and sugary nectar attracts animals such as bees, butterflies, bats and hummingbirds. The animal gets brushed with pollen grains, then carries them to other flowers as it feeds. This is known as animal pollination. In other flowers the pollen grains are so small and light that they blow in the wind. This is wind pollination. Since the flowers of wind-pollinated plants do not need to attract animals, they are usually less colourful and showy. In some water plants, pollen is carried by water currents.

Bee's body gets brushed with pollen grains

Bee collects pollen in pollen 'baskets' on legs

Growing seeds

Inside each seed is a young plant, with the beginnings of tiny stem, root and leaves. The seed also contains stored food, in whitish, lumpy parts called cotyledons. The food enables the young plant to germinate – grow out of its case, set down roots, and send its shoot and new leaves up to the Sun.

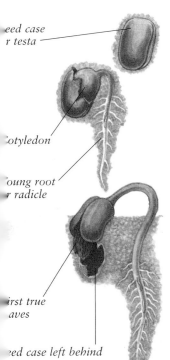

Seed case or testa

Cotyledon

Young root or radicle

First true leaves

Seed case left behind

A typical seed such as a bean has a tough case. It can withstand drying out and lack of water for long periods. But as soon as the seed is exposed to moisture, it begins to develop.

The cells of the baby or embryo plant inside the seed begin to multiply. They begin to use the store of food in the cotyledons. The young root lengthens and grows downwards into the soil.

The root anchors the seed into the soil. The stem begins to straighten. It pulls the shoot and first leaves, sandwiched between the two cotyledons, out of the soil and up into the air.

Forming seeds

The fertilized egg starts to grow into a tiny new plant, known as an embryo, inside a hard protective case, the seed. For the best chance of growing into a new plant, the seed is carried away from the parent plant, to avoid overcrowding. This is seed dispersal.

Animal-dispersed seeds

In some flowers the seed case becomes thick, soft and tasty – a fleshy fruit. In others it becomes extremely hard and thick – a tough nut. Animals of many kinds eat fruits and nuts. The seeds within often pass through the animal's body undigested. They come out of the other end at a new place, ready to grow.

Windblown seeds

In some flowers, the seeds are small and light, and develop wing-like flaps or sails, or fluffy, parachute-like hairs. These help the wind to blow the seeds to new places. Dandelions and sycamores have these types of wind-dispersed seeds.

PRESSING FLOWERS

Identify some colourful common flowers from a garden, using a flower field guide. After getting permission, carefully snip them from their stems and arrange them between two sheets of absorbent paper, such as blotting paper. Put a pile of heavy books on top. Change the absorbent paper each day. After a few days, take out the dried, pressed flowers. You could stick them into a scrapbook and make your own guide book, or use them to decorate pictures or greeting cards.

PLANTS AND PEOPLE

ANIMALS DEPEND ON PLANTS for survival. Many eat leaves, fruits, seeds and other plant parts. Animals also use plants for shelter, such as woodpeckers in tree-trunk holes, and badgers in dens among tree roots. Humans are much the same. We eat plant parts of all kinds, including fleshy fruits such as apples and oranges, nutritious nuts like hazelnuts and peanuts, energy-packed seeds such as wheat (baked into bread) and rice, leaves like lettuce and cabbage, root parts such as potatoes and turnips, herbs and spices like parsley and chilli, even flavourings such as vanilla for ice-cream and cacao for chocolate … The list goes on and is almost endless.

Humans also use plants for shelter. Not by living inside trees, but by cutting down trees and using their wood to make houses and other buildings. Timber also makes furniture, cooking utensils, bowls, toys and decorative items like vases and sculptures. Even this book is printed on paper made from trees, which are plants. Trees for the paper, card and board industry are usually conifers or softwoods. They are specially grown in a sustainable way, with new ones planted regularly to replace them.

On the farm

Farm plants include cereals (grasses) such as wheat, barley, rye, rice and millet. There are also fruits such as pears and apples, vegetables like tomatoes and marrows, berries such as blackberries and grapes, tropical mangoes and melons, and all kinds of nuts. To plant experts, all these are fruits, because they contain seeds. They have plentiful energy and nutrients. In the natural world this is to attract animals to eat them, or to help their own seeds grow and germinate. But we grow these plants to eat ourselves or feed to our farm animals.

Combine harvester in wheat field

Plant products

As well as timber, there are innumerable other plant products. The sticky sap from rubber trees makes natural rubber or latex. Fluffy fibres from cotton plants are spun into cotton cloth. Tough fibres of hemp are twisted into ropes. Olives are pressed to yield olive oil for cooking. Can you add to the list?

Latex sap drips from cuts in rubber-tree bark into collecting bowl

Cotton harves

The many uses of timber

Wood is widely used around the world as a structural material. It is made into huts, sheds, floorboards, bridges, boats, carts, windmills and waterwheels. Bamboo, a very fast-growing grass with a tough, woody stem, makes lightweight scaffolding poles.

Energy from plants

In some places, people cook and heat their homes using fossil fuels such as gas, oil or coal. In other places, the main fuel for cooking and heating is wood. Collecting firewood destroys trees and makes the landscape barren and dusty. However, many people have no alternative for their survival.

Flower ——
Spiny expanded stem ——
Prickly pear (Opuntia)

Plant pests

A weed is a plant growing where we do not want it. Common garden weeds include nettles, bindweed and ragweed. On a larger scale, some plants have been brought to new countries where they have no natural enemies or diseases. So they spread out of control. Prickly pear, a type of cactus, was taken from America to Australia, for use as a spiny hedge-plant. It spread to cover vast areas, driving out local plants and animals. Water hyacinth, originally from tropical America, now chokes lakes and waterways across North America, Africa, Asia and Australia.

Flowers bloom early in artificial daylight and glasshouse warmth

Plant breeding

For centuries, people have chosen or selected plants with features which they wanted, and bred the plants together. This is called selective breeding. The feature may be a special petal colour, bigger fruits, a taller and straighter stem, or resistance to disease. Gradually, the selected plants develop a better version of the feature. The result is thousands of man-made or artificial varieties of plants, in our gardens, parks, farms, fruit orchards, greenhouses, forestry plantations and garden centres.

COMMON BUT RARE

1 The African Violet (which is not closely related to the common violets) is one of the world's most common houseplants.

1 Over many years it has been bred in a huge range of colours and shapes.

1 Yet this plant has all but disappeared from its original wild home, the foothill regions of Tanzania and Kenya in East Africa.

1 Collecting plants from the wild threatens many species, especially cacti.

Medicinal plants

Since stone-age times, people have used leaves, sap, berries and other plant parts to ease suffering and heal disease. By trial and error, they found the most helpful kinds. Today, scientists test thousands of plants for medical use. About one-half of modern medicinal drugs are either purified from plants, or based on substances originally extracted from plants. Many more plants wait to be tested in this way – if they are not destroyed first.

Periwinkle
Opium poppy
Foxglove
White willow
Feverfew

THE ANIMAL KINGDOM

ANIMALS MAKE UP THE BIGGEST kingdom of living things. They include familiar pets like hamsters and goldfish, farm animals such as cows and sheep, and common wild creatures like bugs, slugs, birds, bats and rats. But the animal kingdom also includes very strange living things which look more like space-aliens than Earth creatures. Some live their entire lives in dark caves, inside rocks or tree-trunks, or in the ooze on the sea bed. Many animals can move about actively – but not all. Barnacles and mussels are stuck to seashore rocks. Most animals have sense organs such as eyes or ears – but not all. A sponge cannot see or hear. The key features of an animal are that its body is made of many microscopic cells; it eats or consumes other living things or their parts to obtain energy; it grows or develops; it can move about at some stage in its life; and it reproduces to make more of its kind.

What is this animal?

Is it even an animal? The sea-lily or crinoid looks more like a flower growing on the ocean floor. But it is an upside-down version of the more familiar starfish. The sea lily waves its feathery 'legs' to gather tiny bits of floating food. When young and small, it floats and swims in the ocean, before anchoring to the bottom.

Why animals differ

Each kind of animal has a special body shape and features, which help it to survive in its habitat. For example, a camel in the desert has thick fur to protect against hot sun, wide feet to prevent sinking into soft sand, and a huge stomach to drink vast amounts of water. Its long eyelashes keep windblown sand out of its eyes, and its hump contains stored food in the form of body fat, which the camel can use when other food is scarce. The camel also produces very dry droppings and concentrated urine, to help conserve precious water.

One-humped or dromedary camel

Grabbing a meal

The gulper eel is a deep-sea fish. It has an enormous mouth and can eat a victim bigger than itself. This is useful because food is very rare in the vast, dark depths of the oceans. Any victim that comes near is worth grabbing and eating. The gulper eel's stomach stretches like a balloon to surround its meal.

ANIMAL EVOLUTION

1 Very rare fossils show that the first animals were probably simple, blob-like jellyfish and worms, in the sea more than 700 million years ago.

1 By 500 million years ago, animals with hard body cases, such as trilobites and limpet-like shellfish, inhabited seas and lakes.

1 Around 400 million years ago, the first animals followed early plants on to dry land. These first land-dwelling creatures were probably millipedes and small insects.

1 By 350 million years ago, amphibians walked on dry land. Myriad fish, including sharks, swarmed in the seas.

1 The first reptiles evolved by 300 million years ago.

1 A great extinction 250 million years ago killed off many kinds of amphibians and reptiles, and many types of sea creatures.

1 Around 200 million years ago, reptiles called dinosaurs spread across the land. The first mammals, small and shrew-like, hid from them.

1 Another great extinction 65 million years ago killed off dinosaurs and many other reptiles, as well as sea animals such as ammonites.

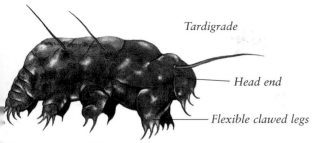

Tardigrade

Head end

Flexible clawed legs

Biggest and smallest

Animals cover a vast range of sizes. The biggest creature ever to live on Earth still swims in the oceans. It is the blue whale, more than 25 metres long and 150 tonnes in weight. Among the smallest animals are water-bears or tardigrades. They resemble short, fat caterpillars with four pairs of flexi-legs, and live mainly in soil or ponds. Some are smaller than the dot on this i.

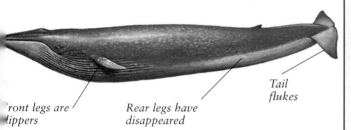

Front legs are flippers

Rear legs have disappeared

Tail flukes

Animals from the past

The dinosaurs lived from about 210 to 65 million years ago. Using the remains of their bones, teeth, horns, claws and other hard body parts, preserved as fossils, we can make informed scientific proposals about how they looked and behaved in life. Their droppings also fossilized, showing what they ate. However, the fossils give no clue to the skin colour of dinosaurs. The colours shown in these types of reconstructions are guesswork.

MAIN GROUPS OF ANIMALS

There are probably at least five million different kinds, or species, of animals. They are divided into main groups, or phyla, by their body structure and main features. The biggest group by far is the arthropods. The various groups are described over the following pages.

SCIENTIFIC GROUP NAME	ORDINARY NAME	NUMBER OF DIFFERENT KINDS, OR SPECIES
Poriferans	Sponges	5,000
Cnidarians (Coelenterates)	Jellyfish, anemones, corals	9,500
Platyhelminthes	Flatworms	6,000
Nematodes	Roundworms	12,000
Annelids	Segmented worms such as earthworms	11,500
Arthropods	Insects, spiders, crabs and other crustaceans, centipedes, millipedes	5 million-plus
Molluscs	Shellfish, snails, squid, octopus	80,000
Echinoderms	Starfish, urchins	6,000
Chordates or vertebrates	Fish, amphibians, reptiles, birds, mammals	40,000

FROM JELLYFISH TO STARFISH

AN INVERTEBRATE IS AN ANIMAL that does not have a backbone or spinal column. More than 30 main groups, or phyla, of invertebrates have soft, jelly-like bodies. The more important and familiar are shown here. They all have a body design which is bilaterally symmetrical – that is, the body has a left and right side. Except for echinoderms, such as starfish. These have a body based on a radial plan, with a centre and parts radiating from it like the spokes of a wheel. (Invertebrates with hard body casings are shown on the next page.)

Starfish and urchins

Members of the large echinoderm group live only in the Their radial or circular body is based on the number fiv most starfish have five arms, or ten, or so on. They mov gliding on hundreds of tiny, sucker-tipped tube-feet on t underside. A sea urchin is like a starfish with its arms c up and in, and joined together on top to form a ball sh Like a starfish, an urchin also has a mouth on the unde which scrapes and rasps food off rocks, and it moves o very long, thin tube-feet. In some kinds of urchins, the protective spines are t with poison.

Inside-out stomach

Starfish are deadly predators. They wrap their suckered arms around a shellfish victim and pull hard and long, to prise the shells apart. Then the starfish pours its digestive juices on to the soft flesh inside the shellfish. Finally the starfish turns its own stomach inside out through its mouth and on to the victim, to soak up the soft, soupy meal.

Tube feet on underside of arm

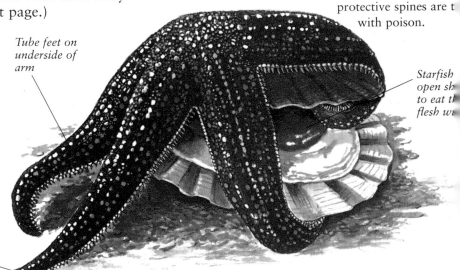

Starfish open sh to eat th flesh wi

Arm tips have simple light-sensitive 'eyes'

Sponges

A sponge has no eyes, ears, brain, mouth, guts or muscles. It is the simplest type of animal – little more than a pile of microscopic cells. It sucks in water though small holes over its body, into a central chamber. Floating particles of food are filtered out using tiny hairs called cilia which line the chamber. The water squirts out through a larger hole, the oscule. Most sponges live in the sea.

Jellyfish, anemones and corals

Anemones have a stalk-like body with a mouth surrounded b waving tentacles. These sting and catch passing animals and them down to the mouth. Corals are smaller versions of ane Each makes a stony cup around its body, for protection. Ove many years, millions of cups build into the rock or a coral re jellyfish has its mouth on the lower side and an umbrella-lik body. Nearly all of these animals live in the sea.

Bath sponge   Breadcrumb sponge   Common jellyfish   Compass jellyfish   Brain coral   Sea an

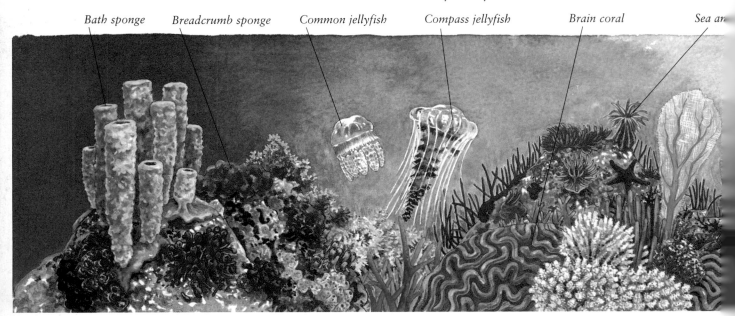

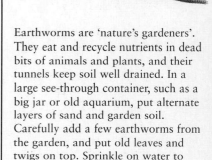

How invertebrates breed

Most animals breed sexually, when a female and male get together. But some invertebrates can reproduce on their own, asexually. A new, small individual grows from the parent animal, just like a new bud grows from a parent plant. Sponges, corals, jellyfish and flatworms do this. Also, in most animals, an individual is either a female or male. But some invertebrates have both male and female parts in the same body. They are hermaphrodites. They include earthworms, leeches, and various molluscs such as snails. A hermaphrodite rarely mates with itself. It usually teams up with a partner and both produce eggs or babies.

Both fathers and mothers

Snails are hermaphrodites. Each has male and female parts. Two snails mate by twining and writhing together in a bath of frothy, sticky, slimy mucus. Each one passes its male cells, or sperm, to the other, to fertilize its eggs. Then each one lays its eggs.

Flatworms

These are mostly small, soft, flattened, leaf- or ribbon-shaped animals. They have simple eyes to detect patches of light and dark. Some dwell in water. Others slide through leaves in tropical rainforests. Still others are parasites, living on or in other animals, including humans, taking nourishment and shelter from them. The parasites include liver flukes and tapeworms.

Roundworms

A handful of soil teems with tiny roundworms, or nematode worms. The mouth at one end eats food, and wastes pass out of the anus at the other end. Unlike true worms, the body of a nematode is not divided into many similar sections, or segments. Many nematodes are parasites, causing diseases such as hookworm and river blindness.

Other invertebrates

The smaller groups or 'minor phyla' of invertebrates are mainly obscure worm-like creatures that live in out-of-the-way places. For example, horsehair worms in the phylum Nematomorpha number only 80 species, compared to 11,500 species of true worms. Horsehair worms are very long and thin, like the strands of a horse's mane or tail. They live in ponds, lakes, canals and other bodies of still, fresh water – including horse troughs. This gave rise to the legend that they are horse hairs come to life. When young, these worms are parasites of small animals such as insects. The adults coil around water plants.

WATCH WORMS AT WORK

Earthworms are 'nature's gardeners'. They eat and recycle nutrients in dead bits of animals and plants, and their tunnels keep soil well drained. In a large see-through container, such as a big jar or old aquarium, put alternate layers of sand and garden soil. Carefully add a few earthworms from the garden, and put old leaves and twigs on top. Sprinkle on water to keep the wormery damp. After a few days, see how the worms mix up the layers and recycle the leaves.

True worms

Annelid or true worms have a body divided into many similar sections or segments, one behind the other. There are more than 3,000 kinds of earthworms, also lugworms and ragworms on the seashore, and fanworms with their crown of feathery feeding tentacles in shallow water. Leeches, which live mainly in lakes and swamps, have a sucker at each end of the body and feed by sucking blood or body fluids.

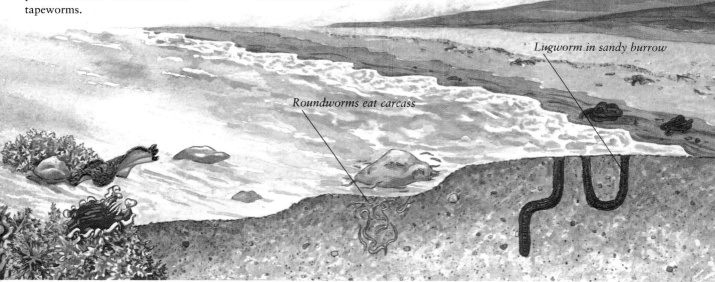

Lugworm in sandy burrow

Roundworms eat carcass

FROM CRABS TO COCKROACHES

OF ALL THE ANIMAL SPECIES in the world, at least nine out of every ten are insects. The insects belong to the major animal group or phylum called the arthropods, a name which means 'joint-legged'. This is because a typical arthropod has a hard, tough body casing, known as an exoskeleton, with flexible joints in the limbs (like our own knees and ankles). These joints allow the creature to walk, run, swim or burrow. Other arthropod groups include the centipedes (chilopods), millipedes (diplopods), crabs and other crustaceans, and spiders and other arachnids.

Inside an insect

Like all arthropods, an insect such as an ant has a strong, rigid outer body casing, the exoskeleton. The insect's body has three main sections. The front, or head, bears two eyes, two antennae or feelers, and mouthparts. The middle, or thorax, has six legs and (in most insects) two pairs of wings. The rear, or abdomen, contains mainly the guts and reproductive parts. The total number of insect species is estimated at more than 5 million.

Antenna

Brain

Heart

Mid gut

Main blood vessel

Malpighian tubes (excretion)

Mouthparts

Main nerve cord

Salivary glands

Hind gut

Acid-making gland

MAIN GROUPS OF INSECTS

There are more than 30 groups (orders) of insects. Biggest by far is the beetles and weevils, with at least half a million species.

SCIENTIFIC GROUP NAME	ORDINARY NAMES
Apterygota	Silverfish, firebrats, springtails and other wingless insects
Orthoptera	Grasshoppers, crickets, katydids
Odonata	Dragonflies, damselflies
Ephemeroptera	Mayflies
Blattodea	Cockroaches
Isoptera	Termites
Mantodea	Mantids such as praying mantis
Dermaptera	Earwigs
Plecoptera	Stoneflies
Phasmida	Stick-insects, leaf-insects
Thysanoptera	Thrips, thunderbugs
Psocoptera	Book-lice
Phthiraptera	Bird-lice, other parasitic lice
Hemiptera	Bugs such as shieldbugs, pondskaters, cicadas, hoppers, aphids, scalebugs
Neuroptera	Lacewings, ant-lions
Coleoptera	Beetles, weevils
Siphonaptera	Fleas
Hymenoptera	Bees, wasps, ants, sawflies
Diptera	True flies such as housefly, gnat, midge, mosquito, cranefly (two wings only)
Lepidoptera	Butterflies and moths

Crabs and other crustaceans

Crustaceans live mainly in the seas and include crabs, lobsters, shrimps, prawns and barnacles. Pond water-fleas, freshwater crayfish and woodlice (sowbugs) are also in this group. So are copepods, which look like pond water-fleas. Copepods live in vast ocean swarms and are among the most numerous animals on Earth. Most crustaceans have two pairs of antennae (feelers), a hard-cased body divided into similar sections or segments, and at least ten pairs of jointed limbs. The total number of crustacean species is about 40,000.

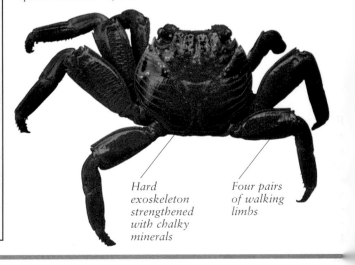

Hard exoskeleton strengthened with chalky minerals

Four pairs of walking limbs

Millipedes

The name means 'thousand-legged', but most millipedes have a couple of hundred legs. There are two pairs on each body segment (unlike centipedes). Millipedes are slow, secretive creatures who prefer the dark and damp, living in forest soil or under bark, eating decaying plant matter. The total number of millipede species is about 8,000.

Centipedes

The name means 'hundred-legged', but most centipede species have fewer than 70 legs. There is one pair per body segment (unlike millipedes). Centipedes are fast, active creatures that prey on worms, insects and other smaller creatures, and kill them with a bite from poison fangs. The total number of centipede species is about 3,000.

Molluscs

On land, familiar molluscs include snails and slugs. But most molluscs live in the sea, such as octopus, squid, cuttlefish, sea-slugs or nudibranchs, and sea-snails like winkles and whelks. Some molluscs have a two-part shell, such as mussels, oysters, clams and scallops. Key molluscan features are a soft, bendy body enclosed in a fleshy 'hood', the mantle. In many molluscs, like snails, the mantle makes a hard protective shell. The total number of mollusc species is about 80,000.

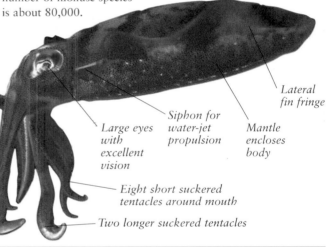

The cuttlefish, a predatory mollusc

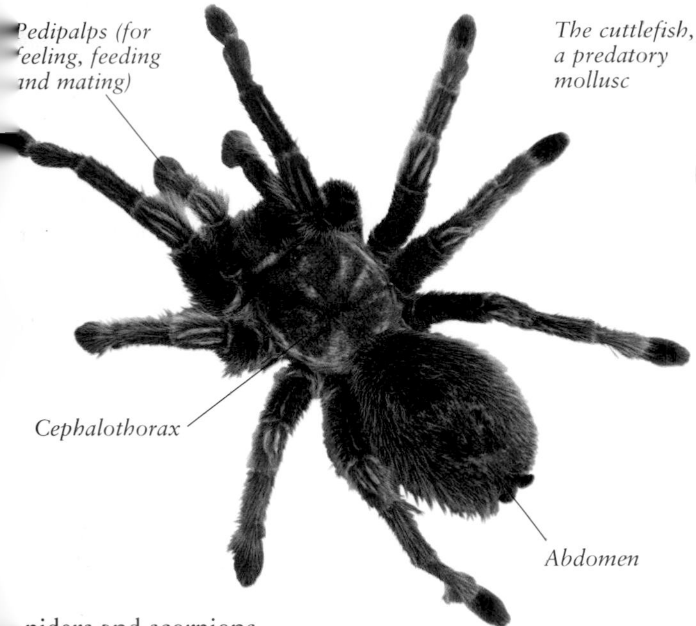

Large eyes with excellent vision

Siphon for water-jet propulsion

Mantle encloses body

Lateral fin fringe

Eight short suckered tentacles around mouth

Two longer suckered tentacles

INSECT RECORDS

1 The longest insects are giant tropical stick-insects. Some are more than 30 centimetres in length.

1 The heaviest insects are large tropical beetles such as the goliath beetle and rhinoceros beetle. They weigh more than 100 grams.

1 The smallest insects are fairy-flies and hairy-winged beetles. They are smaller than the dot on this i.

1 The longest-lived insects are probably beetles. Some have been known to live for more than 40 years.

1 The most numerous insects are tiny springtails (collembolans) in the soil. They have no wings and cannot fly. But they can jump using a hinged, rod-like part at the end of the body. In a handful of soil there may be many hundreds of springtails.

Pedipalps (for feeling, feeding and mating)

Cephalothorax

Abdomen

Spiders and scorpions

Arachnids have four pairs of limbs and a two-part body, the front cephalothorax and the rear abdomen. All spiders catch prey. Many spin silk-strand webs to snare victims and all have a poisonous bite, although less than 50 kinds are dangerous to humans. A scorpion's front pair of legs are large, strong pincers, and its arched tail is tipped with a venomous sting. Tiny mites and ticks are also arachnids. Some of these are parasites and suck blood. The total number of arachnid species is about 70,000.

A SHELL COLLECTION

At the seaside, collect a few empty seashells. Wash them in soapy water and let them dry. Identify them using a guide-book and arrange them in a box or on a card sheet. Look at them closely. Are the two parts of an oyster, clam or mussel shell exactly the same? Study their growth rings (as in tree trunks), usually two each year. In sea-snails like whelks, does the shell always twist the same way in different individuals?

FISHES

MANY ANIMALS HAVE 'FISH' as part of their name, such as jellyfish, starfish and crayfish. But these are not proper fishes. A true fish is a vertebrate – an animal with a backbone or spinal column along the middle of its body. A typical fish also lives in water, has a scaly body, breathes using gills on either side of its head, and has broad, flat fins and a tail for swimming. There are more than 21,000 different kinds, or species, of fish. They form the largest group of vertebrates, Pisces. This is bigger than all the other groups of vertebrates (amphibians, reptiles, birds and mammals) added together. They vary in size from the enormous whale shark, more than 13 m long and perhaps 10 tonnes in weight, to the Philippine dwarf goby which is hardly as big as this word.

Parts of a fish

A fish's body is covered with hard scales, which overlap like tiles on a roof, and are transparent to show the skin colour beneath. Many fish have large eyes to see through gloomy water, and nostrils to pick up floating scents and odours. Along either side of the body is a faint line, the lateral line, which senses currents and swirls in the water. This allows the fish to detect other animals moving nearby. Another sense is tiny electricity-detecting pits over the snout and head, especially in many sharks. These pick up tiny electrical pulses made by active muscles of other creatures.

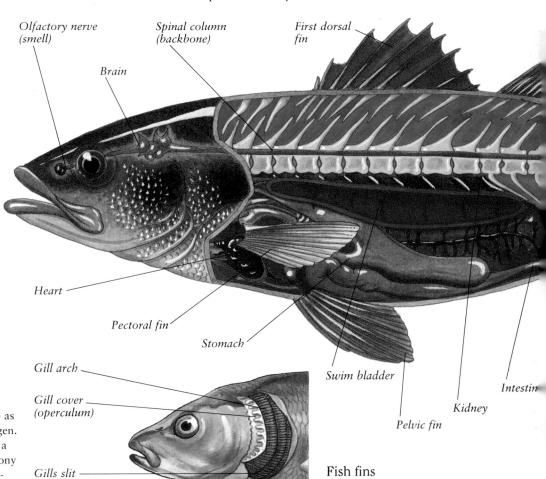

Olfactory nerve (smell)

Brain

Spinal column (backbone)

First dorsal fin

Heart

Pectoral fin

Stomach

Swim bladder

Kidney

Intestin

Pelvic fin

Gill arch

Gill cover (operculum)

Gills slit

Water flows in through mouth

Water flows out through gill slits

Mouth cavity

Fish gills and breathing

A fish's gills do the same job as our own lungs – obtain oxygen. The gills are on each side of a fish's head, protected by a bony flap, the gill cover or operculum, with a narrow opening at the rear, the gill slit. Most fish have four gills on each side of the head, although sharks usually have five. Each gill is an arched, delicate, frilly structure with blood flowing through it. Water flows into the fish's mouth, over the gills and out through the gill slit. Oxygen dissolved in the water passes through the thin covering of the gills, into the blood, and is carried around the body. At the same time, the body waste called carbon dioxide passes from the gills into the water, for removal.

Fish fins

The fish uses its tail fin to go forwards, and its body fins to steer, turn and stop. Fins vary in shape according to lifestyle. Fast ocean fish have fairly narrow, stiff fin and a crescent- or moon-shaped tail. Slow reef fish have wider, more flexible fins, for close control when darting among rocks. Some can even 'row' with their pectoral fins, without using their tail at all. The area, shape and angle of an individual fin is changed by moving the bony rod-like spines, the fin rays, which support it. Muscles in the fish's body at the base of the fin do this. The first fish appeared on Earth some 500 million years ago. As evolution continued, the fins of some fish became legs and these fish developed into amphibians.

Fish without bones

All fish have an inner skeleton with a skull, ribs and similar parts. But in some fish, this is not made of bone. It is cartilage, or gristle, which is slightly softer and bendier than bone. There are about 710 kinds of cartilaginous fish. They include all sharks, from fast, fierce hunters like the great white, to the small and harmless dogfish. cartilaginous fish also include rays such as the manta and stingray, and skates.

Ray's wing-like sides flap to 'fly' through the water

Muscle blocks (myotomes)

Second dorsal fin

Caudal fin (tail)

Stock (base) of tail

Scales on skin

Anal fin

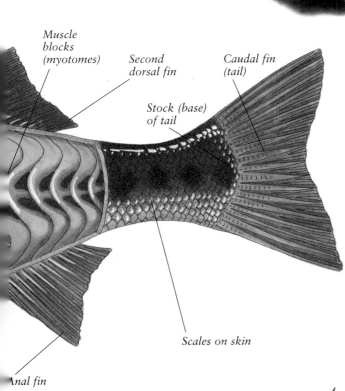

How fish breed

Most fish breed, or spawn, at a certain season. The female lays many eggs, or roe, numbering millions in fish such as cod. She may cast them into the water or hide them in a sheltered place, such as under a rock or among seaweed. The male sheds his sperm, or milt, over the eggs to fertilize them. The eggs then develop and hatch into baby fish, or fry. Only a few fish care for their babies. In the cichlid mouth-brooder, the babies dash inside their mother's mouth when danger threatens.

Tendrils anchor case to seaweed

Egg case of dogfish (a small type of shark)

Embryo (developing baby) in case

In the gloom of deep water, many fish are black, for camouflage in the darkness.

Linophyrne anglerfish

Most ocean fish are streamlined, and silvery or blue-green in colour, for speed and camouflage in the open sea.

Atlantic cod

Eels are long, thin, snake-shaped fish that hide in small cracks or burrow in mud and sand.

Common eel

Some coral-reef fish have amazing patterns of red, yellow, blue and green. These colours advertize the fish's presence, so it can defend its territory or attract a mate.

Clown fish

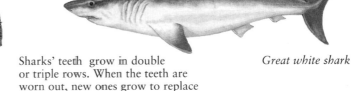

Flatfish are flattened from side to side and lie on one side on the sea bed.

Plaice (or flounder?)

Sharks' teeth grow in double or triple rows. When the teeth are worn out, new ones grow to replace them.

Great white shark

AMPHIBIANS

THE AMPHIBIAN GROUP includes about 4,000 kinds, or species, of frogs, toads, salamanders and newts. The name amphibian means 'two lives', because most amphibians have two-part lives. After they hatch from eggs, they live in water, breathe by gills, swim with a tail, and eat plants such as pondweeds. They are called tadpoles. As they grow up, their bodies change shape, growing limbs and losing the tail. This drastic change in body shape is called metamorphosis. (It happens in other groups of animals too, such as most insects.) Then the growing amphibians leave the water to begin the second, adult, part of their lives. They dwell on land, breathe with lungs, walk or hop on their legs, and eat meat in the form of small creatures such as bugs, slugs and worms. However, they have not left the water for ever. At breeding time, they return to water to lay their eggs, so their offspring can grow up in the same way.

Features of amphibians

Most amphibians have the bony inner skeleton and four legs of a typical vertebrate. In frogs and toads, the toes are partly or fully webbed, for effective swimming. Newts have a long tail for the same purpose. Amphibian skin is thin, flexible and moist in most species. It dries out easily, which could result in death, so most amphibians prefer cool, shady, damp places. The skin also produces slimy, foul-tasting substances to deter predators. In some types, such as arrow-poison frogs, even a small smear of these substances can be deadly poisonous. However, some toads have dry skin and because of this they can survive lack of water for a time.

All adult amphibians catch live prey, usually by spotting it with their large eyes, and then gulping it into the wide mouth. The frog has a long, sticky-tipped tongue which it can flick out to grab a small victim like a fly. Large toads can eat prey as big as rats and lizards. Newts are also fierce predators. They tackle small prey such as worms, tiny fish and young tadpoles – even those of their own species.

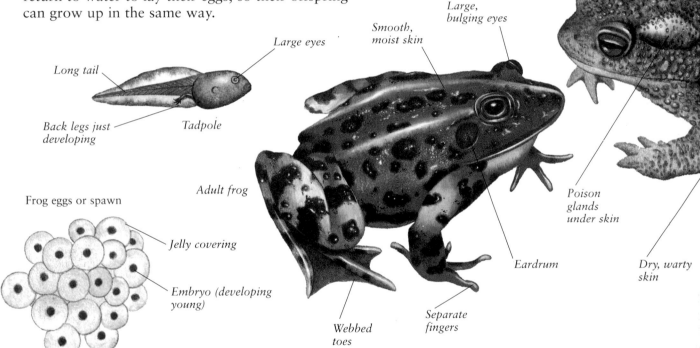

Long tail

Large eyes

Back legs just developing

Tadpole

Smooth, moist skin

Large, bulging eyes

Adult frog

Frog eggs or spawn

Jelly covering

Embryo (developing young)

Poison glands under skin

Webbed toes

Separate fingers

Eardrum

Dry, warty skin

Egg to tadpole to frog

Most adult amphibians return to ponds and pools for the breeding season. In some kinds, males croak or squeak to attract females. A male and female pair up, and the female lays jelly-covered eggs, spawn. The male fertilizes these by adding his milky sperm to them. The jelly coverings of the eggs swell up as they absorb water. The dark, dot-like eggs inside gradually develop and hatch into tiny, feathery-gilled tadpoles, which nibble at pondweed. As the tadpoles grow, the gills shrink and the lungs develop, so the tadpole surfaces to breathe air. The back legs emerge, then the front ones, and the tadpole begins to hunt tiny water creatures. Finally the tail shrinks away and the young adults, or froglets, hop on to land. In the European frog this whole process takes about three to four months, depending on the seasonal temperatures.

Frog or toad?

Most frogs have smooth skin, slim bodies, and move by leaping or jumping. Most toads have lumpy or warty skin, tubby bodies, and move by walking or waddling slowly. In fact there is no single scientific difference between frogs and toads. They all belong to one amphibian sub-group, anurans ('tail-less'). The popular view of the difference between a frog and a toad comes from the common European frog and toad. In other parts of the world, there are toads with smooth, moist skin and frogs with dry skin that tend to waddle. The rear legs of a frog are much longer and stronger than the front legs, for powerful jumping. The front legs soften the landing as the frog finishes its leap. Some sharp-nosed frogs can cover more than three metres in one jump. Salamanders and newts belong to another sub-group of amphibians, the urodelans ('tailed').

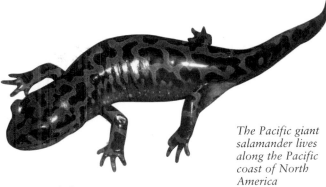

Watery home

In temperate regions, most amphibians breed in early spring. By late spring the adults have returned to damp places on land. In tropical rainforests there is moisture everywhere. So many amphibians simply lay their eggs under logs or stones, or under large leaves.

The Pacific giant salamander lives along the Pacific coast of North America

Giant amphibians

The largest amphibians are giant salamanders. The hellbender of eastern North America lives in streams, hunts other water animals and reaches 75 centimetres in length. Asian giant salamanders of Japan and China grow even bigger, more than one metre long.

Legless amphibians

Besides frogs and toads (anurans), and newts and salamanders (urodelans), the amphibian group also includes about 150 species of caecilians, or apodans. These curious creatures look like large earthworms. Most live in forests in warm places, burrowing in the soil. They are active, fierce predators of small soil animals.

Most caecilians are blind and live in burrows underground.

FROM DESERT TO DEEP CAVE

The great majority of amphibians live in warm, moist places such as tropical rainforests. But some dwell in very different habitats.

● The water-holding frog of Australian deserts stays deep under ground until rains come. Then it digs to the surface, feeds and breeds in temporary pools. As the desert dries again, it burrows back under ground.

● The olm is a rare, white, almost blind salamander that lives in total darkness, in rivers and lakes deep in the caves of southern Europe.

● Tree-frogs have wide, sticky pads on their fingers and toes. These grip slippery leaves in their damp tropical forest homes.

● The spotted mole-salamander of North America burrows in the forest floor and eats earthworms, slugs and other soil animals.

Adult toad

Less webbing on toes

The 'water monster'

The axolotl is a rare amphibian of high-altitude freshwater lakes in Mexico. It grows to about 30 centimetres in length and, like other salamanders, it eats smaller animals. Its name means 'water monster' in the Aztec language. The axolotl is like an amphibian that never grows up. Even when adult and able to breed, it still has feathery gills, like a tadpole.

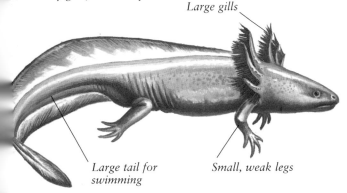

Large gills

Large tail for swimming

Small, weak legs

HOW TO KEEP TADPOLES

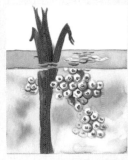
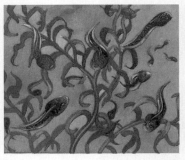

If frogs and toads are common in your area, try keeping some tadpoles for a time, to see how they change their body shape. At the start of the breeding season, ask a knowledgeable adult to collect a fist-sized lump of the spawn. Gather some pond weed from the same place, too. Keep them in an aquarium or similar container, in a cool place away from direct sunlight. Change half of the water every day or two, replacing it with water from the original pond. (Always wear rubber gloves and take great care when handling pond water and wildlife.) Each day, observe the spawn. See how the dark dots grow larger, and then wriggle free of the jelly and emerge as tadpoles. Remove the jelly when this has happened. Keep a diary of when the tadpoles develop their back and front legs. Feed them tiny pieces of dog or cat food. Make sure they have a log or stone to rest on, out of the water, as they begin to breathe air. Finally release them carefully into the wild.

REPTILES

CROCODILES, ALLIGATORS, TURTLES, tortoises, snakes, lizards – all are reptiles. A reptile is a vertebrate animal with a scale-covered body, which lays tough, leathery-shelled eggs. (These do not dry out on land, unlike jelly-covered amphibian eggs.) Most reptiles have four legs, except for two kinds. These are the snakes, and the snake-like reptiles called worm-lizards that burrow in the soil of warm regions. There are about 6,550 kinds, or species, of reptiles alive today. They dwell in most habitats, from lizards in rocky mountains, to turtles and sea-snakes in the middle of the ocean. Many more kinds of reptiles lived in prehistoric times – including the dinosaurs, as shown on earlier pages. It is believed that the first small, shrew-like mammals evolved from reptiles, over 200 million years ago. The first birds probably evolved from reptiles too, more than 150 million years ago. The largest animals ever to walk on Earth were reptiles – giant sauropod dinosaurs from Jurassic times, which weighed over 50 tonnes.

The reptile body

A lizard such as an iguana shows key reptile features. It has an inner skeleton with a backbone, four limbs, a tail, and skin covered with hard, horny scales. The scales do not lie on top of the skin, as in fish. They are embedded in the skin. Most reptiles have big eyes and keen eyesight, ear openings just behind the eyes, nostrils to detect scents in the air (and in water), and a large tongue for tasting food. In some lizards the tongue is very long and can be flicked out to grab small prey.

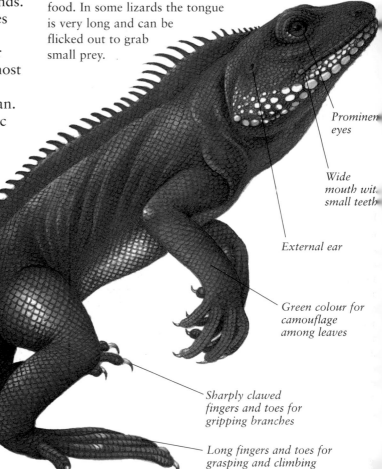

Prominent eyes

Wide mouth with small teeth

External ear

Green colour for camouflage among leaves

Sharply clawed fingers and toes for gripping branches

Long fingers and toes for grasping and climbing

Dry, scaly skin

WHAT DO REPTILES EAT?

Most reptiles eat other animals, either hunting them or scavenging on their dead bodies.

1 Many lizards are quick, darting hunters and pursue insects, worms, small birds and mammals such as mice.

1 Snakes catch living prey, usually by quiet stealth. They cannot chew and must swallow their victims whole.

1 Some turtles lie in wait on the river bed, ready to seize passing fish. Others eat a mixed diet of small animals, carrion, leaves and fruits.

1 Sea turtles like the leatherback consume jellyfish, crabs, mussels and other shellfish, crushing them with their strong beak-like jaws.

1 Crocodiles and alligators lie low in a river or lake, looking like old logs, and ambush animals who come to drink.

1 Very few reptiles eat only plants. One is the marine iguana, a large lizard of the Galapagos Islands in the Pacific, which dives into the sea to chomp on seaweeds.

Turtles

Turtles and terrapins in water, and land-dwelling tortoises, have a body encased in a large, strong, domed shell. The upper part of the dome is the carapace, and the lower part is the plastron. The animal draws its head, legs and tail into the shell for protection. These reptiles are among the longest-lived of all creatures. Spur-thighed tortoises in Europe, eastern box turtles in North America, and giant tortoises on Pacific islands have survived to great ages, some for more than 100 years.

Green turtle

Crocodiles

The largest reptile is the estuarine or salt-water crocodile of the Indian and Pacific Oceans, more than 7 metres long. A croc swims by swishing its tall, flattened tail, and can run surprisingly fast on land. Caimans are crocodilians from swampy areas of Central and South America.

TYPES OF REPTILE		
SUB-GROUP	SCIENTIFIC NAME	NUMBER OF SPECIES
Lizards	Lacertilians	3,750
Snakes	Serpentes	2,400
Turtles, tortoises and terrapins	Chelonians	240
Crocodiles, alligators and caimans	Crocodilians	22
Tuatara	Rhynchocephalians	1
Worm-lizards	Amphisbaenids	140

The Nile crocodile grows to about 6 metres in length.

Sand viper

Deadly snakes

Snakes are reptiles without legs. They move by wriggling and writhing and pushing against tiny bumps in the ground. Some types, like boas, tilt the scales on the lower body for grip. Most snakes creep near a victim and strike with their sharp fangs. Pythons and boas coil around the victim and squeeze or constrict it to death. About 400 of the 2,400 kinds of snakes are poisonous, jabbing venom into the victim with sharp teeth. Feared venomous snakes include cobras, mambas, kraits and tiger snakes, and members of the viper family such as the bushmaster, cottonmouth, rattlesnakes, adders and sidewinders.

How reptiles breed

Reptiles as a group are very quiet, capable only of hisses or hoarse roars, so they rarely make breeding calls. Some male reptiles have courtship 'dances', to show that they are strong and healthy. Male and female mate, and the female lays her leathery-shelled eggs in a suitable place – under stones, in a hollow log, or in soil.

1 Some crocodiles make nests of piled-up vegetation for their eggs.

1 Female turtles come ashore at night and laboriously dig holes in beach sand, lay their hundred or more eggs, and cover them before retreating back to sea.

1 In some lizards and snakes, the babies hatch from the eggs while still inside the mother, and she gives birth to fully formed young.

Tuatara (Sphenodon)

The puzzling tuatara

Tuataras live only on a few rocky islands around New Zealand. They look like lizards, but they are rynchocephalians, a reptile group that was widespread even before the dinosaurs. Tuataras live in burrows by day, and come out at night to eat beetles, spiders and other small animals, and also bird eggs and chicks. Tuataras breed very slowly. Adults do not mate until at least 20 years old, and their eggs do not hatch for 15 months, the longest time for any reptile. Sadly many of the islands where tuataras once survived are now infested with rats, who eat the tuatara eggs. These reptiles are rare and protected.

Baby reptile cuts slit in tough shell with special egg-tooth

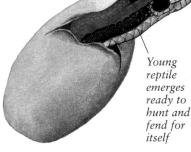

Young reptile emerges ready to hunt and fend for itself

BIRDS

ONLY THREE GROUPS OF ANIMALS can truly fly. They are insects, bats and birds. However, the largest bird, the 2 metre-tall ostrich from Africa, is one of the few kinds of birds that cannot fly at all. The smallest bird, the bee-hummingbird of tropical America, is hardly larger than a bumble-bee. Yet it can fly too fast for us to see, hover and even flit backwards. Birds are vertebrates, with an inner skeleton and backbone, and four limbs. They are warm-blooded, like mammals, and so active even in very cold weather. The unique bird feature is its feathers. They form a light, strong, coloured covering over the body, to keep the bird warm and camouflaged. They also form a large, airtight surface on the wings, for flight. And they can be fanned, twisted and tilted for control in the air, so the bird can soar, swoop, turn and dive with amazing skill.

Parts of a bird

A typical bird is very lightweight, for better flight. Its bones are thin and hollow, and its toothless beak, or bill, lacks heavy teeth and is made of light-yet-strong horn. All birds have large eyes and excellent sight. They can also hear well but their ear openings on the sides of the head are hidden under the head feathers. A few birds, like woodcocks and kiwis, find food by smell, probing their long, nostril-tipped beaks into soil. A bird's front limbs are wings, and the rear limbs are scaly legs with claw-tipped toes.

Primary feathers give main thrust for forward flight

Secondary feathers form aerofoil surface for main lift

Tail feathers can be spread out and tipped down to slow bird down when landing

Wing coverts

Groups of birds

There are nearly 9,000 kinds, or species, of birds, in about 28 sub-groups. The largest is the passerines, or songbirds, with 5,200 species, including familiar wrens, sparrows, tits, swallows, larks, warblers, finches and blackbirds. The smallest sub-group has only one species – the flightless ostrich. Other flightless birds include South American rheas, Australian emus, New Zealand kiwis, and 16 kinds of penguins on the coasts and icebergs of southern oceans.

Skull

Carina (flange or keel on breast bone) for flight muscle attachment

Humerus (upper arm bone)

Ulna and radius (forearm bones)

Carpals (wrist bones)

Carpometacarpus (hand bones)

Digits (finger bones)

Emu, the world's second-largest bird

FLIGHT FACTS

1 The heaviest flying bird is the kori bustard of Africa, which can weigh almost 20 kg.

1 The fastest flying bird is the white-throated spine-tailed swift, which may reach speeds of 160 km/h (100 mph).

1 The bird with the longest wings is the wandering albatross, at 3.5 m total span.

1 But a prehistoric bird from 10 million years ago, the argentavis condor, had wings more than 7 m across.

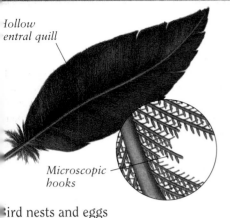

Hollow central quill

Microscopic hooks

Bird plumage

Birds such as sparrows and owls have dull feathers with mottled plumage, often in shades of green and brown, for camouflage among trees and bushes. Other birds, especially males at breeding time, have very bright feathers. They include birds of paradise, peacocks, lyrebirds and trogons. The males sing loudly, and shake and fan their feathers, to attract mates. Most birds moult, shedding their old feathers and growing new ones, twice each year.

Bird beaks

The shape of a bird's beak is adapted to the type of food it eats.

Long down-curved beak of curlew

1 Waders such as curlews and avocets have long, thin, needle-like beaks, and probe into seashore sand and mud for worms, small shrimps and shellfish.

Upper mandible of bill

1 Parrots and finches have large, strong beaks with powerful jaw muscles and extra leverage, to crack seeds and nuts.

Bird nests and eggs

Most birds breed at a certain time of year, usually in spring or the damp season, when food is more plentiful. Male and female court by singing and displaying their plumage, then mate. The female lays hard-shelled eggs, with developing babies inside. Some bird parents put great effort into making a nest for the eggs. Eagles assemble a huge pile of sticks and twigs, called an eyrie, high on a cliff ledge. Weaverbirds twine leaves, grass and stems together to make a strong, flask-shaped, hollow nest hanging from a tree. But guillemots simply lay their eggs on the bare, rocky ledges of seashore cliffs.

Usually, the female sits on or incubates the eggs to keep them warm, while the male fetches her food. Then both parents feed the chicks until they fledge, or learn to fly.

Nest suspended from twig

Red-headed weaverbird in its nest

Nest entrance faces downwards

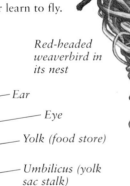

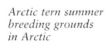

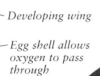

Ear

Eye

Yolk (food store)

Umbilicus (yolk sac stalk)

Developing wing

Egg shell allows oxygen to pass through

Embryo bird inside egg

Lower mandible

1 Birds of prey, such as eagles, falcons, hawks and owls have sharp, hooked beaks (and also sharp claws called talons) for tearing up victims.

Spoon-like or spatulate bill shape

1 Waterfowl such as ducks, geese and swans have spatula-shaped beaks for dabbling in water and mud.

Bird migrations

Some birds fly long distances each year. They breed in one area, when food and conditions are good, and then leave when conditions become bad, usually for somewhere warmer. These regular to-and-fro journeys are called migrations. The champion migrators are Arctic terns. They breed in the Arctic during the northern summer, then fly around the world to Antarctica for the southern summer. The total yearly round trip may be 30,000 kilometres.

Arctic tern summer breeding grounds in Arctic

Migration routes

Summer resting grounds in Antarctic

Treecreeper has upper mandible longer than lower mandible

1 Insect-eating birds, like treecreepers and wrens, have slim, tweezer-like beaks for poking into bark and soil.

MAMMALS 1

MAMMALS ARE PROBABLY the most familiar of all animals. They are generally large, and active in the daytime, like us. They include many pets, farm animals, and also our family, friends and ourselves – since humans are included in the mammal group. A mammal is a warm-blooded vertebrate animal covered with fur or hair, which feeds its babies on milk. The milk is made in the female's milk or mammary glands – the unique feature that gives mammals their name. Mammals vary in size from pygmy shrews, smaller than your thumb, to the biggest animal in the world, the blue whale. The fastest land animal, the cheetah, is a mammal. So is the biggest land animal, the elephant, and the tallest, the giraffe. Mammals live in every habitat on Earth, from bats in the skies, to monkeys in trees, moles underground, seals on seashores, and whales and dolphins in the open ocean. There are three main mammal groups – monotremes, marsupials and placentals (see next page).

European hedgehog has about 5,000 spines

Mammal defences

Plant-eating mammals are prey for meat-eaters. Some have defensive weapons, such as sharp hooves, horns, antlers or tusk-like teeth. Porcupines, which eat roots, fruits, berries and bulbs, have sharp spines called quills, which they rattle to scare the enemy. Hedgehogs also have a spiny covering. The spines are very long, thick, sharp-tipped versions of normal mammal hair or fur. When in danger, the hedgehog tucks in its head and legs and rolls into a ball. Muscles in its skin pull the spines from their laid-back positions into a more upright angle, making it much less tempting as prey. Large mammals such as elephants, rhinos and hippos use their size, bulk and power to overthrow and crush the enemy. The main defences of small mammals like mice and voles are extremely good senses, quick reactions, speed, and small size as they disappear into a little crack or hole. Another form of defence is living in herds (see below right).

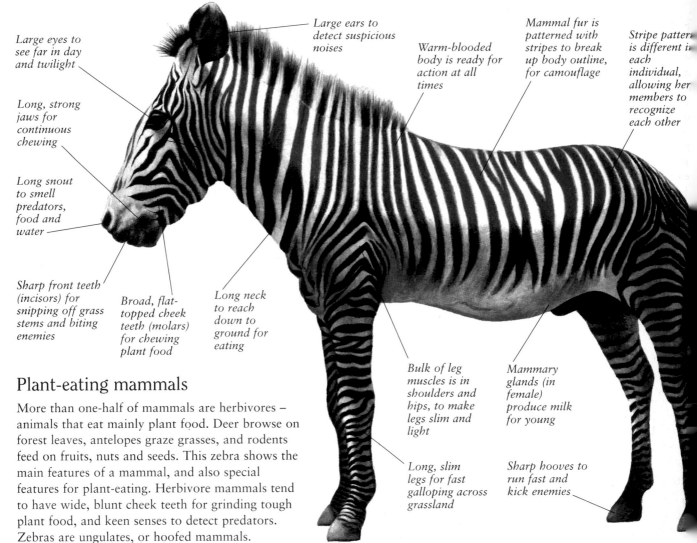

Large eyes to see far in day and twilight

Large ears to detect suspicious noises

Warm-blooded body is ready for action at all times

Mammal fur is patterned with stripes to break up body outline, for camouflage

Stripe pattern is different in each individual, allowing herd members to recognize each other

Long, strong jaws for continuous chewing

Long snout to smell predators, food and water

Sharp front teeth (incisors) for snipping off grass stems and biting enemies

Broad, flat-topped cheek teeth (molars) for chewing plant food

Long neck to reach down to ground for eating

Bulk of leg muscles is in shoulders and hips, to make legs slim and light

Mammary glands (in female) produce milk for young

Long, slim legs for fast galloping across grassland

Sharp hooves to run fast and kick enemies

Plant-eating mammals

More than one-half of mammals are herbivores – animals that eat mainly plant food. Deer browse on forest leaves, antelopes graze grasses, and rodents feed on fruits, nuts and seeds. This zebra shows the main features of a mammal, and also special features for plant-eating. Herbivore mammals tend to have wide, blunt cheek teeth for grinding tough plant food, and keen senses to detect predators. Zebras are ungulates, or hoofed mammals.

Monotremes

A monotreme mammal mother does not give birth to babies, like other mammals. She lays eggs. The babies hatch out and then she feeds them on her milk. There are only three kinds of monotremes: the platypus from Australia, and the short- and long-beaked echidnas (spiny anteaters) from New Guinea and Australia.

Platypus has webbed feet for swimming in creeks and billabongs

Manatee's front limbs are flippers

Long meal-times

Plant food is usually plentiful, but compared to meat, it is tough to chew and difficult to digest. So plant-eating mammals, especially those consuming stringy grasses and woody twigs, spend much more time feeding, compared to meat-eaters. Large herbivores such as elephants, rhinos and sea-cows eat for up to 20 hours daily. The type of sea-cow called the manatee feeds under cover of darkness. It munches water plants in coastal waters for a minute or two and then comes up to the surface to breathe.

Safety in numbers

One form of defence is to live in a large group, such as a herd. Many larger plant-eating mammals, like bison, zebras, wildebeest and Thomson's gazelles (below), do this. At any one time, most members of the herd are feeding or resting. But there are likely to be a few who are alert, watching and listening and sniffing for danger. If trouble is detected, they can warn the others with alarm cries or sudden movements. As the herd rushes to escape, it is difficult for a predator to single out one individual.

Marsupials

There are about 265 species of marsupials, or pouched mammals. They include kangaroos, wallabies, koalas, wombats, bandicoots, possums and opossums, and also fierce hunters such as the native tiger-cat or quoll of Australia. Marsupial babies are born tiny and hairless. They crawl to their mother's pouch (marsupium), where they feed on her milk and continue to grow. Most marsupials live in Australia, with some in South America and a few, such as the Virginia opossum, in North America.

MAIN GROUPS OF MAMMALS

Here are the main groups, or orders, of the mammals known as placental mammals (as explained on the following page). Almost one-half of all mammal species are rodents, and nearly one-quarter are bats.

EVERYDAY NAMES	GROUP NAME	NUMBER OF SPECIES
Cats, dogs, wolves, bears, foxes, weasels, otters, mongooses, hyaenas	Carnivores	230
Whales, dolphins, porpoises	Cetaceans	76
Seals, sea-lions, walrus	Pinnipeds	33
Sea-cows (manatees, dugong)	Sirenians	4
Lemurs, bushbabies, monkeys, apes, humans	Primates	182
Tree-shrews	Scandentians	18
Flying lemurs, colugos	Dermopterans	2
Elephants	Proboscideans	2
Hyraxes	Hyracoideans	11
Aardvark	Tubulidents	1
Horses, zebras, asses, tapirs, rhinos	Perissodactyls	16
Camels, pigs, peccaries, hippos, deer, giraffe, antelopes, gazelles, cattle, sheep, goats	Artiodactyls	187
Squirrels, beavers, gophers, rats, mice, lemmings, gerbils, jerboas, guinea-pigs, chinchillas, porcupines, mole-rats	Rodents	1,702
Rabbits, hares, pikas	Lagomorphs	58
Elephant-shrews	Macroscelideans	15
Moles, desmans, shrews, hedgehogs, tenrecs, solenodons	Insectivores	345
Anteaters, sloths, armadillos	Edentates	29
Pangolins	Philodonts	7
Bats, flying foxes	Chiropterans	950

MAMMALS 2

About one-third of all mammals are mainly carnivorous, or meat-eating. They include the cat family, from tigers to pet cats, as well as the dog family, including wolves, coyotes, jackals and foxes. Other meat-eaters are the generally smaller but very fierce predators known as mustelids – weasels, stoats, polecats, martens, otters, mink, badgers, skunks and similar mammals. The hyaenas and the civets – a group which includes the cat-like civets, genets and linsangs, and the mongooses – are meat-eaters too, and so are raccoons. All of these belong the main mammal group called Carnivora. They are mostly strong and agile, with long, pointed teeth and claws to seize, stab and tear up prey.

Apart from the members of the Carnivora group, many other mammals also eat meat, but in different forms. Dolphins prey on fish and squid. Insectivores, like hedgehogs, moles and shrews, eat meaty but tiny prey, such as insects and worms.

Meat-eating mammals

This lioness shows the main features of a carnivorous or hunting mammal. They include sharp teeth, especially the long, fang-like front teeth called canines, and sharp toe claws. The canines are adapted for grabbing, tearing and ripping prey. The cheek teeth (mainly premolars and molars) of cats and dogs are unlike the broad crushing teeth of herbivorous mammals. They are called carnassial teeth and have strong, sharp ridges. These are used to shear and slice up the food, especially the tough parts of the carcass such as sinews and gristle. In hyaenas, these carnassial teeth are massive. Being close to the joints of the jaws, they have great leverage and can produce huge pressure to crush even bones. Like their prey, carnivorous mammals need keen senses such as sight and hearing. Cats, with their large eyes and long whiskers for feeling the way, tend to be night hunters. Dogs such as wolves hunt mainly by day or at twilight. Bears are also included in the main Carnivora group, but they have a much more varied diet than meat alone (see below right). Strangely, the pandas are also in the Carnivora, because of their general body features and evolutionary links. Yet the giant panda eats almost nothing but bamboo.

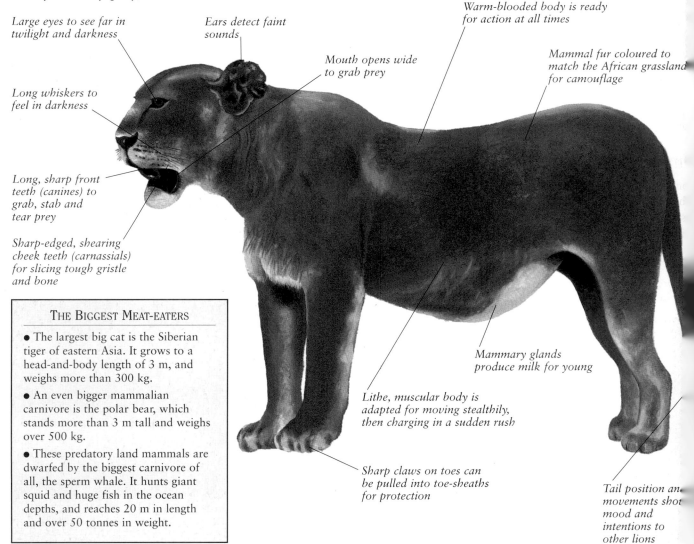

Large eyes to see far in twilight and darkness

Ears detect faint sounds

Mouth opens wide to grab prey

Warm-blooded body is ready for action at all times

Mammal fur coloured to match the African grassland for camouflage

Long whiskers to feel in darkness

Long, sharp front teeth (canines) to grab, stab and tear prey

Sharp-edged, shearing cheek teeth (carnassials) for slicing tough gristle and bone

Mammary glands produce milk for young

Lithe, muscular body is adapted for moving stealthily, then charging in a sudden rush

Sharp claws on toes can be pulled into toe-sheaths for protection

Tail position and movements show mood and intentions to other lions

---

THE BIGGEST MEAT-EATERS

● The largest big cat is the Siberian tiger of eastern Asia. It grows to a head-and-body length of 3 m, and weighs more than 300 kg.

● An even bigger mammalian carnivore is the polar bear, which stands more than 3 m tall and weighs over 500 kg.

● These predatory land mammals are dwarfed by the biggest carnivore of all, the sperm whale. It hunts giant squid and huge fish in the ocean depths, and reaches 20 m in length and over 50 tonnes in weight.

Social mammals

Some mammals live in large groups. They include wolf packs, lion prides, whale schools, monkey troops, and herds of herbivores such as gazelles (shown on the previous pages). In a monkey troop, group members help each other by sharing food, ganging up together against enemies, and grooming each other's fur for lice, fleas and other pests.

Cold body extremities look pinky-blue

Grooming removes skin pests and also strengthens social links

Hibernation

Some mammals enter a deep sleep, hibernation, during the cold season. This helps to save energy and to make them less noticeable to predators. Their bodies cool down from the usual 35–40°C, to 8°C or less, and all body processes happen very slowly. Dormice, ground squirrels such as the chipmunk and marmot, pikas and many kinds of bats undergo hibernation.

Hibernating dormouse

Omnivores

Some mammals eat both meat and plants, depending on what is available. Brown bears eat fish, rabbits and deer, and also feast on roots, fruits and honey. Many monkeys snatch mice, lizards and birds' eggs, but also consume flowers, fruits and berries. These animals are called omnivores, which means they 'eat everything'. Other mammals, such as hyaenas and jackals, and even wolves (below), can be scavengers. They eat dead or dying animals.

Mammal families

In the breeding season, male and female mammals come together to mate. Usually the males display their strength and health by courtship behaviour for the females. Sometimes rival males battle each other, as when male deer rut or male seals fight, to show their strength and win females. Mammal babies develop inside the female's body, in a part called the womb or uterus. In the main subgroup of mammals, the babies receive nourishment through a special body part, the placenta (afterbirth). So this subgroup is called the placental mammals. Usually, the mother feeds and cares for her offspring. In some species, the father helps. Mammals have the longest periods of parental care of any animals. In great apes such as the chimps and gorillas, it lasts for several years.

Flying mammals

A bat's front limbs are large wings, made of very thin, stretchy skin held out by long, thin finger bones. Most bats are small, live in tropical forests and fly only at night, so they are seldom seen by people. They emit very high-pitched squeaks of sound, which bounce off nearby objects. The bat hears the returning echoes and works out what is around, so it can find its way in darkness. (This system, echolocation, is also used by some whales and dolphins.)

Finger bones

Patagium (wing membrane)

Arm bones

PAW-PRINT COLLECTION

You can find out about mammals even when they are not there – by their paw prints. Deer and horses have distinctive hooves. Dog prints are larger than cat prints and have impressions of the claws. Look for paw prints in soft ground such as near a pond. Clean away loose twigs and leaves, press a strip of card in a circle into the soil around the print, and fill it with plaster of paris mixture. Leave it to set. Remove the hard cast and clean it for display in your collection.

ANIMALS AND PEOPLE

EVIDENCE FROM FOSSILS, our own body structure and our genes shows that humans evolved as part of the living world. About two or three million years ago, our very distant ape-like ancestors lived in Africa, hunting animals for meat, and gathering fruits and other plant parts for foods. Our world is now very different. We have clothes, computers, cars and other marvellous inventions. Yet we still rely on animals. We use domesticated species for all kinds of work, such as carrying and pulling. We enjoy the companionship of our tame pets. We appreciate the beauty, sights and sounds of wild creatures such as birds and insects. And billions of people depend on animals for food – whether from the wild or reared on farms.

Farm animals

Farm animals vary around the world. In some regions, cattle are popular. In drier places, goats may be more productive. Pigs and goats are useful because they eat a very wide range of foods, while sheep are fussier, needing mainly grass. In the cold lands of the north, reindeer are reared. Also, people's eating habits and dietary fashions change. If the meat of crocodiles, ostriches, kangaroos, red deer or wild boar becomes popular, it may become worth farming.
On a modern farm, these animals are reared not only for their meat, and perhaps their milk. Their fur, hair or feathers can be made into clothes and textiles. Their skins are treated to produce leathers. Their carcasses are processed into products such as glues, oils and waxes. On a modern intensive farm, very little is wasted.

Changing genes

Many kinds of animals and plants have been altered from their wild ancestors by selective breeding. Most animals on today's farms were produced in this way. In recent years it has been possible to change living things much faster, in one generation, by genetic engineering. Using laboratory methods, animals such as sheep can be cloned – copied exactly, so that all individuals have precisely the same genes, like innumerable identical twins. Or the genes from one species can be extracted from the microscopic cells, in the form of the genetic material DNA, and put into the cells of another species. However, the long-term effects of these changes, such as whether these genetically modified organisms will alter further, or breed with wild relatives, are not known.

Arguments about animals

Some people say that modern, intensive farming methods are cruel. For example, 'battery' chickens are kept in tiny cages with little room, natural light or fresh air. But others say that these methods are useful because they keep food prices low and allow people to buy more varied meals. If all hens roamed freely, the price of poultry produce could soar.

An ostrich farm – ostrich meat can be healthier than many red meats

Learning about life – and death

Millions of people spend billions in money on, and also many happy hours with, their pets. Pet animals can help us to understand about animal needs and the pet's wild relatives. They encourage people to learn about responsibility and caring for others. They can also help us to find out about friendships, and even how to cope with illness and death.

Working animals

Machines such as trucks and tractors do heavy work and haulage in some countries. In other places, animals do this type of work. Llamas, horses, cattle, donkeys and even elephants can be pack animals, carrying heavy loads over rough ground. Horses, oxen, water-buffaloes and elephants are used as draught animals, pulling ploughs, carts and carriages, or dragging logs. Sometimes, animals go where machines cannot. In cold places, dogs or reindeer pull sleds over bumpy snow and jagged ice. In the sandy desert, camels convey loads easily over the soft ground.

ANIMAL USE OR ABUSE?

Are some animals abused and treated cruelly, rather than simply used?

● Rats, mice, rabbits and other animals are bred for research, especially for experiments with new drugs and medicines.

● Without doubt, the animals suffer. Sometimes the suffering is not totally necessary, since the tests may be repeated for checking, or rival companies may be doing them.

● However, without doubt too, people want better medicines and drugs. Tests on cells in test-tubes can help, but cannot yet replace all animal experiments.

● Testing drugs and similar products on animals is still the main way of making sure they are suitable for people. Indeed, it is the law in most countries around the world.

Special uses

Some animals are specially trained to help people. Sniffer dogs smell out illegal substances such as smuggled drugs. Guide dogs are the 'eyes' of people who cannot see properly, and very often, their close companions too. Mounted police patrol on their horses at large events, to aid crowd control. Some people relax and recover their health by stroking specially trained, very docile pet cats and dogs.

FIND OUT ABOUT ANIMAL PRODUCTS

Some people do not eat any type of animal meat or product, including fish, eggs or cheese. Others do not eat meat, but may eat dairy products such as cheese. Still others eat any kind of meat. Such decisions are made for a variety of reasons, including our personal taste, consuming a healthy diet, concerns about animal welfare and the environment, and worries about the way animal products are treated and processed in factories. Look at some animal products, medicines and cosmetics in a local store. What type of information is given on the labelling? Does it have words such as 'organic', 'free-range' and 'cruelty-free'? Are these terms used in the same way by different manufacturers?

LIVING WORLD IN PERIL

WHEN A SPECIES OF LIVING THING dies out, and there are no more left in the world, this is called extinction. It is a natural part of the process of life, death and evolution. Over millions of years, new species have appeared, as others have become extinct. From the evidence of fossils, experts guess that of all the species which have ever existed on Earth, probably more than 95 out of every 100 are now extinct. An average species lasts 5–10 million years, and for much of the history of our planet, a species has become extinct about every 10 years. Extinction still occurs today. But now, it probably happens not at the rate of one species every 10 years, but one species every day. Some estimates are higher, with five species or more disappearing each day. Many of these lost species are small insects and flowers, which science has not even discovered yet, deep in tropical forests. Extinction has speeded up so much because of human activities in the past few hundred years. Various problems facing the living world, and possible answers, are described here.

Hunting and poaching

Some animals are threatened directly by hunting and poaching. They are usually large and powerful species, such as tigers, rhinos, bears, deer, birds of prey, sharks and other big fish. They are shot, poisoned or trapped for various reasons, such as to show the 'bravery' of the hunter and for trophies to sell. They may also be hunted by people who are protecting themselves and their farm animals against attack.

Abundant life

An area of moist tropical forest is home to an enormously complex web of life. It contains at least one hundred times, and perhaps one thousand times, more species than the same area of temperate forest (such as an oak or beech wood). The range of living species in a habitat is known as biodiversity.

Habitat destruction

This is by far the greatest threat to wildlife. People alter natural places for their own use, changing them into farms, factories, mines, roads, houses, schools and other structures. The problem is especially serious in some tropical regions, where the human population is increasing fast, but there are also some of the rarest and most precious wildlife habitats, such as tropical forests, swampy wetlands and coastal coral reefs. The problem of habitat destruction is so serious because it affects not just one or two species, but all species that live in the area. Worldwide changes such as loss of the protective ozone layer in the atmosphere, and the increased greenhouse effect leading to global warming, are also upsetting the delicate balance of nature.

Collecting

Hundreds of species are rare because they are already naturally rare! They are gathered or collected from the wild for people who wish to own and keep rare and exotic species. Of course, this makes them even more scarce. Such

species include cacti and other flowers, colourful birds like parrots, venomous snakes and spiders, and unusual pets like monkeys and apes. Captive breeding of species such as tropical aquarium fish helps to avoid collecting from the wild.

World wildlife laws

International laws help to protect rare species, such as tigers, trees, snails and wildflowers. CITES, the Convention on International Trade in Endangered Species, forbids people to buy, sell or trade protected species, or products from them such as their tusks, flowers, furs or bones, unless they are properly licensed to do so.

Eco-tourism

The idea of eco-tourism is that people pay money to experience rare species in the wild – visit gorillas in their mountain home, stroke whales at sea, or feed sharks on a coral reef. The tourism is carefully controlled so that it affects the wildlife as little as possible, and the money funds more wildlife conservation projects.

Pollution

Vast areas are polluted by unnatural, artificial chemicals. Acid rain damages trees and soil, gets into streams and ponds, and harms fish and other water creatures. Chemicals from industry and our own rubbish and refuse soak into the soil or poison waterways. Intensive farming also pollutes land and water, with pesticides and concentrated fertilizers.

Birds killed by oil pollution

Setting up sanctuaries

National parks, wildlife reserves and nature sanctuaries conserve some wild places. People may be allowed into certain areas, to enjoy the scenery, plants and animals, while other areas are fully protected. Such areas range from a small wood or pond to a vast area of land or sea, the size of a country. In 1994 the Southern Ocean around Antarctica was declared a huge sanctuary where the hunting of great whales and other threatened animals is now forbidden. But sanctuaries must usually be large. A single tiger needs 50 sq km or more of forest to hunt in. And several dozen tigers are needed for a sustainable population that avoids the problems of inter-breeding among close relatives. So a small tiger reserve of a few hectares is less useful for the long term.

THE 'RED LISTS'

1 The IUCN, International Union for the Conservation of Nature, publishes regularly updated 'Red Data Lists' of animals and plants which are threatened in some way.

1 The latest list of animals has more than 5,200 species, including 231 types of bats, 733 fish (one species being the great white shark) – and 806 kinds of snails!

GONE FOR EVER

1 **1665** The dodo, a turkey-sized flightless bird from the Indian Ocean island of Mauritius.

1 **About 1770** Steller's sea-cow, a huge but peaceful plant-eater of the North Pacific Arctic region, 9 m long and weighing 6 tonnes.

1 **1914** The passenger pigeon of North America, once so common that its flocks numbered millions.

1 **1936** The thylacine (Tasmanian wolf or tiger), a dog-like marsupial suspected of attacking sheep.

1 **1952** The Bali tiger, the smallest variety of the tiger species.

LIVING WORLD: QUESTIONS AND ANSWERS

● How many main groups or kingdoms of living things are there? Is it three, five or seven?
Five.

● Brackets, moulds, microscopic single-celled yeasts, rusts and mildews are all in which kingdom of living things?
Fungi.

● When did flowering plants, with their brightly-coloured flowers or blossom, first appear or evolve on Earth?
About 130 million years ago.

● Pines, firs, spruces and larches are in which group of trees? Is it blossom trees, conifer trees or evergreen trees?
Conifers.

● What is the name of the green substance in plants that traps light energy from the Sun?
Chlorophyll.

● When a new plant begins to grow out of its seed case, set down roots, and send its shoots and new leaves up to the Sun, what is this called? Is it pollination, fertilization or germination?
Germination.

● Which type of cactus was taken from America to Australia, for use as a spiny hedge-plant, but spread to cover vast areas, driving out local plants and animals?
Prickly pear cactus.

● The starfish is in which animal group, whose members live only in the sea, and have a radial or circular body is based on the number five?
Echinoderms.

● Earthworms, lugworms, ragworms, fanworms and leeches belong to which main group of worms?
True worms, segmented worms or annelids.

● What is the simplest type of animal, with no eyes, ears, brain, mouth, guts or muscles?
Sponge.

● How many millions of years ago did the dinosaurs die out, along with many other animal groups, and some plants too?
65 million years ago.

● Insects belong to the major animal group or phylum called the arthropods. What does this name mean?
'Arthropods' means 'joint-legged'.

● Their name means 'hundred-legged', but most have fewer than 70 pairs of legs - one pair per body segment. They are fast, active creatures that prey on worms, insects and other smaller creatures, and kill them with a bite from poison fangs. There are about 3,000 different kinds, or species. They are ... ?
Centipedes.

● A shark has a skeleton, but no bones. True or false?
True, a shark's skeleton is made of cartilage (gristle).

● Which 'water monster' is a rare salamander of high-altitude freshwater lakes in Mexico, and grows to about 30 centimetres in length?
The axolotl.

● How many different kinds or species of amphibians (frogs toads, newts, salamanders and similar creatures) are there?
About 4,000 species.

● Which is the largest reptile alive today, growing to more than 7 metres long?
The estuarine or salt-water crocodile of the Indian and Pacific Oceans.

● The tuatara is a strange reptile that looks like a lizard, but it is a rhynchocephalian - a reptile group that was widespread even before the dinosaurs. In which part of the world does the tuatara live?
On a few rocky islands around New Zealand.

HUMAN BODY

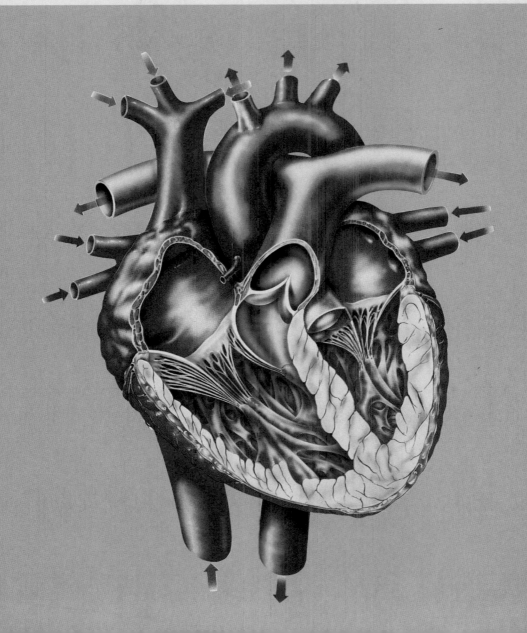

BODY SYSTEMS

THE MOST STUDIED OBJECT in the whole of history is – the human body. More than 2,000 years ago, people began to wonder what was under its skin, and how all the parts worked. Doctors tried to find out why it fell ill, and why it sometimes got better. Artists, painters and sculptors studied the body's shape to produce great works of art. People also asked endless questions about the body. How does it begin? How does it grow from a small and helpless baby into a large, strong, active adult? Why does it become old? Today, many of these questions have been answered, but the body remains a source of fascination and wonder. The body is where we live, move, work, play, eat, drink, think and sleep. The following pages show the main parts of the body and how they work together to keep it alive for 70 years or more.

Studying the body through history

The scientific study of the body's structure is called anatomy. The study of how it works is physiology. The first great anatomist was Claudius Galen of Ancient Rome. He looked after gladiators who fought terrible battles in the Coliseum, so he saw plenty of human insides. Today we use powerful microscopes and scanners to study the body. Yet there is still a great deal left to discover.

Skulls were worshipped in ancient times.

The human animal

There are almost six billion human bodies in the world. They all belong to one group, or species, *Homo sapiens* – 'wise human'. Inside, our bodies are very similar to those of many other animals – especially the great apes, the chimps and gorillas. Scientists agree that humans evolved from a prehistoric ape-like ancestor, by changing gradually over millions of years.

Body cells

Body tissues

Body organs

Body systems

Whole body

How the body is made up
The closer you look at the body, the more you find. The whole body seems like a single object or item. Yet it contains hundreds of organs. Each organ has millions of cells. On an even smaller scale, each cell has billions of molecules, and so on ....

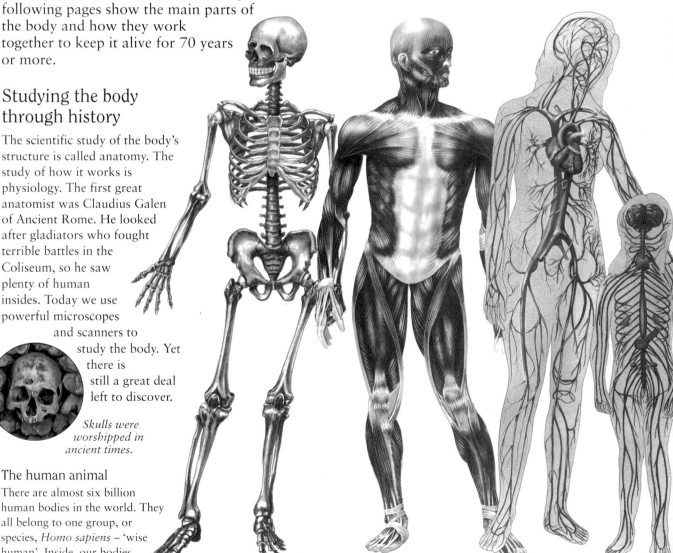

The skeletal system has 206 bones, strong yet light, and linked at joints. They form the body's flexible inner frame.

The muscular system has more than 600 individual muscles. Most pull on bones to cause bodily movements.

The circulatory system is the body's internal transport network, carrying vital substances such as nutrients.

The nervous and hormonal systems are in control of the body. They monitor and coordinate all parts and processes.

Body systems

The body is made up of about 12 major systems. Each of these does one very important job, such as supporting the body, moving it or controlling it. Some systems, such as the nervous and lymphatic systems, spread throughout the body. Others are mainly in one place, like the respiratory system in the head and chest.

Body organs

Each body system consists of several main body parts, called organs. For example, the digestive system is made up of the mouth, gullet, stomach and intestines, plus the liver and pancreas. The circulatory system consists of the heart, the blood, and the immensely complex, branching network of tubes known as blood vessels.

Body tissues

An organ is made of substances called tissues. For instance, the heart has thick walls made of muscle tissue, a tough outer covering, and a thin and flexible lining of blood-proof tissue. It also has nerve tissue to coordinate its pumping movements, and connective tissue to hold all these other tissues together.

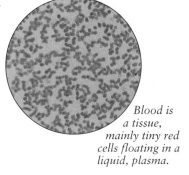

Blood is a tissue, mainly tiny red cells floating in a liquid, plasma.

Body cells

Cells are the microscopic 'building blocks' of the human body. Most kinds are about one-thirtieth of a millimetre across. In epithelial or covering tissue, the cells are box-shaped and joined together strongly, like bricks in a wall. In blood, which is also a kind of tissue, the cells float freely in a fluid. The body consists of more than 50 billion billion cells, of over 200 different kinds.

Molecules

Each cell is made up of yet smaller parts, molecules. These form its outer skin or membrane, its control centre or nucleus, and other parts. A red blood cell contains molecules of haemoglobin – the substance which carries oxygen – 270 million of them.

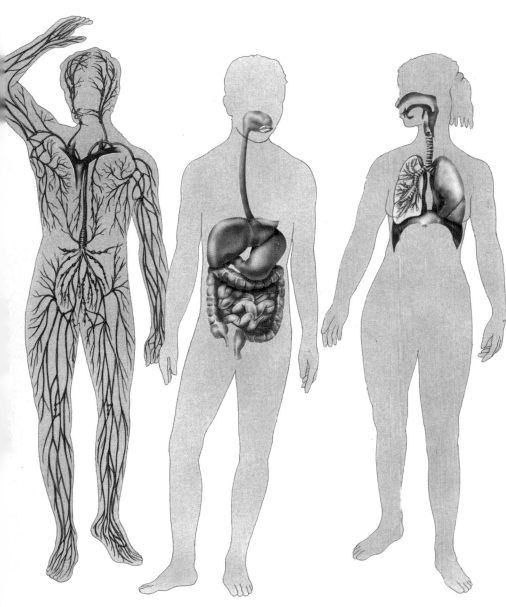

The lymphatic and immune systems are important in fighting disease and germs, and helping the body to recover from injury.

The digestive system takes in and breaks down food, to provide the raw materials for the body's growth and the energy to power its life processes.

The respiratory system breathes in air and takes from it oxygen (which all living things need to survive). It also gets rid of a waste, carbon dioxide.

The same but different

On the outside, people look very different. Some are short, others tall. Some have long legs, others have a long body. Some are light-skinned, others dark-skinned. We can change our appearance with the way we dress. But inside, every body has the same parts, such as a heart, lungs, muscle and bones. Under the skin, we are all very much alike.

SKIN, HAIR AND NAILS

WHEN WE LOOK AT a human body, nearly everything we see on the outside is dead. In fact, it ceased living weeks ago. This dead outer layer is skin, tough yet flexible. It protects the body from knocks, wear and tear, dirt and germs, rain and snow, and possibly harmful rays from the Sun. It also keeps in vital body fluids, salts and minerals. Just beneath this dead surface, skin is very much alive. It is one of the body's busiest organs. It contains tiny blood vessels to keep it nourished, and nerves that detect touch and pain. Skin also helps to control body temperature. When the body is too hot, skin goes flushed and sweaty, to help the body cool down. And the inner layers of skin continually replace the worn-away outer layers, so that the body stays covered and protected.

The size of skin

The skin of an adult person has an area of about two square metres – almost the size of a single bed. It weighs around four kilograms. This makes it the body's largest single part, or organ. Skin varies in thickness from only half a millimetre on the eyelids, to five millimetres or more on the soles of the feet. Skin also responds to changing conditions. Where it is rubbed or pressed regularly, it becomes thicker, to give extra protection. Very thickened patches of skin are called calluses.

The upper layer of skin

The skin's upper layer is called the epidermis. Like the rest of the body, it is made of microscopic cells. At the base of the epidermis, these are very much alive. They multiply to make millions more cells every minute, pushing the cells above them towards the surface. As these cells move upwards, they gradually fill with a hard substance called keratin, then die. About one month later they reach the surface, and are worn away.

The lower layer of skin

The skin's lower layer is the dermis. It contains millions of microscopic touch sensors that detect touch, pressure, heat, cold and pain. Each has a nerve fibre linking it to the brain. The dermis also has tiny blood vessels, and micro-fibres of the tough substance collagen and the stretchy substance elastin. These make skin flexible yet strong.

Hair shaft (composed of dead, keratin-packed cells)

Opening of sweat pore

Dead, keratin-filled cells on surface

Cells move upwards, fill with keratin and die

Rapidly multiplying cells at base of epidermis

Hair follicle

Hair root

Sebaceous (skin wax) gland

Young and old skin

A baby's skin has had little wear and tear. It is soft and smooth, and its hairs are tiny and bendy. Gradually the skin becomes tougher, and body hairs grow larger and thicker. After many years, skin begins to lose its natural stretchiness. Patches which bend a lot develop creases and wrinkles, due to a lack of elastin fibres.

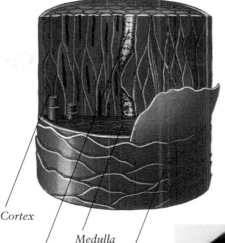

Cortex

Medulla

Hollow centre

Cuticle

Curly or straight?

Hairs that are circular in cross-section tend to grow straight. If the hair is more oval, it grows naturally wavy along its length. If it has a C-shaped cross-section it is curly.

Layers of epidermis

Junction between epidermis and dermis

Sensory nerve endings for light touch

Sensory nerve endings for heavy pressure

Capillary

Sweat duct

Nerve fibre

Collagen and elastin fibres in dermis

Sensory nerve endings for changes in temperature

Sweat gland

Subcutaneous ('under-skin') fat layer

Hair and nails

An average person has about 100,000 head hairs. Like skin, they are made of dead cells. Each hair grows from a pit-shaped follicle in the skin. At the hair's base, or root, living cells multiply rapidly. Gradually they get pushed upwards, cemented into a rod-like shape, filled with keratin, and die. Nails form in the same way, but as a flat plate. This grows from the nail root and slides slowly along, over the living skin below it.

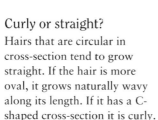

Sweat glands and pores

Sweat is a watery fluid made by around five million sweat glands scattered throughout the skin. Each gland is a tiny knot of tubes, connected to the surface by a corkscrew-like sweat duct. The duct opens at the skin's surface as a hole, the sweat pore (left). All the body's sweat ducts straightened out and joined together would stretch 10 kilometres. An average person produces about 70 millilitres of sweat in cool conditions. This rises to more than one litre per hour for an active person in hot conditions.

HOT OR COLD?

Skin can sense changes in temperature better than actual temperature. Fill three bowls with safely warm water, cool water and cold water. Put one hand into the warm water and the other in the cool water. Then put both hands in the cold water. The hand that was in the warm water should feel colder than the hand in the cool water, because the temperature change was greater.

MUSCLES AND MOVEMENT

ALMOST HALF THE BODY'S weight is muscle. A muscle is a body part specialized to get shorter, or contract, when it receives nerve signals from the brain. Most muscles are long and strap-shaped. They taper at each end into rope-like tendons which attach firmly to bones. When the muscle contracts, it pulls the bone and moves that part of the body. This sounds simple, but the process of moving is incredibly complicated. There are more than 640 muscles, and they hardly ever work alone. They usually work in teams to pull, tilt and twist several bones at once. Also, as one part moves, such as when you hold your arm out sideways, muscles in other parts need to work too. Your back and front muscles tense to take the strain, and your leg muscles shift weight to keep you balanced. The result is a smooth, coordinated movement, without you falling over!

Inside a muscle

A typical muscle is made of bundles of muscle fibres, or myofibres. Each fibre is slightly thinner than a human hair. In turn, each muscle fibre is a bundle of even thinner parts, muscle fibrils or myofibrils. And in turn again, each fibril contains bundles of long thin stringy substances known as actin and myosin. When a muscle contracts, the actins slide past the myosins, like rows of people pulling ropes. As millions of actins and myosins do this, the whole muscle gets shorter.

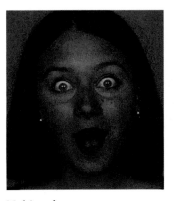 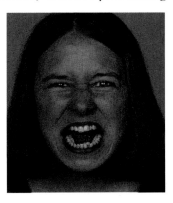

Making faces

About 60 muscles in the face, head and neck produce our huge range of facial expressions. Some of these muscles are joined, not to bones, but to other muscles. For example, the frontalis muscles in your forehead can raise your eyebrows in a questioning way. Smiling is easier than frowning. A grin requires 20 muscles, while a grimace uses more than 40.

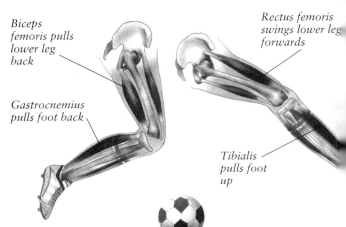

Biceps femoris pulls lower leg back

Gastrocnemius pulls foot back

Rectus femoris swings lower leg forwards

Tibialis pulls foot up

Pull, not push

A muscle can get shorter and pull. But it cannot make a pushing force. So most muscles are arranged in opposing teams. One team pulls the body part one way. Then the other team pulls it back again. As each team pulls, the other relaxes and gets stretched. For example, muscles in the rear of the thigh pull the leg back at the hip and knee. Then opposing muscles in the front of the thigh quickly swing the leg forwards and straighten the knee – KICK!

Power and coordination

In a complicated gymnastic movement, the brain must control almost every muscle in the body. This needs much practice, but gradually the brain part called the cerebellum takes over the control, and it becomes almost automatic.

 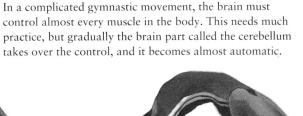

Arms are ready to swing down on to floor just in front of feet

Legs swing up and over with lots of momentum

Legs continue to swing over on to floor and arms push up

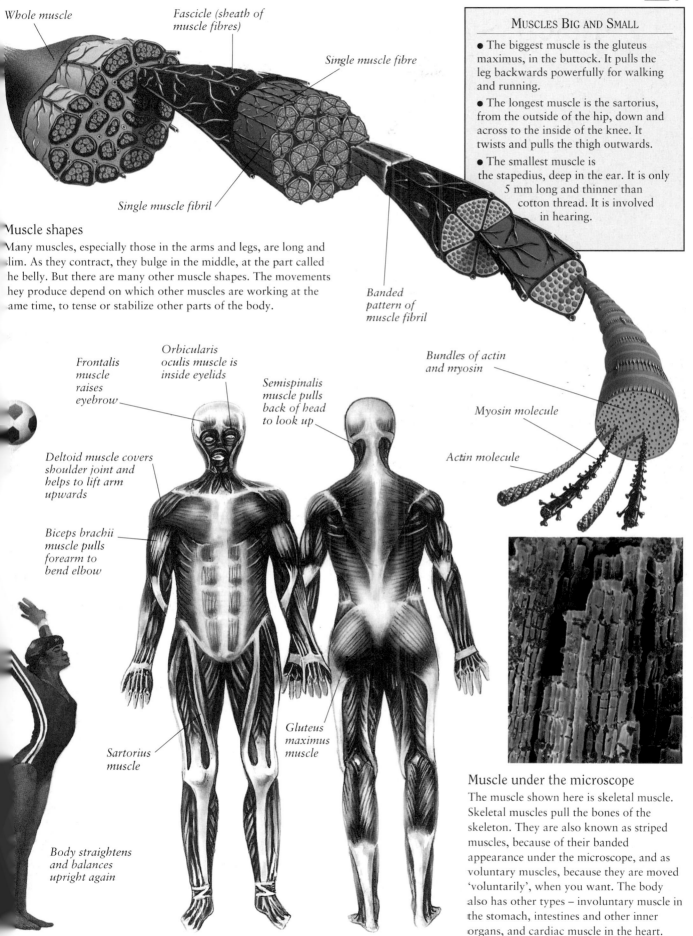

Whole muscle

Fascicle (sheath of muscle fibres)

Single muscle fibre

Single muscle fibril

MUSCLES BIG AND SMALL

● The biggest muscle is the gluteus maximus, in the buttock. It pulls the leg backwards powerfully for walking and running.

● The longest muscle is the sartorius, from the outside of the hip, down and across to the inside of the knee. It twists and pulls the thigh outwards.

● The smallest muscle is the stapedius, deep in the ear. It is only 5 mm long and thinner than cotton thread. It is involved in hearing.

Muscle shapes

Many muscles, especially those in the arms and legs, are long and slim. As they contract, they bulge in the middle, at the part called the belly. But there are many other muscle shapes. The movements they produce depend on which other muscles are working at the same time, to tense or stabilize other parts of the body.

Banded pattern of muscle fibril

Frontalis muscle raises eyebrow

Orbicularis oculis muscle is inside eyelids

Semispinalis muscle pulls back of head to look up

Bundles of actin and myosin

Myosin molecule

Actin molecule

Deltoid muscle covers shoulder joint and helps to lift arm upwards

Biceps brachii muscle pulls forearm to bend elbow

Gluteus maximus muscle

Sartorius muscle

Body straightens and balances upright again

Muscle under the microscope

The muscle shown here is skeletal muscle. Skeletal muscles pull the bones of the skeleton. They are also known as striped muscles, because of their banded appearance under the microscope, and as voluntary muscles, because they are moved 'voluntarily', when you want. The body also has other types – involuntary muscle in the stomach, intestines and other inner organs, and cardiac muscle in the heart.

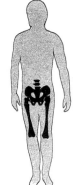

BONES AND JOINTS

MOST BODY PARTS, SUCH AS the guts, nerves and blood vessels, are soft and floppy. The body gets its strength and support from its skeleton. This is an inner framework of 206 bones. Many of them are linked at flexible joints, so they can move when they are pulled by muscles. There are many different shapes of bones, depending on the part of the body they support, and the jobs they do. Long bones in the arms and legs work like stiff girders, so we can reach and hold objects, and walk and run. The skull is a dome-shaped bone that surrounds and protects the delicate brain. The ribs form a moveable cage. This protects the heart and lungs within, yet also allows breathing movements. Without our bones, we would just flop on the floor like a heap of jelly!

Flexible joints
Bones and joints, like other body parts, stay healthy if they are used properly. Exercise and activity can help to develop strong bones and smooth, flexible joints. But if a joint is regularly forced beyond its natural range of movement, it can eventually suffer problems of over-use such as pain and stiffness.

The skeleton

The skeleton has two main parts. The central tower-like axial skeleton consists of the skull, the backbone or vertebral column, and the ribs and breastbone in the chest. The appendicular skeleton is the limbs – the arms and legs. The bones in the legs are long and strong, to hold the body up and carry it when walking and running. The arm bones are very similar to the leg bones, but they are slimmer and lighter, and the joints are more flexible, for grasping and holding.

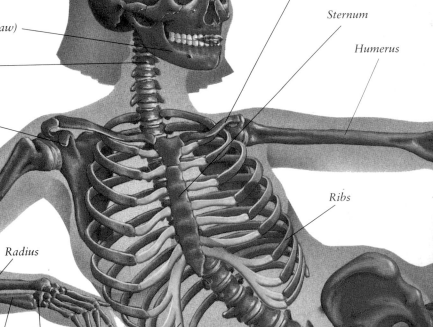

Cranium (brain case) of skull

Mandible (lower jaw)

Cervical vertebrae

Scapula

Clavicle (collar bone)

Sternum

Humerus

Ribs

Radius

Ulna

Carpals (wrist)

Cartilage parts of ribs

Vertebral column

KNOW YOUR BONES

● The largest bone is the pelvis, or hip bone. In fact it is made of six bones joined firmly together.

● The longest bone is the femur, in the thigh. It makes up almost one-quarter of the body's total height.

● The smallest bone is the stirrup, deep in the ear. It is hardly larger than a grain of rice.

● The ears and nose do not have bones inside them. Their inner supports are cartilage, or gristle, which is lighter and bendier than bone. This is why the nose and ears are flexible.

● After death, cartilage rots faster than bone. This is why the skulls of skeletons have no nose or ears!

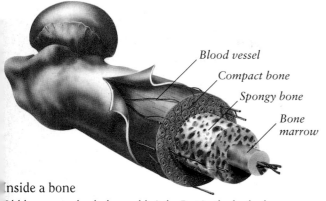

Blood vessel

Compact bone

Spongy bone

Bone marrow

Inside a bone

Old bones are dead, dry and brittle. But in the body, bones are very much alive. They have their own nerves and blood vessels, and they do various jobs, such as storing body minerals. A typical bone has an outer layer of hard or compact bone, which is very strong, dense and tough. Inside this is a layer of spongy bone, which is like a honeycomb, lighter and slightly flexible. In the middle of some bones is jelly-like bone marrow, where new cells are constantly being produced for the blood.

X-Rays

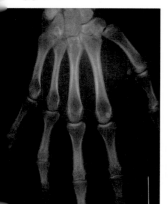

The invisible waves called X-rays can pass through the body's soft tissues, like muscles and nerves. They expose or darken a sheet of photographic film placed on the other side of the body. But the rays are stopped by dense tissues, mainly bone and cartilage. So these show up white. This X-ray reveals the bones in the wrist, palm and fingers.

Joints

Inside a joint like the knee or elbow, the ends of the bones are covered with cartilage (gristle). This is shiny, smooth and slippery, and allows the bones to slide past each other without wear or rubbing. The joint also contains a slippery liquid, synovial fluid, which works like oil to lubricate the movements.

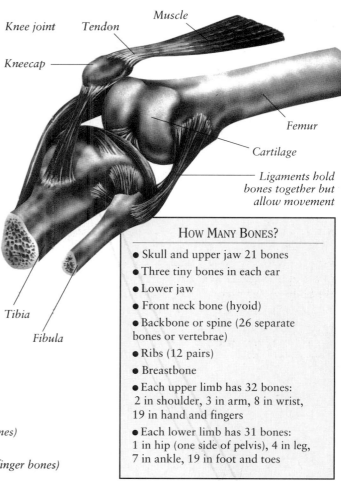

Knee joint

Tendon

Muscle

Kneecap

Femur

Cartilage

Ligaments hold bones together but allow movement

Tibia

Fibula

HOW MANY BONES?

- Skull and upper jaw 21 bones
- Three tiny bones in each ear
- Lower jaw
- Front neck bone (hyoid)
- Backbone or spine (26 separate bones or vertebrae)
- Ribs (12 pairs)
- Breastbone
- Each upper limb has 32 bones: 2 in shoulder, 3 in arm, 8 in wrist, 19 in hand and fingers
- Each lower limb has 31 bones: 1 in hip (one side of pelvis), 4 in leg, 7 in ankle, 19 in foot and toes

WHY ARE MANY BONES LIKE TUBES?

Roll and tape a sheet of card into a tube. Fold another in half many times and tape it into a concertina. Fold and tape another sheet of card into a long box. Now try to bend each long shape. The tube should be strongest. This is why many bones are tubular.

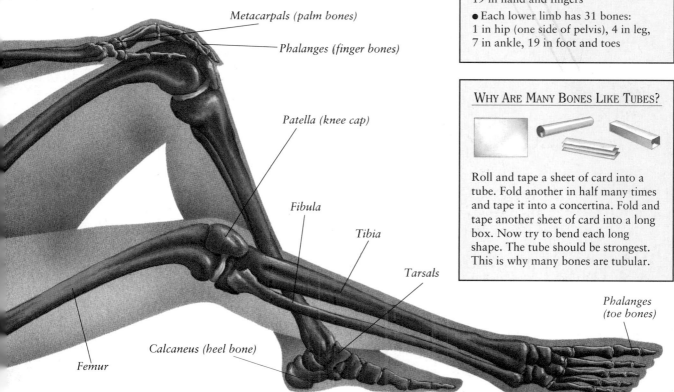

Metacarpals (palm bones)

Phalanges (finger bones)

Patella (knee cap)

Fibula

Tibia

Tarsals

Femur

Calcaneus (heel bone)

Phalanges (toe bones)

LUNGS AND BREATHING

EVERY ANIMAL BODY, including the human body, needs oxygen. This substance is a gas and makes up one-fifth of the air around us. Oxygen is needed because it is an essential part of the life processes inside the body, which break down the food we eat to release energy contained in it. The energy is used for growth, movement and every other body activity. The body system that obtains oxygen from air is called the respiratory system. Its main parts are the two lungs, inside the chest. The movements of breathing suck air into the lungs, where oxygen passes from the air into the blood. The blood flows away and carries the oxygen to all body parts. This is a continuous process, because the body cannot store oxygen for the future. So if breathing stops, the oxygen supply fails. After a few minutes, the body begins to die.

Nasal cavity

Pharynx (throat)

Larynx (voicebox

Trachea (windpipe

Cartilage ring

Lef
bronchu

Left lung

Spac
for hear

Ri

Bronchial tree of branching airways (bronchioles)

Right lung

Diaphragm

More and bigger breaths

During activity or exercise, muscles work harder. This means they use more energy. So they need more oxygen. The body responds by breathing faster and deeper, to take more air deeper into the lungs. At rest, the body takes in and breathes out about 10 litres of air each minute. After running a hard race, this amount can go up almost 10 times.

The respiratory system

This body system consists of the nose and throat, the windpipe or trachea in the neck, the main airways or bronc to each lung, the lungs themselves in the chest, and the mai breathing muscle, the diaphragm. The lungs are light and spongy and contain smaller airways, bronchioles. The bronchioles branch and divide many times, becoming smal and smaller, like an upside-down tree. Each breath draws i air through the nose, or the mouth, or both. Breathing through the nose helps to moisten and warm the air, while nose hairs filter out bits of dust. This helps to keep the lung clean and working efficiently.

Inside the lungs

Deep inside the lungs are more than 500 million microscopic air bubbles, which are called alveoli. These are surrounded by networks of microscopic blood vessels, the capillaries. Fresh air flows through the branching system of air tubes that fills the lungs, and into the alveoli. Oxygen from the air seeps easily through the ultra-thin walls of the alveoli and capillaries, into the blood, and is carried away round the body. Meanwhile one of the body's waste substances, the gas carbon dioxide, passes the opposite way, from the blood to the airways. The stale air is then breathed out.

Artery

Vein

Alveolus

Blood capillaries around alveolus

BREATHING PROBLEMS

In the condition called asthma, the small airways called bronchioles in the lungs get narrower and clogged with fluid. This may be due to an allergy or response to a certain substance, such as house dust or plant pollen, or sometimes due to emotional stress. Breathing grows wheezy. Modern medical drugs breathed directly into the lungs, such as the fine spray from an inhaler, can relieve the problem, and make breathing easier again.

The mouth must be wide open when shouting, to allow the greatest air flow for maximum volume

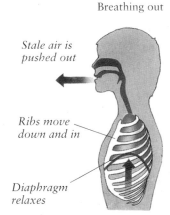

A supply of oxygen

All animals, including those in water, need oxygen. There is oxygen dissolved in water. Fish have gills, which are specialized to obtain the dissolved oxygen. Our lungs cannot obtain this dissolved oxygen. So divers take their own supply, in scuba tanks on their backs, or pumped down a long tube from the surface.

Noises from flowing air

Just below the throat, at the top of the windpipe, is the voicebox or larynx. Air flows through this during breathing. The larynx has two shelf-like folds of cartilage (gristle) in its walls, the vocal cords. In normal breathing these are wide apart. But they can be pulled almost together by voicebox muscles to form a narrow slit. As air flows through the slit it makes the cords shake fast or vibrate, and this produces a noise. Other muscles stretch the cords longer to make the noise higher-pitched, like a squeak. This is how we talk – and sing, shout and make many other noises, both deliberate and accidental!

HOW MANY BREATHS?

How fast do you breathe? And how fast can you breathe? Using a stopwatch, time the number of breaths you take in one minute. Do this first after resting quietly for 10 minutes. Then swim a race. Count the number of breaths every minute afterwards, until it returns to the resting rate. This is the breathing recovery time. It tends to be shorter in people who are physically fit.

Breathing in

Fresh air is sucked in

Ribs move up and out

Diaphragm stretches

Breathing out

Stale air is pushed out

Ribs move down and in

Diaphragm relaxes

Breathing

Breathing involves two sets of muscles. One is a large sheet-like muscle in the base of the chest, the diaphragm. This pulls the lungs down. The other set is the intercostal muscles between the ribs, which pull them up and out. Together, these muscles stretch the lungs and make them suck in air. Then the muscles relax. The lungs spring back to their smaller size and push out the stale air.

FOOD AND DIGESTION

EVERY YEAR, AN AVERAGE PERSON eats about half a tonne of food. But we do not put on half a tonne of weight! We need to eat so much because there is a constant turnover within the body. Cells wear out and die, and new cells are made to replace them. The food we eat is broken down, or digested, into its many and various nutrients. Some of these are used as raw materials for growth, body maintenance and repair. Other nutrients are split apart to release the energy inside them, which is used for moving, breathing and hundreds of other life processes. Any undigested or leftover bits of food, along with various bodily wastes, are then removed from the body at the end of the digestive process and by excretion. Since the body is made from the food it eats, a balanced diet of good foods is important for health.

The digestive system

The main part of the digestive system is the digestive tract. This is like a long tube, some nine metres in total, through the middle of the body. It starts at the mouth, where food and drink enter, and finishes at the anus, where leftover food and wastes leave the body. Some parts of the tract are wide, such as the stomach. Others are narrow and coiled, like the small intestine. Each part has an important digestive task. Also involved in digestion are the liver and pancreas.

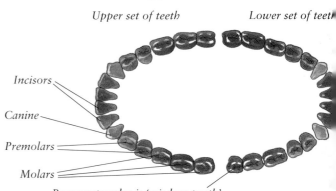

Upper set of teeth   *Lower set of teeth*

Incisors

Canine

Premolars

Molars

Rearmost molar is 'wisdom tooth'

Types of teeth

The adult human body has 32 teeth. The eight chisel-like incisors at the front bite food. The four pointed canines tear and rip it. The eight premolars and twelve molars at the back of the mouth are flattened to crush and chew it. Before the adult teeth grow, the body has a first or 'milk' set of 20 teeth. These begin to grow soon after birth, and are replaced by the adult teeth from the age of about six or seven years.

Fast food, slow eating

Thorough chewing mashes any kind of food into a pulp and makes it easier to digest in the stomach and intestines. Food that is bitten and swallowed with hardly any chewing cannot be digested so well.

Moving food

Lumps of food are pushed through the digestive tract by moving, wave-like contractions of the muscles in its wall, known as peristalsis.

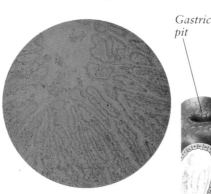

Gastric pit   *Cells make digestive chemicals*

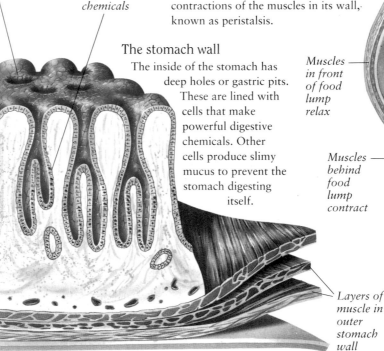

The villi of the small intestine under the microscope

The stomach wall

The inside of the stomach has deep holes or gastric pits. These are lined with cells that make powerful digestive chemicals. Other cells produce slimy mucus to prevent the stomach digesting itself.

Muscles in front of food lump relax

Muscles behind food lump contract

Layers of muscle in outer stomach wall

Layers muscle digestiv tract w

Inside the intestine

The small intestine takes in or absorbs nutrients. The greater the area for absorption, the more effective this process. So the intestine's inner lining has thousands of tiny, finger-like villi. These increase its surface area almost 40 times compared to a flat lining.

Mouth

Teeth bite off and chew food into a soft pulp that is easy to swallow. Chewing mixes the food with watery saliva, from six salivary glands around the mouth and face, to make it moist and slippery. The tongue moves the food around, positioning it between the teeth for thorough chewing and then separates off lumps and pushes them one by one into the throat for swallowing.

Liver

Blood from the intestines flows to the liver, carrying nutrients, vitamins, minerals and other products from digestion. The liver is like a food-processing factory with more than 200 different jobs. It stores some nutrients, changes them from one form to another, and releases them into the blood, according to the activities and needs of the body.

Gall bladder

This small bag-like part is tucked under the liver. It stores a fluid called bile, which is made in the liver. As food from a meal arrives in the small intestine, bile flows from the gall bladder along the bile duct into the intestine. It helps to digest fatty foods and also contains wastes for removal.

Small intestine

This part of the tract is narrow, but very long – about six metres. Here, more enzymes continue the chemical attack on the food. Finally the nutrients are small enough to pass through the lining of the small intestine, and into the blood. They are carried away to the liver and other body parts to be processed, stored and distributed.

Large intestine

Any useful substances in the leftovers, such as spare water and body minerals, are absorbed through the walls of the large intestine, back into the blood. The remains are formed into brown, semi-solid faeces, ready to be removed from the body.

Salivary glands

The three pairs of salivary glands, left and right, are under the tongue (sublingual), under the angle of the lower jaw (submandibular) and just in front of the ear. They produce about 1.5 litres of watery saliva (spit) each day. Some of this is stored, and released when chewing. The rest is released slowly and gradually, to keep the mouth, tongue and throat moist.

Gullet

The gullet, or oesophagus, is a muscular tube. It takes food from the throat and pushes it down through the neck, and into the stomach. It moves food by waves of muscle contraction that pass along its length. These waves are called peristalsis, and they happen all the way along the digestive tract.

Stomach

The stomach has thick muscles in its wall. These contract to squash and mash the food into a sloppy soup. Also, the stomach lining produces strong digestive juices, called acids and enzymes. These attack the food in a chemical way, breaking down and dissolving its nutrients.

Pancreas

The pancreas is a wedge-shaped part behind the stomach. Like the stomach, it makes powerful digestive juices, called enzymes. When food enters the small intestine, the juices flow from the pancreas, along a thin tube, the pancreatic duct, into the small intestine. Along with enzymes made by the small intestine itself, the pancreatic enzymes help to digest food further.

Rectum and anus

The end of the large intestine and the next part of the tract, the rectum, store the faeces. These are finally squeezed through a ring of muscle, the anus, and out of the body.

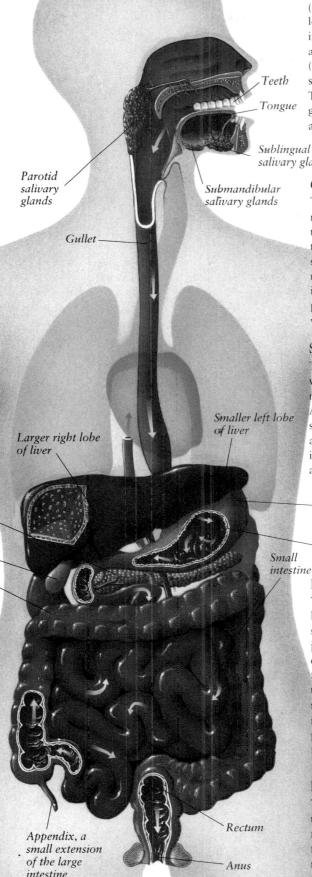

Teeth

Tongue

Sublingual salivary glands

Parotid salivary glands

Submandibular salivary glands

Gullet

Smaller left lobe of liver

Larger right lobe of liver

Stomach

Stomach lining

Pancreas

Gall bladder

Small intestine

Large intestine

Appendix, a small extension of the large intestine

Rectum

Anus

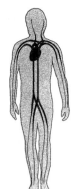

HEART, CIRCULATION AND BLOOD

THE HEART IS USED as a symbol of courage, strength and love. But it's not really involved in any of these. It is simply a hollow bag with muscular walls, which contract about once each second. The contractions squeeze blood from inside the heart, out through the bodywide network of tubes known as blood vessels. The heart, blood vessels and blood are known as the circulatory system, because the same blood goes round and round, or circulates. A typical person has about four to five litres of blood. This thick red fluid carries oxygen from the lungs, and nutrients from digestion, to every body part. It also collects body wastes and takes them to parts such as the kidneys and lungs for removal. In addition, blood carries substances called hormones, which control body processes, and antibodies to fight invading germs.

To head and upper body

From head and upper body

Right atrium

To right lung

From right lung

Pulmonary valve

Tricuspid valve

Right ventricle

Thick muscular wall (myocardium)

From lower body

To lower body

Inside the heart

Your heart is about the size of your clenched fist. It has thick muscular walls and is divided into two pumps by the septum. Each pump has two chambers. The upper, smaller, thin-walled atrium receives blood coming in from the veins. The blood flows through a one-way valve, which makes sure it always moves in the correct direction, into the larger, lower chamber. This is called the ventricle. It has thick, strong walls that contract to squeeze the blood through another valve, out into the arteries.

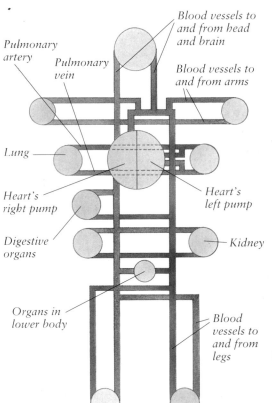

Pulmonary artery

Pulmonary vein

Blood vessels to and from head and brain

Blood vessels to and from arms

Lung

Heart's right pump

Heart's left pump

Digestive organs

Kidney

Organs in lower body

Blood vessels to and from legs

Two-part circulation

The body's circulation has two parts, with the heart as a double pump. Blood from the heart's right pump is dark red and low in oxygen. It goes along pulmonary arteries to the lungs, where it receives fresh supplies of oxygen and becomes bright red. It flows along pulmonary veins back to the heart's left pump. This sends it around the rest of the body, to deliver the essential oxygen to every part.

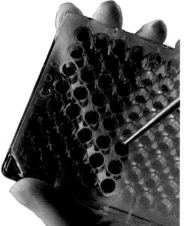

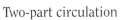

Blood transfusions

If someone loses a lot of blood, through a wound or other injury, one part of the treatment may be a blood transfusion. Blood previously given or donated by another person, the donor, is transferred or transfused into the ill person, or recipient. The blood must be matched. This means making sure it is the correct blood group for the recipient, by laboratory tests (left). Different people have different kinds, or groups, of blood. If blood of the wrong group is given, it may clump together and clot in the recipient's body, making the illness worse or even causing death.

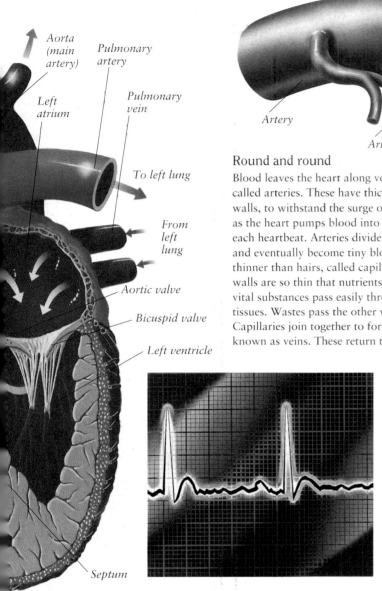

Aorta (main artery)

Pulmonary artery

Pulmonary vein

Left atrium

To left lung

From left lung

Aortic valve

Bicuspid valve

Left ventricle

Septum

Muscular wall

Endothelium (lining)

Lumen (space in middle)

Artery

Arterioles

Blood passes oxygen and nutrients to surrounding tissues

Capillary network

Venules

Vein

Round and round

Blood leaves the heart along vessels called arteries. These have thick, elastic walls, to withstand the surge of pressure as the heart pumps blood into them with each heartbeat. Arteries divide and branch and eventually become tiny blood vessels, thinner than hairs, called capillaries. Capillary walls are so thin that nutrients, oxygen and other vital substances pass easily through them, to surrounding tissues. Wastes pass the other way, into the blood. Capillaries join together to form larger, thin-walled vessels known as veins. These return the blood to the heart.

Heartbeats on screen

As the heart beats, it produces tiny natural pulses of electricity which ripple through body tissues. These pulses can be picked up by metal sensors, called electrodes, pressed on to the skin. A medical machine called the ECG, electro-cardiograph, can display the pulses as spiky lines on a monitor screen or strip of paper. The exact shape of the line tells doctors about the health of the heart.

Blood under the microscope

About half the volume of blood is a pale yellow, watery fluid called plasma. This contains dissolved nutrients, body minerals, salts, hormones and dozens of other substances. The rest of blood is microscopic cells. Donut-shaped red cells pick up vital oxygen in the lungs and carry it to the tissues. White cells are larger and help to protect the body against germs and illness. Platelets are tiny and help blood to clot, to seal a cut or wound. In one drop of blood there are about 5 million red cells, 300,000 platelets, and 10,000 white cells.

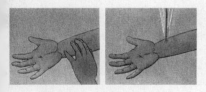

SEE YOUR PULSE!

The heart must pump blood very forcefully, especially up to the head, to overcome the downward pull of gravity. This powerful pumping motion can be felt, using the fingertips as shown, just beneath the thin skin inside your wrist.
To see the effect of your pulse, attach a drinking straw to the inside of your wrist with plasticene. Hold your hand still and you can see that the straw moves in time with the rhythm of your pulse.

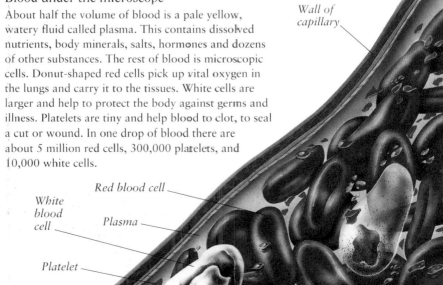

Wall of capillary

Red blood cell

White blood cell

Plasma

Platelet

KIDNEYS AND EXCRETION

HUNDREDS OF LIFE PROCESSES inside the
body produce many kinds of by-products
and wastes. Removal of these is called
excretion. It happens in several ways. The
lungs breathe out carbon dioxide, a
waste made when food nutrients are
broken down to release their energy. The
sweat that oozes on to the skin also
contains some waste salts and minerals.
But the chief method of removing wastes from
inside the body is by the excretory system. Its main
parts are the two kidneys. They 'clean' blood
passing through them, filtering out wastes and
unwanted substances, to form the fluid called urine.
This is stored in a stretchy bag, the bladder, until
it's convenient to remove it from the body.
Strangely, the removal of solid waste from the
end of the digestive tract is not true excretion.
These waste substances have been inside the
tract, but not actually inside body tissues.

The excretory or urinary system

The two kidneys are on either side of
the backbone, shielded by the
lowermost ribs. In most people, the left
kidney is slightly higher than the right
one. Each receives a huge supply of
blood along its wide renal artery. This
blood is filtered and cleaned and
returns along the renal vein. Wastes
and excess water collect as the pale
yellow liquid, urine. This trickles from
each kidney along a pipe called the
ureter, down to the bladder in the
lower body. When the bladder is full,
the urine is released from it and passed
along another tube, the urethra, out
of the body.

Inside a kidney

A kidney has two main layers,
an outer cortex and an inner
medulla. The cortex contains
about one million microscopic
filters. These remove water
and wastes from the blood.
In the medulla, some of the
water is taken back into the
blood, according to the
body's needs and water
balance. Urine dribbles
slowly but continuously into
the kidney's central chamber,
the renal pelvis. Then it passes
along the urethra by the
muscular squeezing process
known as peristalsis, down the
ureter to the bladder.

Cystogram

Body fluids like blood and urine
do not normally show up on an
X-ray image. But in the X-ray
called a cystogram, a person
drinks a special harmless
substance called contrast
medium, which does show up.
As it travels around in the
blood and becomes
concentrated in the urine, it
reveals the shapes of the blood
vessels and urine tubes.

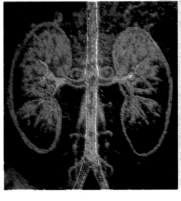

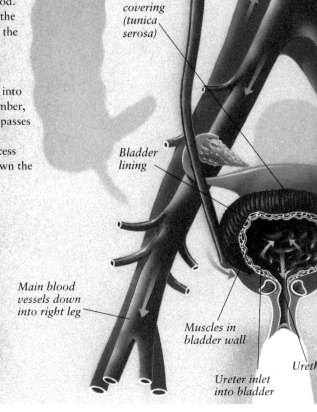

Main vein
(vena cava)

Main artery
(aorta)

Renal artery

Renal vein

Kidney

Bladder
covering
(tunica
serosa)

Bladder
lining

Main blood
vessels down
into right leg

Muscles in
bladder wall

Uretl

Ureter inlet
into bladder

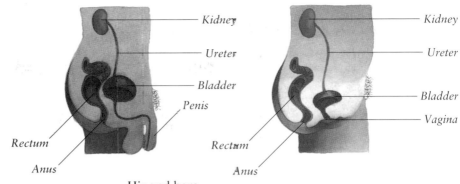

Kidney
Ureter
Bladder
Penis
Rectum
Anus

Kidney
Ureter
Bladder
Vagina
Rectum
Anus

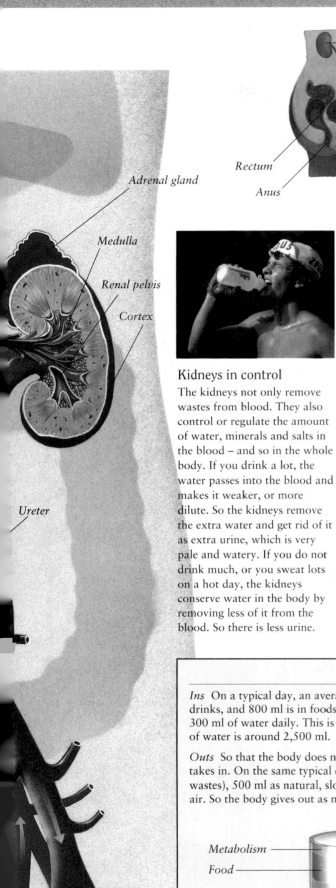

Adrenal gland

Medulla

Renal pelvis

Cortex

Ureter

His and hers

The excretory system has connections and shares parts with the reproductive system. In a man, urine passes along the urethra to the outside. At other times the urethra also carries sperm in their fluid, from the glands called the testes to the outside. The urethra runs along inside the penis, and the urine or the sperm in their fluid pass out of the end. So the reproductive and urinary openings from the body are the same. In a woman, the urethra opens to the outside just in front of the birth canal or reproductive opening, the vagina.

Kidneys in control

The kidneys not only remove wastes from blood. They also control or regulate the amount of water, minerals and salts in the blood – and so in the whole body. If you drink a lot, the water passes into the blood and makes it weaker, or more dilute. So the kidneys remove the extra water and get rid of it as extra urine, which is very pale and watery. If you do not drink much, or you sweat lots on a hot day, the kidneys conserve water in the body by removing less of it from the blood. So there is less urine.

One in a million micro-filters

The kidney's microscopic filters are called nephrons. Each has a knotty tangle of capillaries (tiny blood vessels) called the glomerulus (right), surrounded by a double-layered cup, the glomerular capsule. As blood flows through the glomerulus, wastes and water, plus some useful salts and minerals, are squeezed into the cup. They trickle from the cup along a tiny but long and winding tube, the nephron loop. This is also surrounded by capillaries. Useful substances and the required amount of water pass back into the blood. Wastes and excess water flow on, along larger tubes called collecting ducts, and form urine.

THE INS AND OUTS OF WATER

Ins On a typical day, an average person takes in about 2,200 ml of water. Around 1,400 ml is drinks, and 800 ml is in foods. Also, chemical processes inside body tissues actually make about 300 ml of water daily. This is called the water of metabolism. So, in total, the body's daily intake of water is around 2,500 ml.

Outs So that the body does not swell up like a wet balloon, it must get rid of as much water as it takes in. On the same typical day it loses 1,500 ml of water in urine, 200 ml in faeces (digestive wastes), 500 ml as natural, slow, continual sweating, and 300 ml as water vapour in breathed-out air. So the body gives out as much water as it takes in: 2,500 ml.

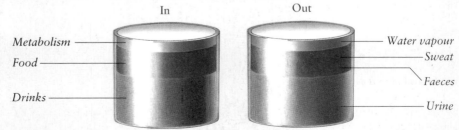

In

Out

Metabolism

Food

Drinks

Water vapour

Sweat

Faeces

Urine

HORMONAL SYSTEM

THE BODY HAS TWO overall control systems, to make sure that its many parts and processes work together smoothly. One is the nervous system. This is based on tiny pulses of electricity called nerve signals. The other is the hormonal or endocrine system. This is based on natural body substances called hormones. There are more than 50 different hormones, and they are all chemicals that 'carry messages'. They are made in hormonal or endocrine glands, and travel around the body in the blood system. Each type of hormone affects a certain part or parts of the body, like the heart, liver or stomach. These parts are called its target tissues or organs. The hormone makes its targets work faster (or slower). The higher the level of hormone in the blood, the faster (or slower) its target parts work. In this way hormones control or regulate the activities of many body parts.

Hormone-making glands

The 10 or so main hormone-making glands are found throughout the head and body, and are shown opposite. They release their hormones directly into the blood flowing through them, rather than along special tubes or ducts. So they are also called ductless or endocrine glands, as opposed to the ducted or exocrine glands like the tiny sweat glands in the skin. However, the pancreas in the upper left abdomen is both exocrine and endocrine. It makes digestive juices that flow along its duct into the intestines, and it produces hormones that pass directly into the blood flowing through this gland.

Scary ride

A rollercoaster ride brings mixed feelings of worry, fear, excitement, even great pleasure! The hormone system is working overtime as various endocrine glands release extra amounts of their hormones into the blood. Along with the actions of the nerve system, they make the heart pound, the muscles tense, the skin sweat and the skin turn pale. Some of these reactions are due to the hormone adrenaline (see opposite). Control by the nerves happens quickly, second by second. The effects of hormones last longer as these chemicals continue to circulate in the blood. This is why the excitement of the ride takes many minutes to die away as the heartbeat gradually slows down, muscles relax and skin returns to normal.

A rollercoaster ride gives you pale, sweaty skin, a pounding heart and tense muscles. These symptoms are caused by a rush of adrenaline, the body's reaction to a scary ride

Hypothalamus

Part of the brain just above the pituitary, it works with it to coordinate the hormone and nerve systems.

Pituitary gland

Makes about 10 hormones that control other hormonal glands; also regulates general body activities and growth.

Thyroid

Makes two hormones, thyroxine and tri-iodothyronine, that affect the speed of chemical processes inside cells, and another hormone, calcitonin, which regulates the mineral calcium.

Pancreas

Makes powerful enzyme-containing juices for the digestive system, and the hormones insulin and glucagon, which regulate energy-rich sugar (glucose) in the blood.

Adrenal

The outer part (cortex) makes the body's natural steroid hormones, which affect levels of water, salts and minerals and help the body cope with stress and disease. The inner part (medulla) makes adrenaline (see above right).

Kidneys

Renin and other hormones help to balance the amounts of water, minerals and salts in blood and body fluids.

Stomach and intestines

Make hormones that work to coordinate the lengthy process of digestion.

Ovaries (female sex glands)

Make hormones that affect growth, including at the time of puberty, when a girl develops breasts and begins the reproductive or menstrual cycle of egg ripening.

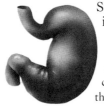

Testes (male sex glands)

Make hormones that affect growth, including at the time of puberty, when a boy develops facial hair and a deeper voice, and begins to produce sperm.

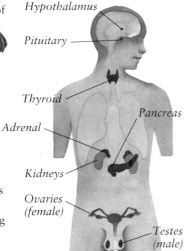

Hypothalamus

Pituitary

Thyroid

Adrenal

Kidneys

Ovaries (female)

Pancreas

Testes (male)

WHAT DOES ADRENALINE DO?

When the adrenal glands release adrenaline in a fight or flight situation, the following things happen to the body to enable it to react properly:

- Blood pressure rises
- Muscles receive extra blood
- Digestive and other organs receive less blood
- Skin receives less blood and so goes pale
- Heart rate increases
- Breathing rate increases
- Tiny airways in lungs (bronchioles) widen
- Liver releases high-energy sugar into bloodstream

Ready for action!

In a stressful or frightening situation, the brain tells the adrenal glands to release their hormone adrenaline. This acts in seconds to increase blood pressure, heart rate, the level of blood sugar, and the blood supply to muscles. These changes prepare the body for physical action, to cope with stress or danger. It's called the 'fight or flight' reaction because the body is prepared to fight or confront danger — or to flee (run away from) it.

TREATMENT FOR DIABETES

In the condition called diabetes, the pancreas does not make enough of the hormone insulin. This means body cells cannot take in blood sugar for energy. The sugar builds up in the blood and is removed by the kidneys. But it needs water to be dissolved in, so lots of water is also removed. The result is that someone with diabetes becomes thirsty and needs to drink large quantities of water, and also produces large amounts of urine containing lots of dissolved sugar.

In 1921 two research workers, Charles Best and Frederick Banting, carried out experiments in Ontario, Canada. They injected the hormone insulin, which had been purified from cattle pancreases, into a dog which had diabetes. The dog survived, the experiments were successful, and injections of insulin became a standard treatment for diabetes.

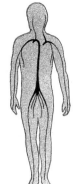

BODY DEFENCES

EVEN IN A CLEAN AND SPOTLESS place, there are probably a few germs. These microscopic living things, such as bacteria and viruses, get on to our skin, and into the food we eat, the drinks we consume, and the air we breathe. They may also get into the body through a cut or wound. If enough germs get into the body, they can start to multiply and cause problems. This is an infection. But the body has several sets of defences against germs. These include the skin, the moist germ-trapping linings of the breathing and digestive passageways, the way blood clots to seal wounds and leaks, white cells and other substances in the blood, the thymus gland in the chest, and small lymph nodes or glands spread all over the body. Together, all of these parts form the body's immune defence system.

The body's germ-killers

The body's immune system includes several kinds of white cells in blood, body fluids and lymph nodes. Some are phagocytes, always on the lookout for germs such as viruses and bacteria. If a phagocyte finds a germ, it flows around it and 'eats' it alive (see opposite). Other white cells, called lymphocytes, make body substances called antibodies. These stick on to the germs and make them helpless or burst open. The white cells recognize germs and other invading substances because the invaders have foreign or 'non-self' substances, antigens, on their surfaces. Antibodies work by attaching to antigens, like keys fitting into locks, to destroy the germ. Also, certain white cells 'remember' the identity of the germs. If the same type of germ tries to invade the body in the future, the immune system recognizes it at once and kills it, before it can multiply. This natural protection against an infection second time around is called immunity.

White blood cells

The Human Immunodeficiency Virus, HIV, attacks the body's immune system – especially certain kinds of white blood cells. These are unable to make antibodies and fight back against the virus, in the normal way. The result is damage or deficiency to the immune system, causing the condition AIDS, Acquired Immuno-Deficiency Syndrome.

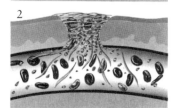

Cuts and clots

A wound or cut in the skin leaks blood from the damaged blood vessels (1). Chemicals released from damaged cells and platelets make dissolved substances in the blood turn into a meshwork of micro-fibres, of the substance fibrin. This network traps blood cells (2). Gradually the meshwork hardens into a clump or clot that seals the leak. The clot then hardens and dries further into a protective scab (3). White cells arrive to attack any germs, and the skin begins to regrow and heal.

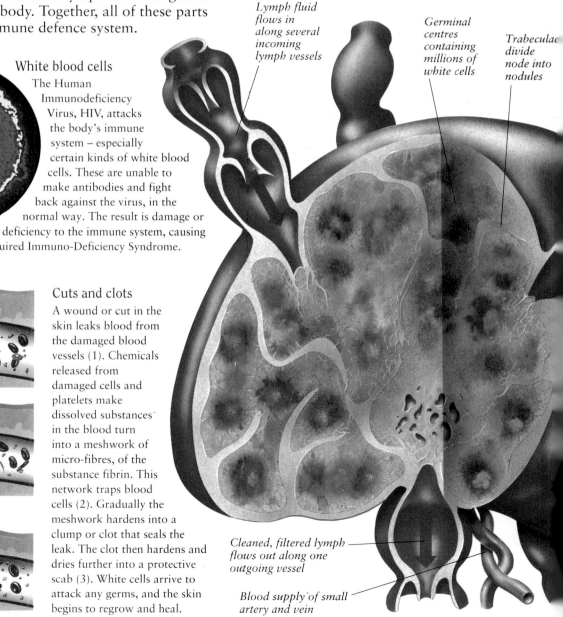

Lymph fluid flows in along several incoming lymph vessels

Germinal centres containing millions of white cells

Trabeculae divide node into nodules

Cleaned, filtered lymph flows out along one outgoing vessel

Blood supply of small artery and vein

The lymphatic system

The lymphatic system is of a network of tubes called lymph vessels, filled with a milky fluid, lymph. At various places around the body – especially the neck, armpits, lower body and groin – these form lumpy-looking lymph nodes. Lymph fluid comes from general body liquids around and between cells, and blood leaked from blood vessels. These collect in lymph vessels and ooze along very slowly. Like blood, lymph fluid delivers nutrients to body tissues, and collects their wastes. It also contains many white cells which defend the body against germs. The lymph vessels come together as large lymph ducts that carry lymph fluid back into the blood system near the heart.

EDWARD JENNER

Edward Jenner (1749–1823), an English country physician, noted that people who had cowpox, a mild disease caught from cattle, seemed resistant to the far more serious smallpox. In 1796 he gave a local boy cowpox. Six weeks later, he deliberately infected the boy's body with smallpox. The boy survived and Jenner's work laid the basis for immunization.

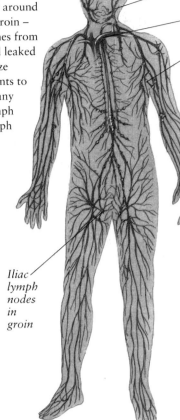

Cervical lymph nodes in neck

Main lymphatic ducts

Axillary lymph nodes in armpit

Iliac lymph nodes in groin

Tonsils and adenoids

The tonsils are patches of lymph tissue at the upper rear part of the throat. They help to destroy foreign substances that are breathed in or swallowed. The adenoids are similar patches at the rear of the nasal cavity inside the nose.

Thymus

The thymus gland in the front of the chest is large during childhood, but shrinks away during adulthood. It helps certain white cells of the immune system, especially lymphocytes, to develop and play their part in the body's defences.

Spleen

The spleen is just behind the stomach on the left side. It makes and stores various kinds of white cells, especially the phagocytes that 'eat' germs. It also makes and stores red cells for the blood, and generally cleans and filters blood.

Eating germs

Several types of white blood cells act as phagocytes. They flow around (1), engulf (2), neutralize (3) and digest (4) any strange or foreign objects, such as germs, before moving on to search for others (5).

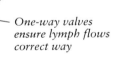

One-way valves ensure lymph flows correct way

Strong outer capsule

Inside a gland

When the body is ill with an infection, various glands swell up. Many of these are lymph nodes. In health they range from pea-sized to grape-sized, but in illness, they can be as big as golf balls. Lymph nodes contain billions of white cells, multiplying rapidly to fight the invading germs. During illness they fill with millions of extra white cells and also dead germs.

Protection for the future

Modern medicine can help the body to become immune or resistant to certain infections, without suffering them first time around. Specially weakened types of a germ, or some of its chemical products, are put into the body, usually by an injection or inoculation (vaccination). The germs are too weak to multiply and cause illness. But they do alert the immune system and produce resistance. This is known as immunization. It is usually carried out during childhood, to give lifelong protection. Which immunizations have you had?

EYES AND SEEING

PEOPLE OFTEN SAY: 'Seeing is believing.' For most people, eyesight or vision is the main sense. More than half of the knowledge inside a brain enters through the eyes – in the form of words, diagrams, pictures and other visual information. (Like now, as you read these words.) So our eyes are our most important sensory organs. A sense organ is specialized to detect some aspect of the surroundings – in the eye's case, light – and produce tiny electrical nerve signals which travel to the brain. The eye records what we see, but does not interpret, analyse or understand it. This happens in the sight centres at the lower rear of the brain. Here, the nerve signals from the eyes are decoded and analysed. The result is that we see the outside world in our 'mind's eye' – in full colour and three dimensions, showing the tiniest movements, intricate patterns and amazing details.

Inside the eye

The eyeball's tough, white outer layer is the sclera. Inside this is a soft, blood-rich, nourishing layer, the choroid. Within this, around the sides and back of the eye, is the retina. This layer detects patterns of light rays and turns them into nerve signals, which go along the optic nerve to the brain. The bulk of the eyeball is filled with a clear jelly, vitreous humour. At the front of the eye is the dome-shaped cornea, through which light rays enter. They pass through a hole, the pupil, in a ring of muscle, the iris. Then the rays shine through the bulging lens, which bends or focuses them to form a sharp, clear picture on the retina.

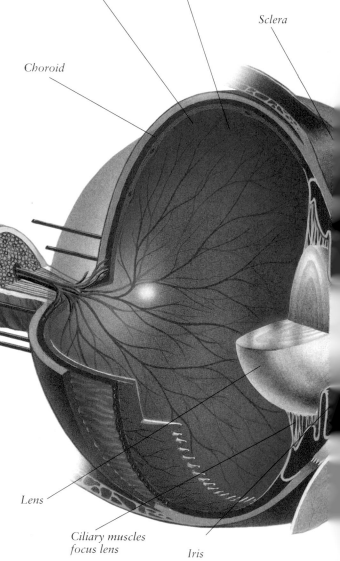

Retina

Blood vessels
on retina

Sclera

Choroid

Lens

Ciliary muscles
focus lens

Iris

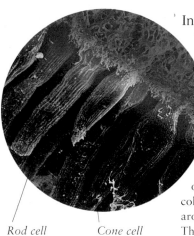

Rod cell   Cone cell

Inside the retina

The retina is about twice the area of a thumbnail. Yet it contains more than 130 million microscopic, light-sensitive cells, called rods and cones because of their shape. Rods number more than 120 million. They work well in dim light, but detect only shades of grey, with no colours. Cones are concentrated around the back of the retina. They see colours and fine details, but only work in bright light.

Colour vision

There are three main kinds of cone cells in the eye. Each type is most sensitive to a particular colour of light – red, green or blue. The thousands of delicate colours and hues we see are combinations of these three primary colours. In some people, a particular type of cone does not work properly, or is absent. This means colour vision cannot work properly. The most common problem is inability to distinguish reds and greens, making the star in the circle difficult to see.

Careful with those eyes

The eyelids close when we blink to smear tear fluid over the eye, washing away dust and germs. The eyelashes also protect the eyes against floating bits and pieces. But eyes are at risk in very dusty or bright places, or when sawing, grinding, and working with chemicals or hot substances that may spray or splash. A mask, goggles or eye protectors are the sensible answer.

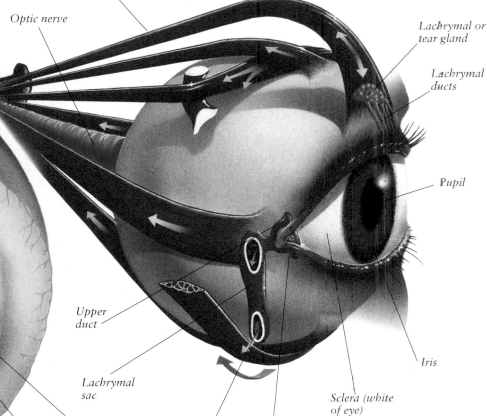

Eye-moving muscles

Optic nerve

Lachrymal or tear gland

Lachrymal ducts

Pupil

Upper duct

Iris

Lachrymal sac

Pupil (hole in iris)

Lower duct

Sclera (white of eye)

Cornea

Naso-lachrymal duct carries tear fluid into nose

Look into my eyes …

The eyeball is partly hidden and protected in the bowl-shaped orbit, or eye socket, in the skull. From the front, we see only about one-tenth of its surface. The white is the tough outer sclera. The coloured disc is the iris. The hole in its centre, the pupil, looks like a black dot. The iris, being muscle, can change shape. It makes the pupil wider in dim conditions, to take in as much light as possible. It contracts to make the pupil smaller in bright conditions, to prevent too-strong light entering the eye and damaging its delicate interior. The whole front of the eye is covered by a very thin, transparent membrane, the conjunctiva, which senses any dust or particles on the eye.

Area of full overlap

Left field of vision

Right field of vision

Area of partial overlap

How far away?

We judge distance or depth in many ways. We have two eyes, and so each sees an object from a slightly different viewpoint. The brain compares these two views. The more different they are, the closer the object. The brain also detects how far the eyes point inwards. Again, the more they do this, the closer the object they are looking at. We also get clues from perspective – the way that lines, such as the two edges of a road, get closer together with distance. Another clue is parallax – as you move your head sideways, nearby objects pass in front of faraway ones. Also, colours fade with distance, and details become hazy. Relative size in another clue. A skyscraper that looks tiny is likely to be far away – not a tiny skyscraper that's very near!

CAN YOU BELIEVE YOUR EYES?

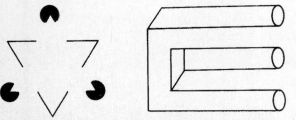

Sometimes our eyes see a scene, but the brain cannot make sense of it. This is usually because the scene could not exist in real life and three dimensions. It is drawn or painted on a flat surface, to trick the brain. For example, is there a clear triangle (left)? Can a C-shaped box have three holes (right)?

EARS, NOSE AND TONGUE

THE HUMAN BODY HAS FIVE main senses. They are sight and touch (dealt with on previous pages), and the three shown here. Each detects a feature of the surroundings and produces nerve signals which travel along nerves to the brain. The ears detect sound waves travelling through the air. The nose detects floating smell or odour particles. The tongue detects flavour particles in foods and drinks. Like sight, these senses can give early warnings of danger, such as the sound of an approaching car, the smell of smoke from a fire, or the taste of rotting food. However, these five main senses are not the only ones. The body also has a range of inner sensors. Their job is to detect its temperature, the levels of chemicals and other substances in the blood, whether the stomach is full or not, and many other essential features.

Smell, or taste, or both?

When we eat a delicious meal, we experience many different sensations. But these are not all tastes and flavours. Many are smells. As we chew, food aromas waft from the back of the mouth, up into the nasal cavity, where they are detected as smells. If you eat food when your nose is blocked, by a cold or clothes-peg, food seems to have much less 'taste'. In fact, it tastes the same, but it lacks the accompanying smells.

Smell is as much a part of the pleasure of eating as taste.

On the tongue

The tongue is covered with dozens of pimple-like projections called papillae. These grip and move food when chewing. Around the sides of the papillae are about 10,000 microscopic taste buds. Different parts of the tongue are sensitive to different flavours: sweet, salt, sour and bitter.

Bitter flavours

Sour flavours

Salt flavours

Sweet flavours

Papille

Olfactory tract   *Olfactory bulb*   *Front of brain*

Olfactory cells

Hypoglossal nerve carries taste information to brain

Muscles inside tongue

Up the nose

Inside each side of the nose is an air chamber, the nasal cavity. Air comes in through the nostril and flows down, around the rear of the roof of the mouth, into the throat. But when you sniff, air swirls up into the top of the cavity. Here is a small patch of about 10 million specialized olfactory (smelling) cells. They have long micro-hairs, or cilia, sticking out from them. Odour particles in the air stick on to the cilia and make the olfactory cells produce nerve signals, which travel to the olfactory bulb. This is a pre-processing centre that partly sorts the signals before they go along the olfactory tract to the brain, where they are recognized as smells.

Taste bud

Each taste bud has some 30 gustatory (taste) cells clustered like the segments of an orange. The cells have micro-hairs, or cilia, sticking up on to the tongue's watery surface. As flavour particles touch the cilia the gustatory cells produce nerve signals. These pass along nerves to the brain, where they are recognized as tastes.

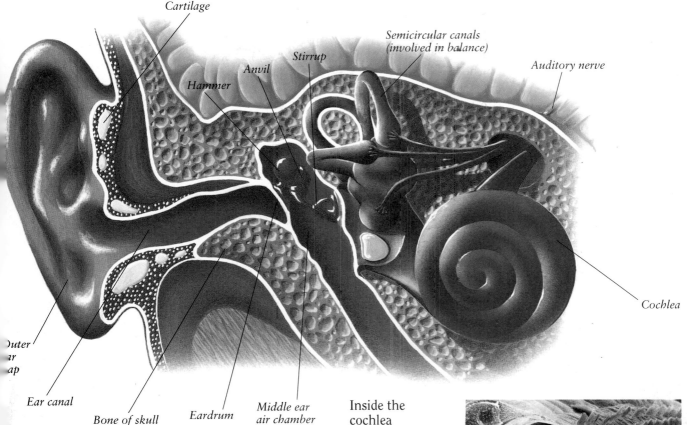

Cartilage

Semicircular canals
(involved in balance)

Stirrup

Anvil

Auditory nerve

Hammer

Cochlea

Outer
ear
flap

Ear canal

Bone of skull

Eardrum

Middle ear
air chamber

In the ear

Sound waves funnel into the outer ear – the flap of skin and cartilage on the side of the head. They pass along a narrow tube, the ear canal, to a small patch of rubbery skin at its end, the eardrum. The sound waves bounce off the eardrum and make it shake to and fro, or vibrate. The eardrum is connected to a row of three tiny bones linked together, the hammer, anvil and stirrup. The vibrations pass along these bones, like rattling the links of a chain. The stirrup presses against a small, fluid-filled, snail-shaped part, the cochlea, deep inside the ear. The vibrations pass as ripples into the fluid inside the cochlea. Here, they shake thousands of tiny hairs that stick into the fluid from hair cells. As the hairs shake, the hair cells make nerve signals, which go along the auditory nerve to the hearing centre of the brain.

Inside the cochlea

There are thousands of hair cells inside the cochlea. And each has dozens of micro-hairs sticking out from it (shown in yellow in the micro-photo, right). Some parts of the cochlea respond to high-pitched sounds, others to low-pitched ones.

A SENSE OF POSITION

Yet another body sense is our inner sense of posture or body position. Try this. Stand up and close your eyes. Hold your arms out straight, to the front. How do you know when you have done this? You can 'feel' the position of your arms and legs, body and head. Hundreds of micro-sensors in your muscles and joints detect the various amounts of stretch and strain in them. This inner sense of posture is called your proprioceptive or kinesthetic sense.

Balance

Balance involves several sets of senses. Deep in the ear, chambers called the utricle and saccule detect the downward pull of gravity, so you know which way up your head is. Other inner ear organs called the semicircular canals contain fluid that swishes to and fro, telling you about head movements. Skin detects pressure as gravity presses body parts down. Eyes see horizontal and vertical lines, like floors and walls. The kinesthetic sense detects body position and posture (see left). All these sense inputs are analysed in the brain, which sends out nerve signals to the muscles, to keep you balanced.

BRAIN AND NERVOUS SYSTEM

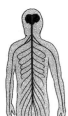

ALL YOUR THOUGHTS, feelings, memories, emotions, wishes and dreams happen in one place inside your body – your brain. It's the place where you are conscious and aware of what's going on around you. It's the place where you think, imagine, have ideas and daydream. Your brain is also the control centre for your whole body. It tells your heart to beat, your lungs to breathe air, your stomach to digest food, and it controls hundreds of other inner body processes. And your brain makes your muscles work, so that you can move around and carry out skilled tasks such as drawing or riding a bicycle. The brain can do these amazing jobs because it is connected to all parts of your body, by an incredibly complicated network of nerves. These nerves look like thin pieces of shiny string. They carry messages, in the form of tiny electrical signals called nerve impulses, between the brain and every other body part.

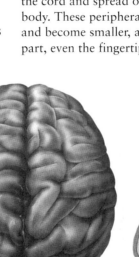

Left cerebral hemisphere

Eye

The brain and nerve network

The brain fills the top half of the head. It is well protected by the strong skull bones around it. The brain's base tapers into a long, thick nerve called the spinal cord. Nerves branch from the cord and spread out through the body. These peripheral nerves divide and become smaller, and reach every part, even the fingertips and toes.

Parts of the brain

The brain looks like a giant, wrinkled walnut. Its most obvious part, making up about nine-tenths of its whole size, is called the cerebrum. It is divided into two halves, known as cerebral hemispheres. Each hemisphere is covered by a pink–grey layer known as the cerebral cortex, which is where thinking happens. Under the cortex is a thick white layer, the cerebral medulla. At the rear of the brain is another wrinkled part, but much smaller than the cerebrum. This is known as the cerebellum. At the brain's base is a narrow part, the brain stem, which tapers into the spinal cord in the upper neck.

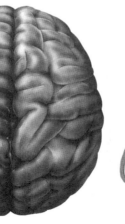

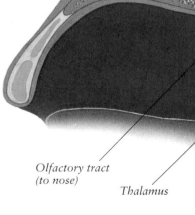

Olfactory tract (to nose)

Thalamus

Pituitary gland

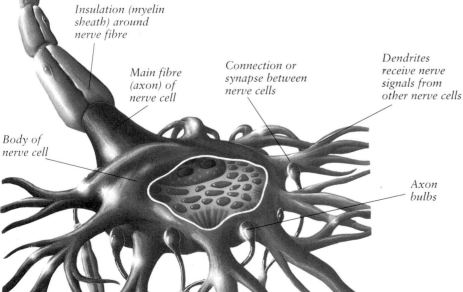

Insulation (myelin sheath) around nerve fibre

Main fibre (axon) of nerve cell

Connection or synapse between nerve cells

Dendrites receive nerve signals from other nerve cells

Body of nerve cell

Axon bulbs

How nerve cells communicate

Each microscopic nerve cell, or neuron, has a blob-shaped main part, the cell body, with thin, spider-like dendrites and one much longer, wire-like nerve fibre or axon. The axon's branched ends have button-shaped axon bulbs which almost touch other nerve cells, at junctions known as synapses. Nerve signals travel along the axon and 'jump' across the synapses to other nerve cells, at speeds of more than 100 metres per second.

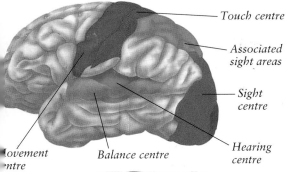

Touch centre

Associated sight areas

Sight centre

Hearing centre

Movement centre

Balance centre

Inside the brain

Different patches or areas of the cortex receive nerve messages from the body's senses, such as the eyes and ears. These are cortical sensory centres. Another patch of the cortex, the motor area or centre, sends out messages to the muscles so that the body can move.

Ultimate control

A person doing a skilled and complex task must concentrate hard. The brain makes thoughts and decisions every second, as information pours in from the eyes, ears and other senses, and signals are sent out to control hundreds of muscles with split-second timing.

Brain waves

Some electrical nerve signals in the brain pass though the skull bone to the skin. They can be detected by sensors and fed into an EEG (electro-encephalograph) machine, which displays them as wavy lines on a screen or paper strip. These 'brain waves' can help doctors to discover any illness or problem affecting the brain.

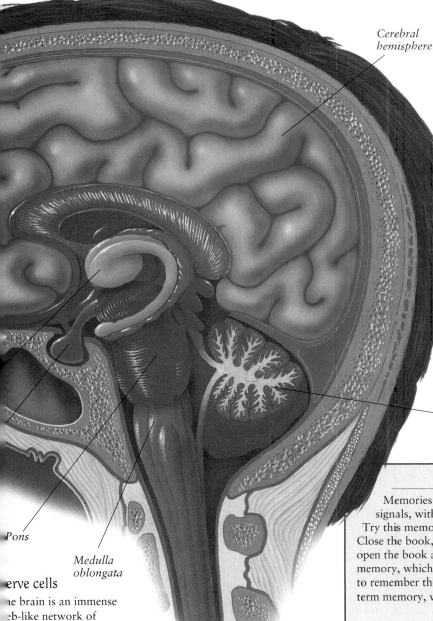

Cerebral hemisphere

Pons

Medulla oblongata

Spinal cord

Cerebellum controls muscle coordination and fine details of movement

Nerve cells

The brain is an immense web-like network of millions of microscopic nerve cells, called neurons. They pass tiny electrical signals amongst themselves. The total number of pathways that signals can take through the brain is unimaginably huge. The signals represent information coming from the senses along sensory nerves, thoughts and decisions and memories in the brain itself, and instructions going out to the muscles along motor nerves.

TEST YOUR MEMORY!

Memories are probably special pathways for nerve signals, within the massive nerve-cell network of the brain. Try this memory test. Study the items below for 20 seconds. Close the book, write down all those you can remember, then open the book again to find your score. This tests short-term memory, which lasts for seconds or minutes. Next week, try to remember the items again, without looking! This tests long-term memory, which can last many years.

REPRODUCTION AND GROWTH

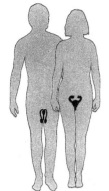

REPRODUCTION MEANS PRODUCING more of your own kind – that is, making babies. The parts of the body involved are called the reproductive system. They work much the same way in humans as in other mammals, such as chimps, cats and horses. The female makes pinhead-sized egg cells called ova. The male makes microscopic, tadpole-shaped cells called sperm. During sex (sexual intercourse), sperm from the man pass into the reproductive system of the woman. One sperm may join with, or fertilize, an egg. If so, over nine months, the egg develops into a baby inside its mother's womb. It leaves the womb at birth. The baby continues to grow into a child, and then into a mature adult, when it can produce babies of its own.

Male reproductive system

The male sex glands are called testes. Each day they produce millions of tiny tadpole-shaped male sex cells, called sperm. These are stored in a tightly coiled tube, the epididymis. As new sperm are produced, the older sperm are gradually broken down and their nutrients recycled in the body. During sex, the man gently pushes his penis into the woman's vagina. After a while, sperm in their milky fluid are forced along the vas deferens tubes, then along another tube, the urethra, which is inside the penis. The sperm pass out of the male body and into the female reproductive system.

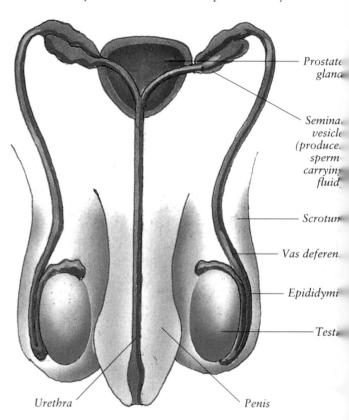

Prostate gland

Seminal vesicle (produces sperm carrying fluid)

Scrotum

Vas deferens

Epididymis

Testis

Urethra

Penis

Egg meets sperm

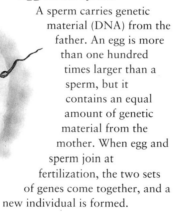

A sperm carries genetic material (DNA) from the father. An egg is more than one hundred times larger than a sperm, but it contains an equal amount of genetic material from the mother. When egg and sperm join at fertilization, the two sets of genes come together, and a new individual is formed.

Amnion (protective membrane)

Foetus (baby)

Uterus (womb)

In the womb

A few hours after fertilization, the fertilized egg splits into two cells, then four, eight, and so on. They form a tiny ball which burrows into the nourishing womb lining. The cells continue to multiply, into hundreds, then thousands. They start to become different, as nerve cells, blood cells and many other types. Eight weeks after fertilization, a tiny baby has taken shape. It is only thumb-sized, but it has a brain, stomach, liver, eyes and other main body parts, and its heart has started to beat.

Ready for birth

Inside the womb, a baby is warm and protected. But it is surrounded by fluid, so it cannot breathe or eat. It obtains oxygen and nutrients from its mother through a plate-shaped part the placenta (afterbirth) in the womb lining. Blood flows from the baby's body along the curly umbilical cord to the placenta. Here it takes up oxygen and nutrients, gets rid of wastes, then flows back along the cord to the baby.

Placenta

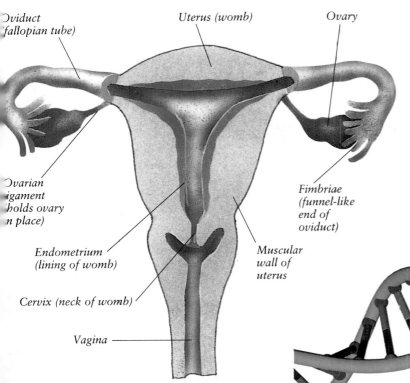

Oviduct (fallopian tube)

Uterus (womb)

Ovary

Ovarian ligament (holds ovary in place)

Fimbriae (funnel-like end of oviduct)

Endometrium (lining of womb)

Muscular wall of uterus

Cervix (neck of womb)

Vagina

Genes and DNA
Genes are instructions for the way the body grows and develops, and physical features such as colour of hair, skin and eyes. Genes are made of immensely long molecules of de-oxyribonucleic acid, DNA. Each molecule has two long parts, backbones, twisted together in a long corkscrew shape called a double helix. The backbones are joined by four kir cross-links, known as nucleotides. The c the cross-links is a chemical code for t' genetic instructions.

Nucleotide cross-link

DNA backbone

Female reproductive system
The female sex glands are called ovaries. They contain tiny egg cells, or ova. Each month (usually) one egg cell becomes ripe and leaves the ovary. It passes along the fallopian tube and into the womb, or uterus. If sex takes place and the egg meets a sperm cell, it may be fertilized. The fertilized egg settles into the blood-rich lining of the womb and begins to develop into a baby. If there are no sperm, the egg and womb lining are lost through the cervix (the neck of the womb) along the passageway to the outside, the vagina. This bleeding is called menstruation, or a period. Once the period is over, the whole process of egg ripening and womb thickening begins again. This is called the menstrual cycle, and is controlled by hormones from the brain and ovaries.

Changing shape
As the body grows, it changes its proportions. A baby's head is much larger, relative to its body size, compared to an adult's head. This is shown clearly if bodies of different ages are drawn to the same size (below).

Inheritance
When an egg and sperm join together at fertilization, each contributes a full set of genes, which number between 100,000 and 200,000 per set. These genes, in the form of DNA, are in the nucleus (control centre) of the fertilized egg. They are copied when it divides, and at every division afterwards. So every body cell has two full sets or pairs of genes. But only one gene of the pair becomes active. This is why a child has some features passed on, or inherited, from the mother and others from the father.

The time after birth is very special, as mother and baby get used to each other by sight, sound, touch and smell.

The new arrival
Birth is an exhausting process for both mother and baby. The womb muscles contract powerfully to push the baby through the cervix, or neck of the womb, and along the vagina, or birth canal, into the outside world. Afterwards, mother and baby rest together and begin to get to know each other. The mother feeds the baby with natural milk from her breasts (mammary glands) or artificial milk from a bottle. This milk has all the energy and nutrients that the baby will need during its first few weeks of life.

Growing up
The human body takes about 20 years to grow to its full physical size and maturity. The first stage is infancy, when the baby needs to be fed, cleaned, carried and cared for. Gradually it learns to smile, crawl, walk and talk. During childhood we learn mental (mind-based) skills such as counting, reading and writing, and physical skills such as running, climbing and riding a bicycle. During puberty the body grows very rapidly, and its sex organs become fully formed or mature.

THE HEALTHY HUMAN BODY

MOST PEOPLE ARE MOSTLY HEALTHY, for most of the time. We can help to improve our chances of a long and healthy life by understanding our bodies and how they work, and what makes them go wrong. Numerous medical studies and surveys have shown how our health is affected by various factors – what we eat and drink, how much and what type of physical exercise we take, the everyday activities we take part in, whether we take in harmful substances such as tobacco smoke, the way we relate to our family and friends, and even the way we organize our daily routine. Most of these factors are under our own control (more or less). So it's up to us to give our bodies the best chance. But there are also factors we cannot change so easily, such as where we live. And we cannot change some factors at all, like the genes we inherit from our parents, which may make us more likely to contract certain diseases.

Body weight
Being severely overweight, or obese, is associated with several kinds of illness. These include heart and blood-pressure problems, breathing difficulties, hormonal disorders such as diabetes, and joint aches and pains. Most people can control body weight by sensible, healthy eating.

Food and drink
The body needs a varied diet. This includes proteins for growth, body maintenance and repair, starches (carbohydrates) for energy, and some fats for energy and maintenance, as well as vitamins and minerals for healthy teeth, bones, skin and other parts. Too much of any single food can cause problems. In general, plenty of fresh fruit and vegetables is helpful. Too much fat, especially animal fats from red meats and rich dairy produce, is not.

MAIN PARTS OF A HEALTHY DIET

Carbohydrates (starches and sugars) – In breads, pastas, potatoes, rice and other grains, especially wholemeal or unrefined types.

Proteins – In plants such as peas, beans and pulses, grains (and so in breads etc.), and in animal food such as meats, especially poultry and fish, and dairy produce such as eggs, milk and cheese.

Fats – In plant oils such as olive, soya, sunflower and safflower oils, also (but less desirable) in animal meats and dairy produce.

Fibre – In most fresh vegetables and fruits, also unrefined or wholemeal grains and their products such as wholemeal bread or rice.

Vitamins and minerals – In fresh fruit and vegetables mainly, also most other foods.

Before
Prior to strenuous exercise, it helps to do some stretching and warm-up exercises, to reduce the risk of sudden strains.

During
Correct clothing and equipment, such as well-fitting shoes, helps to avoid sprains and injuries.

Activity and exercise

The human body has evolved over thousands of years, to live a fairly active life – not to sit in front of a screen 18 hours a day. Most young people get exercise from sports and games. But many adults do not. After a medical fitness check-up, they may be helped by two or three periods of exercise weekly, each about 20-30 minutes long, and strenuous enough to make the lungs pant and the skin sweaty. But remember that some activities strain the same muscles continually, or stretch joints too much, and could lead to over-use injuries in the future.

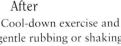

After
Cool-down exercise and gentle rubbing or shaking reduces the risks of stiffness and aches.

Rest and sleep

Lack of sleep can kill a person faster than lack of food. Trying to trick the body into needing less rest or sleep may result in headaches, lack of concentration, and being irritable and forgetful. This is part of the very important area of mental or mind health, which is put at risk by too much stress and worry.

Hygiene

Germs are almost everywhere. Regular hand-washing, especially after using the toilet, and before preparing foods or eating them, reduces the risk of infection – especially of taking germs into the digestive tract, when they could cause stomach or intestinal infection. Brushing teeth twice daily is an enormous help in preventing toothache, tooth decay and smelly breath. Dirty skin or clothes increase the risk of skin spots, smells and other skin problems.

Medical care

Most babies have regular health checks for the first months and years. These continue into childhood and adulthood in the form of visits to the optician for sight tests, to the dentist for tooth care, and to the doctor for check-ups and screening tests. Immunizations in childhood also give protection against various infections. Any health problem is likely to be treated more effectively if it is reported to the doctor earlier, rather than later.

HARMFUL SUBSTANCES

Breathing in tobacco smoke is linked to many serious illnesses. The smoke contains vapours that condense or turn into thick tars. These clog the delicate lungs, increasing the risk of infections such as colds and bronchitis. A drug in tobacco smoke, called nicotine, is highly addictive. Cigarettes also contain cancer-causing substances and chemicals that affect blood pressure and damage blood vessels. There are many other drugs which also damage health.

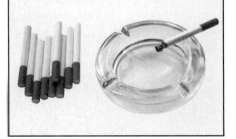

HUMAN BODY: QUESTIONS AND ANSWERS

● Inside the body, many organs (main parts) are in pairs, left and right. Which of the following is not – there being only one? Lung, kidney, pancreas, adrenal.

Pancreas.

● How many bones are there in the body's skeleton?

206.

● Which part of the blood circulation system sends blood to the lungs for fresh supplies of oxygen? Is it the systemic or pulmonary part?

Pulmonary.

● Many body organs and parts have special words to describe them. Which organ is associated with the word 'renal'?

Kidney.

● How long is the body's entire digestive tract or tube, from the mouth to the other end?

Nine metres.

● In which main body part would you find the cerebral cortex and cerebellum?

The brain.

● How many individual muscles are there in the body?

640.

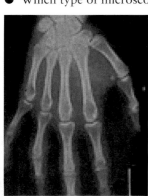

● Which type of microscopic cells are the longest in the body?

Nerve cells.

● In which body part would you find alveoli?

The lungs.

● What is the biggest muscle in the body?

Gluteus maximus (in the buttock).

● How many teeth does a child have, before the adult teeth replace them?

20.

● What are the lymph nodes commonly called, especially when they swell up during illness?

Glands.

● Which part of the tongue tastes sweet flavours best?

The tip.

● Which main sensory part or organ has olfactory cells?

The nose.

● Which main sensory part or organ has rod and cone cells?

The eye.

● Which types of foods are best for health-giving vitamins – fresh fruits, burgers or potato crisps?

Fresh fruits.

● Which hormone (body chemical messenger) gets the body ready for action in the 'fight or flight' response?

Adrenaline.

● Which type of blood vessel carries blood back to the heart? Is it a capillary, vein or artery?

Vein.

● How long does it take for a fertilized egg to grow into a baby ready to be born, in the womb?

Nine months.

● To the nearest billion, how many human bodies are there on Earth?

Six.

● Which is the outer layer of skin, the dermis or epidermis?

Epidermis.

● Where are the hammer, anvil and stirrup.

In the ear (middle ear for a bonus point).

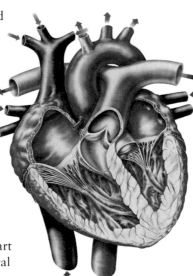

THE WAY WE LIVE

LANGUAGE

EVERY TIME YOU SPEAK you use a complicated system of sounds called a language. A language is a way of organizing the sounds to communicate information and ideas. We use language in so many ways it is impossible to imagine a world without it. Language helps us to describe how we feel, to talk to other people and to learn about them. Finding words for objects and ideas also helps us to make sense of the world. There are probably between 5,000 and 6,000 different languages in the world today. English is spoken by around 1,400 million people, but many other languages are used by just a few hundred people. The languages we use today have taken thousands of years to develop, and they are still changing so that we can describe new ideas, inventions and discoveries.

Language and identity

People feel very strongly about the language they speak. Your language is part of who you are, your history and culture, and people protest strongly if another language is imposed upon them. In some countries, where more than one language is used, there are laws to ensure that one language is not given second place to another. Road signs in Canada, for example, must give information in French before English.

In Israel, street signs appear in Arabic and in English. This sign in Bethlehem must be one of the most photographed in the world

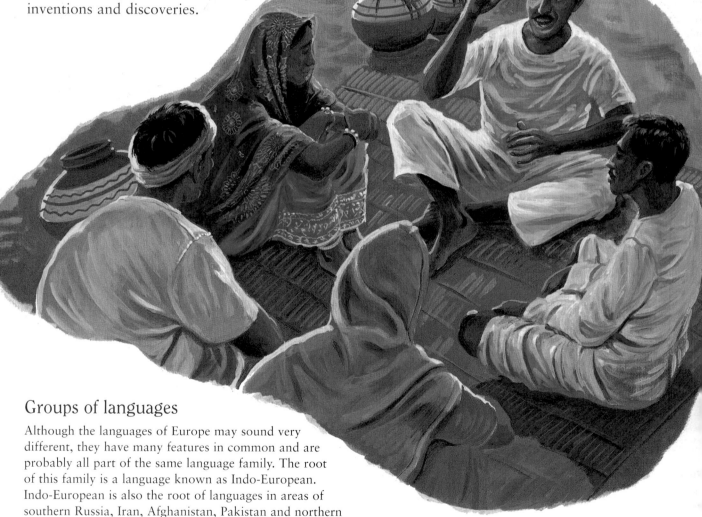

Groups of languages

Although the languages of Europe may sound very different, they have many features in common and are probably all part of the same language family. The root of this family is a language known as Indo-European. Indo-European is also the root of languages in areas of southern Russia, Iran, Afghanistan, Pakistan and northern India. The similarities between these groups of languages could mean that many thousands of years ago tribes from northern Europe moved south into Asia. Over the centuries Indo-European developed into the many different languages spoken in these countries today, but certain words and structures remain the same.

A common language binds people into communities who share a similar cultural history and outlook on life

Latin

Latin was the language of the Romans, whose civilization dominated Europe around 2,000 years ago. Although Latin has not been a living language for centuries, it has continued to be used as a common language in many areas of learning, such as science. There are millions of different species of plants, for example, but biologists all over the world can be sure that they are talking about exactly the same species because they have an international 'master' list of names. On the left is the passionflower, in Latin, Passiflora Kermesina.

We use gestures to signify agreement and anger, as well as to direct someone's attention

Sign language

People who are deaf communicate using a language of hand signs. Some signs represent whole words or ideas, such as 'hungry' or 'animal', other words have to be spelled out using the sign for each letter of the alphabet.

Body language

It is often not just the words that matter when you speak, but the way you say them and the signals you give with other parts of your body, such as the expression on your face or the gesture of a hand. Body language is particularly important when you greet someone, but you have to be careful because, like spoken language, it is often different from country to country. And sometimes body language can cause real confusion. While in Europe you might signal 'no' by shaking your head, in India a shake of the head from side to side means 'yes'.

Tower of Babel

According to the Book of Genesis in the Old Testament of the Bible, the Tower of Babel was built in Babylon with the aim of reaching all the way from Earth to heaven. The god of the Old Testament was angry that people should so arrogantly presume they could get to heaven, and punished them by confusing the language of the builders. This resulted in chaos, and the tower was never completed. Today the word 'babel' means a confusion of noises and voices.

Living languages

It is impossible to give an accurate figure for the number of languages there are in the world. As people explore the world and discover new communities, they find new languages. But languages are also disappearing. When more widely spoken languages are introduced into remote communities the native language often becomes forgotten. A quarter of the world's languages have fewer than 1,000 speakers – often just a hundred or so people – and these languages will almost certainly disappear over the course of the next half-century.

ESPERANTO

In 1889 an artificial language called Esperanto was invented by Ludwig Zamenhof. His idea was to create an international language that would be easy for everyone to learn. Esperanto is used at meetings of international organizations, like the United Nations, and is taught in many schools. There are journals and newspapers in Esperanto, radio broadcasts in Esperanto and the Bible and the Qur'an are among many books translated into that language, but it has not yet been recognized, due to opposition from groups who want English to be accepted as the world language.

WRITING

WRITING IS A WAY of recording information and passing it on to others. Without the writing of ancient peoples, we would know very little about the history of the world. Today, writing is just as important. It allows us to keep in touch through newspapers and the internet. Writing can take different forms. Pictograms use a sequence of pictures to communicate information. Ideograms use marks called characters to describe abstract ideas, such as 'sorrow'. Other scripts, called alphabets, use characters to represent a sound, and create words by putting the sounds together. There are five different alphabets used in the world today: Greek, Roman, Cyrillic, Hebrew and Arabic. The European languages, such as English and French, use the Roman alphabet. Russian and related languages use the Cyrillic alphabet. The advantage of the alphabet system is that you have to learn only a few signs to be able to read – the 26 characters of the English alphabet, for example. With a system of writing that uses pictograms and ideograms, you may have to learn symbols for each of thousands of different words, as in Chinese.

The history of writing

The first writing was probably invented around 5,000 years ago by the Sumerian people of Mesopotamia, which is today part of Iraq. It was called cuneiform, which means 'wedge-shaped', because it was written by pressing a reed into soft clay tablets to make wedge-shaped marks. Cuneiform writing started off as pictures of objects, called pictograms. But over time, the pictures were simplified to make them quicker to write. Chinese writing dates back to around 1500 BC. Chinese used ideograms and sound signs as well as pictograms, and was written using a brush and ink. At around the same time as the Chinese started writing, the Egyptians began to use hieroglyphs – a mix of pictograms and sounds. The Egyptians wrote with reed brushes or pens on papyrus – a type of thick paper made from the stems of the papyrus plant. When papyrus ran out, it was replaced by parchment made from animal skins. Paper from wood pulp was first made by the Chinese in AD 105. Alphabetic script was first invented by the Greeks around 100 BC.

Scribes

In ancient Egypt, scribes were very important people. Their training took up to 12 years and enabled them to get jobs as teachers, librarians or civil servants. In the Middle Ages, all books were handmade by scribes. They illuminated, or decorated, the initial capital letters on a page. They used real gold and silver, as well as inks in many colours. They often used a red lead called minium, which led to small pictures being called miniatures. To copy a book might be a lifetime's work for a scribe.

For many centuries very few people could read or write. Documents were written by hand by a scribe. Books were so valuable that they were often chained to a library desk to stop them from being stolen

This reed pen and baked clay inkpot date from biblical times. Reed pens were easily made with a knife, but wore out quickly

Roman writing tools

The Romans used a metal stylus to inscribe words on to a soft wax tablet. The writing could be rubbed out with the flat end of the stylus and the tablet used again. For writing on papyrus, the Romans used ink made from soot mixed with water. Their ink wells were of clay or stone.

PUNCTUATION

When you are reading text it is important to know where one sentence begins and ends, and where to pause in the sentence. To help make sense of writing, languages have their own system of marks, called punctuation, which shows the reader how the words hang together.

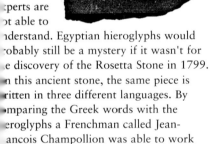

The text on the Rosetta stone is a thank-you to a ruler of ancient Egypt

Unknown scripts

There are still ancient scripts that experts are not able to understand. Egyptian hieroglyphs would probably still be a mystery if it wasn't for the discovery of the Rosetta Stone in 1799. On this ancient stone, the same piece is written in three different languages. By comparing the Greek words with the hieroglyphs a Frenchman called Jean-François Champollion was able to work out the meaning of the hieroglyphs.

Computers

The language of computers is a series of numbers that is practically impossible for a human brain to understand. The computer programme translates the operator's instructions into the machine code that is used inside the computer. It then translates the computer's responses back into the language that the operator can understand. All this happens in a split second.

Arabic

The Arabic alphabet has 28 letters. Seventeen basic characters represent the consonants. Eleven dots were added later in the history of the script for the vowel sounds. The curved characters are written from right to left. Arabic script was probably first used in the 4th century AD. It spread with the spread of the Islamic faith, and was widely used by the 7th century AD. The holy book of Islam, the Qu'ran, says that writing is a gift from God and calligraphy (the art of artistic writing) is highly respected.

АБВГДЕЖЗИ
ЙКЛМНОПР
СТУФХЦЧШ
ЩЪЫЬЭЮЯ

Chinese

Chinese is a very complex written language with over 50,000 characters, which are a mix of pictograms, ideograms and sounds. These have hardly changed for centuries, and the Chinese have little trouble reading ancient scripts. At school a Chinese child will learn around 4,000 characters. The strokes of each character must be made in the right order, and some characters are made up of 26 different strokes.

Russian

The Russian alphabet is called Cyrillic. It is based on the Greek alphabet of the 9th century AD, but gets its name from St Cyril, a churchman of that time who preached the Christian faith to the Slavonic people. The Slavs lived in the area of modern-day Poland, Bulgaria, the Czech and Slovak Republics and Serbia. The Cyrillic alphabet is used to write Bulgarian and Serbian as well as Russian.

WRITE YOUR OWN PICTOGRAMS

You can make your own writing system using pictograms. You could invent pictograms that would be easy for anyone to read, or devise a trickier system that only you and your friends could understand. See if you can read the secret message above. It's an invitation to meet under the tree at midday to go for a day's fishing, then eat the fish for dinner as the Sun starts to go down. Why not start off by writing your own invitation, perhaps to go bowling or skating?

MYTHS AND LEGENDS

MYTHS AND LEGENDS are tales of gods and goddesses, monsters and heroes. But they are also stories that explain the many mysteries of life, such as how life began, what happens when we die or why the Sun rises at dawn and sets at dusk. As well as explaining life, myths teach the rules of life – good triumphs over evil, and weaknesses like greed or vanity are always punished. Many myths have survived for thousands of years, passed down by word of mouth, or in pictures and written words, and these shared stories bind communities together. Every culture of the world has its own myths, and although the stories they tell are very different, they often have the same themes. Legends are different from myths in that they are thought to have some basis in historical fact and to tell of real people. But as they are told over the centuries, the details of the legend are exaggerated and elements of magic may be added to make the story more colourful.

Monsters

Myths are full of fabulous beasts and dreadful monsters. Dragons of all shapes and sizes appear in many mythologies. In most cultures dragons represent the forces of evil that must be overcome, but in Chinese mythology, dragons represent good fortune.

The phoenix

The phoenix was a mythical Greek bird, with shimmering feathers of gold and bright colours. Believed by some to have a life cycle of exactly 500 years, the phoenix is a symbol of immortality and renewal. When the old phoenix reached the end of its life, it would burn itself on a funeral pyre. A young bird would then rise from the flames in its place. The young phoenix would fly with its father to the altar of the Sun god in the Egyptian city of the Sun, which the Greeks called Heliopolis.

The young phoenix rises from the flames of its father's funeral pyre

This stone carving shows the head of Quetzalcoatl, the Aztec serpent god

Quetzalcoatl

Quetzalcoatl was the Aztec god of creation, learning and the winds. The Aztecs said that as god of the winds, he came to sweep the way for the rains that would bring fertility to the earth. The winds made the vegetation of the earth sway like a serpent covered with green feathers.

Sacred places

The most sacred place of the aboriginal people is a huge rock in central Australia, called Uluru (Ayers Rock). The aboriginals believe that their ancestors live in eternity. They call this time before time the Dreamtime. In the Dreamtime the ancestors walk the land along paths known as song lines and all the song lines meet at Uluru.

Uluru is the most sacred place of the aboriginal people of Australia

Charon, the ferryman crosses the river Styx, escorting the dead to the afterlife

Death and the afterlife

Perhaps the greatest mystery of all is what happens to us when we die. The ancient Greeks believed that the souls of the dead travelled to the Underworld, which they called Hades. To get there they had to cross the river Styx with the help of Charon the ferryman. To ensure that the dead reached the Underworld they were buried with a small coin, which would be used in the afterlife to pay Charon.

Creation myths

All over the world, people have tried to explain how the world began and where the first people came from. The Ancient Egyptians believed that at the dawn of time Ra, the Sun god, created the air, moisture, the earth and the sky, and that humans came from his tears. In Norse tradition it is said that the earth was created by the mighty god Odin and his brothers from the flesh of the frost giant that they had killed. They made rocks and stones from his bones, and rivers, lakes and oceans from his blood, and people were created from logs. In Chinese mythology, at the beginning of time there was chaos, which was shaped like an egg. From the egg came yin and yang – the opposite forces of light and dark, male and female, hot and cold – that make up the universe. Out of the egg, too, came P'an-ku, the first being, and he created the Earth and everything in it. The aboriginal people of Australia believe that life was created in the Dreamtime – a time before time. In the Dreamtime the eternal ancestors awoke from their sleep to wander the Earth and transform plants and animals into human beings, before going back to sleep.

Sedna, ruler of the sea, lives with her father and dog-husband in the depths of the ocean. She is both sea goddess and goddess of the dead

The goddess Sedna

The sea was the source of food for the Inuit people of Greenland and northern Canada. Sedna the sea goddess was worshipped for the sea creatures she provided to eat. She was also feared in case she was offended and made the Arctic weather so harsh that hunting and fishing for bears, seals and whales became impossible.

A cunning trickster

The Ashanti people of West Africa have many stories of Ananse the spider. Small and seemingly powerless, she was in fact creator of the world and can outwit any animal, including the lion, python and leopard. When the Ashanti were taken as slaves to America, the legend of Ananse combined with Native American stories of the trickster Great Rabbit, and the Brer Rabbit stories were born.

WAS KING ARTHUR REAL?

The legend of the English King Arthur and the Knights of the Round Table is full of mystery and magic, but it is believed that the real Arthur was a brave Celtic chieftain who lived around AD 500. The first tales of him were written in Latin by monks in the Middle Ages. Among the best known is the one in which he pulled the sword from the stone.

LITERATURE

LITERATURE IS THE ART OF WRITING. It is more than writing just to convey information, it is writing to entertain, to stir the heart, and to explore all sorts of human experience. It offers the best chance we ever get of feeling what it is like to be someone else. Writing is only counted as literature if it stands the test of time. If a piece is really well written and expresses a deep truth it will still be read many years later, and in translation all round the world. There are many different literary forms – stories, novels, poetry, plays, biographies, diaries and journalism. Made-up stories are called fiction, and feature the same themes the world over – adventure, crime, love, horror and fantasy. The events a fiction writer describes are called the plot. The people who take part in the plot are called the characters. The best fiction writers create characters so true to life you feel they are real people. Non-fiction writers may record the lives of great men and women and the effect of historic events. Literature is also an important place for exploring new ideas, for trying to influence politics, and for protesting against injustice.

The first stories

Stories were not always written. They were first told around the fires of cave dwellers, and then passed down by word of mouth through the generations. Each storyteller developed more interesting details and twists of the plot, so the tales grew richer and more vivid with every telling. The tradition of storytelling is called the oral (spoken) tradition. When writing was developed, stories could be written down, but for many centuries only a very few people could read or write, and books had to be written or printed by hand. In the royal courts of Europe singing storytellers, called bards, were employed to write and recite stories and poems. Today in the developed world almost everyone learns to read, and printing technology means that books are cheap, but the oral tradition continues everywhere as people tell each other the stories of their own families and communities.

Alongside singing, music and the antics of a jester, storytelling was a popular form of entertainment in the medieval banqueting hall

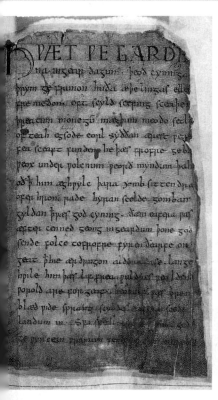

Epic poems

Great legendary heroes have often been celebrated in long poems, called epics (or sagas). At first these poems were not written down, and would have been sung or recited. One of the most famous epics is the Anglo-Saxon poem of Beowulf, a legendary prince who kills Grendel, the man-eating monster who lives in the marshes, and then kills Grendel's mother.

Left, a manuscript of Beowulf. Below, a still from The Thousand and One Nights

etry

etry is a very careful arrangement of
rds that gives them special meaning.
me poetry rhymes, but much does not.
ere are many different forms of poetry: a
net is a poem with 14 lines, a Japanese
ku is a verse with just 17 syllables.
en poets write about very intense
otions, but poetry is also written simply
entertain and amuse.

*s Japanese painting of cherry blossom
inst distant misty mountains echoes the
plicity of the haiku. In just a few
rds, the Japanese poet puts the reader
de his own emotions*

Great classics

Great stories are still read many years after they were first invented. The Thousand and One Nights is a collection of Middle Eastern stories believed to be 2,000 years old. The tales are told by Queen Scheherazade, whose husband wants to kill her. She puts off her death each night by telling him a wonderful tale, such as the story of Sinbad the Sailor. After 1,001 nights of stories, he agrees to spare her life.

The first books for children

It is only in the last 300 years that books have been written especially for children. Until then children simply listened to folk tales and fables. The first important works for children appeared in the 19th century, when Hans Christian Andersen and the Brothers Grimm produced their collections of folk and fairy tales. They were followed by adventure stories, such as Treasure Island by Robert Louis Stevenson, and fantasies, such as Alice in Wonderland by Lewis Carroll.

Above, The Princess and the Pea, a tale told by Hans Christian Andersen. Left, Tenniel was the illustrator of Alice in Wonderland

THE POWER OF BOOKS

Throughout history writers have challenged old ideas and explored new lines of thought, and books have proved an important influence on public opinion. In 1850 Harriet Beecher Stowe wrote Uncle Tom's Cabin, a novel that describes the evils of slavery in the United States. The book played an important part in bringing slavery to an end. But books that criticize governments are sometimes banned or burned and can get the author into trouble. In 1974 the Russian writer Alexander Solzhenitsyn was exiled for his criticism of his country's regime.

THEATRE

FOR THOUSANDS OF YEARS people have enjoyed bringing stories to life by acting them out. The first performances were probably ritual dances by ancient peoples calling upon the spirits to help them and using dance, music, make-up and costume to add force to their message. Today, plays or stories are usually performed by actors in a theatre – a building specially designed for dramatic shows. In the grandest theatres the stage is overlooked by rows and rows of seats so that a large audience can watch the performance. There is a large area behind the stage for scenery, and an area where the orchestra can sit so that live music can accompany the performance. Special lights hung around the stage help to create the atmosphere. Many people work in a large theatre, designing and making the scenery and costumes and preparing the actors for the show. But actors can be just as entertaining when performing plays in a small open space with a few simple props.

Below is one of the most magnificent theatres of ancient Greece, the theatre of Herod Atticus, built on the Acropolis at Athens. In ancient times actors would play several parts in a drama, changing masks to show which character was speaking. Left are the masks of comedy and tragedy

Greek theatre

The earliest theatres that survive today are the open-air Greek theatres built over 2,300 years ago. The actors performed on a stage at the centre – an area called the orchestra – and the audience sat in a semi-circle around them on rows of stone seats. The clever design of the theatre meant that the actors' voices carried clearly to the back rows. Behind the orchestra was an area for costumes and props. The actors were all men and they wore masks depicting a range of set characters, including women.

Puppet shows

Not all plays are performed by human actors. Puppet theatre is very popular all over the world and involves figures that appear to come to life when moved by a human operator. Puppetry dates from at least the 5th century BC. There are many different types of puppet. Glove puppets are worn on the hand, string puppets (sometimes known as marionettes) are operated from above, and rod puppets are operated from below. Punch and Judy shows, a favourite seaside entertainment in Britain, feature glove puppets representing a husband and wife who are always arguing and fighting. Another type of puppet is the string puppet. In Indonesia there are Wayang Kulit shadow puppets. The characters are cut out of leather and their movement is controlled with metal rods. An oil lamp behind the puppets makes their shadows fall on to a screen on which they act out traditional stories. The audience sits in front of the screen and watches the shadow play. Shows usually last many hours and being a puppet master is very demanding work. He not only operates the puppets, he narrates the story, conducts the musicians and may also play an instrument himself.

Shadow puppets are popular throughout Southeast Asia. They are made of leather and moved from beneath by means of metal rods. A light behind them throws their shadows on to a screen, beyond which the audience sits to watch the drama

Travelling theatre

The 10th century saw the rise of Christian religious drama in Europe. Actors took to the road and travelled around performing in the street or in the courtyards of inns. Often the stage was simply the back of the actors' cart. The audience would gather and put money into a hat that was passed around. The actors performed mystery plays, which told stories from the Bible and, later on, morality plays about the battle of good against evil. Some plays were performed in episodes over a number of days.

The townspeople call out their encouragement as good and evil do battle

Pantomime

Pantomimes are plays with music and dancing. They began with the Italian Commedia dell'Arte, travelling players of the 16th century, who told the traditional love story of Harlequin and Columbine. Today the shows take a well-known fairy story such as Cinderella, Aladdin or Red Riding Hood and incorporate a whole range of different acts – such as clowns, singing and magic. The tales are given a comic treatment and usually feature an 'Old Dame' – a foolish, ugly, old woman who is played by a man dressed as a woman.

Frenchman Marcel Marceau, one of the most famous mime artists of all time

Japanese Kabuki theatre

The popular theatre of Japan is called Kabuki. It originated in the 1600s and still plays to packed houses. The shows are lighthearted with lots of singing and dancing, and are performed on an unusual stage with a bridge that runs through the audience, called the flower walk. The actors, who are all men, wear highly decorative costumes, dramatic stylized make-up and wigs that reveal the personalities of the character they are playing.

Mime

Mime is a form of silent theatre. There is usually a musical accompaniment, but the actor does not speak at all. Instead, he or she tells a story using vividly accurate actions and expressions. The art of mime reached a new high in the 20th century with the great French artist, Marcel Marceau.

DANCE

PEOPLE ALL OVER THE WORLD love to move their bodies to the rhythm of music – to dance. People dance for many different reasons. The first dances were probably part of rituals, religious worship and magic. Because dancing is beautiful to watch as well as to perform, it became an entertainment that rich people paid to see, and dancers are known to have performed at the courts of the pharaohs of Ancient Egypt. Dances can also be a powerful form of storytelling. The Maori people of New Zealand use dance to teach their children about their history. Today, many forms of dance are regarded as art. Many of the classical or traditional dances of the world can be performed only by professional dancers who have been specially trained in the correct movements. But there will always be dancing just for fun, that can be enjoyed by anyone who wants to join in.

Religious dance

Kathkali is a sacred Hindu dance of India in which the performers act out the stories of their gods. Every movement and gesture the dancer makes is important, even eye movements. The dancers wear bright costumes and dramatic head-dresses, and dance to the music of drums. Singers with cymbals and a gong act as narrators. The stories usually concern the chaos brought about by human weaknesses until harmony is restored by the gods, and performances often go on all night.

Today kathkali dancing (left) is often performed for the benefit of tourists. But to the Hindu audience and players, it still has strong religious significance

Folk dance

The traditional dances of ordinary people are called folk dances. Flamenco is the national folk dance of Spain. It is performed in spectacular dress to guitar music, singing and clapping. Flamenco has a very dramatic and emotional style – the dancers stand straight and proud, stamp their feet and click their fingers to the rhythm, and shout out to encourage each other. Some dancers shake and tap a tambourine as they move, and others play castanets – wooden clappers held in either hand. Like other folk dances, flamenco can be performed anywhere – outside in a town square or in a bar.

Ritual dance

Dance plays an important part in the rituals or ceremonies of many cultures. The Mbuti children of Africa must learn special dances before they can become adults. Ritual dances are also performed to calm angry spirits or to drive out evil ones. In Sri Lanka when someone is sick a 'devil dance' is performed to rid the body of the demons believed to be causing the sickness. The Aborigines of Australia dance around a magic stone to bring rain, and many of the Native American tribes of North America have traditional war dances that were once performed to prepare the men for battle and call upon the spirits to help them.

Young Mbuti people from Zaire decorate their bodies with white make-up for a dance to celebrate the beginning of adulthood

Flamenco dancers of Spain wear tight dresses that flare out into swirling multi-tiered skirts

Ballet

Ballet is a theatrical form of dance that began in the French court in the 16th century. Over the centuries ballet dancers have perfected a repertoire of classical techniques and movements, which they use to tell stories. Some of the best known are the romantic ballets of the 19th century, Swan Lake, The Nutcracker and Sleeping Beauty. The music for these three ballets was composed by Tchaikovsky.

These ballet dancers perform a pas-de-deux, a traditional romantic sequence for the hero and heroine of the story

ICE DANCING

Ice skating is an Olympic sport as well as a popular entertainment. The craze for ice dancing reached its peak during the 1980s with the gold medal-winning partnership of Jayne Torvill and Christopher Dean. The pair revolutionized their sport by inventing dance sequences with spectacular movements that built up into a story. You may have wondered why skating looks so graceful. The whole weight of the skater is concentrated on the small area of skate that touches the ground – the narrow blade. The enormous pressure under the blade melts the ice, and this reduces friction, so that the skater can glide along.

Ballroom dancing

In the 17th century, while the ordinary people of Europe met at folk dances, the nobility went to balls to dance the minuet. Today the formal dance style lives on as ballroom dancing. The most popular ballroom dance is the waltz. Once a peasant dance from southern Germany, it was considered shocking when first introduced into 18th-century ballrooms, because couples had to dance so close together. The tango (right) calls for even closer contact.

n modern dancing, anything oes. Clubbers dance to a renetic beat and repetitive rance-like music. Some club wners go to extraordinary ngths to surprise their members, including lling the dance hall ith foam!

ve

ew forms of music often spire new ways to dance. In e 1950s, American singers ch as Elvis Presley, Bill Haley d the Comets and Buddy olly began playing an exciting w kind of music called rock roll. New energetic dances d to be invented to keep pace th the music. One technique, led jiving, was particularly ld and demanded stamina as ll as perfect timing. Men ung their partners round and nd, slid them along the floor ween their legs and flung m high up into the air!

DANCE STEPS

These footprints show the basic steps of the waltz. It will help to count to the beat: 'one, two, three, one, two, three, one, two, three...', stressing the 'one' every time as you zigzag round the room. The second step in each section should move to the side, and not be a straightforward walking step. As you relax into the rhythm and start to move more freely, allow your body to sway away from the reaching foot and towards the closing foot. If you tread on your partner's toes, don't worry!

MUSIC

MUSIC IS SIMPLY A PATTERN of sounds that is good to listen to. These sounds can be arranged in many different ways to produce music in a wide range of styles, including classical, jazz, pop or folk. Every culture in the world has its own distinctive tradition of music and song, often played on unique local instruments. But all music is a form of expression – a way to communicate feelings both happy and sad. In particular, people can express their feelings together through music. Today crowds at football matches sing and chant spontaneously with excitement to encourage their team, as in the past slaves labouring in the fields sang together, inventing words and music to keep up a working rhythm and rally their downcast spirits. Music was probably first used in primitive religions, to communicate with the gods and to please them. It is still part of the ritual of most of the major religions today. Music was first written down in the form of notes by monks of the 9th century AD. Before then, all music was learned by listening and repetition. But the discovery of ancient instruments, paintings and written descriptions do give some idea of how it sounded.

Traditional instruments

Many countries and regions of the world have their own unique musical traditions. The music played by the local people of an area is called folk music, and it is often played on traditional instruments. The aboriginals of Australia have an instrument called a didgeridoo, made from a long straight branch that has been buried in the ground until it is eaten hollow by ant-like insects called termites. The didgeridoo makes a low droning noise and is played at night-time ceremonies, called corroborees, when aboriginals gather around a fire to sing, dance and play music.

The didgeridoo is a heavy instrument that has to be played resting on the ground

Melody, rhythm and harmony

Music is made up of sounds, called notes, organized into a pattern that people find pleasing. These patterns are made up of three different elements – melody, rhythm and harmony. The melody is the tune, a pattern of notes in a certain order. It is the part of the music that you recognize and remember. Rhythm is marked by a steady beat – the beat that you follow if you clap or dance to a tune. Harmony is the mixing together of notes to make a more interesting sound. When one person sings a tune there is no harmony, but two voices or a choir can sing different notes at the same time to make a rich harmony of sound.

MOZART

Wolfgang Amadeus Mozart (1756–91) was born in Austria, the son of a violinist and composer. From a very young age Mozart showed extraordinary musical talent. He began composing when he was five, and at six he started to travel round Europe performing harpsichord concerts. As an adult, Mozart made his home in Vienna, where he taught and composed. He wrote a total of 600 pieces in his life, including 41 symphonies, 27 piano concertos and many great operas, such as The Magic Flute and Don Giovanni. Although today he is known as one of the greatest composers ever, he died a poor man at the age of just 35.

String instruments

String instruments are played by making stretched strings vibrate. This can be done by drawing a bow over them, as with a violin (left) or cello, or plucking or strumming the strings, as with a guitar. The shorter the string, the higher the note played. The player makes different notes by pressing the string down on to a fingerboard and shortening it. The sitar is a string instrument from India. It has up to seven strings, as well as 12 secondary strings that create a background drone.

Wind instruments

The family of instruments that are blown to make sound are called wind instruments, and include woodwind instruments, such as the clarinet and saxophone, and brass instruments, like the trumpet and the French horn (left). Woodwind instruments were originally all tubes made of wood, although some today are made of metal. Their sound is made by either blowing across the mouthpiece or over a thin strip of wood in the mouthpiece, called a reed, which vibrates. Different notes are made by opening and closing holes along the tube with your fingers, which alters the length of the tube. Brass instruments are tubes of metal curled round so they are not too long and unmanageable. Notes are usually made by pressing valves to alter how far down the tube the air travels. In the trombone, however, this is done by moving a sliding tube which alters the note.

How many of these instruments do you recognize? They are, from left to right, xylophone, violin, trumpet, clarinet, percussion and double bass

Keyboard instruments

The piano is a keyboard instrument. When you press a key it works like a lever to make a felt-covered hammer hit strings to sound a note. A grand piano (above) has its set of strings laid out horizontally. An upright piano is more compact because its strings are arranged vertically. The piano was originally called the pianoforte, which means soft-loud in Italian, because it can be played very quietly, or make a sound powerful enough to fill a concert hall.

Percussion

The simplest musical instruments are percussion instruments, such as drums, triangles and xylophones. Percussion instruments are struck, either by hand or with a beater, to make sound. There are hundreds of different percussion instruments, often specific to different regions of the world and made of local materials. Traditional African music has a strong rhythm beaten out on drums.

RADIO AND TELEVISION

IN 1901 GUGLIELMO MARCONI first sent signals across the Atlantic using electromagnetic (radio) waves. Radio waves carry information about sound and – as it was later discovered – pictures, and radio and television were born. Up until then news travelled slowly. You could only communicate with distant friends or family by letter or telegraph. National news broke only as quickly as the newspapers could be printed and distributed. In remote areas of the country national events could pass people by unnoticed. The advent of radio and television meant that everyone could be informed about and involved in the events of the country and the world as they happened. Broadcasters have enormous power because they control the flow of information. The way they report the news can also affect people's opinions. But radio and television can also offer unique access to information and entertainment, enabling you to follow the World Cup Final, or events in a remote rainforest.

How television reaches your home

Television programmes are broadcast to homes using radio waves carrying signals about sound and pictures. These signals can reach your home in several different ways. They can be broadcast over a local area from a tall transmission mast to rooftop television aerials. Programmes can also be broadcast over long distances using satellites in space. A television signal is transmitted into space from a large dish aerial, called an Earth station. The satellite picks up the signal, amplifies it and sends it back to Earth. Satellite signals can be picked up by a small dish aerial pointing directly at the satellite. Television signals can also reach homes via underground cables. The cable is made up of dozens of fibre optic cables as thin as a hair, each carrying one channel.

How a television set works

A television set receives radio signals carrying separate information about sound and pictures. Sound signals travel straight to a loudspeaker. Picture signals are sent to the picture tube (known as a cathode ray tube). Here beams of electrons (parts of atoms) are fired at the inside surface of the screen. The screen is made up of thousands of dots of chemicals, called phosphors, which glow either red, blue or green. Combinations of dots build up a full colour picture. Seen in quick succession – 25 to 30 pictures per second – the images give the impression of movement.

A tv set receives electric signals, which it changes into pictures and sound

Streams of particles are fired on to the back of the screen

The picture changes many times a second, giving the effect of movement

The streams of particles build up a picture

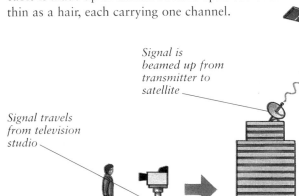

Signal travels from television studio

Signal is beamed up from transmitter to satellite

Signal is beamed back from space to tv mast

Signal arrives inside tv set your home

GUGLIELMO MARCONI

Guglielmo Marconi (1874–1937) was the
Italian scientist who developed long-
distance radio broadcasting, and laid the
foundations for television transmission.
He started experimenting with radio
waves in 1894, aiming to invent a system
that would send messages in Morse Code
over long distances without the use of wires.
By 1899 he had achieved a transmission
of 14 km across the Bristol Channel.
By 1901 he had sent messages from
Cornwall in England to Newfoundland on the other side of
the Atlantic Ocean.

Outside broadcast

To get the most up-to-date news stories, television reporters often
have to film outside the studio at the scene of the action. For a
really big story crews are linked directly to the studio with an
outside broadcast unit in a van or truck that has a transmitter. A
simple news story can be covered by just two people, a reporter
and a camera operator using a video camera.

Inside a studio

Most television programmes are made in a studio. Here the actors,
or a presenter, stand on a set (stage) surrounded by cameras,
microphones and lights. The camera crew wear headphones
linking them to a control room. Monitors in the control room
show exactly what is happening on the set, so the different
material can be co-ordinated for transmission.

How a radio works

A radio set is a radio wave receiver which uses an antenna to pick
up the signals broadcast from a radio transmitter. Radio waves
travel at different speeds, known as wavelengths or frequencies.
Radio stations broadcast each channel using a different frequency,

and a tuner on the
radio set allows you
to select the
programme you
want. An electric
circuit in the radio
set turns the waves
into electronic
signals to make
sound, and an
amplifier makes
these sounds louder.

*This selection of
old radios – now
collectors' items –
shows how radio
design and
technology has
changed. Many
radios today
incorporate a CD
player as well as a
tape deck*

Digital versus analogue technology

In a digital system information is represented by electrical pulses,
instead of smoothly changing electric signals, which are analogue.
Digital pulses represent numbers, which in turn can represent any
type of information, including sound and pictures. Digital systems
use only two numbers, zero and one, which combine in a code.

SOUND-EFFECTS

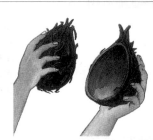

When a radio drama is recorded the actors read a script into
a microphone while a sound-effects technician makes noises
to give an impression of the activity or setting. Sound-effects
are simple to create at home. Try recording a story with the
help of some friends using some of the sound effects below
and see how they add to the atmosphere. A ghost story is
particularly good for this purpose.

For footsteps on the path, fill a tray with gravel and step up
and down on it. For a horse's hooves, knock together two
empty coconut shells. (An old trick, but it's really
convincing!) To make rain, pour water from a watering can
on to a tin tray (preferably outside, or over a sink!). For
thunder and lightning, experiment with tin trays and a
wooden spoon. Bashing a tin tray creates a really good effect,
especially if you have a tray that shudders when you shake it.
For wind, simply blow into a jar.

PHOTOGRAPHY AND CINEMA

THE TECHNIQUES OF PHOTOGRAPHY allow us to capture significant moments in our lives in still images and has filled the world with moving pictures through cinema and television. The camera is a sealed box that allows no light in, except when the shutter at the front opens and you take a photograph. The light reflected by the object in front of the camera passes through the lens, which focuses the light on to a piece of film. The film is a type of plastic coated with chemicals that are sensitive to light. In black-and-white photography there is just one layer of these chemicals, but in colour photography there are three layers, each one sensitive to either blue, green or red. Together, these primary colours make up the full range of colours that we can see. Light alters the chemicals on the film and when the film is developed, the image created by the light is fixed and a picture is revealed, but the light and dark areas are reversed. This is called the negative. Projecting the negative on to light-sensitive paper produces a print with the dark and light areas the right way round.

Moving pictures

Moving pictures – or cinema as we know it today – became possible when George Eastman invented flexible film in 1889. Pictures could be taken in quick succession and when projected at speed the images merged to give the impression of movement. The first movie was shown in Paris in 1895. Early films were silent and in black and white. Music accompanied the story and words appeared on the screen to help the audience follow the plot. Movie actors such as Charlie Chaplin and Rudolph Valentino became stars. In 1927 it became possible to record sound with pictures and in 1932 films were first made in colour. Over the decades techniques have continued to advance to make cinema the popular multi-million dollar entertainment business it is today.

Making a movie

Making a film usually begins with a producer. The producer chooses the storyline and finds the money to film it, picks the director and other technical teams and plans the making of the film. On the set the director is in charge of the large teams of people involved in production. He or she directs the actors and makes the creative decisions that will give the film its character. The set is designed by an art director, a cinematographer is responsible for the cameras, there are sound and lighting crews and many others.

Putting a film together

Once a film has been shot the different individual sequences must be put together in the right order and combined with a sound track. This is done by a film editor who works closely with the director to tell the story in the best way. The editor's choice of which pieces of film to show and what to leave out can affect the character of a film, by building up the suspense, altering the audience's understanding of the plot or speeding up the drama.

Special effects

Part of the magic of cinema is the special effects than enable a director to recreate dramatic action sequences, such as accidents and catastrophes, and fantasy worlds populated by dinosaurs.

CINEMA IN INDIA

India is the biggest cinema-going nation in the world. Around 9 million cinema tickets are sold each day, and more than 700 full-length feature films are made each year. Most Indian films are action-packed and full of romance, singing and dancing, and are made in Bombay – also known as Bollywood. Every Indian city and town is full of cinemas, and travelling cinema vans visit remote rural areas.

Hollywood

American film-making took off at the beginning of this century in a small town outside Los Angeles called Hollywood. The sunny climate meant films could be made all year round. Today Hollywood is the home of the big American film studios (film-making companies) and of many glamorous film stars. Every year, the stars gather at a glittering ceremony, when Academy Awards (or Oscars) are given for achievement in the film industry.

Animation

Animation is the art of bringing drawings or models to life in film. Cartoons are made by filming a sequence of drawings – at least 12 per second – to give the impression of movement. Today computers are able to draw the pictures linking one action to another, making animated films quicker and cheaper to produce. Clay models are animated by repositioning the characters minutely between each frame (individual shot).

Modelling skills can be important in animation

SIMPLE ANIMATION

You can bring a drawing to life by making a flick book. Take a drawing pad or notebook and, starting at the back, draw a character in the top right-hand corner. You don't have to be good at drawing for this to work, a stick person will do. Decide what your character is going to do – walk, jump, or turn a cartwheel, for example.

Then on the next page draw the same character a little further on in their activity, so that you end up with a sequence of between 12 and 20 pictures. Then use your thumb to flick slowly through the pages and watch your character move.

PAINTING AND SCULPTURE

PEOPLE HAVE ALWAYS enjoyed expressing themselves through painting, but they have also painted to record important events or famous people, or simply to decorate their homes or public places. When you look at a painting it is not just the subject matter that is interesting, often it is style that the artist has used – it might be simple or highly detailed, natural or romanticised. It might be a lifelike representation of a scene or the forms may have been changed or distorted. Painters are constantly experimenting with painting materials, giving paintings new textures and forms. Sculpture is three-dimensional art, so as well as looking at it you can often touch and feel and walk around it. There are two basic techniques for making sculptures: either a solid block – often made of stone or wood – is carved out, or liquid metal is poured into a mould, called a cast.

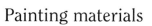

Red, yellow and blue are the primary pigments. Red mixed with blue gives purple. Red mixed with yellow gives orange. Yellow mixes with blue to give green.

Painting materials

The first paintings were done on cave walls using sticks and natural pigments. Today most painters use brushes to apply their paint, but the paints themselves have changed little over the centuries. Pigments or colours may come from berries, bark, roots and earth, shells, beetles or even metals. They can be mixed with a vegetable oil, to make oil paints, or with water to create watercolours. Oil paint is used on canvas, and is very versatile – it can be used thickly or thinly and built up in layers, and produces strong colours that last a long time.

Watercolours are made from pigment dissolved in water, and are used to paint on paper, which absorbs the colour. Watercolours are easy to apply, dry quickly and can be mixed with varying amounts of water to create either strong or light colour.

How colours react with each other

You can experiment with colours by painting squares of different colours, cutting them out and placing them next to each other in different combinations. Notice how the colours change character. Putting black next to white makes the black more black and the white more white. If you put very different colours together, such as green and red, the same effect is achieved. If you put similar colours together, such as blue and violet, the colours will appear to jump and merge in a quite exciting way.

Artists at work in a studio. A constant light source is important to painters. As the Sun goes round from east to west it distorts both colour and form, so a good studio has windows facing north, which get no direct sunlight, and 'artificial daylight' lighting for duller days

COLLAGE

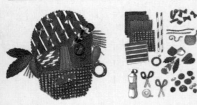

A collage is a picture made up of a combination of materials – paints, different qualities of paper stuck one on top of the other, or any other materials that you think would help to create the effect you are after – printed papers such as newspaper, straws, pieces of fabric, bits of string and even pasta. Try making a collage portrait of yourself (or make a collage of an animal), using as many different textures as you can.

Most artists prefer to mix paints from a tube on a palette (below, on the bench) so they can arrive at their own more subtle colours. Artists' brushes are very expensive items and need to be cleaned and stored carefully after use. The sculptor uses a lump hammer and a flat chisel to put the finishing touches to her work

Abstract art

The word abstract means something that does not have any recognisable shape or form. In the 20th century the term abstract art was first used to describe the paintings of artists who painted ideas rather than objects or scenes. The Swiss artist, Paul Klee, explored ideas such as harmony, rhythm and shape in his works. The painting shown above is called 'Streamers'. What do these shapes and colours suggest to you?

SALVADOR DALI

Salvador Dali was a Spanish artist who lived from 1904 to 1989. He was an expert draughtsman and used a smooth, clean painting technique, but he is best-known for the extraordinary subject matter of his paintings. Dali was one of the leaders of the Surrealist painting movement of the early 20th century. These were painters who wanted to show a world outside the real one ('sur-real' means above the real). Dali filled his work with startling images from his dreams and fantasies, such as a telephone in the shape of a lobster and melting watches hanging limply over a wall.

Looking at pictures

Before the invention of the camera, painting was, and still is, used to record important events or people. Portraits of famous people usually show them in a setting that explains who they were and why they were important. Often, portrait painters had to make their subjects look better than they did in real life. Paintings are often historical documents that show what people wore or ate, their social standing, the jobs they did and how they spent their leisure time.

This artist paints landscapes in a realistic way, but includes abstract shapes that produce a disturbing effect

This discus thrower carved from marble is a Roman copy of a Greek sculpture from 450 BC

Carved sculpture

Carved sculpture is made using chisels and hammers to cut away at a solid block of material. The most common materials are stone, especially marble, and wood. Often the sculptor makes a small model, called a maquette, before embarking on the actual sculpture. The next job is to carve the rough shape, cutting the block with a chisel and hammer. The detail is carved with hand chisels and fine scrapers. Finally, both wood and stone may be polished to give the sculpture a smooth texture.

British sculptor Henry Moore used both stone and bronze. His two-piece reclining figure cast in bronze (below) can be seen in Germany

Cast sculpture

There are many different stages in making a cast sculpture. First, a rough of the sculpture is made from clay. This is covered in a layer of wax, on to which the sculptor can carve the fine detail. Then the whole thing is covered in a layer of heat-resistant plaster with holes at the top and bottom to make a mould. Molten metal is poured into the mould, taking the place of the wax, which melts and runs away. The metal cools, then the mould is cracked open to reveal the culpture.

BUILDINGS

FROM SIMPLE HOMES to mighty monuments, bridges and tunnels, buildings are designed to make life easier, safer, or simply more interesting. All buildings have one thing in common – they were constructed for a specific purpose. In a sports stadium thousands of people must all be able to get a good view of the action. A bridge must get people from one side of a divide to the other. A cathedral must reflect the glory of god, with soaring spires, glowing stained-glass windows and a chamber that resonates with singing and prayer. Building techniques have evolved over the centuries, but much remains timeless, such as the purity of Ancient Greek temples, the beauty of natural materials including wood and marble, and the simple practicality of nomad tents in the Sahara.

Çatal Hüyük in Turkey had buildings of mud brick, with flat roofs and narrow streets

Mud huts and grain stores are built around a yard or compound in this Dogon village in Mali, Africa

Building materials

Homes can be made out of almost anything. The first shelters were made simply out of available natural materials, such as mud, straw, wood, stone, ice, leaves, grass and animal skins, as it was impractical to carry materials far. People began building with bricks around 6,000 years ago, at first using blocks of earth that they dried in the sun. Later, they discovered that baking the bricks at high temperatures made them lighter, stronger and longer-lasting. Today a wide range of building materials is available, including reinforced concrete (concrete around a steel framework), iron, steel, bricks and glass. Sometimes, however, traditional local materials are still the cheapest and most practical alternative. These Dogon huts in Mali, Africa, are made from mud and straw.

BUILDING FACTS

● The limited technical equipment of the builders of the past, compared with the lifting and digging machines available today, did not stop the construction of the awe-inspiring pyramids of ancient Egypt or the European cathedrals of the Middle Ages.

● The biggest cities in the world are in Japan, where large cities have spread and joined up to make giant cities. Japan is made up of islands with high mountains, so most people live on flat strips of land around the coast. To grow, cities have to spread out like ribbons until they finally merge into each other. Over 27 million people live in and around Japan's capital city, Tokyo.

Homes for people

The first people were nomads, who either sheltered in caves or lived in portable homes such as tents made from animal hides. But when people learned to farm they settled down and built more permanent homes. The style of homes varies greatly all over the world, and is determined mainly by climate and local building materials. As communities grow they find different ways for large numbers of people to live together. Today, one solution is to build tall apartment blocks. In 7000 BC in the town of Çatal Hüyük (now in Turkey), 6,000 people lived side by side in homes built of wooden frames and mud bricks. To save on space and building materials, the houses were built one against the other, sharing walls, with few streets between them. The doors were in the roof, and a ladder led down into the living area. This kept the houses cool and kept out animals. It also had the advantage of making the town difficult for a potential enemy to capture.

Classical architecture

The Ancient Greeks and Romans admired buildings that displayed balance, proportion and simplicity. Today this style is known as classical architecture. The Parthenon in Athens, Greece (440–431 BC), is a good example of classical Greek architecture with rows of columns supporting a triangular roof. Three orders of Greek architecture are Doric (plain-topped pillars), Corinthian (pillars decorated with foliage, left) and Ionic (ram's horn pillars, right).

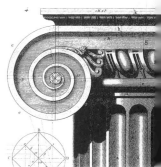

owns first grew up when
eople learned to farm. They
o longer had to run after
erds of wild animals for
eir food

Islamic architecture

The traditional architecture of Islamic countries is influenced by the Muslim religion, and the mosque is not only the place where people worship, but the building at the heart of any community. Mosques often have a simple outline with a central dome, which Muslims believe to be the most perfect shape on earth. They also have towers called minarets, from which people are called to prayer. According to Islamic law, buildings cannot be decorated with images of living things. Instead ceramic tiles and mosaics are used to create geometric designs, or they are decorated using calligraphy (the art of writing). Arches are another common feature of Islamic design, with many variations on the basic horseshoe arch.

A dome decorated with geometric patterns is a classic feature of Islamic architecture

MODEL BUILDING

Collect cereal packets, shoe boxes and cardboard to build a series of beach huts for your window sill. You can cut out the walls and roof in one go, to make the hut stronger. For a square hut, the front, back and two sides should be equal upright rectangles. The front and back need a triangle added on for the roof pitch. The tabs for the roof should be as tall as the height of the pitch. Cut out the hut, stick it together from the inside with tape, then paint the roof red and paint the walls with stripes of bright colour.

Skyscrapers

Towards the end of the 19th century, advances in building technology, new materials and the invention of the lift made it possible to construct buildings taller than ever before. The first skyscrapers were built in Chicago, USA, in the 1880s. They soon became status symbols for American companies and grew taller and taller. The skyline of Manhattan in New York, USA (below), is dominated by skyscrapers. The Chrysler building was completed in 1929 as a symbol of the greatness of the American car manufacturer. The Empire State Building, built in 1931, was for some time the tallest building in New York, with a height of 380 metres. This record was broken in 1972 by the World Trade Centre, which is 419 metres tall.

WORLD RELIGIONS

OUR LIVES ARE FULL of questions, many of which are very hard to answer. Why are we born? Why do we die? How did the world come into being? Why is there unhappiness and suffering in the world as well as joy and love? Religions are sets of ideas and beliefs that try to make sense of these mysteries. In many cases, they also offer principles by which people should live their lives. The first religions were spirit religions dedicated to the many spirits or gods of nature. Spirit religions were not written down, but used stories and myths to explain the world. Today there are many different religions, each with their own god or gods. Three of the major religions – Islam, Christianity and Judaism – believe in only one god. The fourth, Hinduism, has many gods. The principles of these religions are set down in sacred texts – the Christian Bible, the Qur'an of Islam, the Jewish Talmud and Torah, and the Hindu Vedas. Of the thousands of other religions throughout the world, whether institutionalized or private and personal, many share very similar forms of worship – prayer, meditation, singing and chanting.

At Easter Spanish Christians commemorate the last journey of Jesus before his crucifixion by walking in procession through the streets. Often an effigy of Jesus on the cross is carried at the head of the procession

The wearer takes on the spirit embodied in this wooden African mask

Spirit religions

The first religions were based on the worship of the spirits or gods of the natural world – in the animals, plants, rivers and mountains. These are called animist religions and they are traditional religions passed down by word of mouth. Animist religions are still practised all over the world. The people of the Amazon rainforest believe in the spirits of the trees and creatures of the forest they live in, but respect the powerful spirit of the jaguar above all others. Each of the Native American peoples has its own individual religion, but they all share the belief in the great spirit who created the Earth and the spirit in every natural thing. Peoples in the northwestern United States carve animals on totem poles to protect them.

Christianity

Christians are the followers of Jesus Christ, a preacher who lived 2,000 years ago in Palestine in the Middle East (now Israel and Palestine). But many people were suspicious of Jesus and his teachings and while still a young man he was arrested and crucified (hung on a cross to die). Three days after his death his tomb was found empty and he appeared to his followers several times before he finally ascended into heaven. Christians believe that Jesus was the son of God and that he died to release people from their sins. There are 2,000 million Christians living all over the world today and many different branches of Christianity. The most important Christian festivals are Christmas, which celebrates the birth of Jesus, and Easter, which celebrates Jesus rising from the dead. The symbol of Christianity is the crucifix (cross) on which Jesus Christ died.

Islam

The religion of Islam began 1,400 years ago in the city of Mecca (now in Saudi Arabia) when Allah (the Muslim name for god), spoke to Muhammed the prophet. Muhammed wrote down Allah's words in the holy book, the Qu'ran. Islam means submission, and the followers of Islam, called Muslims, submit themselves to Allah's will and try to live in a way that is pleasing to him. When they die, Muslims believe that they are judged and sent to either heaven or hell. Today there are over 00 million Muslims ing all er the orld but ostly in the iddle East, Asia d Africa. Muslims pray five times a day facing towards ecca, but can worship anywhere, even in the street. All uslims must try to make a pilgrimage (called a Haj) to the ly city of Mecca once in their lives.

RELIGIOUS WARS

Throughout history religion has been the cause of many long and bitter wars. Some conflicts have started as disputes over sacred sites. The city of Jerusalem, for example, lies today in the Jewish state of Israel, but it is also a holy city for Muslims and Christians. As a result it has been a hotbed of violence for centuries. Strongly held religious beliefs can also result in intolerance of other religions. Conflict between Muslims and Hindus caused the partition (division) of India in 1947 into the Hindu state of India and the Muslim states of Pakistan and, later, Bangladesh.

Judaism

Judaism began around 4,000 years ago in the Middle East. The Jewish people are descended from the nomadic Hebrews who finally settled in Canaan (now Israel), the land that God had promised them. Throughout their history, the Jews have repeatedly been forced out of the promised land and into exile, and today they live scattered around the world in what is called the diaspora. Jews believe in one god and work towards a just and peaceful life for everyone on earth. They also believe that God will send the world a Messiah to bring peace and harmony. The Jewish holy day is the Sabbath, which runs from sunset on Friday to nightfall on Saturday. This is a day of rest and worship when Jews attend a service in a synagogue.

Hinduism

Hinduism began in India around 5,000 years ago and is one of the oldest religions. Today there are around 733 million Hindus, mostly living in Asia. Hindus believe in a supreme soul or spirit without form, called Brahaman. There are many other Hindu gods, but they all represent different aspects of Brahaman's power and character. The three main gods are Brahma the creator, Vishnu the preserver or protector, and Shiva the destroyer. Hindus believe that when you die your soul is reborn in another body as a person or an animal. This is called the cycle of rebirth, and your actions in this life influence what you become in the next life. Every Hindu seeks to live a good life so that their soul can break out of this cycle and join with the Brahaman. There are many Hindu festivals and celebrations but the main ones are Diwali, Holi and Dusserah. Diwali is a festival of light in late October or early November. Holi is a spring festival when Hindus worship the Lord Krishna. Dusserah is a celebration of the triumph of good over evil, and in South India it is marked by setting fire to a giant paper statue of the demon Ravana.

Hindus look forward to new beginnings at Diwali by putting welcoming lights in their windows, doors and temples and wearing bright clothes to celebrate the triumph of good over evil, and light over dark

Buddhism

Buddhism was founded by Siddhartha Gautama, a royal prince born in Nepal in 563 BC. Unhappy with life, Siddhartha spent many years praying and meditating until he gained enlightenment and finally understood the truths of life. He was given the title Buddha, meaning awakening or enlightenment. Buddhists do not believe in a god but live their lives according to the teachings of the Buddha, following the middle path between luxury and hardship. They believe that after death they are reborn and that the way they live decides whether the next life will be better or worse. Their aim is to escape the cycle of rebirth and find a state of happiness and peace, called nirvana. Most Buddhists today live in Asia, but Buddhism is also practised in Western countries.

Chinese ancestor worship

Around 5 million people in China and the Far East follow Confucianism. This religion is based on the teachings of Confucius (left), who was born in 551 BC in China, and who dedicated his life to teaching people how to live in peace and harmony. Confucius believed that the way to lead a better life was to respect other people and honour your ancestors. Children are taught to respect their parents and elders and to visit temples to worship their long-dead relatives.

FESTIVALS AND TRADITIONS

THE CELEBRATIONS, FESTIVALS and traditions of the world are very varied, but what they all have in common is that they are occasions people share, and this both enriches the lives of the world's communities and makes them stronger. Many festivals offer the opportunity to dress up, dance, sing, tell stories and eat traditional foods. But a festival can also be a solemn time for reflecting on important issues. Some occasions are part of the history of a country or community and mark a key event, such as the day a nation gained its independence or ended a war. Countries also commemorate the lives of important people, such as the great civil rights leader Martin Luther King, who is remembered each year in the United States. The world's religions have their own celebrations such as the Christian Christmas or the Hindu festival of Holi. Seasonal celebrations mark springtime and harvest, and bring light and warmth to the depths of winter. Festivals that are repeated regularly down the generations become traditions that everyone looks forward to.

New Year festivals

In Scotland the New Year begins at midnight on the first day of January, and is called Hogmanay. Scottish people hold hands in a circle, sing a song called Auld Lang Syne and wish each other good luck. For Jewish people, New Year is also a religious festival called Rosh Hashanah. They reflect on the things they have done wrong in the past and promise to do better in future. For the Chinese, New Year is a spring festival. People get together for a big meal and to exchange presents, and there are celebrations in the streets, with men dancing inside an enormous dragon costume. There may also be acrobats and jugglers, and firecrackers are exploded to frighten away evil spirits.

Religious festivals

Festivals are often an important part of religious celebrations. The most important event in the Christian year is Holy Week. It takes place in the spring and remembers the last week of Christ's life. Palm Sunday marks the day on which Christ entered Jerusalem riding a donkey, and people laid palm leaves in his path. Maundy Thursday commemorates the last supper Christ ate with his followers, and Good Friday (meaning god's Friday) marks the day Christ died on the cross. The week ends on Easter Sunday, the day he rose from the dead. One of the most important Hindu festivals is Holi, which is also a spring festival of rebirth. As part of the celebrations, Hindu children throw coloured powder and water over each other. This custom is particularly associated with Krishna, the playful young god.

Playful Hindus sprinkle each other with coloured powder to welcome spring

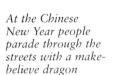

At the Chinese New Year people parade through the streets with a make-believe dragon

Corn dollies are woven in all sorts of shapes and are symbols of fertility

Harvest festivals

Harvest festivals are celebrated the world over to give thanks for a successful harvest. Thanksgiving in the United States is also an important part of remembering America's history. It echoes the harvest celebrations of the early settlers in America. They survived only with the help of the Native American Indians who taught them to farm, to catch turkeys and to find wild foods like cranberries. Thanksgiving is still celebrated today with turkey and cranberry sauce. A harvest tradition in Britain is to make a corn dolly from the last sheaf of wheat to be cut, where the spirit of the corn is believed to be hiding. The dolly may be burned in the spring and its ashes scattered as the field is ploughed, so returning the spirit of the corn to the soil and nourishing the earth. Every year in October the Germans celebrate the hops harvest with a beer festival. In Mexico they have a radish festival. On Christmas Eve the largest radishes are carved into shapes and set out to decorate restaurant tables and market stalls.

Marriage customs

Weddings are important celebrations marking the new beginning for two people. Promises are made, and family and other guests join in the well-wishing. Often weddings are religious ceremonies full of rituals and symbols. At a Hindu wedding there is always a sacred fire as a symbol of the presence of god and his wisdom. At a Jewish wedding the bride and groom drink from the same glass, then crush it underfoot to remind them that love is fragile and they must work hard to keep it. In both Jewish and Christian tradition rings are exchanged as symbols of the marriage. Rings are symbols of eternity, being circles with no beginning and no end, reminding the couple that they have pledged to love each other for ever.

A CHILDREN'S FESTIVAL

● In Turkey, 23 April is Children's Day. A child even gets the chance to sit at the desk of the country's prime minister! There are puppet shows, dances and kite-flying competitions.

● In Japan, Children's Day is 5 May. Paper kites in the shape of fish are hung from poles to stream in the wind.

Fasting

Not all special occasions are marked with meals and parties. Several important religious festivals are remembered with a period without food, known as a fast. The Jewish New Year is a solemn time when Jews remember the past and ask forgiveness. After nine days, the ceremonials are brought to an end with Yom Kippur, which is a day of fasting. The most important festival of the Muslim year is Ramadan. The Muslim holy book, the Qur'an, calls for all Muslims to fast from dawn to dusk for one month to commemorate the time when Allah gave his teachings to the prophet Muhammed. The end of Ramadan is celebrated with a special feast called Eid (below).

Seasonal festivals

The changing seasons are also an occasion to celebrate. In Sweden they celebrate the longest day of the year – Midsummer. People dress in traditional costume to dance and sing around a pole decorated with flowers and leaves. In northern Sweden the Sun does not set all night and celebrations go on right through till morning.

Remembrance

November 11 is Remembrance Day in Britain, when people remember those who died in the wars of this century. The day marks the end of World War I (1914–18). Today paper poppies – a reminder of the poppies that grew on many of the battlefields of World War I – are sold to raise money for the families of those killed in that war, and the wars that have followed it. Wreaths of poppies are laid at a special memorial by the Queen and other important figures, and a two minutes silence is observed to remember those who gave their lives.

The Swedes celebrate midsummer by dancing all night

GOVERNMENTS

IT IS NOT POSSIBLE to involve everyone in the decisions made every day in running a country. Instead a group of people, known as a government, make these decisions on behalf of the people. Governments have many responsibilities, including taxation, health care, education, defence, welfare, and environmental policy. A government's priorities and the way it runs the country are decided by the political views – the beliefs and ideas about running the country – of its members. There are many different ideas and theories about how this should be done, but people who share similar views group themselves into a political party. There are two main types of government: democratic government and autocratic government. In a democracy people are able to vote for the political party which best represents the views they hold about running the country. In an autocracy there are no elections, or there might only be one party and no choice of candidates.

Democracy

Countries where the people can choose their government are called democracies. At a general election each person puts a cross on a piece of paper to make their choice known. Then their votes are counted up to see who has won. India is the largest democracy in the world. Every citizen is able to vote for people to represent them in the national parliament. At the election in 1996 over 343 million people cast their votes out of a total electorate of over 592 million. Organizing an election in India is extremely difficult. There are 15 different languages and 21 states, so there had to be 565,000 polling stations and 3 million polling officers.

Over 340 million out of a total of 590 million voters queued to take part in India's 1996 general election

Monarchy

A monarchy is a country that is ruled, or a whose government is headed by a king or queen. In many traditions this right to rule was and still is believed to have been granted by God, and throughout history monarchs have had great power deciding the laws of the country and collecting taxes. A monarch's right to absolute power was first challenged by the people of France in the 18th century. In a series of events known as the French Revolution the people finally executed their king and France became a republic. Today there are still many monarchs, but few have real power. These monarchs have a more diplomatic role, representing their country abroad or acting as figureheads at events of national importance.

The oba (king) of Akure wears traditional robes and a beaded crown for occasions of state. He is the ruler of the Yoruba people of Nigeria

---

GOVERNMENT FACTS

● The world's oldest parliament is in Iceland. Called the Althing, it was started by Viking settlers in AD 930.

● The people of ancient Athens, in Greece, started the first democratic assembly nearly 2,500 years ago. But it wasn't completely fair, because women and slaves weren't given the right to vote.

● Traditionally the king or queen of England owns all the swans on the River Thames, except for those marked in a special annual ceremony.

Dictatorship

In a dictatorship one person or group holds all the power and does not allow any opposition. The power might be held by an individual, a family, a political party or a military group. From 1939 to 1975 Spain was a dictatorship, ruled by General Francisco Franco (right). He seized power after the country was divided by civil war, and succeeded with the help of the military in crushing all opposition. He continued to rule until his death in 1975.

Republic

A republic is a state, which means that it is not ruled by a monarch but by the people, who elect their government representatives and a head of state, such as a President. The United States of America is a republic and it is governed according to a constitution (laws setting out how the country should be run) written in 1787. The constitution set out three branches of government: the President, Congress and the Supreme Court. The President leads the executive branch, which decides and carries out the government's policy. Congress makes the laws of the country and the Supreme Court makes judgments according to the law. The government was set up in this way to prevent any one branch becoming too powerful.

The White House in Washington DC is the official residence of the President of the United States

Communism

The ideas of communism are based on the works of Karl Marx (1818–1883). Communism means 'belonging to all' and Marx believed that working people would revolt against the ruling classes that exploited them, and together take ownership of everything. He held that people should work in cooperatives and share all goods and services. The communist party has ruled China since 1949 when Mao Zedong (1893–1976) took power. Although the regime has improved conditions of the mainly agricultural society of China, the powerful state government restricts the freedom of the individual.

This statue of heroic workers is one of many in communist North Korea

The United Nations

The United Nations (UN) is an organization dedicated to world peace. Most countries have a representative at the UN General Assembly, which meets in New York. The UN helps the world's governments to work together and sends peace-keeping troops to war zones and trouble spots.

Capitalism

A capitalist system is one that is based on the belief that those who have money or 'capital' should be allowed to use it to generate more money. This might be done by starting up businesses or investing money in other businesses to allow them to generate more profit, which the investor takes a share of. The financial systems of many countries, such as France (below) are based on the general principal of capitalism, but rules and regulations are needed to keep this in check so that a rich minority is not allowed to exploit a poor majority.

NELSON MANDELA

Nelson Mandela (born 1918) was a South African lawyer. In 1948 South Africa adopted a policy called apartheid, which meant the segregation of the races, and rule by the white minority. Mandela joined a black nationalist party called the African National Congress (ANC), which opposed apartheid. In 1962 he was arrested and sentenced to life imprisonment. Throughout his 27 years in jail he continued to speak out against apartheid and became a symbol of the injustice of the regime. In 1990 Mandela was finally released, aged 71. In a referendum in 1992 South Africans voted to end apartheid rule, and in 1994 Mandela was elected the first black president of South Africa.

TRADE AND MONEY

Trade is the exchange of goods and services – buying and selling. Coins were invented when overseas trading began and merchants used weights of precious metals, such as silver, to buy and sell. Overseas trade has shaped the world. When European traders found rich markets in foreign lands they made great efforts to protect their interests. Sea-faring nations such as Britain, Portugal and Holland established colonies in distant lands with their own armies and police forces and so, through trade, built huge empires and became world powers. The world today survives on trade. Few countries are self-sufficient, so they sell what they have to raise money to buy what they need. Products are visible items such as food or cars, or 'invisible' items such as the labour or manufacturing expertise that makes a product, or a financial service, such as insurance. In international trade today little actual money changes hands, as transactions take place on paper or over the telephone and are managed using computer systems.

Money

Money is a recognized form of payment. Today units of money are represented by notes and coins, but they have taken many other forms. Cowrie shells were once used in China, India, Thailand and Africa. Other forms of money include copper rings, salt, beads, stone dishes, cocoa beans and axes. When the first coins were issued, it was the weight that determined their value. Paper money was first used by the Chinese in the 10th century as an alternative to dealing with large quantities of metal coins. At first paper money was simply a handwritten receipt, but later receipts of fixed values were issued by governments.

Markets and bazaars

Markets are still at the heart of communities all over the world. Every day people travel to the village markets of India and Africa to buy and sell, to meet friends and exchange news. In Thailand there are floating markets, with vegetables, fruit, flowers and spices being sold from boats called sampans. A bazaar sells craft goods. Moroccan bazaars are famous for their brassware (left).

Trade

Early people could make, find or grow most of the things they needed for everyday life, but as civilization developed and communities grew, people began to need more things. Craftsmen, such as potters or weapon-makers, developed businesses. Peddlers and local farmers would meet once a week at a market to sell their wares. The first permanent shops probably appeared in Europe in the Middle Ages, but they were only the front room of someone's house. People did not use money, but bartered or exchanged items they judged to be of equal value – a quantity of wood, or food, an axe or a day's labour. Today we calculate the value of something in terms of units of money, but the value of something may not be fixed, and haggling over prices is still very much part of buying things in markets the world over.

In an Indian street market, a trader waits for customers to buy her fresh produce

How trade shaped the world

The world as we know it today has been shaped by trade. The first so-called explorers were in fact traders sent on missions to find new trade routes, markets and products. The Portuguese sailor Christopher Columbus, who is credited with being the first European to reach America in the 15th century, was in fact on a mission to find a shorter trade route route from Europe to India and the East Indies where valuable spices grew. Merchants also travelled a route called the Silk Road to bring back precious silks and porcelain from rich Chinese cities. They faced a gruelling journey across the Gobi desert, through the mountains of Central Asia to trading ports in the Middle East and around the Mediterranean Sea.

In Arabia, camels belonging to travelling merchants made long journeys across the desert laden with valuable goods to sell

Imports and exports

The goods and services that a country sells abroad are its exports, and the goods and services that it buys in are its imports. Imports and exports are compared to calculate a balance of payment between two countries. If one country exports more to another country than it imports from it, it is said to have a trade surplus. If it imports more than it exports, that is called a trade deficit.

Trade centres

Trade centres have traditionally grown up in places where transport is good and there is no shortage of materials, goods or labour. The busiest and largest port in the world today is Rotterdam in the Netherlands. It thrives on its connections to the river Rhine and to the sea. A key centre in the East is Hong Kong (left).

Containers are unloaded at Southampton Docks, UK

Stocks and shares

The initial cost of starting up a business is called the financial capital, and often this money is borrowed. The people who lend the money all hope to have a share in the company's profits in the future. The capital is divided into a number of shares, and each share has a certain value. This value may go up or down, depending on how the company performs. The only place shareholders may sell their shares (or a unit of shares called stock) is through a Stock Exchange (right). Here they are traded (bought and sold) by a broker who is a member of the Stock Exchange.

MONEY FACTS

● A currency is a money system, such as the Japanese yen, the French franc, the US dollar, the Mongolian tugrik or the Bhutan ngultrum. The exchange rate is what it costs to buy or sell one currency for another. This changes on a daily basis,

● The process of stamping a design on to a coin is called minting. One side of the coin usually shows the head of the monarch or the symbol of the body that guarantees the value of the coin. Only an authorized producer, known as a mint, is allowed to manufacture and stamp coins. Coins not made at a mint are forgeries.

THE WAY WE LIVE: QUESTIONS AND ANSWERS

● What else has been used as money apart from coins and banknotes?

Many things, including cowrie shells, copper rings, salt, beads, stone dishes, cocoa beans and axes.

● How did trade shape the world?

The first explorers were traders looking for new trade routes, markets and goods. When European traders found rich markets overseas, they often turned them into colonies, which they ruled with their own soldiers and police. In this way, countries such as England, Holland and Portugal built up powerful empires across the world.

● Who was Salvador Dali?

A Spanish painter who lived from 1904 to 1989 and was famous for his surreal style. His subjects included a lobster telephone and melting watches.

● What is a maquette?

The small model that a sculptor makes before starting to work on the subject full-size.

● What was Çatal Hüyük?

It was one of the world's first towns, built in what is now Turkey in 7000 BC. The houses were built next to each other, sharing walls to save space, and the doors were in the roofs, with ladders leading down to the living area.

● Can you name some features characteristic of Islamic architecture?

Dome, minaret, horseshoe arch, ceramic tiles, mosaics, geometric designs, calligraphy.

● Who believed that working people should share all labour, goods and services?

Karl Marx (1818–1883), the founder of communism.

● What is a republic?

A state. This means it is not ruled by a monarch, but by the people, who elect their government representatives and a head of state, such as a president.

● Who invented democracy?

The people of Athens in ancient Greece.

● What happens at Chinese New Year?

This is a spring festival, when people get together for a big meal and to exchange presents. There are celebrations in the street – acrobats, jugglers and fireworks, and men dance inside a huge dragon costume.

● What happens in Sweden on Midsummer's Eve?

The Swedes celebrate the longest day of the year by dancing all night, sometimes round a maypole decorated with flowers. In the north of Sweden it stays light all night.

● Who was George Eastman?

George Eastman invented flexible film in 1889. This was the birth of moving pictures, or cinema, as we know it.

● What is Mecca?

Mecca is the holy city of Islam. It is in present-day Saudi Arabia. Muslims pray five times a day facing Mecca, and aim to make a pilgrimage there at least once during their lives.

● How would you make a sound effect of horse's hooves?

Bang two halves of a coconut shell together.

● When were radio waves discovered?

In 1901, by Guglielmo Marconi.

● Where should you be careful of shaking your head?

In India. If you shake your head from side to side in India, it means 'yes', not 'no'.

● What is the Rosetta stone?

This ancient stone was discovered in 1799. On it, the same piece is written in three languages, Greek, Egyptian hieroglyphics and a language that so far no one has been able to decipher.

SCIENCE AND TECHNOLOGY

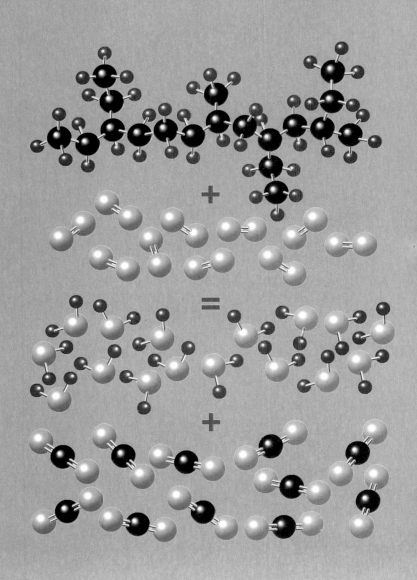

MATTER

STEEL, WATER AND AIR are all examples of matter. Like most matter around you, they are made of tiny particles called atoms. Atoms are much smaller than the smallest speck of dust – a single one is far too small to see. About 90 different types of atom occur naturally. Substances made of only one type of atom are called elements. The gold of an earring, the copper of a water pipe and the helium gas in a party balloon are all elements. Substances made of more than one type of atom are called compounds. In many compounds, atoms join together in groups called molecules. Water, for example, is a compound that consists of molecules. Each is made up of two atoms of the element hydrogen and one of oxygen, H_2O. A tiny drop of water consists of billions of these three-atom molecules. Most matter normally exists as one of three states: solid, liquid or gas. Many solids are crystals, where the atoms or molecules are joined in a regular, repeating pattern.

Everyday examples

These diagrams show the atoms or molecules in all three states of matter. The air that you breathe in is a mixture of several different gases, including the element oxygen, and the compound carbon dioxide. Tea is a liquid solution that is a complex mixture consisting mainly of water. Steel is a solid that is a mixture of the elements iron and carbon, along with small amounts of other elements.

Gases, liquids and solids

A gas spreads out or expands to fill any space it can. The gases of air fill even the tiniest corners of a room. In a gas, the particles move randomly at high speed, bumping into each other and the walls of their container – like a small number of people blindfolded, running around a playground! If a gas cools down, the particles move more slowly, and come closer together. To be like a liquid, there would be more people in the playground, and they would walk around, occasionally linking arms. In a solid, the particles only move slightly around fixed positions. So the playground would be filled with people, linking arms and rocking to and fro on the spot! Most materials can exist in more than one state, depending on temperature. For example, liquid water freezes at zero degrees Celsius, 0°C, into solid ice.

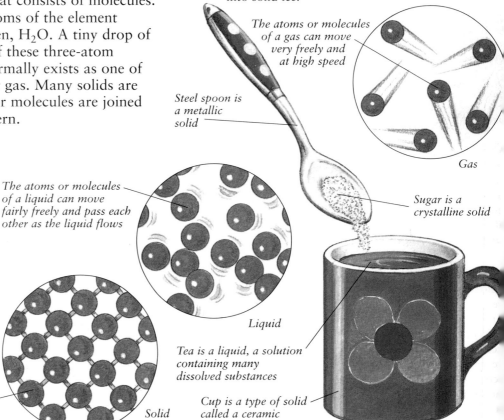

The atoms or molecules of a gas can move very freely and at high speed

Steel spoon is a metallic solid

Gas

Sugar is a crystalline solid

The atoms or molecules of a liquid can move fairly freely and pass each other as the liquid flows

Liquid

Tea is a liquid, a solution containing many dissolved substances

The atoms or molecules of a solid are fixed in position and can move very little

Solid

Cup is a type of solid called a ceramic

Elements, compounds and mixtures

Pure substances may be elements or compounds. Pure water and pure salt are examples of compounds, while pure iron and pure hydrogen are elements. Most substances familiar from daily life are mixtures. Milk, for example, is a mixture of many compounds including water and fats. Adding sugar to water forms a type of mixture called a solution. The molecules of sugar break away from each other and mix with the water to become part of the liquid. Mixtures can be separated in many ways. A mixture of salt (a compound) and iron filings (an element) could be separated by adding to water, to dissolve the salt, or by placing a magnet nearby to attract the iron. To separate mud from muddy water, you can pass the muddy water through a filter.

FACTS ABOUT MATTER

● The same elements that we find on Earth exist throughout the Universe.

● Plasma, a mixture of charged particles, is often called the fourth state of matter. On Earth, plasma is not common. Stars are made almost entirely of plasma, however.

● Pure hydrogen gas consists of molecules each made of two hydrogen atoms joined together, H_2. On average, a hydrogen molecule travels as fast as a speeding jet plane.

● Carbon has the highest melting point and boiling point of all elements. Helium has the lowest.

● Atoms are so small that it would take about ten million of them in a line to measure 1 mm.

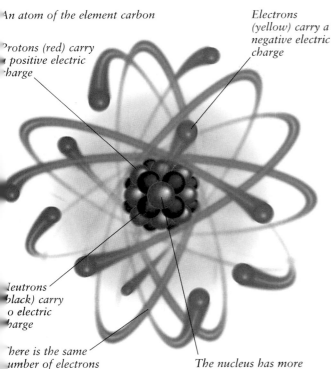

An atom of the element carbon

Protons (red) carry a positive electric charge

Electrons (yellow) carry a negative electric charge

Neutrons (black) carry no electric charge

There is the same number of electrons around the nucleus as there is of protons inside it

The nucleus has more than 99 per cent of the mass of the atom

Hydrogen atom

Oxygen atom

Molecules of water

Different molecules

The simplest molecules consist of just two or three atoms. Substances called polymers consist of molecules made of hundreds or thousands of atoms. They are formed when smaller molecules join together. Plastics, such as polythene, consist of polymer molecules.

Molecule of polythene

Carbon atom

Hydrogen atom

What's inside?

Atoms are not the smallest particles of matter. Each atom consists of even tinier particles called neutrons, protons and electrons. The neutrons and protons are together in the centre, or nucleus. Different elements have atoms with different numbers of protons in their nuclei and different numbers of electrons going around the nucleus.

Probing matter

Protons and neutrons are not the smallest particles of matter. In devices called particle accelerators, particles are made to collide at incredibly high speed. Showers of subatomic particles – those even smaller than atoms – are produced in these collisions. From the way these particles behave, physicists are discovering more about the matter that makes up not only our whole world, but the whole of the surrounding Universe.

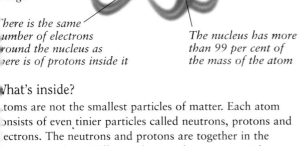

Hot liquid

We normally think of the metal iron as a solid. At temperatures above 1,535°C, iron melts to become liquid, or 'molten'. It remains liquid until the temperature falls again, or until it rises above 2,750°C, when the liquid iron becomes a gas!

A regular arrangement

In a crystal, the regular way in which the atoms or molecules join together is the reason for the uniform appearance. Most crystals have a regular shape with flat sides or facets, angled edges and sharp corners. Crystals form as a liquid cools and solidifies, or as particles from a solution join together.

Molten iron is liquid and pours easily, as in this steelworks

GROWING SUGAR CRYSTALS

Ask an adult to heat half a litre of water in a saucepan, until it is hot but not boiling. Carefully add as much sugar as will dissolve in the hot water. Ask the adult to stir the solution, and then allow it to cool. Once the solution has cooled, pour it into the glass jar. Leave the jar somewhere where it will not be disturbed for a few weeks. The sugar molecules in the solution will gradually join up, forming beautiful crystals.

CHEMICAL REACTIONS

HYDROGEN GAS IS HIGHLY FLAMMABLE, and burns rapidly with a POP or even a loud explosion when mixed with air. Yet the result of this rapid, even violent burning is – water. Atoms of hydrogen (H) combine with atoms of oxygen (O) to make millions of tiny molecules of water (H_2O). The hydrogen and the oxygen are called the reactants, and the water is the product of the reaction. When a candle burns in air, the reactants are wax and oxygen from the air, while the products are water and carbon dioxide. Chemical reactions always make new substances from old ingredients, by rearranging the atoms and molecules of the reactants. For example, substances found in oil can be made to react in just the right way to make plastics such as polythene or nylon.

Fast burner

Chemical reactions occur at different rates. An explosion is a very fast reaction. It produces gases so quickly that it causes a blast which can destroy buildings. This explosion was created by a reaction involving a material called dynamite.

Three into two

Candle wax is made from just two elements: carbon (C) and hydrogen (H). When a third element – oxygen (O) from the air – gets involved inside the flame, atoms of the three elements rearrange, forming water (H_2O) and carbon dioxide (CO_2). Heat energy released by the reaction produces light and vaporizes more wax, ready to continue the reaction.

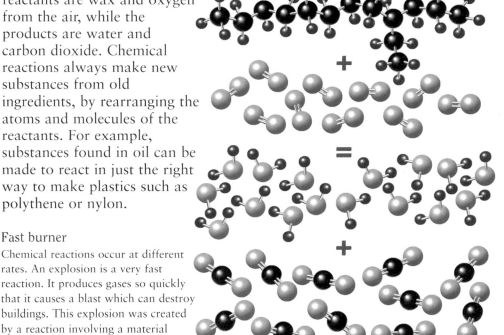

Wax is made up of huge molecules that contain the elements carbon and hydrogen

Oxygen gas is made up of molecules, each containing two atoms of the element oxygen

Water molecules are formed when some oxygen atoms join with hydrogen atoms

Carbon dioxide gas is formed when other oxygen atoms react with carbon atoms

Energy and reactions

All reactions involve a transfer of energy. In some cases, such as a burning reaction, energy is given out as heat or light. In others, the reaction needs energy to make it happen. It may take heat from its surroundings, for example. Such a reaction is found in a type of cold compress used to treat sporting injuries. Reactants inside the compress are mixed together when needed. They take heat they need to react from the injured part of the body. So the place where the compress touches the body is cooled. Another reaction that requires energy is used in photography. Silver compounds in photographic film produce pure silver to form the picture, but they need energy to do so. They get the energy from the light that falls on the film.

HENRY CAVENDISH (1731-1810)

French-born English physicist and chemist Henry Cavendish was the first person to identify hydrogen gas, which he called 'inflammable air'. Later, he worked out that water is produced when hydrogen and oxygen react together. He discovered this reaction at about the same time as it was discovered by the French chemist Antoine Lavoisier. The idea that water was made from hydrogen and oxygen contradicted the long-held belief that it was a pure element. Cavendish also devised a clever experiment to calculate the mass of the Earth. And he worked out how to calculate the forces between electric charges. Cavendish was an extremely shy man, had few friends, and worked mainly alone.

Slow reaction

When oxygen and water mix with iron, a chemical reaction occurs. The iron slowly combines with the oxygen and water forming a reddish compound called hydrated iron oxide. This is more commonly known as rust.

Seeing the light

When light falls on a compound of silver on a photographic film, a chemical reaction occurs which frees, or liberates, silver metal from the compound. The silver forms tiny dark grains on the surface of the film that make up the photograph. The individual grains can only be seen under a microscope.

Black and blue

Many chemical reactions involve acids. Most metals, for example, fizz when placed in acids, dissolving to form a solution and giving off hydrogen gas. A solution of sulphuric acid dissolves the compound iron oxide, forming a blue solution of copper sulphate. If this solution is heated and then cooled, the copper sulphate forms into beautiful crystals.

Electric reaction

All chemical reactions involve electricity, because they are caused by the exchange of the electrically charged particles called electrons, between atoms. On a larger scale, electric current can cause certain reactions to happen. This metal trophy has been coated by a layer of pure silver from the silver solution it was in, as an electric current passed through the solution. It is much less expensive than making the whole trophy from solid silver. The process is known as electroplating.

Billions of silver atoms have attached to the surface

Synthetic dyes

Chemists carry out research to invent or discover new chemical reactions that may be useful. About 150 years ago, the first synthetic or artificial dyes were produced by chemical reactions. This work has given us many more and brighter coloured dyes, than using natural dyes from plants and animal products.

FIZZY BUT SAFE

There are many simple and safe chemical reactions that you can perform at home or in school. One is the reaction between ethanoic acid, more commonly known as vinegar, and a compound called sodium hydrogen carbonate, more familiar as bicarbonate of soda ('bicarb'). A mixture of these two chemicals fizzes. Each of the bubbles of the fizz is filled with carbon dioxide gas produced by the reaction. To make the reaction look more impressive, add a few drops of green or red food colouring.

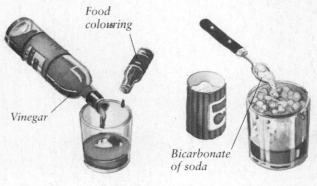

Food colouring

Vinegar

Bicarbonate of soda

MATERIALS

AMONG THE MOST USEFUL MATERIALS in the modern world are wood, concrete and steel for buildings, paper for writing and printing, and glass for windows and bottles. Most people use the word 'material' to describe substances like these, which we use to make things. To a scientist, however, a material is really any solid, liquid or gas – even the air you breathe. Some materials come from plants or animals or from underground. Examples of these natural materials are paper, leather and marble. Other materials are made by chemical reactions in factories. Metals are examples of such 'synthetic' materials. They are obtained from rocks in which they are chemically combined with other elements. Plastics are also synthetic materials, because they are made when compounds in oil undergo carefully controlled chemical processes. Scientists are always striving to find new materials for an ever-increasing variety of products.

Properties of materials

The way in which a material behaves helps us decide how to use it. Glass, for example, is transparent and this makes it suitable for windows. Textiles are soft, opaque and easy to cut to size. This makes them perfect for keeping out light as curtains or blinds. The quality, or property, of a material can be changed by mixing it with other materials. When metals are mixed together, they are called alloys. Some alloys are stronger than individual metals and may have been produced for a specific purpose. Another way in which materials are combined is in composites. An example of a composite is fibreglass, which is a combination of plastic and glass, used to make small boats.

There's so much in it

Modern consumer products are often made from a bewildering array of different materials. The people who made this games console used glass, metals, plastics and fabrics. The plastic materials have only beome available in the last hundred years, while glass and metals have been used for many centuries.

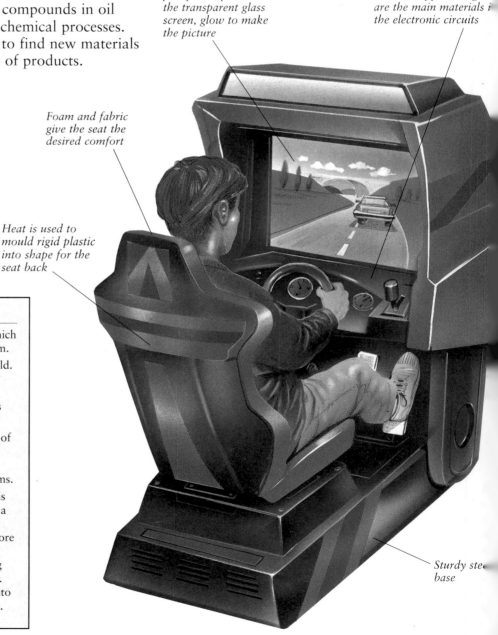

Special materials called phosphors, painted on the transparent glass screen, glow to make the picture

Silicon, copper and gold are the main materials in the electronic circuits

Foam and fabric give the seat the desired comfort

Heat is used to mould rigid plastic into shape for the seat back

Sturdy steel base

KNOW YOUR MATERIALS

● The first plastic was celluloid, which was used to make photographic film.

● The first metal to be used was gold. This is because it occurs naturally, whereas most other metals must be smelted to remove them from rocks called ores.

● Whereas water molecules consist of just three atoms each, plastics have very large molecules, each one of which consists of thousands of atoms.

● Rubber is a natural material – it is solidified latex, which is the sap of a rubber tree. Its properties can be changed to make it stronger and more elastic, by a process called vulcanization. This involves heating rubber under pressure with sulphur. The process can also turn rubber into a harder substance, called vulcanite.

What's it made of?

It may surprise you to know that glass is made of sand. In a glassworks, sand is mixed with other substances, and heated until it melts. As it cools, it becomes thicker, and can be moulded or blown (right) into shape before it hardens to form glass. Metal-containing compounds may be added to make coloured glass.

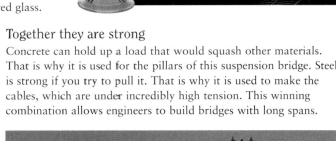

The ingredients of glass, from the top, are calcium carbonate, sand and sodium carbonate

Together they are strong

Concrete can hold up a load that would squash other materials. That is why it is used for the pillars of this suspension bridge. Steel is strong if you try to pull it. That is why it is used to make the cables, which are under incredibly high tension. This winning combination allows engineers to build bridges with long spans.

lloy there!

mixture of two metals, or a metal and another material, is called
n alloy. Steel, for example, is an alloy of iron, carbon and a
ariety of other elements. The body, or fuselage, of jet airliners is
ormally made from alloys of aluminium. These alloys are ideal
ecause they are light yet strong.

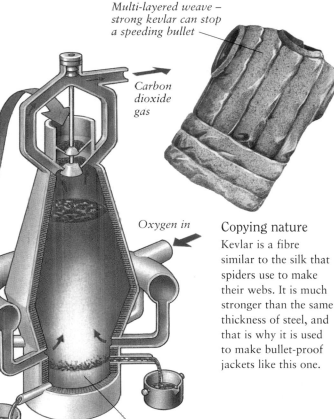

gain and again

e use millions of tonnes of materials to make things every day.
hen their useful life is over, some of these things are buried in
landfill sites, where they slowly decay. Others can be recycled – the materials from which they are made are processed again and made into new things. Empty drinks cans are separated into those made of steel and those made of aluminium, before being melted down.

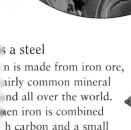

Multi-layered weave – strong kevlar can stop a speeding bullet

Carbon dioxide gas

Oxygen in

Copying nature

Kevlar is a fibre similar to the silk that spiders use to make their webs. It is much stronger than the same thickness of steel, and that is why it is used to make bullet-proof jackets like this one.

s a steel

n is made from iron ore,
airly common mineral
nd all over the world.
en iron is combined
h carbon and a small
ount of other chemical
ments, it makes steel,
ich is more durable
n pure iron.

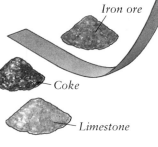

Iron ore

Coke

Limestone

A blast furnace

Molten steel and waste products are tapped off

ENERGY

SCIENTISTS DEFINE ENERGY as 'the ability to do work', in other words, to make things happen. The Sun supplies most of the Earth's energy, as electromagnetic radiation that includes light rays and infra-red or heat rays. Some of the light energy is absorbed by plants, and stored in their leaves and stems as energy-rich chemicals such as sugars. When we eat plants, some of the energy is released inside our bodies, to help us grow and stay alive.

Energy is never created. It merely changes from one form to another. For example, the moving, or kinetic, energy of the wind turns a wind turbo-generator, which converts it into electrical energy. This energy can make light in light bulbs, heat in a toaster, or movement in an electric motor.

Electricity can also be made from plants and animals that died millions of years ago. As they rotted, they formed fossil fuels – coal, oil and natural gas. The energy of those plants and animals is still contained in the fossil fuel, which is burned in power stations. It forms heat that is used to generate electricity.

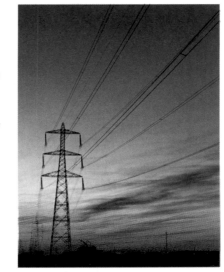

Power to the people

Most of the electricity that we use is made, or 'generated', in power stations. The electrical energy is distributed to where it is needed by long, thick metal cables. These are usually high above the ground, for safety, and supported on towers called pylons. The network of cables criss-crossing the landscape is known as the electricity distribution grid.

Energy transfer

Energy from the Sun is absorbed by plants by a process called photosynthesis. When a cow eats grass, it takes in this chemical energy. The cow uses some to grow and stay alive, and stores some in its body. When a person eats the cow's meat or drinks its milk, he or she takes in some of the energy from the cow. And some of this energy is converted again when a person runs, into kinetic energy. To stop, the person uses friction between the running shoe and the ground, producing heat energy.

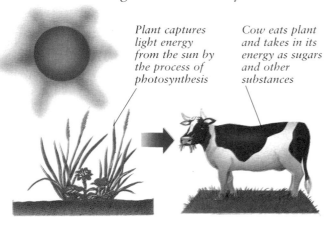

Plant captures light energy from the sun by the process of photosynthesis

Cow eats plant and takes in its energy as sugars and other substances

Person eats burger and takes in cow's meat with its stored energy

Energy in food is changed by muscles into energy of movement

Energy needs

Most of our energy needs are supplied by burning fossil fuels. These fuels can be burnt and used only once. Scientists have shown that supplies of fossil fuels are being used up extremely fast. The race is on to harness safe and cheap 'alternative' energy sources, such as solar, wind or water power. These alternatives are 'renewable'. For example, the kinetic energy of the wind is produced by the Sun heating different parts of the Earth's surface and so causing the air to move. More of this energy is released every day by the Sun, so wind power will never run out. Another alternative is nuclear power, produced in nuclear power stations by a reaction called fission. This is the controlled splitting of the atomic nuclei of 'heavy' elements such as uranium, and it releases huge amounts of heat energy. This can be used to generate electricity. However, there are hazards involved in fission, including the release of harmful radioactivity.

Wind turbines swivel on their towers, always to face into the wind

Wind power

Wind energy has been used for centuries, in windmills that use the energy to grind corn. Today, we use wind turbines to turn generators that supply electricity. They rely on strong winds, which only blow steadily in certain places. Wind power stations known as wind farms, with lots of wind turbines (or aerogenerators), are usually built in high, remote sites. Unlike fossil fuel power stations, they do not produce any air pollution. But they alter the look of the landscape, which has been called 'visual pollution'. They may also make loud humming or whooshing noises.

Hot or cold

When things feel cold to the touch, it is because they are at a temperature which is lower than that of your skin. This is normally 37°C, the average temperature of the human body. But it varies slightly around the body, as shown by this thermograph or computer-coloured heat-photograph. Warmer parts of the body are shown in redder colours, and cooler parts such as the scalp and ears in blues and greens. Temperature is a measure of the internal energy of an object's atoms and molecules – how much and how fast they move. In a hot solid object, the atoms and molecules vibrate more and faster than when the object is cool. Heat energy transfers from hot things to cold things in three different ways. These are called conduction, convection and radiation.

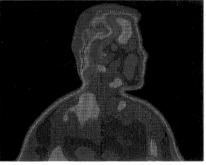

Future energy?

Inside this experimental fusion reactor, the nuclei from the centres of hydrogen atoms join, or 'fuse', to form the nuclei of helium atoms. (This is the same process that happens inside the Sun.) Nuclear fusion releases huge amounts of energy, and produces virtually no waste, pollution or radioactivity. But at present, the process requires more energy input than it produces.

Up and down

When you climb up to a high ridge, you need energy, to work hard as you ascend against the pull of gravity. The energy is not lost: it can be retrieved by jumping off the ridge! The energy which comes from a certain position, being higher than you were, is known as potential energy. It becomes kinetic or moving energy, as you jump and speed downwards. This energy is then stored in the bungee rope as it stretches, in the form of potential energy. It is retrieved again when the rope pulls and bounces you back up!

Potential energy is stored in the stretchy rope

The larger the blades, the more energy captured

Generator inside the turbine produces electricity as the blades spin

Wires in towers link turbines to wind farm control room

Control room

FORCES AND MOTION

A FORCE IS A PUSH OR A PULL. We can observe how forces can change motion by considering everyday objects such as shopping trolleys. A trolley moving through outer space will not speed up, slow down or change direction, because no force acts on it. Back on Earth, a trolley outside a supermarket will not move unless someone pushes or pulls it. A full trolley is much harder to start and stop, and to steer, than an empty one. English scientist Isaac Newton observed these same effects, as detailed below. He described them as the Laws of Motion (even though he never used a shopping trolley!) The two most important forces in everyday life are gravity and friction. Gravity gives trolleys weight, and makes them roll downhill. Friction is produced when two surfaces in contact slide or rub. It is friction inside the trolley's wheels that makes it eventually slow down and stop.

Newton's Laws

Isaac Newton published his Laws of Motion in 1687. The First Law explains how an object's motion does not change unless there is a force acting on it. The Second Law considers how the motion of a heavier object requires more force to change it than the motion of a lighter one. The Third Law states that forces come in pairs. So when a force is applied on an object, the object produces an equal force in the opposite direction. This means that the Earth's force of gravity pulls on you – and your own gravity pulls back on the Earth, with an equal but opposite force.

ISAAC NEWTON (1642-1727)

English mathematician and physicist Isaac Newton is one of the best-known scientists of all time. He described his Laws of Motion in 1687, in Latin, in his book 'Philosophiae naturalis principia mathematica' (The Mathematical Principles of Natural Philosophy). As well as working out these laws, Newton designed an important type of telescope. He was the first person to realize that white light is made of light rays which are all the colours of the rainbow. He suggested that gravity was a universal force, possessed by all forms of matter, from atoms to planets. Newton's ideas about gravity may have been inspired in about 1666 by an apple falling from a tree in his garden at Woolsthorpe Manor, Lincolnshire.

Pressure

A person makes more of a dent in a soft floor wearing narrow heels than wide ones. The same force – the person's weight – pushes down on the floor in each case. But it is more 'concentrated' with narrow heels, because these make contact over a smaller area compared to wide heels. A scientist would say that the narrow heel exerts more pressure than the flat heel. Pressure is a measure of how much force is exerted on a certain area, usually measured in square metres or square centimetres. Not only solids exert pressure – liquids and gases do, too. The pressure of air inside an inflated balloon pushes outwards in every direction. If it did not, the balloon would deflate as the air was squashed by the force produced by the stretched rubber.

What is weight?
What we call 'weight', and we measure in grams o kilograms, is actually a force. It i due to the pull of gravity. Being a force, it should be measured in the units called newton

The weightlifter pushes upwards on the bar, w a force equal to gravity pulling down on the b

The floor pushes upwards on the weightlifter and weights, with a fo equal to gravity pulling them both downwards

Mr Universe

Gravity is a force of attraction (pulling things together) that acts everywhere in the Universe. It holds stars and galaxies together. allows the Moon and artificial satellites to orbit the Earth. It als keeps us from falling off the Earth and flying away into space. This weightlifter has to work hard against the pull of gravity to and hold up the weights on the bar.

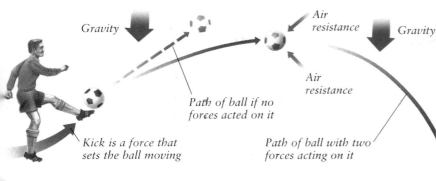

Gravity

Air resistance

Gravity

Path of ball if no forces acted on it

Air resistance

Gravity and air resistance make ball curve and fall back to the ground

Kick is a force that sets the ball moving

Path of ball with two forces acting on it

Something in the air

Kicking a football shows Newton's Laws of Motion in action. The kick is a force that gives kinetic or moving energy to the ball. This overcomes its inertia, or tendency to resist movement. The ball sets off through the air. It would carry on for ever in a straight line, but two forces act on it. One is gravity pulling down. This slows the ball's ascent, makes it change direction, and accelerates it downwards. The horizontal motion of the ball is unaffected by gravity, which can only pull downwards. But another force acts, which is air resistance. This is caused as the ball pushes its way through air, knocking into the molecules. Air resistance makes the ball slow down. So the path of the ball through the air is a curve.

Pull of air

Inside these balloons are countless millions of gas molecules, which make up air. They are dashing around at high speed. When these molecules hit the inside surface of the balloon, they produce pressure. This pressure keeps the balloon inflated. The rubber of the balloon itself pushes back with an equal but opposite pressure.

Air compressed or squeezed inside balloon

No force

There is no overall force on this parachutist. Gravity pulls him downwards. But air resistance, caused by the parachute pushing past air molecules, acts in the direction opposite to motion. This upwards force of air resistance, also called drag, exactly balances the downwards force of gravity. So the parachutist carries on falling at the same speed. A bigger parachute would produce greater air resistance, and so the speed of the fall would be slower.

Weight a minute

The gravity of the Earth pulls this apple closer to the Earth's centre. The gravity of the apple pulls back on the Earth with an equal but opposite force. We can see and feel the resulting balance of forces as the weight of the apple. The more mass an apple has – that is, the more atoms or matter it contains – the greater its weight.

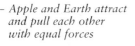

Apple and Earth attract and pull each other with equal forces

FLOATERS AND SINKERS

The pressure of water around an object, such as a ball, produces an upwards force called upthrust (green arrow). The weight of the object is a downwards force (yellow arrow). Heavier objects have a greater downwards force. If this downwards force is less than the upthrust, the object floats.

MACHINES

WHAT WE THINK OF as machines – bicycles and washing machines, for example – normally consist of many simpler machines working together. Scientists use the term 'simple machines' to refer to levers, pulleys, wheels, screws, gears and inclined planes (slopes). Simple machines make our work easier, usually by 'magnifying' forces. For instance, a seesaw is a lever. If a person sits near the pivot of the seesaw, you can lift them up by pushing down on the opposite end. (A lever's pivot is its fulcrum.) It is harder to lift the person by pushing down nearer the middle. It is even harder lifting the person straight up, without using a seesaw at all! Even a simple slope (inclined plane), such as a ramp for a wheelbarrow, is considered to be a machine. You can raise the load in the wheelbarrow by one metre, by simply pushing it up a long gentle slope. To lift the barrow and load directly, by a height of one metre, would need a greater force. A corkscrew is another example of a device that uses simple machines. The screw thread twists into the cork as you turn it, while levers and gears make it easy to pull the cork out of the bottle.

Force and distance

You can reach the top of a hill by walking straight up its steep slope, or by walking up a less steep path that winds to and fro. The gentle slope is easier – but you have to walk farther. This link between force and distance is found in all simple machines. For example, a crane uses a combination of cables and pulleys called a block and tackle. The crane's engine can lift a very heavy weight by pulling on the cable with a relatively small force. However, the cable must move farther than the heavy object itself, because it passes up and down over several pulleys. The result is that the same amount of work is done in both cases. Lifting with block and tackle is easier than lifting without, but takes longer. The same applied to levers, such as using a screwdriver to prise open a paint tin (see right). You move the screwdriver handle easily over a longer distance. The tip pushes the lid over a shorter distance, but with greater force.

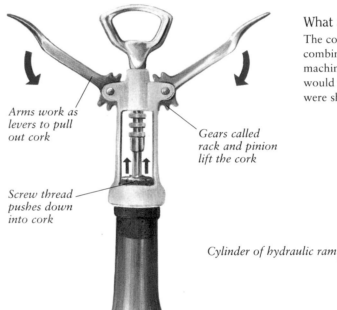

Arms work as levers to pull out cork

Gears called rack and pinion lift the cork

Screw thread pushes down into cork

What a combination
The corkscrew is a clever combination of several simple machines. Imagine how it would work if its arms (levers) were shorter.

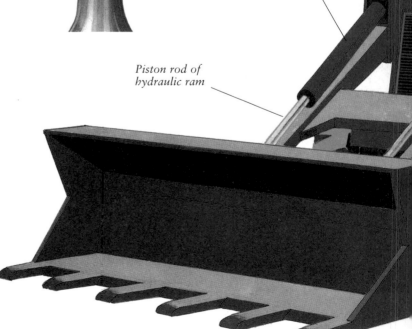

Cylinder of hydraulic ram

Piston rod of hydraulic ram

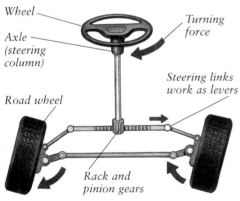

Wheel

Axle (steering column)

Turning force

Road wheel

Steering links work as levers

Rack and pinion gears

You-turn
Some large vehicles, such as trucks and buses, have large steering wheels. They are easier to turn than a small steering wheel. But you have to spin them around a long way, perhaps several times, to turn the road wheels only a small distance. Steering wheels are examples of a type of simple machine called the wheel and axle.

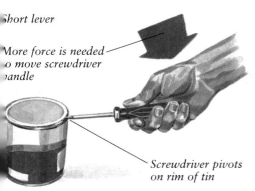

Short lever

More force is needed to move screwdriver handle

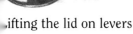

Long lever

Less force is needed to move screwdriver handle

Screwdriver pivots on rim of tin

Screwdriver handle must move over greater distance

Lifting the lid on levers

Some paint tins are really tough to open. Using a screwdriver as a lever makes it much easier. The longer the screwdriver, the less force you need to apply to the handle – but the farther you have to push it.

A complicated machine

The main arms of the digger each consist of three levers, linked at pivots. Each lever is pushed by devices called hydraulic rams, which are worked by fluid under high pressure. The digger's steering wheel is another simple machine, the wheel and axle, as shown on the right.

Slow down

Machines can make movements slower and more controlled. Inside this watch, shown with its back plate removed, an uncoiling spring turns the gears that turn the hands. Without gears, the hands would speed around the face, and the clock would not keep good time.

Screw thread

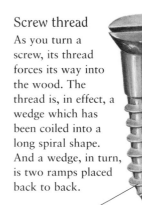

As you turn a screw, its thread forces its way into the wood. The thread is, in effect, a wedge which has been coiled into a long spiral shape. And a wedge, in turn, is two ramps placed back to back.

Screw thread

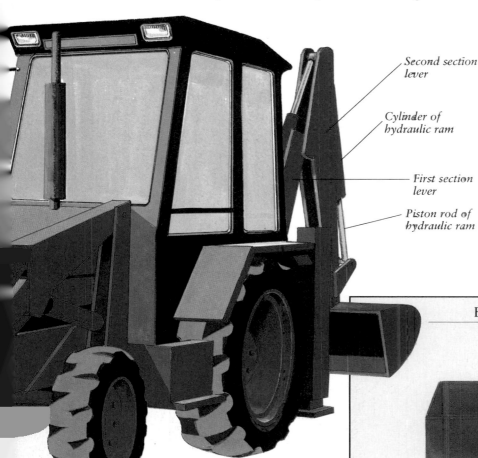

Second section lever

Cylinder of hydraulic ram

First section lever

Piston rod of hydraulic ram

EXPERIMENTING WITH LEVERS

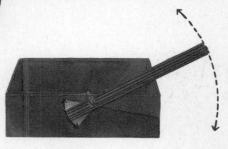

Cut a strip of corrugated cardboard from a box lid. Make it about 2 cm wide, and about 20 cm long. Push a paper fastener through it, about 3 cm from one end, and through one of the sides of the box. Now, hold the short end of the lever, and move it up and down. See how the other end of the strip moves farther. Next, move the longer end. Feel how it is easier to push – but the shorter end moves less.

ELECTRICITY AND MAGNETISM

WHEN YOU SWITCH ON A TORCH, billions of tiny particles called electrons move from the negative terminal of the torch's battery, through the metal wires and the bulb, and back to the positive terminal of the battery – a complete circuit. This is an electric current since each electron, which is part of an atom, carries a negative electric charge, and movement of electric charges makes up a current. We use these moving electrons to do many useful things, including lighting and heating our homes, and powering televisions, music systems, computers and hundreds of other electrical appliances that modern life depends on.
Static electricity, on the other hand, is caused by electric charges remaining in a fixed position. When you rub a balloon in your hair, electrons transfer from hair to balloon, and stay there. This leaves the hair positively charged, and the balloon negatively charged. The hair clings to the balloon because positive and negative charges attract each other. Two objects with the same charge – two rubbed balloons, for example – repel each other (push apart). Magnets also attract and repel each other, like electric charges. In fact, electricity and magnetism are very closely linked.

Magnets

All magnets have two ends, or poles. One end is called the north-seeking pole, or simply the north pole, and the other is called the south-seeking or south pole. A magnet's north pole always points north if a magnet is free to turn. When two north poles or two south poles are close together, they push apart. When a north pole and a south pole are brought close, they attract each other. A steel paper clip brought close to the north pole of a magnet becomes a magnet, with its south pole nearest to the magnet. This is how paper clips, and other objects made of iron or steel, cling to magnets.

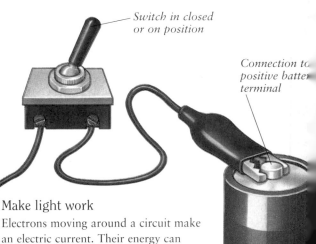

Switch in closed or on position

Connection to positive battery terminal

Filament (thin coiled wire) inside bulb gets hot and glows as electricity passes through it

Connecting wires

Plastic insulating cover stops electricity leaking from wire

Make light work

Electrons moving around a circuit make an electric current. Their energy can make things happen. For example, when electrons flow through the filament of a bulb, they heat it up and cause it to glow. A switch can turn electric current on and off. If it is opened or off, the circuit is broken, and the electric current can no longer flow.

Connection to negative battery terminal

Electric charges

Electric charges are carried by electrons, which are particles found in every atom. All atoms have a central nucleus, which carries positive electric charge, surrounded by the negatively-charged electrons. Within any one atom, there is normally the same amount of positive and negative charges, so the atom has no overall charge. It is said to be neutral. If electrons are lost or gained, then the balance of charge is upset, and the atom becomes charged. Inside a torch battery, electrons are separated from their atoms by chemical reactions. The electrons emerge at the negative terminal of the battery and move around a circuit. They are pushed by the negative charges of other electrons there, and pulled around the circuit by positive charge at the other terminal.

Back and forth

The electric current that is supplied to our homes, to power appliances such as hair-driers, is called alternating current, AC. This is because the electrons inside the cables move back and forth many times every second. The current supplied by a battery is direct current, DC, because the electrons move in only one direction (from the negative to the positive terminal).

Lines of force

You can imagine the invisible magnetism or magnetic field around a magnet, as lines of magnetic force. The closer the lines, the stronger the magnetism. The lines are closest, and so the magnetism is strongest, at the two poles of the magnet.

Electricity cables to electromagnet

Electromagnets

When an electric current flows through a wire, it produces a magnetic field around the wire. The magnetic field can be made stronger by winding the wire into a coil, the solenoid, and putting an iron bar in it. This is an electromagnet.

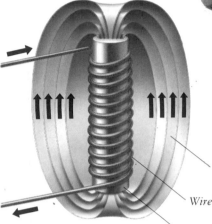

On and off

Ordinary or permanent magnets exert their magnetism all the time. An electromagnet only does so while electricity flows, so it can be switched on and off. Electromagnets have hundreds of uses, from automatic door locks to cranes in car scrap yards.

Lines of magnetic force

Wire wound into coil

Soft iron core

What a line-up

There is a good reason why a compass needle lines up north-south. Electric currents deep in the Earth's core make the Earth into a huge electromagnet. The compass needle is attracted to the poles of the Earth-magnet, which are found near the Earth's geographical North and South Poles.

Hair-raising

Static electricity can be produced by rubbing or friction. If a person becomes charged with static, each strand of hair has the same charge on its surface as all the other strands. Like charges repel, and so all the strands of hair repel each other and the main body. This makes the strands of hair stand up and 'flyaway'. Gradually the charge leaks away into the air. This happens faster if the air is damp. Walking on a nylon carpet can also charge the body. When you touch a metal door handle, the charge leaps to it, with a small spark and shock.

EXPERIMENT: MAGNETIC FORCES

Find any two magnets, and investigate the forces between them. You can find out which end of each magnet is the north pole by hanging the magnet from a cotton thread. Use a compass to find out which way is north, and mark the north pole of each magnet in the same way. Then see what happens when you bring different combinations of poles together. What happens, for example, when you put a north pole next to another north pole? Or two south poles together? Does the pushing (repulsion) or pulling (attraction) force become stronger as the magnets move nearer each other?

LIGHT AND COLOUR

INSIDE A TOASTER there is a wire called an element. When electric current passes through it, the element starts to glow with an orange light. If the toaster's element became hotter still, it would glow first yellow, then white like the filament of a light bulb. Light that is produced by hot objects is called incandescent light, and includes light created at the surface of the Sun. Sunlight is a jumbled mixture of many different colours of light, and you can see these colours in a rainbow. Light travels very fast, in straight lines, through many materials, including air, glass and water. It bends or refracts as it passes from one material to another. This is useful in making lenses, which bend light in just the right way to produce spectacles, telescopes and microscopes. When light cannot pass through a material, it may be absorbed, or it may be reflected or bounce back. Coloured surfaces absorb some colours while reflecting others. A red jumper, for example, reflects only red light.

Reflection and refraction

Reflection is light bouncing off an object. Refraction is light bending as it passes from one material to another. Both are very useful. For example, if light did not reflect from objects that do not produce their own light, we would only be able to see light sources. To see a book in a dark room, for example, we must position a lamp so that light falls onto the book and reflects off it into our eyes. Mirrors and other shiny surfaces reflect light uniformly, and this means that you can see images in them, such as your face, for example. You can observe refraction if you look at an object under water. Light from the object bends as it passes from the water to the air. We make use of refraction by shaping glass into lenses that can produce images by focusing light.

Lens system of multiple lenses

Diaphragm controls amount of light entering camera

Path of light rays

Screw mechanism for focusing

View through viewfinder

Photographic film

What a picture

At the back of a camera there is a flat piece of photographic film. Light passes through the lens at the front, and reaches the film so that light from any one point of the scene in front of the camera falls on the same point on the film inside it. This is called focusing. The film records the pattern of light making up the image, by undergoing chemical changes where light hits it. (In a digital camera, the photographic film is replaced by light-sensitive electronic panel called a CCD, or charge coupled device.)

FACTS ABOUT LIGHT

● It takes only a hundred-millionth of a second for light to travel 1 m.

● The spectrum does not consist of seven distinct colours, as many people believe. It is a band of colours that varies gradually from red through to purple.

● There are three different types of colour-sensitive cell in the eye. People who are colour-blind have one type of cell that does not work properly.

● The surface of the Sun is at a temperature of about 6,000°C. At this temperature, it gives off white light. As sunlight passes through Earth's atmosphere, air molecules bounce some of the blue light in all directions, which is why the sky is blue.

● Lenses that bulge out in the middle are said to be convex. Magnifying glasses are convex lenses.

A colourful spread

The colours of the rainbow are all present in white light. They separate as they pass through a triangular piece of glass or plastic, called a prism, because they all bend by different amounts. This spread of colour is called the light spectrum. Millions of raindrops in the sky do the same job, which is why you only see rainbows when the Sun shines on a rainy day. The colours are known by tradition as red, orange, yellow, green, blue, indigo and violet.

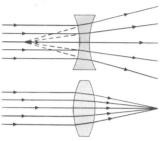
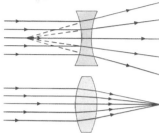

Prism

White light enters prism

Colours of light spectrum

Upside down

When you look through a lens, objects beyond the lens may look larger (magnified) or smaller (diminished) and upside down. This is because the lens refracts or bends the light rays passing through it.

Concave lens diminishes image

Convex lens magnifies image

Watching television

Our eyes contain three types of colour-sensitive cell: red, green and blue. The tiny dots or phosphors on the inside surface of a television screen come in the same three varieties: red, green and blue. By mixing light from these phosphors in different combinations, it is possible to fool the eye into seeing any colour.

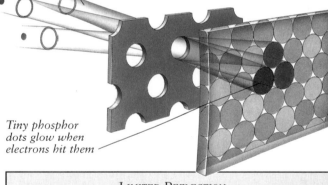

Electrons from red, green and blue guns

Tiny phosphor dots glow when electrons hit them

On reflection ...

Light that falls on your face reflects off it in all directions. If some of the light hits a nearby mirror, it will reflect uniformly. Some of that reflected light then enters your eyes, and you see an image of your own face. Flat or plane mirrors give undistorted images. The mirror in this picture is curved, and so it produces a wobbly or distorted image.

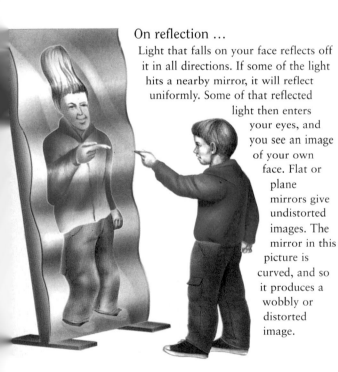

Glow in the dark

Incandescence is not the only way of producing light. There are dyes on the inside surface of a television screen called phosphors, which give out light without being hot. They glow by a process called luminescence. Other luminescent sources of light include glow-in-the-dark signs and some types of fluorescent lamps. The light is produced by electrons inside the atoms that make up a luminescent material. Electrons that gain energy, by absorbing light or electrical energy (but not heat), for example, give out light as they lose that energy. In a glow-in-the-dark sign, electrons gain energy from light that falls on them during the day. During the night, the billions of electrons give out their extra energy as an eerie green glow of light.

LIMITED REFLECTION

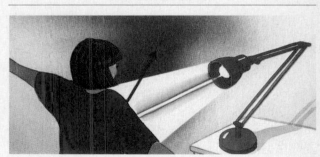

Hold a brightly coloured object, such as a red jumper, near a white wall in a dark room. Shine a torch or lamp onto the object, and look at the wall. You should see a patch of light illuminating the wall. What colour is the light on the wall? With a red jumper, it should be red. Only certain colours of light reflect off coloured objects. White objects (such as the wall) reflect all colours. This is why you can see the patch of light reflected from a coloured object, whatever its colour. With a matt black object, you should get no reflection, because black objects do not reflect any light.

SOUND

IF YOU TOUCH THE SIDES of your neck as you speak, you will feel small movements or vibrations. Inside your throat, there are two flaps of skin called vocal cords. These move to and fro (vibrate) thousands of times every second when you speak. Plucked guitar strings produce sounds when they vibrate, too. In fact, all sound is caused by vibrations. A vibrating object disturbs the air around it, sending waves of sound out in all directions, like ripples on a pond. The vibrations pass through the air, and those that enter our ears, we hear as sound. The vibrations of sound also pass through liquids such as water (you can hear under water) and through solids (you can hear sound through walls). How loud or quiet a sound is depends on how far away you are from the source of the sound, and how much the sound source moves to and fro as it vibrates. Sound may also be high- or low-pitched. A rapidly vibrating object produces a higher-pitched sound than an object vibrating more slowly.

Vibrations

Vibrations of sound can be recorded using microphones, which make copies of the vibrations as varying electric currents. When the sound waves reach a microphone, they cause a tiny magnet to move to and fro within a coil of wire, inside the microphone. The electrical signals are produced inside this coil (see opposite). The signals from a microphone can be made larger by an electronic device called an amplifier. The output of an amplifier is a bigger, more powerful version of the varying electric currents. These make a cone inside a loudspeaker vibrate in exactly the same way as the original source of sound – but much louder. The output from the microphone can also be recorded as tiny patterns of magnetic patches on magnetic tape. There are many other ways of recording sounds, such as on optical discs (CDs). But each one involves making a copy of the original electrical signals, like those from a microphone.

Sound waves

Vibrating objects, like drums, disturb the air in a similar way to a finger moving to and fro at the surface of a still pond. Sound waves travel out in all directions. The bigger the vibrations, the taller the waves, which means louder sounds. The height of a wave is called its amplitude. The faster the vibrations, the higher the sounds in pitch. The speed of vibration is called the frequency. Gradually the energy of sound waves fades, which is why things sound louder when you are closer to them.

Cymbal vibrates fast and produces high-pitched (high frequency) sound

Drum vibrates slowly and produces low-pitched (low frequency) sound

Bass drum vibrates very slowly and produces very low-pitched (low frequency) sound

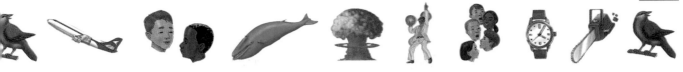

Sounds good

The scientific study of sound is known as acoustics. Experts called acoustic engineers help to design and build recording studios, theatres and other sound and music venues. They predict how sound waves will travel through the space, and how they will be absorbed or reflected by the walls, ceiling, floor – and people. They advise on materials to direct sound clearly to the audience.

Turn it down

The loudness or intensity of sound is measured in units called decibels (dB). You can just about hear a sound with a loudness of 10 dB, such as rustling leaves. Sounds of 85–90 dB can affect hearing, especially if they continue for a long time. In many places there are limits on the loudness of sound and noise. A sound of 130 dB, such as a jet plane very close by, is painful and has a very high risk of permanently damaging the ears.

Diaphragm

Magnet

Coil of wire

Amplifier

Small loudspeaker (tweeter) for high-pitched sounds

Large loudspeaker (woofer) for low-pitched sounds

...otective ...nd cover

Handle

...ood vibrations

...side most microphones is a ...n piece of flexible material ...led a diaphragm, which ...rates to and fro as sound ...ves hit it, a bit like a cork ...bbing up and down with the ...ples in a pond. The ...phragm is fixed to a coil of ...re which is near a magnet. ...e movements of the coil in ...e magnetic field produce ...ctric currents in the wire.

Coil of wire   *Magnet*   *Diaphragm or cone*

Under control

The cone or diaphragm of a loudspeaker works in the opposite way to a microphone. It produces sound as it is made to vibrate by powerful electrical signals from the amplifier.

RUBBER BAND GUITAR

Tape two pencils across an upturned shoe box, one near each end. Stretch a thin rubber band over the pencils and pluck the rubber band. The rubber band vibrates and disturbs the air around it. The vibrations are also passed on to the box, and this makes the sound louder than it would be without the box. Now press a finger about halfway along the rubber band. Now, the rubber band vibrates more times every second when you pluck it, and the note is higher.

ELECTRONICS

COMPUTERS, HI-FIS, TELEPHONES, and even some washing machines and toasters use electronics – the careful control of often tiny electric currents. Inside a computer, these tiny electric currents represent numbers, letters and commands. They move around complicated electronic circuits which consist of components – small devices that affect the currents in different ways in various parts of a circuit. A component called a resistor is used to reduce the current flowing through its part of a circuit. A capacitor stores electric charge as current flows through it, ready for release at the correct time. A diode allows electric current to pass through in one direction only. Combining the various functions of these many different components, in complicated circuits, allows us to have a host of electronic devices for everyday use. Hundreds or thousands of components can now be made out of a single sliver or wafer of the material called silicon. The components are microscopic in size and are made ready-connected to each other, or integrated. Most modern electronic equipment includes these integrated circuits, also known as microchips or silicon chips.

Making the connection

Inside all modern electronic devices are circuit boards like the one on the right. These boards hold electronic components, which are connected together by metal tracks to form a complicated electric circuit. Most electronic devices contain integrated circuits.

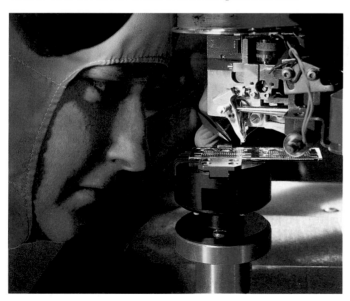

Making a circuit

The manufacture of integrated circuits is a sophisticated process, involving many stages of treatment to a slice of pure silicon crystal. During the process, the silicon is subjected to heat and attack by acid and ultraviolet light.

Semiconductors

Most metals allow electric currents to pass through them easily. They are said to be good conductors of electricity. Plastics, wood, glass and many other materials do not conduct electricity very well at all. They are insulators. Some materials are in between – they conduct electricity fairly well, or only in some circumstances. This makes them very useful in electronic devices. For example, some semiconductors carry electricity if light falls on them, so they are used in light-sensitive equipment such as video cameras.

Diodes are made from two different types of semiconductor, as a combination that conducts current in only one direction. Transistors are also made of semiconductors (see opposite). They can be used to make an electric current larger. This is amplification, and is important in sound recording and playback. Transistors are also used as switches, to turn currents on and off. This is put to use in calculators and computers, which process numbers as electric currents that are either 'on' or 'off'.

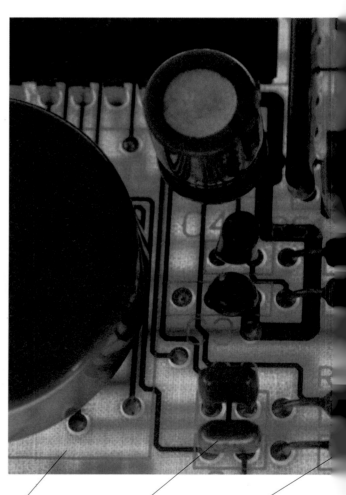

Circuit board is made from an insulating material such as plastic, ceramic or fibre-board

Capacitor stores electrical energy as electric charge, until it reaches a certain level or for a specific time, then releases it

Resistors resist the flow of electric current and reduce the amount passing through that part the circuit

Just testing

A circuit may need to be tested, to make sure it is working properly. The probes of this multimeter touch different points in the circuit, and the meter displays how much current flows through that part of the circuit.

Low prices!

Since it has been possible to manufacture integrated circuits cheaply, the range and availability of electronic goods has increased dramatically. There are few houses in developed countries without a television and a telephone, for example.

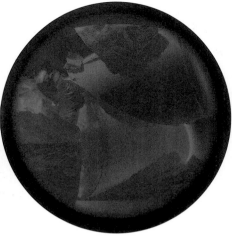

The chips are down

The best-known semiconductor is silicon, shown above as wafers of silicon crystal. It is the basis of many electronic components, including tiny integrated circuits. This is why integrated circuits are sometimes called silicon chips.

Variable electronic components

The metal 'legs' of each component carry electric current to and from metal tracks or pins on the circuit board. A variable resistor, like an ordinary fixed resistor, controls the current flow through a circuit. But a variable resistor can be adjusted for higher or lower resistance. Volume knobs and similar controls on music systems are normally variable resistors. Turning the volume control up allows more current to flow to the loudspeakers, making the loudspeakers produce a louder sound. Variable capacitors are also adjustable and are often used for the tuning controls on radios. Transistors, like diodes and integrated circuits, are made of semiconductor materials such as silicon. They have three connections or wires. The current flowing into one controls the amount of current flowing between the other two. Transistors can work as switches, amplifiers, oscillators (to reverse the direction of electricity rapidly) and photocells to control current in response to light levels.

LED

As its name suggests, a light-emitting diode (LED) is a type of diode that gives out light. The light is of a very precise colour which is determined by the materials from which the diode is made. LEDs are normally encased in a plastic of the same colour, to protect them from damage. They are not usually as bright as light bulbs, but they use much less electricity. They are also extremely reliable, rarely burning out.

Metal tracks 'printed' on the circuit board (PCB) act as wires to carry electricity to certain components

Resistors are colour-coded, the order and colour of the bands indicating their resistance in units called ohms

Solder connections link the circuit board via wires to other components such as the electricity supply

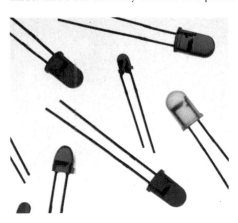

COMPUTERS

WHEN YOU TYPE WORDS using the keyboard of a personal computer, (PC), pulses of electricity pass along wires into the main computer unit. Inside this is the central processing unit (CPU), which processes data (pieces of information) put into it. The data are in the form of 'on' (1) and 'off' (0) electrical pulses that represent letters, numbers and simple instructions. For example, the code for the letter w is 01110111. The 1s and 0s are called bits, short for binary digits. A group of eight bits is a byte. One kilobyte (kB) is about one thousand bytes, one megabyte (MB) is about one million bytes, and one gigabyte (GB) is 1,000 million. As well as signals from the keyboard, mouse, scanner, camera or other input device, the CPU receives data or information from the computer's memory. There are two main types of memory inside the computer, RAM and ROM (see right). In addition, data and programs are stored on disks, including the main or hard disk. Text, numbers, pictures and sounds can all be 'digitized', represented by bits. A high-quality sound that lasts one second, for example, can be represented by about 700,000 bits (90 kB). The results of processes inside the CPU are sent to output devices such as the screen, printer or loudspeaker.

How computers remember

There are many different devices for storing computer data. Some are integrated circuits (microchips) which have arrays of millions of electronic components called capacitors. Each capacitor can hold either a tiny electric charge (bit 1) or no charge (bit 0). RAM, random access memory, is this type. It holds a temporary store of sets of instructions called programs, along with the results of calculations carried out by the CPU. ROM, read-only memory, is similar, but its data cannot be changed or overwritten. ROM holds the basic system programs that the computer needs to start, or boot up. A CD-ROM is very different. It is a compact disk (CD) that holds huge amounts of data. This may be programs, text, pictures, animations and sounds, as for an encyclopedia. A similar disk, DVD or digital versatile disk, holds even more than a CD-ROM.

What's inside?

The main unit of a PC contains various microchips, including the CPU, and several RAM and ROM chips. All the parts within the unit are attached to the main circuit board or motherboard and connected by metal tracks called buses or ribbon connectors.

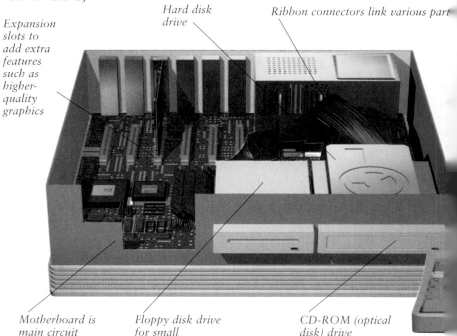

Expansion slots to add extra features such as higher-quality graphics

Hard disk drive

Ribbon connectors link various parts

Motherboard is main circuit board

Floppy disk drive for small magnetic disk

CD-ROM (optical disk) drive

Magnetic personality

A computer's hard disk is actually several disks revolving together. Each is coated with a magnetic substance. A read–write head produces a magnetic field that creates tiny patches of magnetism on the disk surface, to store bits 0 and 1.

Mouse

Using a mouse, a computer-user can select particular programs or choose on-screen options. A ball inside the mouse rolls around as the mouse moves. The ball rubs against two rollers, and this tells the computer the position and speed of the mouse.

Ball rolls as mouse is pushed along

Roller

Screen

A screen, or monitor, allows a computer-user to view the processes and results happening inside the machine, and also to interact with the computer. When the user moves the mouse (see below left), a pointer moves across the monitor screen. The words or numbers typed on the keyboard appear on the monitor, too. The screen can display pictures, diagrams, movies and animations as well as words and numbers. Monitors work in the same basic way as the screen of a television set. However, some screens, especially those on small laptop computers, have much flatter, lightweight screens which are liquid crystal displays (LCDs).

Keyboard

The main way of inputting words and numbers into a computer is by typing them on a keyboard. Each time a key is pressed, electrical contact is made – so each key is like a switch. When a particular switch is activated, a series of electrical pulses is sent to the computer. However, the time of the keyboard may be limited. In the future, we may well simply speak our instructions and data to computers. It is already possible to talk to some computers, if they have microphones connected and they are loaded with programs called voice-recognition software.

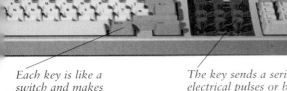

Each key is like a switch and makes electrical contact when pressed

The key sends a series of electrical pulses or bits when pressed

Fast worker

Modern computers can handle enormous amounts of data very quickly. This means that they can be used to create and show animations or to edit and play video and sound. The use of sounds, animations and videos as well as text and images is called multimedia.

On the desktop

The most familiar computers are desktop PCs (personal computers), consisting of a main unit with the hard disk, a monitor screen, a keyboard, a mouse and loudspeakers. There is often a printer too, which can make hard copy – printed documents such as letters or pictures. There may also be a scanner, which works like a photocopier, and allows a drawing or photograph to be converted into computer data. Computer programs are called software, while hardware is the computer and other devices connected to it. Applications are programs that allow the computer to be used for a particular task.

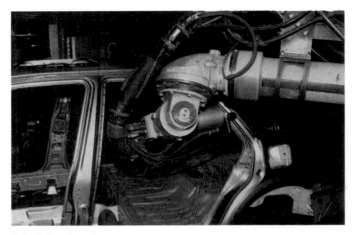

A helping hand

The data output by a computer can be used to control machines called robots. A computer-controlled robot can carry out the same task in precisely the same way, thousands of times daily. It can also carry out dangerous tasks. But these robots can also sometimes put people out of work.

On the move

Many people who work use computers, if only to write letters, and store names, addresses and other information. For those who spend much time on the move, a lightweight portable or laptop computer like this one, powered by rechargeable batteries, is very useful.

Flow of information

The arrows on this diagram show the relationship between the CPU, RAM and ROM, and input and output devices such as the monitor, keyboard and printer.

Input

ROM

CPU

RAM

Memory

Output

CARS

MOST CARS ARE POWERED by engines that run on petrol, which is made from oil. Hundreds or thousands of times every second, tiny sparks inside each cylinder of a car's engine ignite a mixture of petrol and air. The mixture explodes and that pushes a piston to the bottom of the cylinder. The piston is connected to a shaft, called the crankshaft, which turns as the piston is pushed down. Most cars have four or six cylinders, each with a piston. As the shaft turns, it brings pistons up to the top of the cylinders again, ready for the next explosions. The rotation of the shaft – powered by the explosions in the cylinders – turns gears in the gear box. The gears turn another shaft, which turns the car's wheels. Cars have batteries, which supply electric power for lights, and to produce the sparks to ignite the fuel in the piston. Some cars have diesel engines, in which there is no spark. The fuel and air mixture ignites when it is squashed by the piston rising up the cylinder.

The way out of the jam

The number of cars in the world has risen continuously over the past hundred years, and there are now so many cars in towns and cities that there are frequent traffic jams. Burning petrol or diesel pollutes the air by releasing carbon dioxide gas and other substances. Most car designers attempt to make their cars more efficient, so that they drive just as far using less fuel. In the future, we may be driving solar-powered electric cars that receive their power from the Sun. As well as producing noise, traffic jams and pollution, cars can be dangerous. Thousands of people are killed on the roads each year. Designers are always trying to find new ways of making cars safer for the driver, passengers and pedestrians. Assisted brakes, seat belts and airbags are all used to make cars safer.

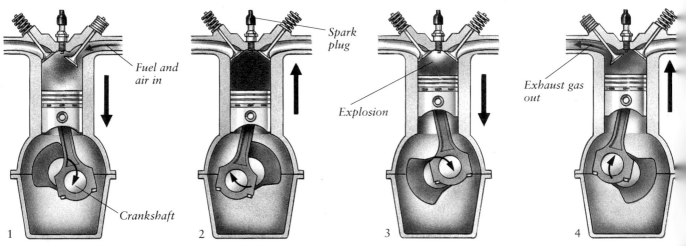

The first car

The first really practical car to be produced was the three-wheeled Motorwagen. It ran on petrol but had a top speed of just 20 kilometres per hour. The Motorwagen was designed and built by Karl Benz in 1885. Since then, more than 300 million cars have been built.

Inside the cylinders

The pictures below show the order of events inside a particular cylinder. There are four stages to the four-stroke cycle of a petrol engine, beginning with the intake (1) of the petrol–air mixture. The mixture

On track

Speed is the most important feature of racing cars. To achieve this, they must have powerful engines and streamlined bodies that push through the air with least resistance. Racing cars are normally close to the ground, which makes them easier to control as they speed round corners.

becomes compressed (2) as the piston moves upwards, and then it is ignited (3) by a spark. As the piston comes round again, it forces the exhaust gases out of the cylinder (4).

Fuel and air in

Spark plug

Explosion

Exhaust gas out

Crankshaft

1   2   3   4

Testing the flow

As a car moves along the road, it has to push its way through the air. The smoother – or more aerodynamic – the shape of the car, the easier it is for it to push through the air, and the less fuel it uses. Below, a model of a car is being tested. A stream of mist passes over the body of the car in an artificial wind (as if the car were moving through still air at high speed). The less the car disturbs the mist stream, the more aerodynamic it is.

heer weight of traffic

egular traffic reports on radio d television use the phrase heer weight of traffic' to plain why particular roads e at a standstill. Within wns and cities, public ansport such as buses and ams is a very effective way of ducing traffic.

Cushioning the blow

Most modern cars are fitted with airbags. These are installed in the steering wheel or the dashboard, and they automatically fill with air if the car is involved in a crash. When the driver is thrown forwards, he or she hits the airbag, which cushions the blow. An airbag will only work in a head-on collision, and will not be effective in a side impact or a roll.

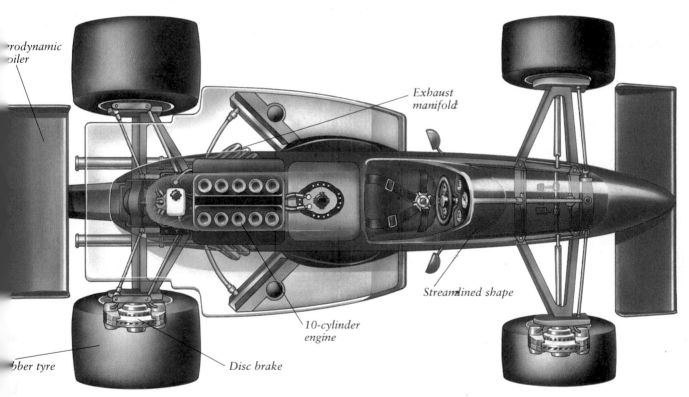

rodynamic oiler

Exhaust manifold

Streamlined shape

10-cylinder engine

bber tyre

Disc brake

Driving force

As well as the engine, gearbox and the shafts that turn the wheels, a car needs brakes to stop it, lights to see and be seen in the dark, a cooling system for the engine, and windscreen wipers and demisters to allow the driver to see clearly. All of the different systems of a modern car work together to make driving as safe and easy as possible. Formula one racing cars like this one (above) do not have the same systems as a modern family car. They do not need headlights or demisters, for example. But they do need very powerful engines, so that they can move at more than 320 kilometres per hour.

KNOW YOUR CARS

● Some cars run on compressed air, which is carried in tanks in the car.

● The main problem with electric cars is that they do not have the same range as petrol or diesel cars.

● Grand Prix motor racing began nearly 100 years ago, in 1906.

BOATS AND TRAINS

THERE ARE MANY TYPES of boats and ships. They carry people or cargo, or are used for sport and leisure. Boats stay afloat because of a force called upthrust, which is produced by the pressure of water pushing on the hull of the boat. To produce enough upthrust to float, the boat sits quite low in the water. It displaces, or pushes aside, huge amounts of water. Most boats have some source of power in order to move through water. This may be oars to push the boat along by human power, an engine-powered propeller under the water, or sails. In order to navigate, many boats have sophisticated systems controlled by computers. They have radar and sonar systems that use radio waves or sound waves to detect the depth of the water, and to avoid collisions with other craft, floating objects like icebergs, and rocks hidden just below the surface.

Hoist the sails

The wind pushes sails, and the sails are attached to a boat, and this is how a sailing boat moves. The direction of movement depends on the direction of the wind, the angle of the sails, and the position of the boat's steering rudder under the water. By changing direction repeatedly in a zig-zag manoeuvre called tacking, a boat can sail gradually into the wind.

Pushing through

Most boats have propellers, which ar[e] shaped like fans. Ju[st] as fans move air as they turn, a propell[er] pushes the water backwards, forcing the boat forwards.

Containers of standard size allow boats to be loaded and unloaded efficiently

Floating low in the water

A boat or ship floats lower in the water if it is heavily laden. A line on the side of a ship, called the Plimsoll line, shows what lev[el] the water should reach on the boat's hull, in various types of water. If the water level is higher than the Plimsoll line, the boat [is] too heavily laden and could sink.

Radar mast

From steam to electric

The first trains were powered by steam engines. Their invention changed travel and industry completely. Cargo could be transported by train and people could move around much faster than in the past. Most modern trains are electric or diesel-electric. Electric trains pick up electric power from an extra rail or an overhead cable. Diesel-electric trains produce their own electrical power, in generators that are driven by diesel engines. In each case, the electrical power drives electric motors that turn the train's wheels. Trains are more efficient than cars. They use less fuel per person per kilometre. Travelling from city to city in a train instead of a car means that there are fewer cars on the road, too.

Under its own power

Most modern trains are powered by electric motors. The electric motor is very efficient, turning more than 90 per cent of the energy fed into it, as electricity, into the energy of movement. A petrol engine is only about half as efficient.

Air craft

Powerful fans produce a cushion of air underneath the flexible 'skirt' of a hovercraft. This lifts most of the craft above the water, reducing water resistance (a type of friction) that slows down most boats. Propellers, like those on a plane, push the hovercraft forwards.

Over the points

Unlike cars or buses, trains cannot steer in the direction they want to go. At certain places the tracks cross over, allowing trains a choice of destination. These are called points. In a modern railway system the points are controlled by computers with safety back-ups.

The right shape

The shape of train wheels is very important. If they were flat, the wheels would slide off the tracks.

Flange on side prevents wheel slipping off rail

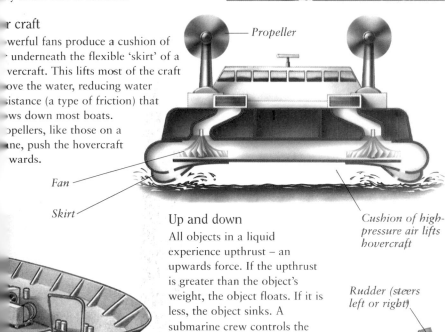

Propeller

Fan

Skirt

Cushion of high-pressure air lifts hovercraft

Up and down

All objects in a liquid experience upthrust – an upwards force. If the upthrust is greater than the object's weight, the object floats. If it is less, the object sinks. A submarine crew controls the weight of the craft by varying the volume of air in the sub's buoyancy tanks.

Rudder (steers left or right)

Hydroplane (steers up or down)

Hovering train

The motors or engines of a train are needed to fight against friction (rubbing) between the wheels and the axles. But some trains use powerful magnets to lift, or levitate, them above the track. These maglev (magnetic levitation) trains need no wheels, and are very quiet.

BOAT AND TRAIN FACTS

● A double-hulled boat is called a catamaran. A triple-hulled boat is called a trimaran.

● The speed of a boat through the water is normally measured in units called knots. One knot is one nautical mile per hour. A nautical mile is 1.15 miles (1.85 km).

● The first railways carried coal out of mines in horse-drawn carriages more than 200 years ago.

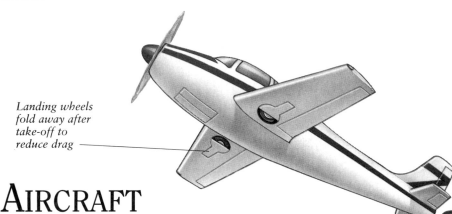

Landing wheels fold away after take-off to reduce drag

Light aircraft

The body of an aeroplane is called the fuselage. Most small planes – called light aircraft – are pushed through the air by propellers turned at high speed by powerfu engines. There is a variety of moveable control surfaces on the aeroplane. Ailerons on the main wings help an aeroplane to roll or bank (tilt to the side) into a turn. The rudder on the aeroplane's fin (tail) is used to steer left or right. The elevators on the tailplane make th plane climb or descend.

Cabin fo pilot and passenge.

Propeller (air screw) produces thrust

AIRCRAFT

There are four main forces that affect an aeroplane. The most important is the upwards force called lift. This is produced by the wings of the aircraft as they move quickly through the air. It must be greater than the second main force, which opposes lift – the downwards pull of gravity that gives the aircraft weight. The third main force is thrust, that pushes the aeroplane forwards through the air. Thrust is produced by propellers or jet engines. It must overcome the fourth force, which opposes thrust. This is drag, also called air resistance. It is a type of friction caused by air rubbing against the plane as it moves along. Most aircraft wings have flaps that can be raised or lowered to alter the flow of air. These are especially important at lower speeds, when the aeroplane is taking off or landing. A helicopter uses the same idea to make its lift, but in this case, the wings are its rotor blades, which spin around very quickly. The angles of the blades can be changed, to make the helicopter hover in one place without moving, or travel backwards or forwards.

Lighter than air

Some aircraft, such as hot-air balloons, are called lighter-than-air craft. They are buoyant, in the same way as an object that floats in water. They float because the main par or 'envelope' of the balloon weighs less than the same volume of normal air. So the envelope floats upwards in normal air, like a bubble in water. In a hot-air balloon, a burner heats the air in the envelope. The heated air expand so that there is less air inside the envelope than before, and the balloon can then rise because it weighs less. Balloon flights are normally made during the morning and evening, when the air is cool. This produces the greatest difference between the air insid and outside the envelope, giving the greatest lift. Airships, on the othe hand, are filled with a lighter-than-air gas called helium.

Envelope

Montgolfier balloon on its first flight

No power

A hang glider is not powered by a propeller or a jet engine. Its wings do not produce lift in the same way as a powered aeroplane. So a hang glider is more like a steerable parachute than an aeroplane. It always sinks slowly compared to the air around it. However, if the pilot can steer it into a column of rising air, called a thermal, the hang glider can rise compared to the ground – even though it is still sinking in the air around it.

Full of hot air

More than 200 years ago, people first experimented with hot-air balloons. Two French brothers, Joseph-Mic and Jacques-Etienne Montgolfie made a balloon that rose into the a on 21 November 1783 in France, in fr of an astonished crowd. The balloon wit its two brave volunteer pilots, Pilatre de Rozier and the Marquis d'Arlandes, rose about 900 m into the air, and sank back again gently ten minutes and 8 km later.

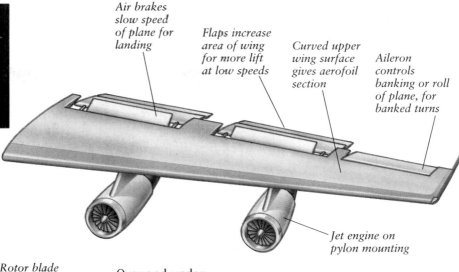

Air brakes slow speed of plane for landing

Flaps increase area of wing for more lift at low speeds

Curved upper wing surface gives aerofoil section

Aileron controls banking or roll of plane, for banked turns

Jet engine on pylon mounting

Rotor blades

The rotor blades of a helicopter produce lift as they turn. The blades can be tilted – either individually or together – to steer the helicopter, or to rise, hover or descend. A system of control bars at the centre of the rotors controls the angle, or pitch, of the blades. Because the whirling blades produce lift as well as controlling direction, helicopters are known as rotary-wing craft.

Rotor blade

Rotor head tilts blades to control helicopter's flight

Drive shaft from engine

Over and under

As a wing moves through the air, it splits the air in two. Air that passes over the wing moves faster than air that passes below it, because the upper surface is more curved. This shape is known as the aerofoil section. The fast-moving air produces less pressure on the upper wing surface than the slower-moving air underneath. So there is an overall upwards push – lift. The amount of lift depends on the speed the aeroplane moves, the area of the wings, and the curvature of the aerofoil section. Heavy aeroplanes, such as jumbo jets, need large wings and powerful jet engines to push them through the air quickly enough.

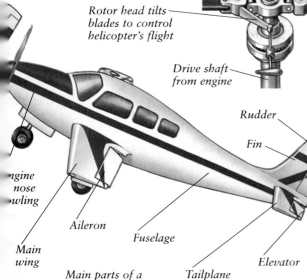

Rudder

Fin

Engine nose cowling

Aileron

Fuselage

Main wing

Main parts of a light aircraft

Tailplane

Elevator

Light aircraft taxis to take-off position

Taking to the skies

There has been a tremendous increase in air traffic over the past 50 years. Most large cities now have airports, and air traffic controllers use sophisticated radar to track the position of aeroplanes in the sky, in an attempt to prevent accidents. At a busy airport there is one movement – a plane taking off or landing – almost every minute. Usually movements are fewer or stop at night, to reduce noise pollution.

MAKING LIFT

How can you make a piece of paper rise without touching it to push it upwards? Cut out a strip of paper about 3 cm wide and 15 cm long. Hold one end of the strip between one finger and the thumb of each hand, just in front of and below your bottom lip. Now blow over the top of the paper, and you will see it lift into the air. As you blow, you are creating fast-moving air over the paper, like the air passing over the top of a wing. The still air underneath the paper pushes upwards more than the faster-moving air above the paper pushes downwards, lifting the paper.

COMMUNICATIONS

THERE ARE MANY different ways of communicating in the modern world. People within speaking distance use words and gestures. But what about telecommunications – getting a message to someone far away? In the past, flags and smoke signals were used to pass information over large distances. Today, we can use the telephone. It is an instant way to communicate, and has a microphone that converts sound into electrical signals. Television and radio are other ways to communicate. Television, radio and telephone signals pass along metal wires or fibre-optic cables. Printing – in books, magazines, newspapers and letters – is another way of communicating. Today, the written word can be sent instantly across the world, from computer to computer. The Internet is a vast, world-wide network that allows people on opposite sides of the globe to exchange information between their computers. Information – words, sounds and pictures – must be digitized (see opposite) before it can be stored, transmitted or received by computers. In the near future, most communication will be digital, allowing even easier exchange of information.

ALEXANDER GRAHAM BELL
(1847-1922)

In March 1876, Scottish inventor Alexander Graham Bell sent the world's first telephone message to his assistant, Thomas Watson: 'Mr Watson, come here, I want you!' Bell was calling for help to Watson in the next room at his workshops in Boston, Mass., USA. Other researchers including Thomas Edison were trying to develop the telephone, and had some success. However, Bell became famous because he was the first to apply for a patent (a document that claims an invention as yours).

Bouncing back from space

Satellites have revolutionized the way we communicate. They circle the Earth far above the ground, and pass signals from one place to another that may be on the opposite side of the world. Satellites are covered with solar cells, which convert sunlight to electric current. This is used to power all the equipment in the satellite. Satellites are used for many different purposes. Comsats (communications satellites) allow us to make telephone calls to people far away, or see television pictures made in other countries. The signals from the ground are sent up to a satellite and bounced back down to Earth to receiving 'dishes'. These collect the signals, and pass them to your telephone or television set. Other satellites send information down to Earth, about weather, about other countries and about space itself.

A satellite sends signals on the downlink to a mid-oceanic island

Comsats

Most communications satellites orbit the Earth more than 35,000 kilometres above ground. At this height, they orbit once every 24 hours, so that they appear to stay in a fixed point in the sky. Radio signals from Earth are picked up (received) by dishes on the satellite, made stronger (amplified) and sent (transmitted) to receiving dishes in a different part of the world.

The Internet

Perhaps the most exciting and convenient way to communicate is on the Internet. It is a huge network of interconnected computers. Most people connect their computers to the Internet using modems that convert digital signals into analogue signals (right) that can pass along ordinary telephone cables.

Telephone signals

Inside the mouthpiece, a microphone produces an electrical signal that is a copy of the sound of your voice. The signal passes down cables, through exchanges and to the earpiece of the other telephone, where a loudspeaker produces the sound.

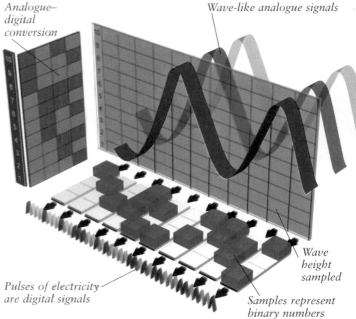

Analogue–digital conversion

Wave-like analogue signals

Pulses of electricity are digital signals

Wave height sampled

Samples represent binary numbers

Diaphragm

Coil of wire

Earpiece

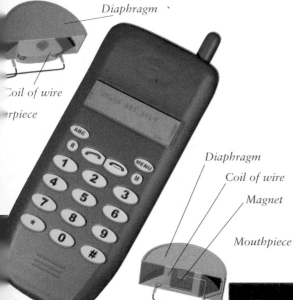

Diaphragm

Coil of wire

Magnet

Mouthpiece

The digital world

Microphones produce continuously varying electric currents that are copies of sounds they pick up. These wave-like signals are analogue. They must be digitized – represented as a series of on and off pulses – before they can be used by computers or sent through modern digital telecom networks. This is done by sampling the analogue signal thousands of times each second, and representing the value of each sample as a binary digital number.

On the move

Mobile telephones allow people to stay in touch even when they are not at home. The signals to and from the telephone are carried by radio waves to a local receiving cellular station, which is connected to the normal telephone network.

Tomorrow's world

In the near future, most communications equipment will send and receive huge amounts of digital information through the fibre-optic cables of ISDN – Integrated Services Digital Network. This will give people access to the Internet, digital television and radio, and a videophone which will allow them to see the people they talk to.

● What is the difference between an element and a compound?

An element is made of atoms of only one type, while a compound is made of more than one type. Iron is an element, made only of iron atoms; rust is a compound, made of atoms of iron, oxygen and hydrogen joined together.

● What is the easiest way to separate the mud from muddy water?

Passing muddy water through a paper filter is the best way to separate mud and water. The filter holds back the muddy particles, while allowing the water to pass through.

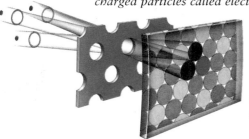

● What are the three states of matter?

The three states of matter are solid, liquid and gas.

● Why do crystals have regular shapes?

Crystals have regular shapes because the atoms or molecules of which they are made are joined together in regular, repeating ways.

● How is glass made?

Glass is made by melting sand and then allowing it to cool.

● Which properties of concrete and steel make them ideal for building a suspension bridge?

The pillars of a suspension bridge are made of concrete, which can support a heavy load pressing down on it. The bridge is supported by steel cables, because steel is strong when it is pulled.

● What is the name of the force that pulls everything together?

The force that pulls everything together is called gravity. It is the force of gravity between you and the Earth that keeps you on the ground.

● What is an electric current?

An electric current is the movement of electric charges. Current in a wire is caused by the flow of electrically charged particles called electrons.

● What is incandescence?

Incandescence is the production of light by objects that are very hot.

● What causes sound?

Rapid vibrations of objects disturb the air, and the disturbance travels out in all directions through the air, as sound waves. When the waves enter the ear, they are heard as sound.

● What is the word 'bits' short for?

'Bits' is short for 'binary digits'. A bit can be either '0' or '1', and groups of bits inside a computer represent words, numbers and instructions.

● What is the job of a spark plug inside a car's engine?

Spark plugs produce sparks that ignite the mixture of petrol and air inside the cylinders of a car engine. The petrol and air mixture explodes, pushing the piston down.

● What is the name of the upward force that keeps boats afloat, and what causes it?

A boat is kept afloat by a force called upthrust, which is caused by the pressure of water pushing on the boat's hull.

● What are the four forces that act on an aeroplane in flight?

An aeroplane is acted upon by weight (downwards), lift (upwards), thrust (forwards) and drag (backwards).

● Which of the following are 'lighter-than-air' craft: a jet aeroplane, a hot air balloon, a helicopter, an airship?

A hot air balloon and an airship are examples of 'lighter-than-air' craft.

● What does the word 'modem' stand for?

'Modem' stands for 'modulation-demodulation', which describes what a modem does: it changes (modulates) the digital signal from a computer into an analogue signal that can travel through the telephone network.

● What does a decibel meter measure?

The loudness of a sound is measured in decibels, so a decibel meter is an instrument that measures the loudness of sound.

HISTORY

THE FIRST CIVILIZATIONS

TODAY'S MEN AND WOMEN are descended from ape-like creatures who lived in Africa about four million years ago. Unlike earlier apes, these creatures (known as Australopithicus, 'southern ape') walked upright. By 2.5 million years ago, their descendants (Homo habilis, 'handy man') had discovered how to make simple tools. Modern humans (Homo sapiens sapiens, 'wise man') first appeared about 100,000 years ago. They had large brains and used words to communicate, instead of signs and cries. By around 35,000 years ago, modern humans were living in Europe, Asia, and Australia; they migrated to America some time before 13000 BC. Early humans lived as hunters and gatherers, but some time around 9000 BC groups of men and women began to settle in villages and plant seeds of wild grains for food. This 'Agricultural Revolution' happened in the Middle East, but between 6000 and 3000 BC, farmers in Asia, America and Africa discovered how to grow rice, potatoes and yams. By around 7000 BC, the world's first towns had appeared.

Hand-axes like this one made of flint were some of the world's earliest tools. They were invented by Homo erectus around two million years ago

Dating systems

Like many other history books, this encyclopedia uses a calendar that divides the past into two separate eras. BC (initials standing for before Christ) and AD ('Anno Domini', Latin words, orginally used by the Christian Church that mean 'In the Year of our Lord'). According to this calendar, the year that Jesus Christ was born is counted as Year 1 AD. You count forwards from Year 1 in the AD era, and backwards from Year 1 in the BC era. There is no year zero.

A ziggurat, a pyramid-shaped tower of mud-brick, stood at the centre of each Sumerian city.

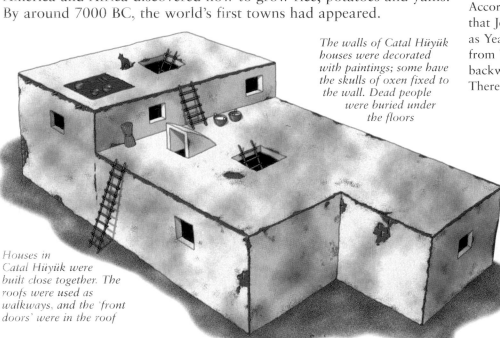

The walls of Catal Hüyük houses were decorated with paintings; some have the skulls of oxen fixed to the wall. Dead people were buried under the floors

Houses in Catal Hüyük were built close together. The roofs were used as walkways, and the 'front doors' were in the roof

The first towns

The first towns we know about were Catal Hüyük, in Turkey, and Jericho, in Israel. Both were at their biggest and strongest around 7000 to 6000 BC. They were surrounded by pounded earth ramparts covered with mud-plaster; inside, the houses were tightly packed together. The townspeople grew grain for food, but made most of their wealth through craft and trade. Farmers and hunters brought animals, furs and skins to towns, to exchange for craft goods such as pottery, jewellery, metalwork and cloth. Catal Hüyük (above) was a market centre for obsidian – a valuable black volcanic stone used to make knife blades. In early towns, people did not use coins; they had not yet been invented. Instead, they bartered (swapped) the goods they wanted to sell for other useful items. After around 6000 BC, these first towns became less important, as many new farming villages were built nearby.

SUMERIAN FACTS

● Sumerian kings were buried in huge 'death pits', together with their splendid furniture, jewellery, weapons – and many of their servants, who died alongside their royal masters.

● King Sargon of Akkad, a city to the north of Sumerian lands, was the first to unite the whole of Mesopotamia under one ruler, around 2300 BC.

● As well as inventing writing, the Sumerians also invented the wheel. But to begin with, they used it only for making pottery, not for transport.

Pyramids

Pyramids are massive monuments containing tombs. They were built in ancient Egypt, between 2686 and 1550 BC to house the bodies of dead pharaohs – the Egyptians' god–kings. The pyramids' shape was important. It represented the rays of the Sun. The Egyptians believed that dead pharaohs were carried to everlasting life in the land of the dead by the Sun's rays.

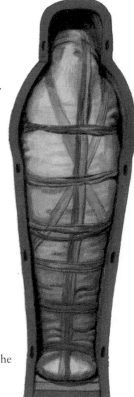

City life

Around 5000 BC, a group of people called the Sumerians arrived in Iraq. They settled in Mesopotamia – the land between the river Tigris and the river Euphrates. Grain, fruit and vegetables grew well there in irrigated fields. The Sumerians got rich by selling their farm produce to neighbouring peoples. Their population increased, and by around 3500 BC, their villages had developed into big, busy cities.

The Sumerians built ziggurats as homes for their gods. There was a temple at the top of each one

Making mummies

The Ancient Egyptians believed that people's spirits could only survive after death if their bodies survived as well. So they preserved dead bodies by removing the innards, drying the flesh and bones with chemicals, then wrapping the remains in bandages. Wealthy families also paid for fine painted mummy cases, or for stone caskets, called sarcophagi. Finished mummies were buried in tombs decorated with pictures of the dead person and their family enjoying life in the world of the dead. The word 'mummy' comes from the Arabic for bitumen (sticky black tar, found in the Egyptian desert). Mummified bodies often looked black and sticky because they were coated in resin – not tar, but scented gum from trees.

WRITE IN PICTURES

The first known writing system was invented by the Sumerians who lived in Mesopotamia around 3500 BC. It used picture-signs to represent objects, such as houses or birds or fish. Later, picture-signs were used to communicate ideas – the picture-sign for mouth (a pair of lips) could also mean 'speak'. Two picture signs could be combined to create a new meaning: for example, when written side by side, the signs for 'food' and 'mouth' meant 'eat'. Design some picture symbols of your own, and use them to write this message: 'I love learning about history.' (You can use a heart for 'love'.)

THE MEDITERRANEAN WORLD

FOR OVER 2,000 YEARS, the Greeks were the most powerful people in Mediterranean lands. From around 3000 BC, kings based on the island of Crete controlled Mediterranean sea routes, and demanded tributes from neighbouring lands. Around 2100 BC, new settlers arrived in Greek lands from the north and east. They set up powerful kingdoms ruled by warriors. Then, around 800 BC, Greece was divided into city-states. These were ruled by tyrants (strong men), oligarchs (groups of rich men) or, increasingly, by the citizens themselves. Over the centuries, a splendid Greek civilization developed. The Greeks were skilful designers, builders and craftworkers, and made many great discoveries in science, mathematics, medicine and philosophy. Greek writers also composed wonderful poems and plays. Greek power collapsed when the Romans invaded in 146 BC, but Greek ideas continued to flourish.

Great nations

Many other civilizations developed in the lands around the Mediterranean Sea, and in neighbouring Central Asia. Often, they fought one another, but they also formed close links through trade. The mighty Babylonian empire ruled Mesopotamia, and traded with India and Arabia. Further north, the warlike Assyrians were powerful from around 1100 to 612 BC. In 539 BC, another warlike people, the Persians, conquered the Babylonians. Persia also took over the nearby Greek colonies in Asia Minor, and the rich kindgom of Media on the shores of the Caspian Sea. The greatest trading nations were the Canaanites, who lived in present-day Syria, Lebanon and Jordan, from about 2000 to 1200 BC, and the Phoenicians who occupied the same lands after them.

The Hebrews

The Hebrews were nomads, who kept flocks of sheep and goats in eastern Mediterranean lands. Ancient stories, recorded in the Bible, tell how they were made to work as slaves in Egypt from around 1800 to 1200 BC. Led by Moses, a prophet or religious teacher, they escaped across the Red Sea and returned to their homeland. Around 1020 BC, they founded the nation of Israel, which was ruled by mighty kings. In 922 BC, Israel was divided in two; the southern part became known as Judah, and its inhabitants were called the Jews.

According to the Bible, Yahweh (God) gave the prophet Moses two slabs of stone with the Ten Commandments (holy laws for living a good life) written upon them

The Parthenon

The glittering white marble temple known as the Parthenon was dedicated to Athene, guardian goddess of the Greek city-state of Athens. It was built between 448 and 432 BC on top of the Acropolis, a high cliff-fortress in the centre of Athens, and was part of a grand rebuilding scheme planned by General Pericles (495–429 BC) after the Persians had invaded. Pericles was the leading Athenian statesman, who encouraged science, learning and the arts and wanted to make Athens the most beautiful city in Greece.

The Parthenon housed a gold and ivory statue of the goddess Athene. Every four years, the people of Athens held a ceremony to present the goddess with a new robe, called a peplos

The Olympic Games

The first recorded Olympic Games were held to honour the gods and took place in 776 BC, in southern Greece. To begin with, running was the only sport. Later, wrestling, boxing, horse-racing and chariot-racing were added, also pentathalon (wrestling, running, discus, long-jump and javelin), plus music, poetry and drama competitions.

King Nebuchadnezzar built the magnificent Hanging Gardens close to the royal palace in Babylon, and filled them with exotic plants and flowers to please his wife

Hoplites were armed with swords and spears, and protected by metal breastplates and helmets, leather greaves (leg-guards) and round shields. Each soldier had to buy his own weapons and armour

Babylon

Babylon was a rich city-state in Mesopotamia, to the north of Sumerian lands. It first became powerful around 1750 BC, when it was ruled by King Hammurabi, a famous lawgiver. The city had wide streets, rich palaces, huge ziggurats and temples, splendid gateways and massive walls. Babylon reached its greatest glory during the reign of the warrior king Nebuchadnezzar (605–562 BC).

Greek soldiers

Greek city-states were defended by armies of foot-soldiers, called hoplites. They were recruited from male citizens. In Athens, for example, young men aged 18 had to spend two years in army training. Only army commanders and rich citizens rode horses and chariots to war. On the battlefield, hoplites fought side by side in long lines (called phalanxes), holding out a wall of spears towards their advancing enemies.

Phoenician graves were decorated with extraordinary masks, like this one, made of pottery. They were probably meant to frighten evil spirits away

The Phoenicians

From around 1200, the Phoenicians lived in Canaan, at the eastern end of the Mediterranean. They were farmers and skilful craftworkers, making beautiful purple cloth and delicate glass. Phoenician scribes invented an early form of the alphabet we still use today. The Phoenicians were also expert sailors and shipbuilders, travelling to trade all round the Mediterranean Sea.

ALEXANDER THE GREAT

Alexander the Great (356–323 BC), king of Macedon, was a brave and brilliant army commander who had ambitions to rule the world. After conquering Greece and the mighty Persian empire, he led his army on a long march (about 30,000 km) across Central Asia to India and back. This journey took over 10 years, and helped spread Greek language, art and ideas over a very wide area. Alexander died of a fever aged only 33. His empire was divided among his generals after his death.

THE ROMAN EMPIRE

ORIGINALLY, THE ROMANS were farmers who lived in central Italy. Their neighbours were the powerful Etruscans. As the Romans grew stronger, they fought against the Etruscans, until around 753 BC they won control of the city of Rome. At first, the Romans were ruled by kings, but in 509 BC Rome became a republic, ruled by consuls – officials elected by the citizens. Senators, chosen from among top citizens, also helped shape government policy and make new laws. Over the years, the well-trained Roman army began to conquer more land, and by around 264 BC the Romans ruled all Italy. Soon, they controlled a vast empire overseas. In 47 BC, quarrels among power-hungry citizens led to a civil war. It ended in 27 BC, when an army commander, Octavian (later known as Augustus), took control. From then on, Rome was ruled by emperors. Some were wise and just – others were weak and cruel. Roman power finally collapsed in AD 476, after the city was attacked by tribesmen from Central Asia.

In 218 BC the Carthaginian general Hannibal led 40,000 men and 37 war-elephants on a long march through Spain and across the Alps to attack the city of Rome. Many men and elephants died in the winter snows

Carthage

In 814 BC, Phoenician traders founded the city of Carthage, on Africa's north coast. Carthage grew rich and powerful, and came into conflict with Rome. Between 264 and 146 BC Carthage fought and lost the three Punic Wars against the Romans. The Romans destroyed Carthage, and made all its citizens slaves.

The Romans as builders

The Romans were great builders and engineers. Rome was full of fine temples, palaces and monuments – and also aqueducts (to carry fresh water), public baths and sewers. Throughout the empire, Roman army engineers built roads, bridges and fortifications.

The city of Rome

Rome grew from a collection of farming villages around 750 BC to a city housing over one million people by AD 300. A survey made around that time listed 2 circuses (racetracks), 2 great arenas, 8 bridges, 28 libraries, 1,352 drinking-water fountains, 11 public baths, 144 public lavatories, 29 warehouses and over 46,000 private homes. There were also temples, forums (shopping centres) and government offices.

Rome was the centre of a vast network of international trade

Celtic gold necklace, shaped like a new moon

The Celts

The Celtic peoples of northwestern Europe were enemies of Rome. Celtic civilization first appeared around 750 BC in Austria but soon spread, through trade and migration, through France and northern Italy to Ireland, Britain and northern Spain. The Celts were farmers, warriors, poets, story-tellers and skilful craftworkers, making wonderful weapons and jewellery from bronze and iron. They fought fiercely against invading Roman armies. By around AD 200, Celtic civilization had disappeared from most of Europe.

Roman soldiers fought with spears, swords and daggers. To protect themselves, they wore padded leather helmets, metal or leather breastplates, and kilts made of strips of leather and metal. Underneath, they wore a wool or linen tunic, and (in cold climates) woollen socks and underpants. For the winter they had leather boots and a thick cloak

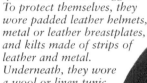

Roman soldiers

The Roman empire was guarded by large numbers of soldiers, recruited from citizens of the empire and from friendly lands. Recruits had to be fit, strong and under 25; they agreed to serve for long periods of up to 20 years and more. If they survived to retirement age, they were given a lump sum or a pension, and a 'diploma' recording their fighting years. On campaign, Roman soldiers lived in well-organized camps, or in semi-permanent forts – blocks of wooden buildings surrounded by earthworks and strong walls. An elite group of soldiers, called the Praetorian Guard, was created in AD 27 to protect the emperor and the city of Rome.

Rise and fall

By around AD 100, the Roman empire stretched from southern Germany to North Africa and the Middle East. Lands conquered by Rome were ruled by Roman governors, and guarded by the Roman army. Everyone living there had to pay taxes to Rome, and to obey Roman laws. In AD 395, the empire was divided into two parts, east and west. A new, eastern, capital city was built at Constantinople (present-day Istanbul).

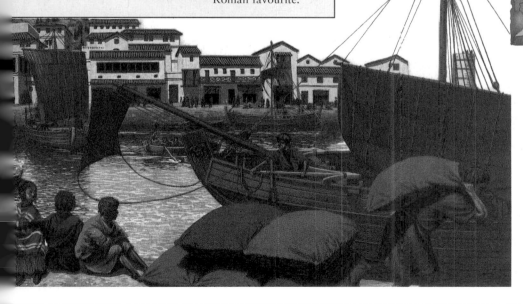

MEDIEVAL EUROPE

IN WESTERN EUROPE, from around 800 to 1400, society was organized according to the feudal system. Almost everyone, from the greatest noble to the lowliest peasant, was bound by ties of loyalty and obedience to a superior lord. In return for performing duties for him, they were rewarded with food, money or, more usually, land. Their duties varied: peasants had to work on the lord's farms, nobles and knights (trained soldiers from noble families) were expected to fight by his side. European society was also shaped by another powerful organization – the Christian Church. Priests and monks were the best-educated people in medieval Europe; they played an important part in government, scholarship and the arts.

Barbarian invaders

From around AD 300, the Roman Empire was threatened by barbarian invaders. Vandals and Goths attacked from the north and west; Huns and Alans invaded from the east. In AD 410, barbarians set fire to the city of Rome. They were driven away, but returned. In AD 476, they forced the last Roman emperor to give up his throne. Europe was in chaos, but after AD 700, new kingdoms took shape, ruled by warrior kings like Charlemagne.

Freedom in the towns

The feudal system had very little effect on people who lived in towns. They made their living from craftwork, or by trade, and did not owe obedience to a lord. In AD 800, townspeople were a tiny minority of the European population. But towns grew in wealth and importance throughout the Middle Ages. Town councils built fine churches, cathedrals and council chambers; buyers and sellers from miles around hurried to weekly market days.

CHARLEMAGNE

Charlemagne (ruled AD 768–814) was king of the Franks, a warlike people who lived in southwestern Germany and France. He conquered a rich empire in Italy, Austria, Hungary and northern Germany, and on Christmas Day AD 800 was crowned Holy Roman Emperor by the Pope in Rome. Charlemagne was a great law-maker, and a patron of learning and the arts. He encouraged trade, repaired Europe's old Roman roads, and standardized the empire's system of weights, measures and coins.

Viking warriors fought with swords and battle-axes. Sometimes, they worked themselves up into a frenzy before battle, so they would fight extra fiercely. This was called 'going berserk'

The Vikings

The Vikings lived in the cold, harsh land of Scandinavia. They were skilful sailors and bloodthirsty pirate raiders, who brought death and destruction to many countries in northern Europe between AD 793 and 1100. But Viking people were also peaceful farmers, traders and craftworkers, who developed the world's first parliament and a system of strong laws.

Medieval lords employed well-trained officials to run their estates and supervise the peasants who worked there

Castles

Castles were first built around AD 1000 as military strongholds. Later they became important family homes.

Living on the land

Most people in medieval Europe earned their living from the land. Peasant men, women and children laboured in the fields, ploughing, sowing and harvesting, making hay, picking grapes for wine, and making butter and cheese. Some peasants were not even free to leave their lord's farm.

Pilgrimages

In the Middle Ages, pilgrims made journeys to say prayers at Christian holy places throughout Europe and the Middle East. A pilgrimage had a serious purpose, but it could also be fun. Pilgrims stayed at inns to rest and refresh themselves, and to enjoy good food and ale. They travelled in groups for company, but also for protection against bandits and thieves.

Town houses were mostly built of wood, straw and plaster. They had thatched or tiled roofs. In busy cities, they were built tightly packed together. This often led to disastrous fires

The Black Death

The Black Death was a terrible epidemic (outbreak of disease) that arrived in Europe from Asia in 1347. The germs that caused it were carried in the blood of rats and fleas (mostly living in dirty, crowded towns) and passed on to humans by flea-bites. Medieval people did not understand this; they tried many different remedies, such as saying special prayers, washing in herb-scented vinegar, or carrying lucky charms. But none of them worked. The Black Death killed millions of people.

Spread of the Black Death

	1347
	1348
	1349

British Isles

Russia

Germany

France EUROPE

Spain

Italy

Greece Turkey

AFRICA ASIA

N
0 Kms 800
0 Miles 500

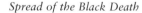

THE MUSLIM EMPIRE

THE PROPHET MUHAMMAD was a religious leader who lived in Arabia from AD 570 to 632. Muhammad taught people to worship Allah (God) and to live good lives. His teaching led to the growth of a major world religion, called Islam ('obedience to God'). It is still followed by millions of people today. In AD 622 Muhammad was forced by enemies to leave his home city, Mecca. He went to Medina, an Arabian market town, where he and his companions developed a new lifestyle, based on their faith. They became known as 'Muslims' – the people of Islam. Muhammad returned to Mecca with an army in AD 630, and captured it. Soon, Muslim soldiers took control of all Arabia, spreading their faith wherever they went. By AD 750 they had conquered a vast empire, stretching from southern Spain to the borders of China.

A great Muslim city

The Muslim lands were ruled by princes called caliphs, and governed by Muslim laws. At first, the caliphs' capital was at Medina, then at Damascus (in Syria), but they soon moved it to Baghdad, a magnificent new city (now in Iraq). Baghdad was founded by Caliph al-Mansur in AD 762. It was a circular city with a great mosque at the centre, and the caliph's palace nearby. Within the city walls there were schools, colleges, hospitals, bath-houses, libraries, gardens, fountains, markets, shops, and an observatory for studying the stars. In 1258, Baghdad was destroyed by invading Mongol armies.

Muslim science

Muslim rulers encouraged learning and Muslim scholars were skilled at medicine, mathematics, astronomy, philosophy and science. They got their knowledge from ancient Greek texts, which they translated into Arabic, the language used by scholars all over the Muslim world. They also made many important discoveries themselves. The numbers we use today (1, 2, 3 etc.) were developed by Muslim scholars around AD 850 from earlier Indian originals. We also use many Muslim scientific words, such as 'chemistry' and 'algebra'.

This Muslim star-diagram shows a constellation (an imaginary figure in the night sky).

Decorating a mosque

Muslim artists were forbidden to portray people or animals (only God could create life). Instead, they decorated buildings with graceful patterns, based on mathematical shapes. They also used words from the Qur'an, the Muslim holy book.

Muslim engineers discovered how to build high curving domes above square or rectangular prayer-halls – no one else had been able to do this properly before.

ecca

he city of Mecca, in Arabia, was an
cient holy site. After AD 630, when the
ophet Muhammad and his soldiers
ptured Mecca, it became the holiest place
the Muslim world and an important
ntre of pilgrimage. At the heart of the
y stood the Kaaba ('cube'),
building housing a holy relic known as
e Black Stone. Muhammad taught that
e Jewish Prophet Abraham had
orshipped God there, long ago. Today,
uslim people aim to make a pilgrimage
Mecca at least once in their lives.

*Christian knights
were soldiers from
noble families
who fought the
Muslims on
horseback. The
Church taught
that it was a
knight's duty to
protect the
Christian
faith.*

The Crusades

The Crusades were wars fought
between Christian and Muslim
armies over who had the right
to rule the city of Jerusalem
(in present-day Israel) and the
surrounding lands. This area was
holy to Muslims, Christians and Jews.
The Crusades began in 1096, when a
Christian army set out for Jerusalem
from Europe. They ended in 1291, when
Muslim soldiers from Asia, North Africa
and the Middle East drove the last
Christian army out of the Holy Land.

*Muslim Crusading armies
(soldier, right) formed a
tough, well-trained fighting
force. Muslim army
engineers invented siege
engines and fire-bombs, and pioneered a
useful way of sending messages from the
battlefield, by pigeon post.*

*Muslim rulers issued fine gold and
silver coins, decorated with
Arabic writing. They were used
by traders in many different
Muslim
lands.*

GENGHIS KHAN

During the 13th century, the Muslim lands
were conquered by fierce Mongol armies.
The Mongols were nomads, who lived in
central Asia. In 1206, all the Mongol tribes
joined together under the leadership of a
soldier prince called Temujin, and set off to
conquer new lands. Temujin took the title
'Genghis Khan' (it means 'world ruler').
He united all the lands conquered by the
Mongols into a mighty empire, made new
laws and encouraged trade. When he died in 1227, he ruled
ll Asia, and half China, too.

Crafts and trade

Many important international trade routes passed
through Muslim lands. Ships carrying spices, cotton
cloth and precious stones from India, Africa and the
East Indies arrived in the Persian Gulf and the Red Sea.
Merchants led camel-trains across Asian mountains and
deserts to bring silks from China. All these goods were
sold in markets or bazaars (shopping centres) in Muslim
lands, along with fine locally made craft goods, such as
glass, pottery, metalwork and carpets.

*Muslim scientists and engineers
designed and constructed many
beautiful buildings, especially
mosques (buildings for worship),
palaces and schools.*

EARLY CHINA AND JAPAN

CHINESE PEOPLE CALLED THEIR NATION the 'Middle Kingdom'. They believed it was the centre of the world. From AD 618 to 1279, under the Tang and Song dynasties (families of emperors), China was one of the richest and most advanced civilizations on Earth. The Chinese built huge, splendid cities, and developed new and better varieties of rice. The population increased rapidly, and the army conquered large areas of land. Chinese scientists made many important inventions and discoveries, such as printing, paper-making, gunpowder, rockets and clockwork. Chinese craftworkers made silk cloth and porcelain (which we call 'china'), that were highly prized in Europe, Africa and Asia.

Neighbours

Japan and Korea were two of China's neighbours. Japan was ruled by emperors, who claimed to be descended from the gods. Ordinary people grew food in tiny garden plots, and caught many kinds of food from the sea. Korea was home to many famous scholars and scientists, and Korean craftworkers pioneered many pottery-making and ironworking techniques.

Chinese cities were administered by government officials. They collected taxes and made sure the laws were obeyed

The Great Wall of China

For centuries, China was divided into many separate states, which were often at wa[r]. In 221 BC, Prince Cheng from the state of Qin, conquered all the others and united them. H[e] became China's first emperor, and reigned until 210 BC. Cheng was a formidable ruler. He imprisoned or killed all his enemies, burned books he did not agree with, passed new laws, built roads and canals, and introduced a new system [of] coins, weights and measures. He also rebuilt earlier, small-scale earthworks to create a huge Great Wall to defend his empire from enemy attack.

In warm South China and sheltered lowland Japan, rice grew very well. In cold North China and the Japanese mountains, wheat and barley were the usual crops

The emperor's palace was built of wood and decorated in bright red lacquer. Red and yellow were royal colours

Rice farming

Chinese and Japanese farmers grew rice in flooded paddy-fields. It was exhausting work. Each seedling had to be carefully planted by hand, and workers had to wade ankle-deep in mud to pull out weeds that might damage the crop. For extra food, Chinese and Japanese farmers bred fish in the flooded fields, and raised waterfowl, such as geese and ducks.

Folding paper fans were invented in Japan. Draw a rectangle (about 15 x 40 cm) on paper. Decorate each side with felt-tips or paint. Make 20 2cm-wide zig-zag folds in the painted paper. Cut 10 strips of card about 20 cm long and 2 cm wide. Punch holes in one end. Glue one strip of card to the left-hand side of each zig-zag fold.

Push a paper-fastener through the holes in the card strips. Fold back paper-fastener tips.

Use your fan to keep cool.

The Silk Road

Valuable goods made in China – especially silk cloth and porcelain (fine pottery) – were carried overland to Europe, North Africa and the Middle East along the 'Silk Road'. This was not a single pathway, but a series of rough tracks over 7,000 kilometres long leading across high mountains and treacherous deserts. It took merchants many months to travel from one end to another. Bandits, lack of food, and bad weather made the journey very dangerous at times. Along the way, travellers rested in 'khans', or boarding houses.

Samurai fought with swords, bows and arrows, and were expert horse-riders. They wore strong but lightweight armour, made of leather and wicker (woven bamboo). Their helmets were often decorated with splendid crests

Faith and worship

The Buddhist faith originated in India around 500 BC. It taught that people will only ever achieve peace and calm if they learn not to be ruled by selfish desires. Buddhism was introduced to Japan by monks and scribes from China and Korea around AD 550. The Japanese emperors and their courtiers all decided to follow this new faith.

Temples were made of carved and painted wood. Unlike most other Japanese buildings, they might be several storeys high – a sign that they were special. Often, they contained huge statues of the Buddha – the founder of the Buddhist faith

War and peace

Samurai were elite Japanese fighting men, who served in private armies belonging to great 'daimyo' (warlords and landowners). They were meant to follow a strict code of conduct, called 'bushido' (the way of the warrior), which taught that it was nobler to die fighting than to surrender.

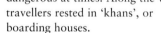

EARLY AMERICA

OVER 300 DIFFERENT NATIVE PEOPLES lived in North America. Each people spoke their own language, followed their own customs and made their own laws. Their lifestyle depended on where they lived. In the icy Arctic regions, Inuit hunters survived by catching walrus and seals. On the grass-covered Great Plains, the Sioux and the Comanche hunted herds of buffalo. The Iroquois of the cold northeastern forests grew corn and hunted deer. In the harsh desert lands of the Great Basin, the Paiute people lived as nomads, hunting rabbits and gathering grubs, seeds and nuts. Native peoples of South and Central America ruled several great empires. The Olmecs, the Maya and the Aztecs ruled in Mexico; the Nazca and the powerful Incas reigned in Peru.

This Aztec knife, made of semi-precious stone, was used for killing victims for sacrifice.

Sacrifices to the gods

Many Meso-American civilizations, such as the Aztecs and the Maya, practised human sacrifice. They killed prisoners captured in war as offerings to the gods of the Sun, the rain and growing plants. They believed that blood from the sacrificed captives would feed the Sun, make the crops grow in the fields and encourage the rains to fall.

Mesa Verde

The Anasazi people of southwestern North America managed to survive in hot, dry, semi-desert lands. They dug irrigation ditches to carry water to their fields and built large communal dwellings, like this one at Mesa Verde (Colorado), in the cool shelter of overhanging cliffs.

CIVILIZATIONS
IN CENTRAL AMERICA:
Olmecs 1200 BC–400 BC
Early Maya 1000 BC–AD 300
Classic Maya AD 300–600
Zapotecs AD 300–900
Mixtecs AD 600–500
Toltecs AD 900–1200
Aztecs AD 1300–1530
IN ANDES MOUNTAINS:
Chavin and Paracas 900 BC–200 BC
Nazca 200 BC–AD 600
Mochica 100 BC–AD 700
Huari AD 600–900
Chimu AD 1000–1450
Incas AD 1420–1540

The Maya people

The Maya lived in Central America, in today's Mexico, Guatemala and Belize. They were most powerful around AD 200–900, though Maya states existed for centuries afterwards, and many people still maintain Maya traditions and languages today. Maya lands were divided into city-states, each ruled by a warrior king who was honoured like a god. Ordinary people grew maize and beans, raised turkeys and kept bees, collected wild plants for food and medicines and hunted for jaguar furs, snake-skins and coloured feathers from tropical birds in the rainforest.

Totem pole

Tall totem poles, carved from the trunk of a single massive tree, were made by Native American peoples who lived in the rain forests along the Northwest American coast. They hunted bears and beaver, and caught salmon in rivers and streams. Each totem pole tells a family's history; it also portrays protective ancestor spirits and gods.

The Inca empire

This little statue of a llama (an animal related to deer) was made by the Inca people who lived in the high Andes mountains of Peru. The Incas relied on llamas to carry heavy loads – they had no wheeled transport – and to provide them with soft, warm hair, which they spun and wove to make clothes. For almost 100 years, from 1438 to 1532, the Incas ruled a mighty empire, including parts of present-day Colombia, Bolivia and Chile. Under Inca rule, everyone in the empire was given work to do – growing food like maize and potatoes, working at crafts, building roads or fighting in the army.

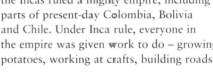

Moveable homes

Native American nomad peoples like the Blackfoot and the Dakota (Sioux) lived in moveable tipis (leather tents) when buffalo-hunting on the Great Plains. This vast area of grassland stretched from the Mississippi River to the Rocky Mountains. After around 1690 they hunted on horseback and used horse-power to move their tipis and follow the buffalo herds.

Maya kings and queens were buried in magnificent pyramid-shaped temples, decorated with carvings and glyphs (picture symbols).

Maya learning

The Maya were the first Americans to invent a system of writing and keep detailed records. They used glyphs (picture symbols) written in codexes (folding books) to describe important events, myths and legends, and the achievements of their kings. The Maya were also expert astronomers and mathematicians, using just three numbers (1, 5 and 0) to perform complicated calculations, and to predict the movements of stars and planets in the night sky. They developed two very accurate calendars, one for farmers and government officials, with 360 days, and another, for priests and religious scholars, containing 260 days.

Religious wars

In 16th- and 17th-century Europe, many people quarrelled about religion. Campaigners, known as 'Protestants', broke away from the Roman Catholic Church to set up new churches of their own. They disagreed with Roman Catholic beliefs, wanted to worship in their own languages, and to decide how their local churches were run. For over 150 years, between around 1500 and 1650, Europe was torn apart by bitter religious wars. They were fought between rulers and peoples who supported the rival Protestant and Roman Catholic branches of the Christian faith.

Exploring the world

In 1419, explorers from Portugal began to sail along the west coast of Africa. It was the start of 200 years of pioneering voyages in ocean-going wind-powered ships. These voyages had dramatic consequences. For the first time, Europeans and peoples from America, India, Southeast Asia and the Far East came into regular contact; sometimes they worked peacefully together, sometimes they fought.

EUROPEAN UPHEAVALS

THE 16TH AND 17TH CENTURIES were a time of rapid change throughout Europe. There were upheavals in religion and government, and in ideas about art and science. New inventions like printing and new information about the rest of the world brought back by explorers raised questions in many people's minds. These were exciting, but disturbing, too. People no longer agreed about how they should live and worship. Some, like the Mayflower settlers, left home to set up new communities in distant lands. Others began to question how their countries should be run. Most rulers held fast to traditional beliefs. But in some countries, terrible poverty and economic problems led to calls for government reform.

IMPORTS

Explorers' pioneer voyages also led to an enormous increase in international trade between 1600 and 1800. Many plants, such as tomatoes and potatoes, and animals from America were introduced to Europe and Asia. In return, Asian plants like sugar and African plants like coffee were carried to America, where they were grown on plantations worked by slaves.

Magellan's crew sailed in a battered second-hand cargo-vessel called the Vittoria. It became the first-ever ship to sail round the world

After Columbus's Atlantic voyage in 149... explorers from Europe pioneered new se... routes and set out to conquer the world

Renaissance

The word 'Renaissance' is used to describe the period from around 1400 to 1600. It was an exciting time when new ideas in art, architecture, science and learning flourished in many European lands. The Renaissance began in Italy. Many of the greatest Renaissance artists, such as Michaelangelo (who painted this chapel ceiling), lived there.

Thirty Years' War

One of the worst religious conflicts was the Thirty Years' War (1618–48), between Austria and Spain (Catholics) and some German states, Denmark and Sweden (Protestants). Spain and Austria ruled parts of Germany, and wanted to ban the Protestant faith from their lands. The war caused dreadful damage and terrible loss of life. No one could 'win', but when it ended, the German states were given freedom to worship as they chose.

Civil War

King Charles I of England believed he had a divine (God-given) right to rule. Many of his people did not agree, and this led to a civil war (1642–8). Parliament won, and King Charles was executed. England became a republic, and an army commander, called Oliver Cromwell, ruled England as 'Lord Protector'. He, in turn, was replaced by the King's son, who ruled as Charles II.

PUMPKIN SOUP

Pumpkins were one of the vegetables that Native American people helped the Mayflower settlers grow after they landed on the eastern coast of North America. Today, American people eat pumpkins on Thanksgiving Day (the last Thursday in November), a national holiday held each year to remember a special meal cooked by the settlers in 1621. The settlers wanted to give thanks to God for a plentiful harvest which provided them with stocks of food to last through the coming winter. To make a nourishing pumpkin soup, you will need: 500 g pumpkin flesh, 1 large onion, 2 medium potatoes, 2 large carrots, 2 sticks celery, 1 small red pepper. Chop all the vegetables and cook very gently in oil. Add 500 ml water and simmer until soft. Whizz the vegetables in a blender until they make a pulp. Add enough milk to make a thickish soup. Heat through, stirring all the while. Serve with bread and cheese.

Pilgrims

In 1620, a group of 102 men, women and children with strong Christian beliefs decided to leave England for far-away America, where they could set up a new community, run their own church, and make their own laws, based on the Bible. They sailed in a cramped, leaky ship called the Mayflower, and endured a long, stormy voyage across the Atlantic Ocean. They landed (in Massachussetts) as a bitter winter began. Over half of them died; the rest only survived because friendly Native American people gave them food and showed them how to grow American crops like pumpkins and maize. The next year, 1621, they managed to gather a plentiful harvest which gave them food for the winter and made them safe.

Ever since 1799, when an American writer invented the name, the religious pioneers who sailed in the Mayflower have been called the 'Pilgrims' – people who made a long, dangerous journey because of their faith

PETER THE GREAT

Peter the Great became Tsar (emperor) of Russia in 1689, when he was 17 years old. He had ambitious plans to modernize Russia. He introduced new skills and techniques in navigation and shipbuilding, copied from western Europe. He encouraged Russian exploration into Siberia, and founded a new capital city, called St Petersburg, on the Baltic Sea coast. But his rough, brutal behaviour made him very unpopular. He died in 1725.

EARLY AFRICA

FOR OVER 1,000 YEARS, rich, powerful kingdoms flourished in many parts of Africa. They mostly owed their wealth to trade. African workers discovered how to mine precious metals, such as gold and copper, and also emeralds and other precious stones. Products from magnificent African animals, such as elephant ivory and rhinoceros horn, were also highly prized in many other lands. The African rulers who controlled this trade used their wealth to pay for many fine buildings and works of art, and to support strong, well-trained armies to defend their lands. Many peoples in Africa followed ancient traditional religions, but, after around AD 800, kingdoms in North and West Africa became converted to Islam.

This Nok terracotta sculpture shows a man with a decorated hairstyle. He may be a priest or a king.

The Nok

The Nok people lived beside the mighty Niger River in West Africa. They were at their most powerful between around 800 BC and AD 200. The Nok were farmers, metalworkers and potters, who made huge, sometimes lifesize, figures out of terracotta (baked clay). These statues portray people (left), as well as wild and domesticated animals. They were probably made for religious purposes.

Between 1200 and 1300, ten Christian churches were cut out of the solid rock in the kingdom of Ethiopia, Northeast Africa. The were excavated by workmen using only simple mallets and chisels. It was an astonishing feat of construction. Most of the churches were shaped like crosses, th holy symbol of the Christian faith. They soon became great centres of pilgrimage.

Links with other lands

Africa is a vast continent, and travel overland from north to south or east to west was almost impossible at most times in the past. As a result, many regions of Africa were linked more closely to other countries and continents than they were to distant African lands. Most of these links were formed by sea travel. Ethiopians travelled to Arabia and Central Asia across the Red Sea, East African kingdoms bordered the Indian Ocean, and North African nations made contact with countries in Europe and the Middle East by sailing across the Mediterranean Sea.

The Kingdom of Axum

The kingdom of Axum, in Ethiopia, traded with Arabia, India an the Mediterranean lands. It exported many precious goods, including gold, ivory, precious stones, live monkeys, tortoiseshell and spices. Axum was ruled by all-powerful 'Kings of Kings', wh paid for many wonderful buildings, including tall stone pillars an churches hewn from rocks. Axum was one of the first countries t become Christian, around AD 300.

Trade and wealth

Between around AD 700 and 1600, merchants from the rich Muslim lands of North Africa led camel-trains laden with salt on long journeys across the Sahara to trade with people living in the powerful West African kingdoms of Mali, Ghana and Songhay. In return, they carried back cargoes of gold, leather and slaves. West African rulers used this wealth from trade to build fine palaces, mosques, schools and universities in cities on the edge of the desert, such as Jenne and Timbuktu.

The Shona

The fortress-city of Great Zimbabwe was built for the Shona kings of East Africa, who ruled a powerful empire from around 1200 to 1600. Within its strong stone walls, Great Zimbabwe contained houses, palaces and tall stone towers for storing grain. The Shona people were farmers, who raised herds of cattle and planted crops of millet. They also mined iron, gold and copper, and hunted elephants for ivory. They traded all these goods at East African coastal ports. There, they met Arab merchants, who sailed to Africa across the Indian Ocean with precious cargoes of glass and perfumes from Arabia, jewels from India, and silks and porcelain from China.

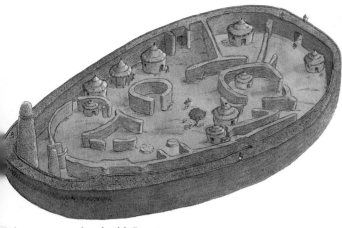

The stones used to build Great Zimbabwe were carefully shaped and fitted by hand. No mortar was used to hold them together.

North Africa

Rich, powerful dynasties ruled the fertile lands along the coast of North Africa (in present-day Morocco, Algeria and Tunisia). They built splendid cities, with fine palaces, libraries and mosques, and busy markets. Further inland, clans of nomad Berber people, called the Tuareg, managed to survive in the desert. They lived as nomadic herdsmen, keeping camels, sheep and goats and travelling across the desert from oasis to oasis in search of water.

Camels were the only animals that could survive long enough without food and water to make exhausting journeys across the hot, dry desert, laden with valuable goods to sell. Their wide, flat feet did not sink into the desert sand, and they could store enough nourishment in their humps to last for about 10 days. Although camels were often smelly, stubborn and bad-tempered, they were highly prized.

Market towns grew up at oases along the edge of the Sahara desert, where people and animals had access to reliable water supplies.

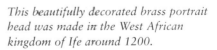

This beautifully decorated brass portrait head was made in the West African kingdom of Ife around 1200.

Artists and metalworkers

African artists were skilled at many crafts, especially stonework and metalwork. Between around 1200 and 1900, metalworkers living in the rainforest kingdoms of Ife and Benin (part of present-day Nigeria) made beautiful portrait statues and plaques (square picture-panels) of shiny golden metals called brass and bronze. The plaques were used to decorate the royal palace in Benin city; the portrait statues were placed on royal family altars to honour dead ancestors.

INDIA

OVER THE CENTURIES, the vast sub-continent of India has been home to many great civilizations. Some of the world's first cities were built by farming peoples who lived in the Indus Valley, in present-day India and Pakistan. They disappeared around 1500 BC, perhaps because their land was over-used, or because they were attacked by Indo-Aryan invaders. The Indo-Aryans introduced a new religion, called Hinduism. For years, India was divided into many small Hindu kingdoms, but by 322 BC, kings belonging to the Mauryan ruling family had conquered a large empire. The next great Indian empire was ruled by the Hindu Gupta dynasty, which came to power in AD 320. They encouraged science, learning and the arts. Hindu kings reigned in southern India for almost the next 1500 years, though they were often threatened by invaders, and sometimes fought among themselves.

The Muslims

In 1175, the first Muslim rulers came to power in India. They ruled kingdoms in the north and the west. Then, in 1526, India was invaded by Muslim warriors descended from the Mongol peoples of Central Asia. They became known as the 'Mughals', and, by 1600, had conquered most of India. The Mughals ruled India for more than three centuries. The first Mughal emperors were strong and warlike; they aimed to create a brilliant civilization by encouraging all that was best in India, regardless of social background, religion or race. But after around 1700, Mughal emperors gradually lost power. The last Mughal emperor was forced to give up his throne when the British government took control in 1858.

The picture shows the first Mughal emperor, Babur, who ruled from 1526 to 1530. He was a famous collector of books and paintings.

Court painters

The Mughal emperors encouraged the finest artists from India and the neighbouring lands to come and work at their courts. Mughal painters created exquisite miniature paintings in brilliant jewel-like colours. Some were portraits and scenes of royal life at court; others were carefully observed studies of plants and animals.

Cities of the Indus Valley

Around 40,000 people lived in Mohenjo-Daro and Harappa, the two largest cities in the Indus Valley, between 2500 and 1500 BC. Both cities were well planned, with wide streets, spacious houses, running water and drains. In the centre of each city was a huge fortress, built on an artificial mound, where the rulers lived. This striking stone statue (right) was made around 2000 BC, in Mohenjo-Daro. It probably portrays a priest-king.

The way of peace

Hindu King Ashoka ruled the Mauryan empire in India from 272 to 231 BC. He began life as a warrior, but became sickened by the violence of battle. He turned to Buddhism, seeking understanding by peaceful means. He paid for Buddhist holy laws to be carved on rocks throughout India, and for many Buddhist monuments. This decorated gateway marks the entrance to the Great Stupa at Sanchi, a dome-shaped holy site.

Trade with the West

The first European ship to sail to India reached the Malabar (western) coast in 1498. After that, European merchants made regular voyages to India. They purchased valuable Indian spices, cotton cloth, drugs and dyestuffs to sell in Europe. In 1600, a group of leading British merchants set up the East India Company, to organize and protect long-distance trade. It became immensely rich and powerful, and had its own private army.

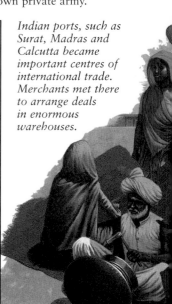

Indian ports, such as Surat, Madras and Calcutta became important centres of international trade. Merchants met there to arrange deals in enormous warehouses.

TIMELINE

- 2500–1500 BC Indus Valley civilization.
- 1500 BC Hindu civilization begins.
- 500 BC Buddhist faith develops.
- 330 BC Alexander the Great brings Greek ideas to India.
- AD 50 Kushan empire powerful.
- AD 320 Gupta dynasty powerful.
- AD 750 Three Empires era.
- 1175 First Muslim empires.
- 1526 Mughals conquer India.
- 1858 India becomes part of British Empire.
- 1947 India becomes independent; new nation of Pakistan created.

Magnificent Mughal architecture

Many people think that the Taj Mahal (above), near Agra, in India, is one of the most beautiful buildings in the world. It is made of gleaming white marble, decorated with delicate flower patterns made of semi-precious stones. It was built by Mughal emperor Shah Jahan (ruled 1627–1658) as a tomb for his wife, Mumtaz Mahal. She died giving birth to their fourteenth child.

The British in India

Britain took control of India after Indian soldiers working for the British East India Company rebelled in 1857. In the following years, many British government officials, doctors, engineers, tea-planters and estate managers went to live and work in India. Often, their families accompanied them. The British community in India lived sheltered, privileged lives, looked after by Indian servants. They became known as the 'British Raj' (ruling class).

Members of the British Raj continued to follow an upper-class British lifestyle in India.

TIPU SULTAN

Tipu's name meant 'Tiger'. He gave orders for this life-size model of a tiger killing an Englishman to be made for one of his palaces.

Hindu Tipu Sultan was ruler of the South Indian state of Mysore from 1782 to 1799. Like many other Indian rulers, he fought against the British, who were trying to take control of India. Tipu lost half his kingdom after invading a nearby state which was protected by Britain. He was killed fighting British soldiers who were besieging his lands.

European merchant ships were built with huge wide hulls, to carry the maximum amount of cargo. Because of the strong monsoon winds blowing across the Indian Ocean, they could make the long voyage from England to Europe only once or twice a year.

PACIFIC LANDS

THE PACIFIC OCEAN is the largest body of water on earth. It covers an astonishing 180 million square kilometres. For thousands of years, the islands of the Pacific were remote from the rest of the world, cut off by wild waves and stormy seas. But the people living there – the Aboriginals, Polynesians and Maoris – developed unique and well-adapted civilizations. They found ways of surviving in environments that were often difficult and even hostile. The Aboriginals of Australia lived as hunters and gatherers, eating animals, insects and grubs they had caught, and many wild roots, berries and seeds. The Polynesians and Maoris (Polynesian settlers in New Zealand) lived by fishing and farming. In warm Pacific islands, close to the Equator, they grew yams, bananas, breadfruit and coconuts, and kept pigs, dogs and chickens. In colder New Zealand, they planted sweet potatoes, gathered seaweed and shellfish, and caught whales, seals and fish from the seas around their islands.

Maori forts

Groups of Maori settlers in New Zealand often fought against each other. To protect their families, they built their villages on well-defended hilltop sites and surrounded them with walls made of strong wooden poles. The Maoris were expert woodworkers, and decorated their most important buildings with wood-carvings in elaborate swirling designs.

The Aboriginals

The Aboriginal people settled in Australia over 50,000 years ago. With great skill, they discovered how to live in Australia's harsh natural environments – coastal swamps, rainforests and deserts. They dug shallow wells to find underground water, and used tools such as digging sticks (for finding grubs and tubers underground) and grinding stones (for crushing seeds and grains). They made cloaks and tents from skins and furs, spun thread from pounded tree bark, and hollowed out tree-trunks to make canoes.

Australian Aboriginal hunters used spears and throwing sticks, called boomerangs, to hunt emu and kangaroo. They also used nets and traps to catch fish and birds

Easter Island

Some time between AD 1100 and 1450, the people who lived on remote Easter Island carved 600 strange stone heads almost 10 metres tall. The statues probably represented ancestors, gods or kings. But because the entire population of Easter Island died out soon after 1500, no one knows for sure! Historians also do not know why Easter Island became deserted. Possibly, an environmental disaster struck after the inhabitants had cut down all the trees for building and firewood.

Easter Islanders arranged their huge statues in rows, to make a very impressive monument, thought to have magical power

MAKE A 'SKELETON' PICTURE

For many thousands of years, the Aboriginal people created paintings on cave walls in an amazing 'skeleton' style. Their artwork showed the bones and inner organs of different wild creatures, as well as the outer skins. They believed this way of painting helped them show the life-force and spirit of the animals they saw all around.

To make a skeleton picture, draw the outline of your animal on white paper. Trace the outline on to dark-coloured paper. Cut out the outline, then glue it on to the white paper. Cut out the shapes of bones, heart, lungs etc. in dark paper. Glue them on to the white paper. Decorate with paint or felt-tips.

IMPORTS

For hundreds of years, merchants from India, Europe and the Middle East sailed to the rich Spice Islands (present-day Indonesia) to purchase sweet-smelling spices and medicinal herbs. In the 16th century, they began to venture beyond the Spice Islands and into the Pacific Ocean. The first European sailors sighted Australia in 1642.

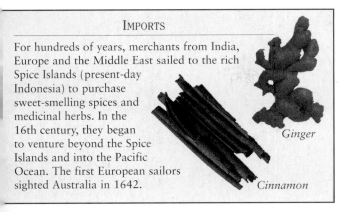

Ginger

Cinnamon

All ships travelling to the Spice Islands, or to China and Australia, had to pass through the narrow Malacca Straits. Rich trading towns grew up here and on the nearby islands, selling silks, spices and gems. After around 1500, they were conquered and ruled by European nations

Trading routes from Europe to the Spice Islands. After around 1850, many Chinese sailors, shopkeepers and farm labourers followed the Europeans to this area

The Maoris

The Maori people were very skilful sailors. The first Maori settlers made the long voyage across the Pacific to New Zealand from other Polynesian islands in wooden outrigger canoes. The largest ocean-going canoes might be over 30 metres long. They could carry up to 500 men, women and children, plus their animals, farm tools and seeds. They were pushed through the water by wooden paddles, or sometimes fitted with big triangular sails made of palm-leaf matting. Smaller canoes were also used by Maori fishermen, or by fierce Maori warriors on raids.

Australian settlers

It took nine months for sailing ships to travel from Europe to Australia. That was one of the main reasons why, in 1788, the British government decided to send convicted criminals there. Once in Australia, there was little chance that they would ever return to cause trouble! But Australia was a vast, exciting country which offered many opportunites, and before long the convict settlers were joined by willing migrants from Europe. Over 342,000 arrived between 1852 and 1861, some of the peak years for migration. Settlers hoped to make their fortunes as farmers, sheep-ranchers or gold-diggers.

AMERICA

ON 4 JULY 1776, a new nation was born – the United States of America. It consisted of only 13 states. They declared independence from Britain, which had ruled them as colonies for over 150 years. During the 19th century, the USA grew rapidly as more states joined the Union. Some were purchased from other European powers; some were conquered in wars. Some were given away in peace treaties, and others were simply taken over by pioneer farmers, who settled on uncultivated lands. American industry and business grew rapidly after oil, coal and steel were discovered in the northwest, and valuable gold in California. Millions of migrants arrived from Europe, hoping to make their fortunes in the 'land of the free'. By 1900, the USA was so successful that it was the richest country in the world.

Wagon train

From around 1850, many families left Europe and East Asia to make a new life in America. Some settled in cities along the east coast, others trekked westwards to reach the Great Plains, the Rocky Mountains and California. Settlers travelled in 'trains' of covered wagons, pulled by oxen or horses. During the long and dangerous journey, many died from hunger, thirst and disease, or in fights with Native Americans. Life in new western ranches, farms and mining settlements could be lonely and very hard.

The settlers and the Native Americans

When the first European settlers arrived in the 1540s, North America was home to around 300 different Native peoples. Sometimes, Native Americans and European settlers arranged to lived peacefully, side by side. They traded together, and occasionally helped one another with local information and offers of food. But more often, there were quarrels between them, because the European settlers felt they had a God-given right to take over Native peoples' lands. As more and more settlers arrived in America from Europe and Asia, these quarrels turned into war. The Native peoples fought bravely, but settler troops and settlers had bigger, better weapons, and drove most Native Americans from their homes. The last battle to defend Native peoples' land was fought in 1890 at Wounded Knee, South Dakota.

A replica of the Mayflower

Early migrants

The first Europeans to settle in America sailed there in ships like the Mayflower (a replica is shown right). In the 1540s, the Spanish settled in present-day Florida and California. In the 1580s, the French and English settled in present-day Virginia.

Railroad

Railways were vitally important in the new United States of America. By 1890, over 260,000 kilometres of track had been laid. They linked northern industrial cities and east-coast ports with the vast ranches and farmlands of the west and south. Building the railways was a great engineering achievement; lines had to be laid across mountains, deserts and swamps. In 1869, the first transcontinental railway line was completed. At a special ceremony the final sections of rail were joined together with a golden nail (left).

Civil war soldiers

Northern (Unionist) soldier

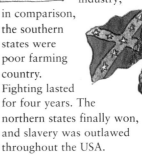

From 1861 to 1865, the northern and southern states of the USA fought a bitter civil war. The two sides quarrelled over slavery. They also had different views about law-making, politics and trade.

The northern states were growing rich by developing industry; in comparison, the southern states were poor farming country. Fighting lasted for four years. The northern states finally won, and slavery was outlawed throughout the USA.

Southern (Confederate) soldier

GEORGE WASHINGTON

Britain, France, Spain and Portugal claimed the right to rule the lands where Europeans had settled in North and South America. They also claimed the right to collect taxes there. The settlers thought both these claims were very unfair. In 1776, a group of 13 British colonies in North America decided to break away from British rule. The British sent soldiers to fight against the rebels, but were defeated in 1783. General George Washington (1732–99) led the American colonists in this War of Independence. In 1789, he became the first president of the USA.

Covered wagons were given the romantic name 'prairie schooners', because their canvas roofs, which billowed and flapped in the wind, reminded people of graceful sailing ships

Slavery

Since around 1500, black men, women and children from Africa were shipped to the Caribbean and to neighbouring regions of North and South America. They were sold to owners of plantations, huge estates where sugar and cotton were grown in very large quantities to be shipped back to the fast-growing towns and cities in Europe. The slaves had no freedom and no rights. They were often very cruelly treated, especially if they tried to run away. In 1807, Britain banned all her citizens from taking part in the slave trade anywhere in the world, and tried to encourage other European nations to ban slavery in the lands they ruled. But in the USA, slavery was not finally abolished until 1865.

INDUSTRIAL EUROPE

THE INDUSTRIAL REVOLUTION began around 1770 and lasted for almost 100 years. It was a time of rapid change in the way things were made. Engineers invented big machines to mass-produce goods quickly and cheaply in factories. At first, these new machines were only designed for spinning thread and weaving cloth, but they were soon used for making all kinds of useful things, such as shoes, paper, pottery and metal tools. They were also used to produce large quantities of strong materials for construction, ship-building and weapons production, such as bricks, iron and steel. The Industrial Revolution also brought many changes to the way people lived. Men, women and children working in huge factories replaced old-fashioned craftworkers, who used to make things at home, slowly and carefully by hand.

Railways

Railways helped the Industrial Revolution by carrying goods made in factories to shops and markets far away. They also carried fresh food from the countryside to feed families who worked in factory towns. The world's first passenger railway was opened by British inventor George Stephenson in 1825. Soon, railways were built in many parts of Europe.

Farm machinery

After around 1700, many people in Europe and America became fascinated by science. Farmers and estate-owners experimented with new ways of breeding animals and sowing crops. Alongside industrial scientists, they began to invent new machines to make farming quicker and more profitable. The seed drill (above) made a hole and planted a seed in one go.

Mines

The owners of mines often employed children to work for them. They were very useful for crawling down tight tunnels, or squeezing in between huge machines. Many working children were killed in accidents with machinery, or died from illnesses caused by breathing coal dust, cotton fibres or chemical fumes.

IMPORTED EMPIRE PRODUCE

Until the late 1800s, large parts of Africa, East Asia and Australia were cut off from the rest of the world. But, once European explorers had travelled across them, European nations hurried to seize rich, distant lands and claim them as part of their empires. Local people were not consulted. They found their lands ruled as colonies by far-away countries. European government officials, miners, ranchers, and farmers moved to live there and began to grow rich, exporting goods such as coffee beans back to their homelands.

Industrial towns

The first factories were built close to supplies of coal, iron-ore and water. These were necessary for making big new machines and providing power to run them. Often, they were found in the countryside, far away from existing towns. So, to provide housing for industrial workers, new towns were built next to the factories. Conditions there were often grim.

Schools

In the early years of the Industrial Revolution, many children were forced to work long hours in dangerous conditions in factories and mines. But after around 1830, governments passed laws to protect child workers, and charities set up many more 'ragged' schools, where factory children could study after work and at weekends. By the 1870s, European governments began to set up state-funded schools, where pupils under 12 received free, compulsory education. By around 1900, most factory workers could read and write.

KARL MARX

Karl Marx (1818–1883) was a German writer living in London. In 1848, he published a book called 'The Communist Manifesto'. In it, he demanded political freedom and better pay and working conditions for ordinary people. He called on workers to claim their rights: 'Workers of the world, unite! You have nothing to lose but your chains!'

After around 1800, thousands of poor, hungry, unemployed men and women migrated from the countryside to live in fast-growing factory towns. They hoped to find regular work and better pay. Wages in factories were better than those on farms, but working conditions in factories were often dirty and dangerous, and houses in factory towns were noisy, crowded and full of disease.

WARS & REVOLUTIONS

MORE THAN ANY OTHER TIME in history, the early 20th century was an age of wars and revolutions. In South Africa, from 1899 to 1902, Boer farmers (descended from Dutch settlers) rebelled against British colonial rule. In the Far East, a war broke out between Russia and Japan in 1904. Both wanted to be the strongest power in East Asia. The last Chinese emperor was forced to give up power by rebels who wanted a new, republican form of government which would give more power to ordinary people. In Europe, rival nations fought a devastating war from 1914 to 1918, shattering old beliefs about how societies should be run. In Russia, Communist revolutionaries overthrew the government in 1917. Then, from 1924 to 1939, brutal Communist dictator Stalin reorganized the country in a series of Five Year Plans.

The outbreak of the 1914–18 war was marked by massive troop movements, as British and French armies hurried to stop the Germans reaching the Channel coast. Both sides met face to face in Belgium and northern France. They dug lines of trenches (deep, narrow holes in the ground) to shelter their troops from cannon and machine-gun fire. The opposing armies remained in their trenches, gaining – or losing – very little territory, for the next four years

Women munitions workers

While men were away fighting during World War I, women took over many of their jobs. These included heavy, dirty tasks, such as making weapons and driving lorries, that people had considered unsuitable for women until then. Women also served as volunteer nurses, sometimes in dangerous war-zones.

World War I

By 1900, the strongest European nations – Britain, Germany and France – were jealous of each other's industrial wealth, and envied each other's colonies overseas. They also quarrelled over the future of Serbia and other Balkan states. In 1914, war broke out between them. Germany, Austria–Hungary and Turkey fought against Britain, Russia and France. Other European nations, plus the USA, Canada, Australia, New Zealand and South Africa, soon joined in. Fighting lasted until 1918, when Germany surrendered.

Russian Revolution

Many Russians hated their government, headed by Tsar Nicholas II. They thought him cruel, unfair and foolish. In 1917, he was overthrown by protesters called Bolsheviks. They were members of the Communist Party, led by a writer called Lenin. The Bolsheviks executed the Tsar and his family and took land away from rich nobles. After three years' civil war, the Communists controlled all Russia. They gave it a new name – the USSR (Union of Soviet Socialist Republics).

CHAIRMAN MAO

The last Chinese emperor was forced out of power in 1912. After that, there were many quarrels between rivals for the Chinese government. From 1916 to 1938 there were civil wars. In 1948, the Communists took control of China, led by Mao Zhedong (1893 – 1976). He made ambitious plans to modernize China. Today, Mao is often criticized, because his plans caused hardship for many Chinese people.

Irish nationalists confront British soldiers during the Easter Rising of 1916.

MAKE FLANDERS POPPIES

In many countries, red poppies have become a symbol of remembrance. They honour the millions of young soldiers who died in Flanders (present-day Belgium) in the 1914–18 war. To make Flanders poppies, cut thin strips of black paper about 10 x 2.5 cm. Make fringes along one long edge. Wind each strip round one end of a cork; fasten with sticky tape. Wrap a length of wire in green sticky tape, leaving 2.5 cm bare at one end. Push bare end of wire into cork. Cut 6 petals (about 10 x 10 cm) out of red paper. Use sticky tape to fasten petals to cork.

Easter Rising

Ireland had been ruled by Britain for centuries. In 1912, the British government said it would let Ireland have 'Home Rule' – its own parliament for making decisions about purely Irish affairs. But the majority of people living in the north of Ireland did not want to break away from mainland Britain; in the south, the majority wanted complete independence. At Easter 1916, about 1600 anti-British rebels seized important buildings in Dublin, and declared an Irish Republic. They were defeated by the British, and their leaders were shot. There were many more years of fighting and negotiations before the southern part of Ireland became an independent nation in 1937.

Many poor Spanish farmers supported the Republicans during the Civil War. They became guerrillas, hiding in wild countryside to attack Fascist soldiers, and creeping out at night to raid Fascist camps and weapons stores

Spanish Civil War

In 1936, civil war broke out in Spain. It was fought between Republicans (who wanted the people to have the right to choose the government) and Fascists (who supported a dictator who would keep citizens firmly under control). Young people from all over Europe travelled to Spain to fight for the Republicans, but many European governments supported the Fascists. The Fascist leader, General Franco, became ruler of Spain in 1939, and stayed in power until 1975. The Spanish Civil War saw the first-ever bombing raid from the air on unarmed civilians, at the Republican town of Guernica in 1938.

FAST-CHANGING WORLD

SINCE THE BEGINNING of the twentieth century, the world has changed more quickly than ever before. European empires in Africa and Asia have disappeared, and new independent nations have taken their place. New scientific knowledge has allowed people to reach the Moon and to find out more about the secrets of life on Earth. New medical discoveries have saved millions of lives. Fast cars and planes make it easy to travel long distances; telephones and televisions send information rapidly all round the world. But all this progress has brought new problems, such as overcrowding and pollution. Sadly, there is still a vast gap in living standards between rich and poor people. And many wars are still being fought.

World War II

In 1939, Hitler (see below) sent armies to invade Czechoslovakia and Poland; Britain, France and Russia decided to help the Czech and Polish people defend their lands. This marked the beginning of World War II. Italy and Japan allied with Hitler; Canada, Australia, New Zealand, South Africa and the USA joined Britain to fight against him. The war soon spread to British colonies in the Far East, and to China and the islands of the Pacific Ocean. Fighting continued until 1945. During the whole course of the war, over 15 million troops and at least 20 million civilians were killed.

From riches to rags

'Stocks' are shares of businesses. They can be bought and sold, and are often very valuable. In a 'crash', the value of stocks falls rapidly; they can become almost worthless. In 1929, the US stock market 'crashed'. Unemployment and poverty followed, in Europe as well as America. Charities ran soup-kitchens, and governments offered welfare payments, but throughout the 1930s many families went cold and hungry.

Civilians under attack

The first powered flight took place in 1903. After that, engineers began to design many new and better aircraft. Because of these planes, World War II was the first in which civilians faced mass attacks from the air. Whole cities were flattened by bomb-blasts, or destroyed in 'firestorms'. Mass bombings were designed to cause panic and fear among ordinary people, and to force their leaders to surrender. But ordinary people on both sides of the war, as well as first-aid workers and fire-fighters, showed enormous courage. During raids, they hid in underground bomb-shelters – or under their kitchen tables. When the danger was past, they lived as best they could among the ruins.

HITLER

Austrian-born Adolf Hitler (1889-1945) became Chancellor (head) of the German government in 1933. He was leader of the extreme right-wing Nazi political party and had two aims: to make Germany the strongest nation in the world, and to get rid of all Jewish people and other minority groups. In 1934 he began to persecute all the Jews in Germany. They had to give up their jobs and businesses and wear special badges on their clothes. Later, he sent them to concentration camps (appalling prisons) where about 6 million died. When Germany was defeated in 1945, Hitler killed himself to avoid being captured and put on trial for his war crimes.

GANDHI

Mohandas Gandhi (1869–1948) devoted his life to ending British rule in India. He was a deeply religious man, who followed the Hindu faith, and a shrewd and intelligent politician. He won the support of millions of ordinary people in India, and led them on non-violent protest marches. After over 20 years of these campaigns, India finally became independent in 1947. Gandhi was shot dead the next year, by an Indian who disapproved of his support for religious toleration. He was given the name 'Mahatma' (Great Soul).

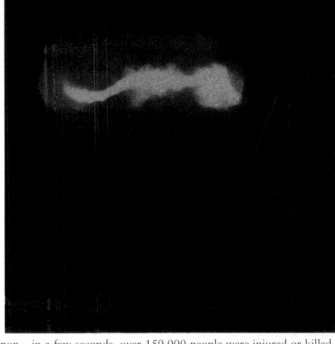

Atom bomb

The first atomic bomb exploded over the city of Hiroshima, in Japan, on 6 August 1945. It was dropped by the USA. The world had never seen such a terrible weapon – in a few seconds, over 150,000 people were injured or killed. After a second atomic bomb was dropped soon afterwards, on the port of Nagasaki, Japan surrendered. This led to the end of World War II.

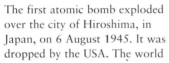

Fall of the Berlin Wall

After 1945 a dangerous tension developed between the capitalist USA and communist USSR. This was the 'Cold War'. Nations all round the world took sides. In 1961, a wall was built through Berlin in Germany to divide capitalist Western Europe from the communist East. The wall came down in 1989, when the communists lost control of the USSR, and the Cold War ended.

Space exploration

During the 1950s and 1960s, the USA and the USSR made astonishing advances in rocket technology and space exploration. In 1957, the USSR launched the first space satellite, and in 1961, sent the first person into space. The USA landed the first person on the Moon. American astronaut Neil Armstrong took his historic step on to the Moon's surface on 20 July 1969.

Russia's Mir space station

Computers and communications

The world's first computers were invented for army use during World War II. They were huge (the size of rooms) and very slow. Today, computers fly aircraft, control factories, and store vast amounts of data.

When linked by telephones to the Internet, they allow people all round the world to communicate with each other and share information.

During the 1990s more people than ever owned PCs (personal computers).

THE SPACE RACE

1957 First satellite in space (USSR).

1961 First man in space (USSR).

1969 First landing on the Moon (USA).

1981 First Space Shuttle flight (USA).

1986 First Mir Space Station (USSR).

HISTORY: QUESTIONS AND ANSWERS

● Where were the first farms?

In the Middle East. Around 9000 BC, people there began to clear little plots of land, scatter seeds of wild grain on the ground, and harvest it when it was ripe.

● Why did the Egyptians build pyramids?

The ancient Egyptians believed that peoples' spirits could only survive after death if their bodies were carefully preserved. So they turned the bodies into mummies, and buried them in a dry place. Wealthy people, like pharaohs (kings) could afford magnificent tombs. These were often pyramid-shaped, like the life-giving rays of the sun.

● When were the first Olympic Games?

No one knows for sure. The Ancient Greeks believed that the first Olympic Games was held in 776 BC, but sports festivals may have been held at the Greek village of Olympia for hundreds of years before that.

● Who lived in the world's first high-rise buildings?

Citizens of Rome, and the nearby port of Ostia. They lived in 'insulae' – big blocks of flats.

● Did the Vikings reach America?

Yes, around AD 1000. A bold Viking adventurer, named Lief Ericsson, sailed westward from Greenland until he reached 'Vinland' (present-day Newfoundland). He built a farmstead there, but quarelled with the local people, and returned home.

● What was the Black Death?

A terrible disease that spread throughout Asia, North Africa, Europe and the Middle East in the 1340s and 1350s. It was caused by germs, spread by fleas that lived on rats. Millions of people died.

● Who lived in a circular city?

The citizens of Baghdad, a splendid city in Iraq, founded by Muslim ruler Caliph al Mansur in AD 762. His royal palace and a great mosque stood at the centre of the city, surrounded by parks and gardens. Government office and army barracks were nearby. There were mosques, hospitals, schools, libraries, markets, fountains and gardens. Craftworkers and all kinds of traders lived on the outer rim of the city.

● Where did the Silk Road run?

From rich cities in China, across the Gobi Desert, to the shores of the Black Sea. Merchants from many lands travelled along this route to buy and sell valuable goods, such as silk and porcelain.

● Who wrote in pictures?

Maya and Aztec scribes who lived in Mexico and the nearby lands. The Maya invented the first writing in America, using a system of picture-writing called glyphs.

● Which kings built strong stone towers?

The Shona kings of south-east Africa, who built the walled city of Zimbabwe around 1400. They ruled a rich empire based on cattle-farming, metal-working and trade.

● Which Indian king changed his mind?

King Ashoka, who came to power in India around 227 BC. He was a famous warrior, but became sickened by the violence of battle, and devoted his life to peace.

● Who were the first people to reach New Zealand?

The Maoris, who sailed in big canoes from Polynesian islands in the Pacific Ocean to settle in New Zealand around AD 800.

● Which side won the American Civil War?

The Unionists, from the northern states, who wanted to ban slavery. They defeated the Confederates, from the southern states, in 1865.

● How many soldiers took part in World War I?

About 65 million. Over 10 million were killed and 20 million were injured.

● When did the world's first atom bomb drop?

On 6 August 1945. It was dropped by planes from the USA on the Japanese city of Hiroshima.

● Who led India to independence?

Peaceful protester Mohandas (Mahatma) Gandhi (1869–1948).

WORLD ATLAS

SCANDINAVIA AND FINLAND

FACT BOX

◆ **Denmark**
Area: 43,075 sq km
Population: 5,300,000
Capital: Copenhagen
Official language: Danish **Currency:** Danish krone

◆ **Sweden**
Area: 449,790 sq km
Population: 8,000,000
Capital: Stockholm
Official language: Swedish **Currency:** Krona

◆ **Norway**
Area: 323,895 sq km
Population: 4,400,000
Capital: Oslo
Official language: Norwegian **Currency:** Norwegian krone

◆ **Finland**
Area: 337,030 sq km
Population: 5,100,000
Capital: Helsinki
Official language: Finnish **Currency:** Markka

TWO PENINSULAS extend from northwestern Europe, shaped rather like the claws of a crab. The southern peninsula, extending from Germany, is called Jutland.

Together with a chain of islands which includes Fyn, Sjælland, and Lolland, Jutland makes up the nation of **Denmark**. Most of Denmark is flat and low-lying, a country of green farmland. It exports bacon and dairy products.

Across the windy channels of Skagerrak and Kattegat, between the North and Baltic Seas, lies the long northern peninsula occupied by **Sweden** and **Norway**. This is a land shaped by movements of ice in prehistoric times. Glaciers carved out the deep sea inlets called fjords along its ragged western coast. Ranges of mountains run down the peninsula like a backbone. They descend to a land of forests, bogs and thousands of lakes.

Summers can be warm, but winters are bitterly cold, with heavy snow. Norway lives by fishing and its North Sea rigs make it Western Europe's largest producer of oil and natural gas. Sweden is a major exporter of timber, paper, wooden furniture and motor vehicles.

The three nations of Denmark, Sweden and Norway form the region of Scandinavia. It was from here that the seafarers known as Vikings set out about 1,200 years ago. The Vikings raided and settled the coasts of Western Europe, traded in Russia and the Middle East, settled Iceland and Greenland and even reached North America. Today's Danes, Swedes and Norwegians are all closely related, as are the Germanic languages that they speak.

The Arctic lands of northern Scandinavia are home to the Saami (or Lapps), a people who traditionally lived by herding reindeer. Their neighbours are the Finns and the Russians.

Finland is a land of lakes, with coasts on the Gulfs of Bothnia and Finland. Its forests make it a leading producer

FINLAND

ICELAND

RUSSIA

ICELAND

Grimsey
Raufarhöfn
Kópasker
Húsavík
Vopnafjörður
Seyðisfjörður
Neskaupstadur
Búðir
Djúpivogur
Höfn
Ísafjörður
Þingeyri
Ólafsfjörður
Akureyri
Eskifjörður
Vatneyri
Hólmavík
Saudárkrókur
Blanda
Myvatn
Jökulsá á Fjöllum
VATNAJÖKULL
▲ Hvannadalshnúkur 2,119m
Skjálfandafljót
HOFSJÖKULL
Stykkishólmur
Blönduós
Hvítá
Þjórsá
Þórisvatn
Borgarnes
LANGJÖKULL
Hvítá
▲ Hekla 1,491m
Akranes
Þingvallavatn
MYRDALSJÖKULL
Vík
Ólafsvík
■ **Reykjavík**
Stokkseyri
Heimaey
Surtsey
Keflavík
Vestmannaeyjar

North Cape

Vadsø
Kirkenes
Polmak
Utsjoki
Inarijärvi
Sodankylä
Pelkosenniemi
Rovaniemi
Kemi
Oulu
Alta
Karasjok
Enontekiö
L A P L A N D
Hammerfest
▲ Mt. Halti 1,324m
Vittangi
Tornio
Luleå
Tromsø
Kiruna
Gällivare
Boden
Piteå
▲ Mt. Kebnekaise 2,111m
Jokkmokk
Skellefteå
Narvik
Sorsele
LOFOTEN VESTERÅLEN
Storuman
Bodø
Mosjøen

FINLAND

Joensuu
Outokumpu
Kuopio
Jakobstad
Kokkola
Jyväskylä
Seinäjoki
Vaasa
Tampere
Pori
Rauma
Hämeenlinna
Lahti
Hyvinkää
Turku
Helsinki
Kouvola
Kotka
Mariehamn
ÅLAND

SWEDEN

Dorotea
Umeå
Örnsköldsvik
Kramfors
Östersund
Sundsvall
Ljusdal
Hudiksvall
Bollnäs
Söderhamn
Falun
Mora
Borlänge
Gävle
Särna
Västerdal
Västerås
Uppsala
Örebro
Eskilstuna
Stockholm
Södertälje
Norrköping
Linköping
Jönköping
Växjö
Karlstad
Vänern
Vättern
Trollhättan
Boras
Göteborg
Uddevalla
Strömstad
Halmstad
Helsingborg
Kristianstad
Kalmar
Karlskrona
Västervik
Visby
GOTLAND
Borgholm
ÖLAND
Bornholm
Rønne
Ystad
Trelleborg
Malmö

BALTIC SEA

NORWAY

Steinkjer
Trondheim
Røros
Sunndalsøra
Kristiansund
Ålesund
Dombås
Galdhøpiggen
2,469m
Lillehammer
Gjøvik
Voss
Bergen
Uskedal
Haugesund
Drammen
Oslo
Fredrikstad
Skien
Larvik
Stavanger
Arendal
Egersund
Kristiansand
Mandal

NORWEGIAN
SEA

Skagerrak
Kattegat

DENMARK

Ålborg
Holstebro
Viborg
Randers
Århus
JUTLAND
Horsens
Esbjerg
Kolding
Odense
Copenhagen
GERMANY

SWEDEN
NORWAY
DENMARK

N

Stockholm, the heart of Sweden

The Swedish capital, Stockholm, is built between Lake Mälar and the Baltic Sea. The city covers several islands. It includes the mediaeval Old Town, merchants' houses from the 1900s and many modern factories and offices.

People of the Arctic

The Saami people live in Lapland, a region which extends right across the Scandinavian Arctic. Traditionally they are a nomadic people, who follow their herds of reindeer.

The Little Mermaid

This bronze statue in the Danish capital, Copenhagen, shows a character from one of the children's stories by Hans Christian Andersen (1805-75). Andersen created some of the world's best loved fairy tales.

LOW COUNTRIES

FACT BOX

◆ **Netherlands**
Area: 41,160 sq km
Population: 15,600,000
Capital: Amsterdam
Official language: Dutch
Currency: Guilder

◆ **Belgium**
Area: 30,520 sq km
Population: 10,200,000
Capital: Brussels
Official languages: Flemish, French
Currency: Belgian franc

◆ **Luxembourg**
Area: 2,585 sq km
Population: 400,000
Capital: Luxembourg
Official language: French, German, Letzebuergesch
Currency: Luxembourg franc

THE COUNTRY OF THE NETHERLANDS is sometimes called Holland, but that is really the name of just two of its provinces, North and South Holland. This is a very flat, low-lying part of northern Europe. Long barriers and sea walls have been built to protect the countryside from North Sea floods. Large areas of land called polders have been reclaimed from the sea over the ages.

After a period under Spanish rule, the **Netherlands** became wealthy in the 1600s by trading with Southeast Asia. Its capital city, Amsterdam, still has many beautiful old houses and canals dating back to this golden age. The Netherlands today remain a centre of commerce, exporting bulbs and cut flowers, vegetables and dairy products, especially cheese, and also electrical goods. Rotterdam is the world's busiest seaport. Peoples of the Netherlands include the Dutch and the Frisians, as well as people whose families came from former Dutch colonies in Indonesia and Surinam.

The Flemish people of **Belgium** are closely related to the Dutch and their two languages are very similar. Belgium is also home to a French-speaking people, the Walloons, who mostly live in the south of the country. Much of the countryside in Belgium is also low and flat, but the land rises to the wooded hills of the Ardennes in the south. The country is heavily industrialized, and is also known for its fine foods – chocolates, pâtés, hams and traditional beers.

Luxembourg is a tiny country, a survivor of the age when most of Europe was divided into little states, principalities and duchies. However, modern industry and banking have made Luxembourg wealthy and successful. The people of Luxembourg speak French, German and a local language called Letzebuergesch.

The three countries have close ties. In 1948, after the terrible years of World War II (1939-45), Belgium, the Netherlands and Luxembourg set up an economic union called 'Benelux'. In 1957 they went on to what

Bruges skyline

The brick gables of old merchants' houses make a pleasing skyline in many historical towns of the Lowlands. Bruges has been famous through the ages for its lacemaking. The city is linked by canal to the seaport of Zeebrugge.

Wetlands butterfly

The Large Copper butterfly is on the endangered species list in both Belgium and the Netherlands. The butterfly thrives in flooded fields. Its caterpillar can survive underwater for many weeks. However draining of wetlands by farmers and roadbuilders threatens its survival.

NETHERLANDS

Enschede
Almelo
Emmen
Assen
Groningen
Zwolle
Meppel
Leeuwarden
Sneek
North-East Polder
Flevoland Polder
IJsselmeer
Ameland
Terscheling
West Frisian Islands
Vieland
Waddenzee
Markerwaard Polder (planned)
Barrier Dam
Texel
Hilversum
Haarlem
Zaanstad
Alkmaar
■ Amsterdam

'When it's spring again...'
The classic Dutch landscape includes fields of brilliantly coloured tulips and old-fashioned windmills. Both attract the tourists and are seen here near the town of Haarlem.

Dutch cheese
Another popular attraction in the Netherlands is the cheese market at Alkmaar. The Netherlands exports mild cheeses such as Edam and Gouda around the world.

GERMANY

Arnhem

Nijmegen

Waal

Lek

s'Hertogenbosch

Delft

Rotterdam

Dordrecht

Breda

Tilburg

Eindhoven

Venlo

Heerlen

Maastricht

Vaalserberg 321m

Verviers

Liège

Genk

Hasselt

Huy

Namur

Sambre

Meuse

Dinant

Botrange 694m

Spa

ARDENNES MOUNTAINS

Buurgplatz 559m

GERMANY

Bastogne

Libramont

LUXEMBOURG

Luxembourg

Esch-sur-Alzette

LUXEMBOURG

Antwerp

Mechelen

Leuven (Louvain)

Brussels

Waterloo

Charleroi

La Louvière

Mons

BELGIUM

St. Niklaas

Aalst

Ghent

Tournai

Schelde

Kortijk

Roeslare

Bruges

Zeebrugge

Vlissingen

Westerschelde

Oosterschelde

NETHERLANDS

Ostend

BELGIUM

FRANCE

N

The future – 1958 style
This strange looking landmark is the Atomium. It was built for the World Fair held in Brussels in 1958 and was meant to be a symbol of a new age of atomic science and technology.

EUROPE

BRITISH ISLES

THE BRITISH ISLES lie off the northwestern coast of Europe, between the shallow waters of the North Sea and the stormy Atlantic Ocean. Their western shores are warmed by an ocean current called the North Atlantic Drift. The climate is mild, with a high rainfall in the west.

The largest island is called **Great Britain**, and its three countries (**England**, **Scotland** and **Wales**) are joined together within a United Kingdom. The second largest of the British Isles is called **Ireland**. Most of Ireland is an independent republic, but part of the north is governed as a province of the United Kingdom.

Great Britain has a landscape of rolling farmland. There are rugged highlands in Wales and Scotland, while England has rich farmland in the southeast, bleak moors in the north, flat fields in East Anglia and wild old villages and towns, but also large cities and ports.

The Irish landscape is less crowded. It has green fields, misty hills and, in the west, steep cliffs pounded by Atlantic breakers. Its capital, Dublin, lies on the River Liffey.

English is spoken throughout the British Isles, but other languages may be heard too – Welsh, Irish and Scots Gaelic, and the various languages spoken by British people of Asian and African descent.

Both the UK and the **Republic of Ireland** are members of the

Fact Box

◆ **United Kingdom:**
England, Scotland, Wales,
N. Ireland
Area: 242,480 sq km
Population: 58,000,000
Capital: London
Official language: English
Currency: Sterling pound

◆ **England**
Area: 130,420 sq km
Population: 48,675,119
Capital: London
Official language: English
Currency: Sterling pound

◆ **Scotland**
Area: 77,170 sq km
Population: 5,111,000
Capital: Edinburgh
Official language: English
Currency: Sterling pound

◆ **Wales**
Area: 20,770 sq km
Population: 2,899,000
Capital: Cardiff
Official language: Welsh,
English
Currency: Sterling pound

◆ **Northern Ireland**
Area: 74,120 sq km
Population: 1,610,000
Capital: Belfast
Official language: English
Currency: Sterling pound

◆ **Republic of Ireland**
Area: 70,283 sq km
Population: 3,552,000
Capital: Dublin
Official language: English, Irish
Currency: Irish pound (punt)

Highland games
Scottish pipers parade in the Highland Games. This competition has been taking place since the early nineteenth century, but has its roots

Wren
One of the most widespread birds of Britain, this short drab coloured bird with a cocked tail, has a loud warbling song. Wrens feed on caterpillars, beetles and bugs.

NORTH SEA

SHETLAND ISLANDS
Unst
Yell
Lerwick
Foula
Sumburgh Head

Fair Isle

ORKNEY ISLANDS
Westray
Kirkwall
South Ronaldsay
Hoy
John o'Groats
Thurso

SCOTLAND

Cape Wrath

NORTH-WEST HIGHLANDS

Butt of Lewis
Stornoway
Lewis

OUTER HEBRIDES
North Uist
South Uist
Barra

North Minch

Fraserburgh
Peterhead
Aberdeen
Dee
Don
Spey
Inverness
Loch Ness
GRAMPIAN MTS.
Montrose
Dundee
Tay
Perth
SIDLAW HILLS
OCHIL HILLS
Forth
Loch Lomond
Firth of Forth
Edinburgh
St. Abbs Head
Berwick-upon-Tweed
Holy I.
Tweed
Jedburgh
Glasgow
Clyde
Greenock
Kilmarnock
Ayr
Arran
Kintyre Pen.

SCOTLAND

Ben Nevis 1343 m
Mallaig
Oban
Mull
Skye
Rhum
Coll
Tiree
Jura
Islay
INNER HEBRIDES

NORTHERN IRELAND

Malin Head

OCEAN

Erris Head
Achill Head
Donegal
Donegal Bay
Sligo
Lough Conn
Chew Bay
Lough Mask
Lough Corrib
Galway Bay
Galway
ARAN ISLANDS
Loop Head
Gt. Blasket I.
Dingle Bay
Carrauntoohill 1,041 m
Killarney
Bantry Bay
Mizen Head
Kenmare River
Old Head of Kinsale
Cork
Blackwater
GALTY MTS.
Tipperary
Limerick
Shannon
Lough Derg
Athlone
Lough Ree
Lough Allen
BOG OF ALLEN
Nore
Barrow
Carlow
Waterford
Hook Head
Wexford
WICKLOW MTS.
Wicklow Head
Dublin
Dun Laoghaire
Liffey
Boyne
Dundalk
Armagh
Slieve Donard 852 m
Belfast
Lower Lough Erne
Upper Lough Erne

NORTHERN IRELAND

IRELAND

Durham
Middlesbrough
Scarborough
Flamborough Head
Spurn Head
Kingston upon Hull
NORTH YORK MOORS
Swale
York
Leeds
Bradford
PENNINES
Rotherham
Sheffield
Oldham
Manchester
Preston
Blackpool
Walney I.
Morecambe Bay
Lake District
Scafell Pike 978 m
Eden
Solway
Isle of Man
Douglas
IRISH SEA
Holyhead
Anglesey
Llandudno
Caernarfon
Snowdon 1,085 m
Cardigan Bay
Bardsey I.
Aberystwyth
Cardigan
CAMBRIAN MTS.
Wrexham
Stoke on Trent
Wigan
Liverpool
WALES
Carmarthen
St. Brides Bay
Milford Haven
Gower Peninsula
Swansea
Cardiff
Newport
Wye
Severn
Cheltenham
Gloucester
Bristol
Bristol Channel
MENDIP HILLS
Bridgwater
EXMOOR
Ilfracombe
Lundy
Bude
DARTMOOR
Plymouth
Torbay
St. Ives
Penzance
Lands End
Lizard Point
ISLES OF SCILLY

NORTH SEA

ENGLAND
Derby
Nottingham
Trent
Leicester
Welland
Peterborough
THE FENS
The Wash
LINCOLN WOLDS
Norwich
EAST ANGLIA
Ipswich
Colchester
Chelmsford
Cambridge
Northampton
Milton Keynes
Coventry
Birmingham
Wolverhampton
Walsall
CHILTERNS
Oxford
Swindon
Reading
London
Thames
Luton
Southend-on-Sea
NORTH DOWNS
Canterbury
Dover
Folkestone
THE WEALD
Hastings
SOUTH DOWNS
Brighton
Isle of Wight
Portsmouth
Bournemouth
Southampton
Winchester
HAMPSHIRE DOWNS
Basingstoke
Salisbury
Portland Bill
Lyme Bay
Exeter
COTSWOLD HILLS

ENGLISH CHANNEL

Alderney
CHANNEL ISLANDS
Guernsey
Jersey

WALES

Tower of London
Built in the eleventh century by William the Conqueror, this ancient fortress on the river Thames was once a royal home. It is now a museum and houses the crown jewels. It was here that Anne Boleyn, wife of Henry VIII, was beheaded. Yeomen of the Guard, or Beefeaters, still guard the Tower.

N

Ladies' View, Killarney, Eire
This famous beauty spot in southern Ireland enjoys wonderful views of Macgillycuddyis Reeks (a mountain range) and the lakes of Killarney. Of these lakes Lough Learne, or lower lake, is the largest with over 30 islands.

FRANCE AND MONACO

Château de Charumont
France has many historical castles, palaces and stately homes, or châteaux. Some of the finest are in the Loire valley.

FRANCE IS A LARGE, beautiful country which lies at the heart of Western Europe. Its western regions include the massive peaks of the Pyrenees, vineyards and pine forests, peaceful rivers and Atlantic shores.

The north includes the stormy headlands of Brittany, the cliffs of Normandy and the Channel ports. Rolling fertile plains are drained by the winding river Seine, over whose banks and islands sprawls the French capital. Paris is one of the world's great cities, with broad avenues, historic palaces and churches.

The west of **France** is bordered by wooded hills which rise to the high forested slopes of the Jura mountains and finally the spectacular glaciers and ridges of the Alps. The rocks of the Massif Central, shaped by ancient volcanoes, rise in central southern France, to the west of the Rhône valley. The sun-baked hills of southern France border the warm seas of the Mediterranean Sea. This coast includes the wetlands of the Camargue, the great seaport of Marseilles and the fashionable yachting marinas of Cannes.

France has played a major part in history, and the French language is now spoken in many parts of the world. The French people are mostly descended from a Celtic people called the Gauls and Germanic peoples, such as the Franks and Vikings. Within France are several other peoples with their own languages and distinct cultures, such as Bretons, Basques, Catalans, Alsatians, Corsicans and Algerians.

France is a republic belonging to the European Union (EU) and is an important industrial power, producing cars, aerospace equipment, chemicals and textiles. The country is renowned for its wines, its cheeses, and its fine cooking.

Part of the Mediterranean coast is occupied by a very small principality called **Monaco**. It has close links with its large neighbour and shares the same currency. The state is famous for its casino.

Cape Corse
Bastia
CORSICA
Gulf of Sagone
Ajaccio
Bonifacio
Strait of Bonifacio

Cherbou
Carent.
Gulf of St-Malo
Gra
Morlaix
St.-Malo
Brest
St-Brieuc
Dinan
Foug
Douernenez
Quimper
Pontivy
Rennes
Lorient
Vannes
Redon
St. Nazaire
Belle-Ile
Nant
La Roche-sur
Isle d'Yeu
Les Sables-d'Ol
Ré I.
La Roch
Roch
Oléro
R
P

Sacré-Coeur
The gleaming domes of this church soar above the Parisian district of Montmartre, once famed as the haunt of artists and writers.

Bay
Biarritz
P
S P

Shape of the future
The Futuroscope theme park and study centre, near Poitiers, is one example of France's many experimental modern buildings. This theatre looks like a huge crystal.

Vineyard harvest
Grapes are gathered at a vineyard in Alsace, on the slopes of the Vosges. Grapes, grown in many regions of France, are made into some of the world's finest wines.

FRANCE

Dunkerque
Calais
Boulogne
Lille
Montreuil   Arras   Douai
Valenciennes
Abbeville   Cambrai
Dieppe   St. Quentin   Hirson
Amiens   Charleville-Mézières
Fécamp   Montdidier
Bolbec

Bay of
the Seine

Le Havre   Rouen   Compiègne   Reims   Verdun   Metz
Caen   Louviers   Meaux   Pont à Mousson
Lisieux   Evreux   Châlons-sur-Marne   Nancy   Strasbourg
Argentan   Paris   Versailles   St.Dizier   Toul
St. Germain-en-Laye   Rambouillet   Epinal   Colmar
Mayenne   Chartres   Fontainebleau   Troyes   Mulhouse
Laval   Nemours   Sens   Langres   Montbéliard
Le Mans   Orléans   Montargis   Auxerre   Dijon   Besançon
Angers   Tours   Blois   Gien   Avallon   Dôle
Saumur   Vierzon   Autun   Pontarlier
Châtellerault   Bourges   Nevers   Le Creusot   Chalon-sur-Saône
Poitiers   Châteauroux   La Châtre   Monceau les Mines   St.Claude
Niort   Moulins   Mâcon   Annecy
Civray   Montluçon   Bourg-en-Bresse   Chamonix
FRANCE   Vichy   Villefranches   Mont Blanc
Cognac   Limoges   Lyon   Villeurbanne   4,807m
Angoulême   Clermont-Ferrand   Chambéry   Val d'Isère
Nontron   Puy de Sancy   Vienne   Grenoble
Barbezieux   1,886m   St.-Etienne
Périgueux   MASSIF   Annonay   Romans-sur-Isère
Libourne   CENTRAL   Valence
Bergerac   Souillac   Aurillac   Prives   Gap
Bordeaux   Cère   Montélimar
Marmande   Lot   Mende   Carpentras
Agen   Rodez   Avignon
Mont-de-Marsan   Cahors   Millau   Nîmes
Montauban   Albi   Arles   Aix-en-Provence   Nice   MONACO
Gaillac   Castres   Montpellier   Cannes
Auch   Toulouse   Sète   St.Raphael   St.Tropez
Tarbes   Carcassonne   Béziers   Brignoles
Lourdes   Narbonne   Marseille   Toulon   Côte d'Azur
St. Gaudens   Foix   Perpignan

ANDORRA

BELGIUM
LUXEMBOURG
GERMANY
SWITZERLAND
ITALY
MONACO

Seine
Marne
Meuse
Moselle
Saône
Loire
Cher
Loire
Dordogne
Lot
Aveyron
Tarn
Garonne
Ariège
Aude
Rhône
Isère
Drac
Durance
Verdon
Doubs
Rhine
VOSGES
JURA
ALPS
LANGRES PLATEAU
LANGUEDOC
CEVENNES
NORMANDY HILLS

N

MONACO

FACT BOX

◆ **France**
Area: 543,965 sq km
Population: 58,600,000
Capital: Paris
Official language: French
Currency: French franc

◆ **Monaco**
Area: 1.9 sq km
Population: 28,000
Capital: Monaco
Official language: French
Currency: French franc

Quiche Lorraine
A speciality of north-eastern
France, this is a baked pastry
tart filled with eggs, cream,
cheese and bacon.

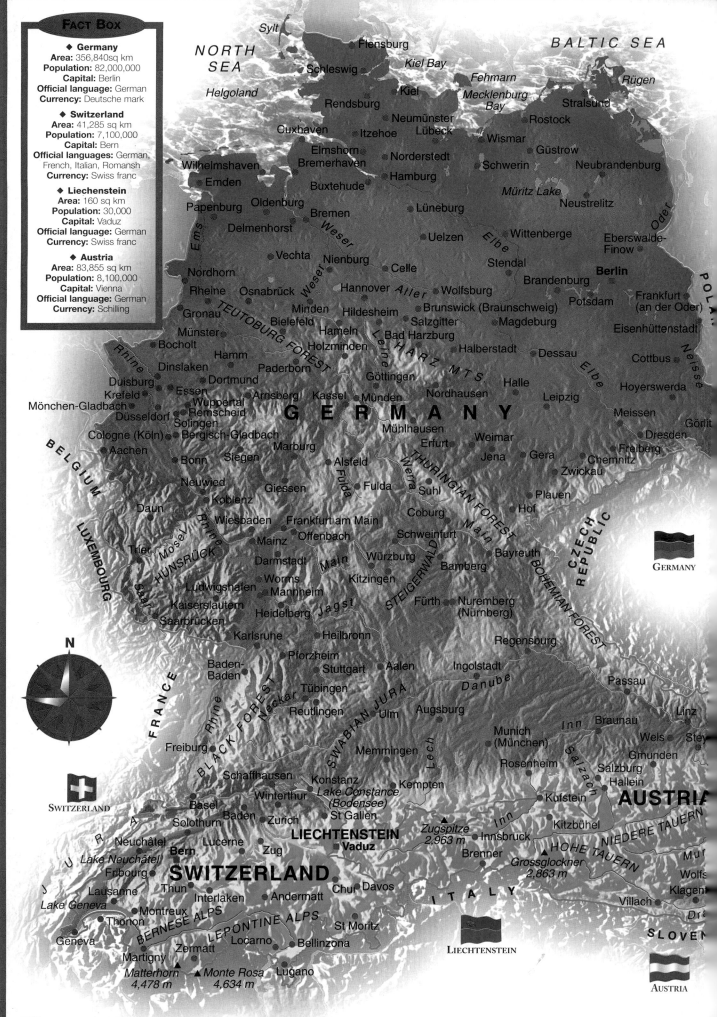

NORTH SEA
BALTIC SEA

Sylt
Flensburg
Schleswig
Kiel Bay
Fehmarn
Rügen
Helgoland
Kiel
Mecklenburg Bay
Stralsund
Rendsburg
Neumünster
Wismar
Rostock
Cuxhaven
Itzehoe
Lübeck
Güstrow
Schwerin
Elmshorn
Norderstedt
Neubrandenburg
Wilhelmshaven
Bremerhaven
Hamburg
Emden
Buxtehude
Müritz Lake
Neustrelitz
Papenburg
Oldenburg
Bremen
Lüneburg
Eberswalde-Finow
Delmenhorst
Uelzen
Wittenberge
Oder
Vechta
Nienburg
Celle
Stendal
Berlin
Nordhorn
Weser
Hannover
Aller
Wolfsburg
Brandenburg
Potsdam
Frankfurt (an der Oder)
Rheine
Osnabrück
Minden
Hildesheim
Brunswick (Braunschweig)
Magdeburg
Eisenhüttenstadt
Gronau
TEUTOBURG FOREST
Bielefeld
Hameln
Bad Harzburg
Salzgitter
Halberstadt
Dessau
Cottbus
Neisse
Münster
Bocholt
Hamm
Paderborn
Holzminden
HARZ MTS
Elbe
Hoyerswerda
Dinslaken
Dortmund
Göttingen
Halle
Duisburg
Essen
Arnsberg
Kassel
Münden
Nordhausen
Leipzig
Meissen
Krefeld
Wuppertal
GERMANY
Görlitz
Mönchen-Gladbach
Remscheid
Mühlhausen
Weimar
Dresden
Düsseldorf
Solingen
Bergisch-Gladbach
Marburg
Erfurt
Jena
Gera
Freiberg
Cologne (Köln)
Bonn
Siegen
Alsfeld
THURINGIAN FOREST
Chemnitz
Aachen
Neuwied
Giessen
Fulda
Fulda
Werra
Suhl
Zwickau
Plauen
Daun
Wiesbaden
Frankfurt am Main
Coburg
Hof
Koblenz
Offenbach
Schweinfurt
Bayreuth
Mosel
Rhine
Mainz
Main
Würzburg
Bamberg
CZECH REPUBLIC
Trier
HUNSRÜCK
Darmstadt
STEIGERWALD
BOHEMIAN FOREST
Worms
Kitzingen
Saar
Ludwigshafen
Mannheim
Main
Fürth
Nuremberg (Nürnberg)
Kaiserslautern
Heidelberg
Jagst
Saarbrücken
Karlsruhe
Heilbronn
Regensburg
Pforzheim
FRANCE
Baden-Baden
Stuttgart
Aalen
Ingolstadt
Passau
Neckar
Tübingen
Danube
Linz
Rhine
BLACK FOREST
Reutlingen
Ulm
Augsburg
Braunau
Wels
Stey
Freiburg
SWABIAN JURA
Memmingen
Lech
Munich (München)
Inn
Salzach
Gmunden
Rosenheim
Salzburg
Schaffhausen
Konstanz
Kempten
Hallein
AUSTRIA
Basel
Winterthur
Lake Constance (Bodensee)
Kufstein
Baden
St Gallen
Kitzbühel
NIEDERE TAUERN
Neuchâtel
Lucerne
Zurich
LIECHTENSTEIN
Zugspitze 2,963 m
Innsbruck
HOHE TAUERN
Mur
Lake Neuchâtel
Bern
Zug
Vaduz
Brenner
Mu
Fribourg
SWITZERLAND
Grossglockner 2,863 m
Wolfs
Lausanne
Thun
Chur
Davos
ITALY
Klagen
Lake Geneva
Interlaken
Andermatt
SLOVEN
Montreux
BERNESE ALPS
St Moritz
Dr
Geneva
Thonon
LEPONTINE ALPS
Villach
Martigny
Zermatt
Locarno
Bellinzona
Matterhorn 4,478 m
Monte Rosa 4,634 m
Lugano

BELGIUM
LUXEMBOURG

GERMANY

SWITZERLAND

LIECHTENSTEIN

AUSTRIA

N

GERMANY & THE ALPS

GERMANY LIES BETWEEN Western and Central Europe. In the south the high peaks of the Alps are flanked by belts of forest.

The rolling hills and heathland of the centre stretch to the North Sea, while in the west the rivers Rhine and Moselle wind through steep valleys planted with vines. In the northeast a vast plain is bordered by the Baltic Sea and by the rivers Oder and Neisse.

For most of its history Germany has been divided into different states. Today's united Germany dates from 1990. Germany is a federal republic, which means that its regions or Länder have considerable powers. The country is a leading member of the European Union and is a major world producer of cars, electrical and household goods, medicines, chemicals, wines and beers.

Switzerland is a small country set amongst the lakes and snowy peaks of the Alps and the Jura ranges. Its beautiful landscape and historical towns attract many tourists. Industries include dairy produce, precision instruments and finance. Zurich is a world centre of banking, while Geneva is the headquarters of many international agencies, such as the Red Cross and the World Health Organization.

To the east, the tiny country of **Liechtenstein** is closely linked with Switzerland and uses the same currency. The land of **Austria** descends from the soaring peaks of the Alps to the flat lands of the Danube river valley. Austria once ruled a large empire which stretched eastwards into Hungary and southwards into Italy. Today Austria still plays an important part in Europe, making its living from tourism, farming, forestry and manufacture.

German is spoken through most of the region, with a great variety of dialects. In parts of Switzerland there are people who speak French, Italian and Romansh.

(map labels) ems · nube · Vienna · Pölten · Bruck · Baden · Neusiedler See · ener Neustadt · fenberg · raz · HUNGARY

Edelweiss
This small herb, with its pretty white flower, grows in the European Alps. High mountain meadows are filled with wildflowers in spring and summer.

Brimming with beer
Munich, capital of Bavaria in southern Germany, hosts a famous beer festival every October. Regional dress is still common in the region.

River of ice
This impressive glacier grinds its way down the Alps near Zermatt. Many tourists and climbers visit Switzerland to enjoy the spectacular views.

Medieval revelry
Festival costumes recall the Middle Ages in Baden Württemberg. During that period Germany was made up of many small states.

IBERIAN PENINSULA

N

Bay of Biscay

Cape Ortegal

Cape Peñas

La Coruña • El Ferrol • Gijón
Llar
Carballo • Villalba
Oviedo •
CANTABRI
Cape
Finisterre
Fonsagrada •
Santiago de Compostela • Lugo
Sarria
Lalin • • León
Monforte de Lemos
SIERRA Astorga •
Vigo • Orense • CABRERA
Miño
La Gudina • Villada
Baltar • Esla
Braga • Bragança
Tâmega • Mogadouro • Vallad
Tuela
Vila Real • Zamora •
Porto • Douro Medina del Camp
Lamego • Tormes
PORTUGAL Salamanca •

THE IBERIAN PENINSULA
is in southwestern Europe, and
juts out into the Atlantic Ocean.
It is bordered to the north by
the stormy Bay of Biscay and to
the south by the Mediterranean
Sea and the Balearic Islands.
Across the Strait of Gibraltar, just
13 kilometres away, lies the continent of Africa.

Aviero • Viseu •
Guarda • Cuidad Rodrigo •
Coimbra • Covilhã • Béjar •
SIERRA DE GRED(
Plasencia •
Castelo Branco • Tajo
Leiria • Tajo
Tomar • Cáceres • Trujillo •
Caldas da Rainha
Tagus Portalegre •
Santarém •
Lisbon Badajoz • Don Benito •
Setúbal • Évora • Almendralejo •
Pozoblan
Ardila Azuaga •
Beja • SIE
Guadiana Cór
Constantina •
Chança Nerva •
Guadalquiv
Huelva • Seville • Puente (
Lagos • Osuna •
Faro Costa de la Luz Morón de la Fron
Cape Algarve Gulf
Saint Vincent of Cadiz Ronda •
Jerez de la Frontera •
Cádiz • SIERRA
DE RONDA Mar
Gibraltar (l
Algeciras •
Cueta (Sp
Strait of Gibral

The north coast, green from high rainfall, rises to the
Cantabrian mountains, while the snowy Pyrenees form a high
barrier along the Spanish-French frontier. Another range, the
Sierra Nevada, runs parallel with the south coast. Inland, much
of the Iberian peninsula is taken up by an extremely dry, rocky
plateau, which swelters in the heat of summer. To the west are
forested highlands and the fertile plains of Portugal, crossed
by great rivers such as the Douro, Tagus and Guadiana.

The Iberian peninsula is occupied by four countries or
territories. There is **Gibraltar**, a British colony since 1713,
and the tiny independent state of **Andorra**, high in the
Pyrenees. The two main countries of the region are
Spain and **Portugal**. Both have a history of overseas
settlement, and both Spanish and Portuguese have
become the chief languages of Latin America. Many
people speak other languages, including Basque and
Catalan, and have their own traditions and history.

Both Spain and Portugal were ruled by dictators
for much of the 20th century, but today both are
democracies and members of the European Union. Spain
produces olives, citrus fruits, wines and sherries, and has a
large fishing fleet. Portugal also produces wine and port takes
its name from the city of Oporto. Fishing villages line the
coasts and cork, used for bottle stoppers and tiling, is cut from
the thick bark of the cork oak tree.

PORTUGAL

Feria in Seville
At the Feria, held in the Spanish city of Seville
every April, people ride into town dressed in
traditional finery. The river is lined with tents
and pavilions. The festival is celebrated with
bullfights, flamenco music and dancing.

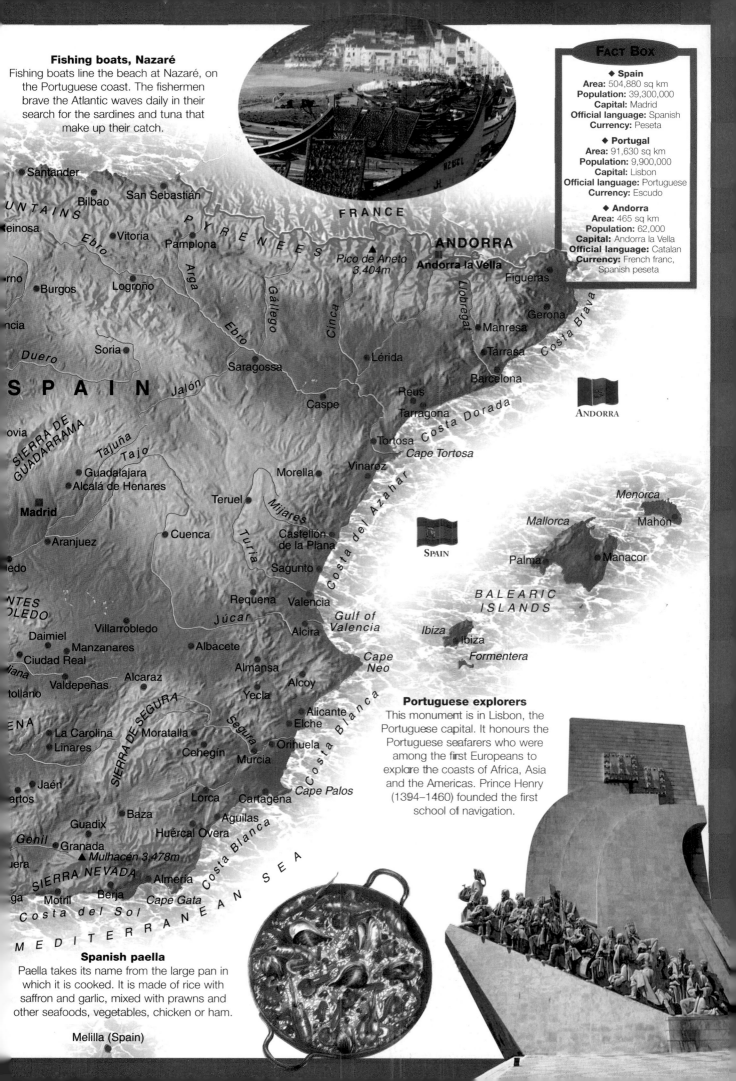

Fishing boats, Nazaré

Fishing boats line the beach at Nazaré, on the Portuguese coast. The fishermen brave the Atlantic waves daily in their search for the sardines and tuna that make up their catch.

FACT BOX

◆ **Spain**
Area: 504,880 sq km
Population: 39,300,000
Capital: Madrid
Official language: Spanish
Currency: Peseta

◆ **Portugal**
Area: 91,630 sq km
Population: 9,900,000
Capital: Lisbon
Official language: Portuguese
Currency: Escudo

◆ **Andorra**
Area: 465 sq km
Population: 62,000
Capital: Andorra la Vella
Official language: Catalan
Currency: French franc, Spanish peseta

Santander
Bilbao
San Sebastián
UNTAINS
einosa
Ebro
Vitoria
Pamplona
PYRENEES
FRANCE
Pico de Aneto 3,404m
ANDORRA
Andorra la Vella
Figueras
Arga
rno
Burgos
Logroño
Gállego
Ebro
Cinca
Llobregat
Gerona
Manresa
Costa Brava
Tárrasa
ncia
Duero
Soria
Saragossa
Lérida
Barcelona
ANDORRA
SPAIN
Jalón
Caspe
Reus
Tarragona
Costa Dorada
Tortosa
Cape Tortosa
ovia
SIERRA DE GUADARRAMA
Tajuña
Tajo
Guadalajara
Alcalá de Henares
Teruel
Morella
Vinaroz
Mijares
Menorca
Mallorca
Mahón
Madrid
Cuenca
Castellón de la Plana
Turia
SPAIN
Palma
Manacor
Aranjuez
edo
Sagunto
Costa del Azahar
BALEARIC ISLANDS
NTES OLEDO
Requena
Valencia
Gulf of Valencia
Júcar
Alcira
Ibiza
Ibiza
Villarrobledo
Daimiel
Albacete
Cape Neo
Formentera
Ciudad Real
Almansa
iana
Valdepeñas
Alcaraz
Alcoy
Yecla
tollano
SIERRA DE SEGURA
Alicante
Elche
ENA
La Carolina
Moratalla
Segura
Orihuela
Costa Blanca
Linares
Cehegín
Murcia
Jaén
Lorca
Cartagena
Cape Palos
artos
Baza
Aguilas
Guadix
Huércal Overa
Costa Blanca
Genil
Granada
▲ Mulhacén 3,478m
uera
SIERRA NEVADA
Almería
Costa Blanca
ga
Motril
Berja
Cape Gata
MEDITERRANEAN SEA
Costa del Sol

Portuguese explorers

This monument is in Lisbon, the Portuguese capital. It honours the Portuguese seafarers who were among the first Europeans to explore the coasts of Africa, Asia and the Americas. Prince Henry (1394–1460) founded the first school of navigation.

Spanish paella

Paella takes its name from the large pan in which it is cooked. It is made of rice with saffron and garlic, mixed with prawns and other seafoods, vegetables, chicken or ham.

Melilla (Spain)

ITALY AND ITS NEIGHBOURS

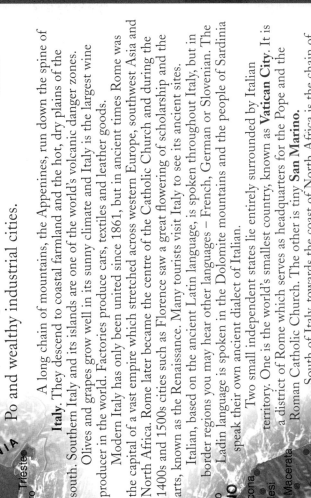

ITALY OCCUPIES a long, boot-shaped peninsula which stretches south from the snowy peaks and blue lakes of the Alps into the Mediterranean Sea. The country also takes in the large islands of Sardinia and Sicily. The northern regions of the mainland include the wide, fertile plains around the river Po and wealthy industrial cities.

A long chain of mountains, the Appenines, run down the spine of **Italy**. They descend to coastal farmland and the hot, dry plains of the south. Southern Italy and its islands are one of the world's volcanic danger zones. Olives and grapes grow well in its sunny climate and Italy is the largest wine producer in the world. Factories produce cars, textiles and leather goods.

Modern Italy has only been united since 1861, but in ancient times Rome was the capital of a vast empire which stretched across western Europe, southwest Asia and North Africa. Rome later became the centre of the Catholic Church and during the 1400s and 1500s cities such as Florence saw a great flowering of scholarship and the arts, known as the Renaissance. Many tourists visit Italy to see its ancient sites.

Italian, based on the ancient Latin language, is spoken throughout Italy, but in border regions you may hear other languages – French, German or Slovenian. The Ladin language is spoken in the Dolomite mountains and the people of Sardinia speak their own ancient dialect of Italian.

Two small independent states lie entirely surrounded by Italian territory. One is the world's smallest country, known as **Vatican City**. It is a district of Rome which serves as headquarters for the Pope and the Roman Catholic Church. The other is tiny **San Marino.**

South of Italy, towards the coast of North Africa is the chain of islands which make up **Malta**. The Maltese have their own language and live from building and repairing ships and from tourism.

Spaghetti Bolognese

Spaghetti is a kind of pasta. Made from wheat and eggs, pasta is eaten in all kinds of shapes and sizes, each with its own name. Here it is served with a meat and tomato sauce, invented in the city of Bologna. Italians who have left their homeland have made their cooking popular around the world.

Sun and sea

Portofino is a small town on the Gulf of Genoa, in Italy's Liguria region. Its pretty waterfront and fishing boats attract many tourists in the hot Mediterranean summer.

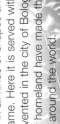

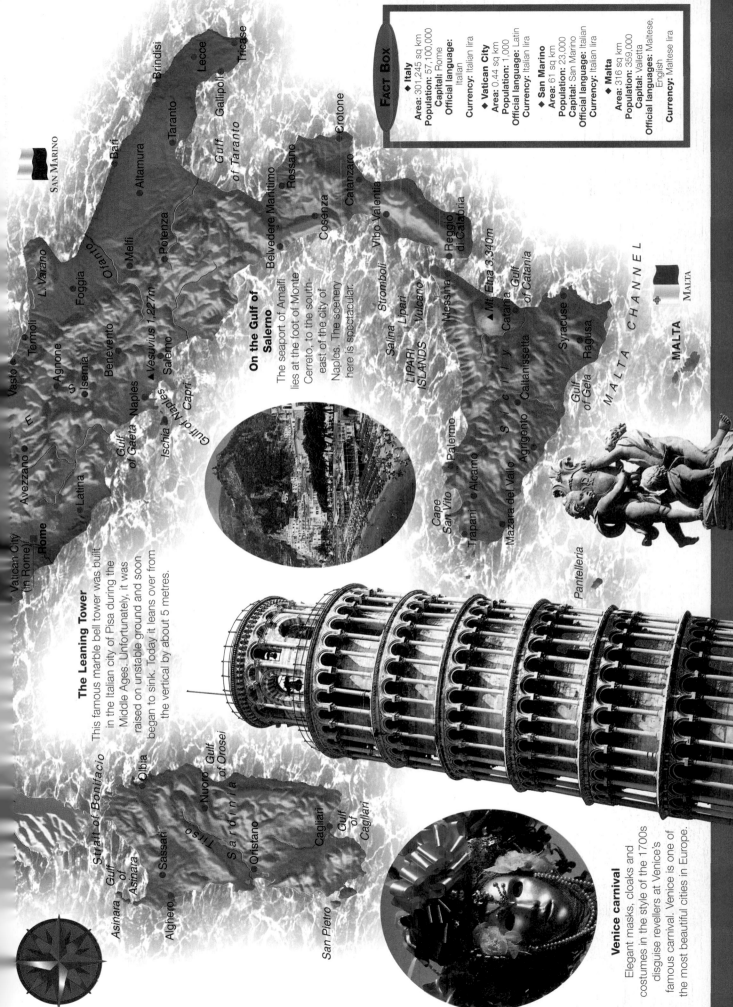

◆ **Italy**
Area: 301,245 sq km
Population: 57,100,000
Capital: Rome
Official language:
Italian
Currency: Italian lira

◆ **Vatican City**
Area: 0.44 sq km
Population: 1,000
Official language: Latin
Currency: Italian lira

◆ **San Marino**
Area: 61 sq km
Population: 23,000
Capital: San Marino
Official language: Italian
Currency: Italian lira

◆ **Malta**
Area: 316 sq km
Population: 359,000
Capital: Valletta
Official languages: Maltese,
English
Currency: Maltese lira

SAN MARINO

MALTA

MALTA

MALTA CHANNEL

On the Gulf of Salerno

The seaport of Amalfi lies at the foot of Monte Cerreto, to the south-east of the city of Naples. The scenery here is spectacular.

Tricase
Lecce
Gallipoli
Brindisi
Gulf of Taranto
Taranto
Bari
Altamura
Crotone
Rossano
Belvedere Marittimo
Catanzaro
Cosenza
Vibo Valentia
Reggio di Calabria
▲ Mt Etna 3,340m
Stromboli
Salina
Lipari
Vulcano
Messina
LIPARI ISLANDS
S i c i l y
Catania
Gulf of Catania
Syracuse
Ragusa
Caltanissetta
Agrigento
Gulf of Gela
Gela
Palermo
Alcamo
Cape San Vito
Trapani
Mazara del Vallo
Pantelleria

Foggia
L. Varano
Ofanto
Melfi
Potenza
Benevento
Isernia
Agnone
Temoli
Vasto
▲Vesuvius 1,227m
Naples
Salerno
Ischia
Capri
Gulf of Naples
Gulf of Gaeta
Latina
Avezzano
Vatican City (in Rome)
Rome

The Leaning Tower

This famous marble bell tower was built in the Italian city of Pisa during the Middle Ages. Unfortunately, it was raised on unstable ground and soon began to sink. Today it leans over from the vertical by about 5 metres.

Strait of Bonifacio
Gulf of Asinara
Asinara
Alghero
Sassari
Olbia
Nuoro
Gulf of Orosei
Sardinia
Tirso
Oristano
Cagliari
Gulf of Cagliari
San Pietro

Venice carnival

Elegant masks, cloaks and costumes in the style of the 1700s disguise revellers at Venice's famous carnival. Venice is one of the most beautiful cities in Europe.

213

CENTRAL EUROPE

THREE SMALL COUNTRIES cluster around the eastern shores of the Baltic Sea. **Estonia, Latvia** and **Lithuania** were part of the Soviet Union (today's Russian Federation) from 1940 until 1991, when they became independent. Their lands include forests and lakes, farmland and industrial cities.

Poland, which has historic links with Lithuania, is a large country which has also known invasions and foreign rule through much of its history. Despite this, the Poles, a Slavic people, have kept a sense of independence and a pride in their traditions. The lands near Poland's Baltic coast are dotted with lakes. The north is a flat land of pine forests, part of the great plain which stretches from eastern Germany into Russia. It is cold and snowy in winter, but warm in summer. In southern Poland the land rises to highlands and the jagged peaks of the Tatra mountains, along the Slovakian border.

Slovakia and the **Czech Republic** were a single country until 1993. Slovakia is a land of high mountains dropping to fertile farmland around the River Danube, which forms its southeastern border. When the two countries divided, most industry lay on the Czech side of the border. The Czech Republic produces beer, glass, ceramics, steel and machinery. The country is bordered by mountains and, in the east, by the Bohemian centre of learning and the arts.

The Czechs and Slovaks are both Slavic peoples, but the Hungarians are Magyars, a people who invaded and settled in the region about 1200 years ago. **Hungary** is a country of wide open plains and low mountains. Its fertile farmland produces fruits, grains and grapes for making strong red wine. Its beautiful

Historical Prague

Prague, capital of the Czech Republic, is a fine old city on the River Vltava. Prague was the chief city of independent Bohemia in the Middle Ages.

ESTONIA

LATVIA

LITHUANIA

RUSSIA

Lake Peipus

Kohtla-Järve

Tartu

Tallinn

Munamagi 318 m ▲

Parnu

E S T O N I A

Hiumaa

Saaremaa

Gulf of Riga

Ventspils

Jurmala

Saldus

Liepāja

▲ *Gaizina 311 m*

L A T V I A

Daugavpils

Riga

Jelgava

Siauliai

Panevezys

Utena

Ukmerge

Kaunas

Vilnius

L I T H U A N I A

Nemunas (Neman)

Klaipeda

POLAND

Kaliningrad (RUSSIA)

Gulf of

N

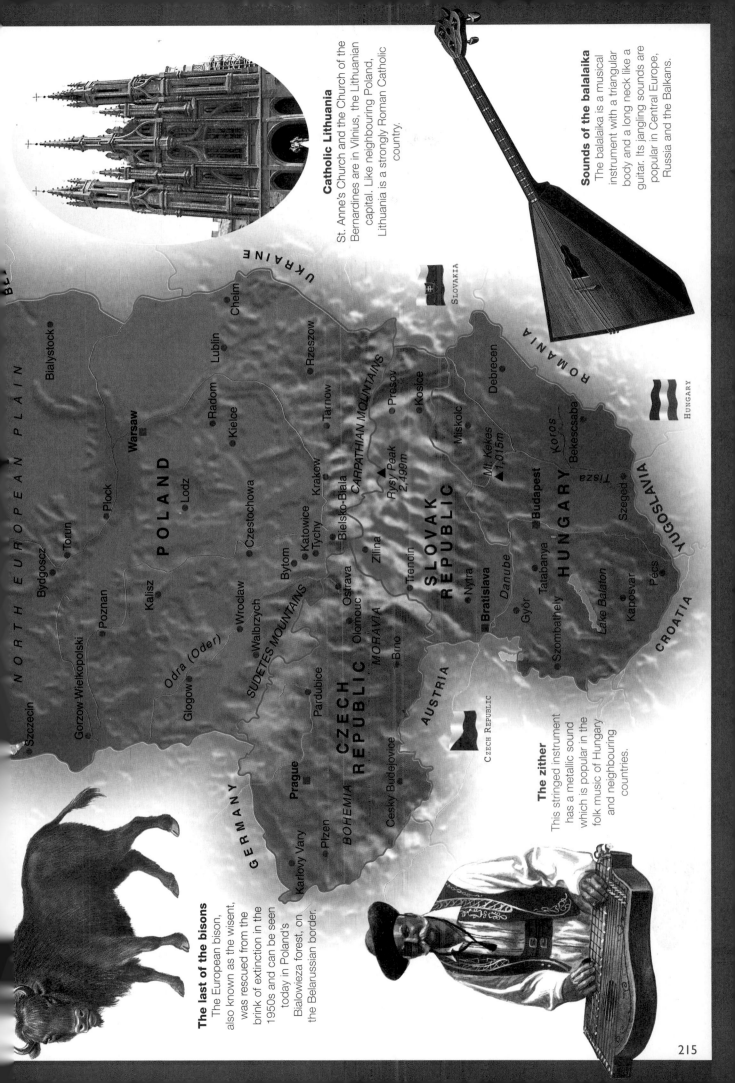

Catholic Lithuania

St. Anne's Church and the Church of the Bernardines are in Vilnius, the Lithuanian capital. Like neighbouring Poland, Lithuania is a strongly Roman Catholic country.

Sounds of the balalaika

The balalaika is a musical instrument with a triangular body and a long neck like a guitar. Its jangling sounds are popular in Central Europe, Russia and the Balkans.

The zither

This stringed instrument has a metallic sound which is popular in the folk music of Hungary and neighbouring countries.

The last of the bisons

The European bison, also known as the wisent, was rescued from the brink of extinction in the 1950s and can be seen today in Poland's Bialowieza forest, on the Belarussian border.

UKRAINE

NORTH EUROPEAN PLAIN

- Bialystock
- Cheim
- Lublin
- Radom
- Rzeszow
- Kielce
- Warsaw

POLAND

- Lodz
- Plock
- Torun
- Bydgoscz
- Poznan
- Kalisz
- Czestochowa
- Katowice
- Tychy
- Bielsko-Biala
- Krakow
- Tarnow
- Presov
- Kosice
- Miskolc
- Debrecen

CARPATHIAN MOUNTAINS

▲ Rysy Peak 2,499m

SLOVAK REPUBLIC

- Zilina
- Trencin
- Nytra
- **Bratislava**
- Gyor
- Szombathely
- Tatabanya
- **Budapest**

HUNGARY

Koros
Bekescsaba
Tisza
- Szeged
- Kaposvar
- Pecs

Lake Balaton

Mt. Kekes ▲ 1,015m

ROMANIA

YUGOSLAVIA

CROATIA

SLOVAKIA

HUNGARY

CZECH REPUBLIC

- Szczecin
- Gorzow-Wielkopolski
- Glogow
- Odra (Oder)
- Wroclaw
- Walbrzych

SUDETES MOUNTAINS

BOHEMIA
MORAVIA

CZECH REPUBLIC

- Pardubice
- Olomouc
- Ostrava
- Brno
- **Prague**
- Plzen
- Karlovy Vary
- Cesky Budejovice

GERMANY

AUSTRIA

Danube

BALKANS AND ROMANIA

SLOVENIA

THE STATES OF SOUTHERN Central Europe are known as the Balkans. They take their name from the Balkan peninsula, a great wedge of land which stretches south into the Mediterranean.

The warm, blue waters around the Balkan coast form the Adriatic, Aegean and Black Seas and are popular with tourists. The region is mountainous, with hot, dry summers. Winters are severe in the north of the region, but generally mild in the south. Earthquakes are common. The Balkan countries produce fruit, wines and spirits, dairy products such as yoghurt and cheese, olives, sunflowers and tobacco.

In the early 1990s the northwest of the region saw bitter fighting as the large nation of Yugoslavia broke up into separate independent states. These took the names of **Slovenia**, **Croatia**, **Bosnia-Herzegovina**, **Yugoslavia** (Serbia and Montenegro), and **Macedonia** (which is also the name of the northernmost province of Greece). The small and very poor country of **Albania** also suffered from political unrest and civil war in the 1990s.

The northeast of the Balkan peninsula is occupied by **Bulgaria,** a land of fertile farmland to the south of the river Danube, crossed by the Balkan and Rhodope mountain chains. Its northern neighbour is **Romania**, lying around the forested Carpathian mountain range and the Transylvanian Alps. On the Black Sea coast, the river Danube forms a marshy delta region.

The Balkan peninsula narrows to the south, breaking up into the headland of the Peloponnese and scattered island chains. **Greece** was the centre of Europe's first great civilizations, between 4,000 and 2,000 years ago. The rock of the Acropolis, with its temple, the Parthenon, still towers above the Greek capital, Athens.

Off to market
Romanian farmers gather for a cattle fair at Sugatag. The population as a whole is made up of Romanians, whose language is linked to the Latin language of the ancient Roman empire, as well as Magyars and Gypsies.

The sunflower crop
Sunflowers are grown in many parts of southern Europe. Their seeds may be roasted and eaten as snacks, turned into cooking oil or used to make margarine.

Old-fashioned style
Traditional Bulgarian costumes, with waistcoats, aprons and skirts may still be seen at many festivals or folk dances.

UKRAINE

ROMANIA

YUGOSLAVIA

HUNGARY

Satu Mare
Baia Mare
Oradea
Cluj-Napoca
Somes
Tîrgu Mures
ROMANIA
Alba Iulia
Arad
Mures
Sibiu
Brasov
Deva
Moldoveanu ▲
2,543 m
TRANSYLVANIAN ALPS
Timisoara
Resita
Subotica
Tisza
VOJVODINA
Novi Sad
Belgrade
Sabac
Smederevo
Craiova
Vallevo
Negotin
Dunarea (Danube)
Kragujevac
Vidin
Cacak
Mikhaylovgrad
Pleven
Krusevac
Nis
Vratsa
Lovech
BALKAN MOUNTAINS
Novi Pazar
SERBIA
Leskovac
Sofia
Kazanluk
YUGOSLAVIA
MONTENEGRO
Pristina
BULGARIA
Pec
KOSOVO
Pernik
Pasardzhik
gorica
Urosevac
Musala Peak
2,925 m ▲
Lake Scutari
Plovdiv
Khaskovo
Skopje
Smolyan
Mt Korabit ▲
2,751 m
Tetovo
MACEDONIA
RHODOPE MOUNTAINS
Vardar
Siruma
PIRIN MTS
Drama
Komotini
Tiranë
Prilep
Palikastron
Xánthi
Elbasan
Lake Ohrid
Bitola
Sérrai
Kaválla
Alexandroúpolis
ALBANIA
Lake Prespa
Edhessa
Kilkís
Vlore
Náousa
Thessaloníki
Thasos
Gjirokaster
Ptolemaïs
Samothrace
Aliakmon
Mt Olympus
▲ 2,917 m
Mt Athos
2,033 m
Limnos
GREECE
Joánnina
Trikkala
Lárisa
Vólos
Skíathos
Mitilíni
Kérkira
Párga
Kardhítsa
Skopelos
Skíros
Lesbos
Corfu
Arta
Lamía
Euboea
AEGEAN
Pálairos
Parnassus
Kími
SEA
Chios
Leukas
▲ 2,547 m
Khalkís
Astakós
Agrínion
Cephalonia
Ithaca
Pátrai
Marathon
Ándros
Samos
IONIAN
Mégara
Athens
SEA
Lámbia
Corinth
Piraeus
Tinos
Ikaría
Zante
Amaliás
Alfios
Argos
Layrion
Kéa
Pirgos
Tripolis
Návplion
Kíthnos
Síros
Mikonos
Patmos
Galatás
Sérifos
Páros
Léros
PELOPONNESUS
Naxos
Kálimnos
Kalamáta
Sparta
Sífnos
Cos
Areópolis
Mílos
Íos
Astipálaia
Tílos
Rhodes
Neápolis
Thíra
Rhodes
Lindos
Cythera
SEA OF CRETE
Kárpathos
Khaniá
Réthimnon
Iráklion
Mt Ida
2,456 m
Crete

BULGARIA

MACEDONIA

GREECE

ALBANIA

Islands from volcanoes
The Greek island of Santorini (or Thira) is one of the islands that form the Cyclades in the Aegean Sea. Once a volcano, the island has steep cliffs and narrow, winding streets. It has become a popular destination for tourists.

Clear waters
A waterfall sparkles in the sunshine in Croatia. This is a small country of many landscapes.

RUSSIA AND ITS NEIGHBOURS

FOR A LARGE PART OF THIS CENTURY all the countries on this map were part of one huge country, the Soviet Union. That nation was formed in the years after November 1917, when communists seized power from the czars. Communist rule ended in 1991 and many of the regions around the former Soviet borders then broke away to become independent countries.

St Basil's Cathedral, Russia
Moscow is famous for the onion-shaped domes of St Basil's Cathedral. It was built in 1555 by Czar Ivan IV to commemorate the defeat of invading Tartars.

The remaining part of the former Soviet Union was renamed the '**Russian Federation**'. It is still by far the largest country in the world, stretching across two continents, Europe and Asia. Eighty percent of the population are Russians, but the rest belong to one of the many other ethnic groups who live in this enormous region.

Northern Russia is a land of tundra, where deep-frozen soil borders the Arctic Ocean. To the south is the great belt of forest known as taiga, whose spruce trees are heavy with snow during the long, bitter winter. Southern Russia and the **Ukraine** have the fertile black earth of the rolling grasslands known as steppes. The lands to the south of Russia's new borders take in warm, fertile valleys, thin grasslands grazed by sheep and goats, deserts and high mountains.

Russia is rich in minerals, oil, natural gas and timber. Its industries were developed in a hurry during the Soviet years, but at great cost to its people and environment. Russia is still an economic giant, producing machinery, textiles, chemicals and vehicles.

BELARUS

UKRAINE

MOLDOVA

GEORGIA

ARMENIA

AZERBAIJAN

UZBEKISTAN

TURKMENISTAN

KYRGYZSTAN

TAJIKISTAN

Franz Josef Land

FINLAND
ESTONIA
LITHUANIA
LATVIA
RUSSIA

Murmansk *BARENTS SEA*
Novaya Zemlya
KARA SEA
Dikso

L. Ladoga
Archangel
Amderma
L. Onega
N. Dvina
Salekhard

BELARUS
Minsk
Smolensk
Yaroslavl'
Kirov
Pechora
Ob'
SIBERIAN LOWLAND

Gomel
St Petersburg
Chernobyl
Moscow
Volga

UKRAINE ■Kiev
Nizhniy Novgorod
Kazan Perm
Khanty-Mansiysk
R   U   S

MOLDOVA
Chisinau
Dnepr
Voronezh
Kama
Nizhniy Tagil
Irtysh

Khar'kov
Syzran
Ufa
Tobol'sk
Ob'

Odessa
Don
Saratov
Yekaterinburg
Tor

Donetsk
Volga
Samara
Chelyabinsk

Sevastopol
Volgograd
Magnitogorsk
Omsk

Rostov-on-Don
Ural
Orsk
Novosibirsk

BLACK SEA
Astrakhan
Ishim

Mt. Elbrus
5,642 m
Groznyy
Aqmola
Irtysh

Batumi
CAUCASUS MTS
Caspian Sea
KAZAKHSTAN
Karaganda

GEORGIA
Tbilisi
Semey

ARMENIA
Yerevan
Aral Sea
SA

AZERBAIJAN
AZER.
Balkhash

Baku
Nukus
TURANIAN PLATEAU
Lake Balkhash

Tashauz
Almaty
CHINA

Syr Darya

TURKEY

IRAN

TURKMENISTAN
Ashgabat
Bukhara
UZBEKISTAN
Bishkek
KYRGYZSTAN

Amu Darya
Tashkent

Dushanbe
TAJIKISTAN

AFGHANISTAN

218

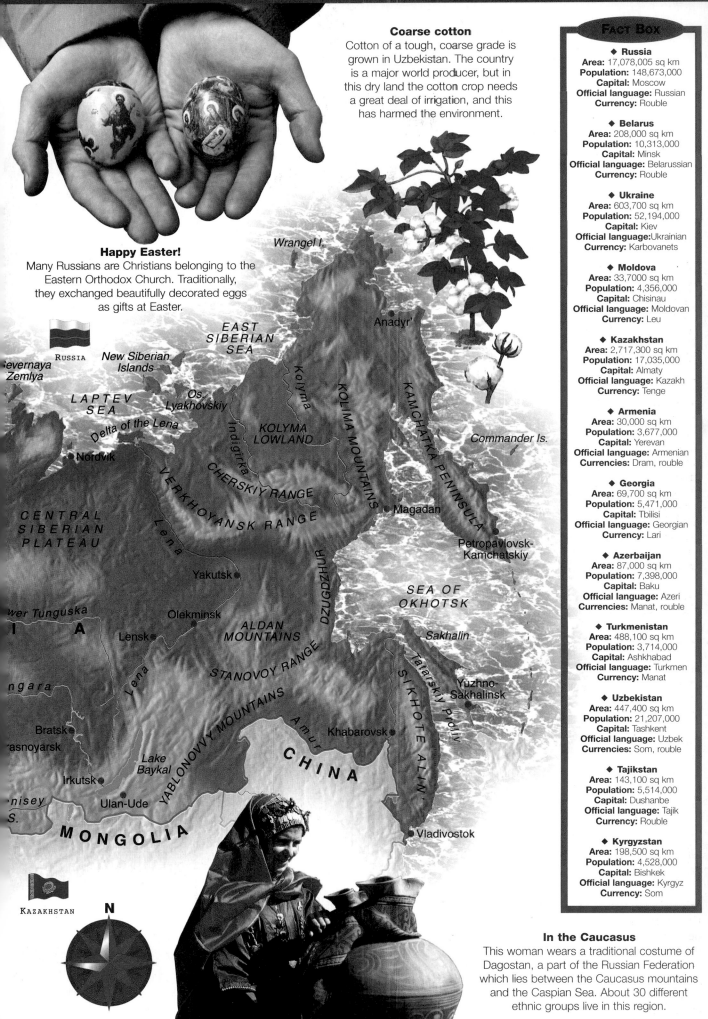

Coarse cotton

Cotton of a tough, coarse grade is grown in Uzbekistan. The country is a major world producer, but in this dry land the cotton crop needs a great deal of irrigation, and this has harmed the environment.

Happy Easter!

Many Russians are Christians belonging to the Eastern Orthodox Church. Traditionally, they exchanged beautifully decorated eggs as gifts at Easter.

RUSSIA

KAZAKHSTAN

N

In the Caucasus

This woman wears a traditional costume of Dagostan, a part of the Russian Federation which lies between the Caucasus mountains and the Caspian Sea. About 30 different ethnic groups live in this region.

Map labels:

Wrangel I.

EAST SIBERIAN SEA

Anadyr'

New Siberian Islands

Severnaya Zemlya

LAPTEV SEA

Os. Lyakhovskiy

Delta of the Lena

Nordvik

Kolyma

KOLYMA LOWLAND

Indigirka

CHERSKIY RANGE

KOLIMA MOUNTAINS

KAMCHATKA PENINSULA

Commander Is.

Magadan

Petropavlovsk-Kamchatskiy

CENTRAL SIBERIAN PLATEAU

VERKHOYANSK RANGE

Lena

Yakutsk

DZUGDZHUR

SEA OF OKHOTSK

wer Tunguska

Olekminsk

ALDAN MOUNTAINS

Lensk

A

Lena

STANOVOY RANGE

Sakhalin

SIKHOTE ALIN.

Tatarskiy Proliv

Yuzhno-Sakhalinsk

ngara

YABLONOVVY MOUNTAINS

Amur

Khabarovsk

Bratsk

asnoyarsk

Lake Baykal

CHINA

Irkutsk

nisey S.

Ulan-Ude

MONGOLIA

Vladivostok

FACT BOX

◆ **Russia**
Area: 17,078,005 sq km
Population: 148,673,000
Capital: Moscow
Official language: Russian
Currency: Rouble

◆ **Belarus**
Area: 208,000 sq km
Population: 10,313,000
Capital: Minsk
Official language: Belarussian
Currency: Rouble

◆ **Ukraine**
Area: 603,700 sq km
Population: 52,194,000
Capital: Kiev
Official language: Ukrainian
Currency: Karbovanets

◆ **Moldova**
Area: 33,7000 sq km
Population: 4,356,000
Capital: Chisinau
Official language: Moldovan
Currency: Leu

◆ **Kazakhstan**
Area: 2,717,300 sq km
Population: 17,035,000
Capital: Almaty
Official language: Kazakh
Currency: Tenge

◆ **Armenia**
Area: 30,000 sq km
Population: 3,677,000
Capital: Yerevan
Official language: Armenian
Currencies: Dram, rouble

◆ **Georgia**
Area: 69,700 sq km
Population: 5,471,000
Capital: Tbilisi
Official language: Georgian
Currency: Lari

◆ **Azerbaijan**
Area: 87,000 sq km
Population: 7,398,000
Capital: Baku
Official language: Azeri
Currencies: Manat, rouble

◆ **Turkmenistan**
Area: 488,100 sq km
Population: 3,714,000
Capital: Ashkhabad
Official language: Turkmen
Currency: Manat

◆ **Uzbekistan**
Area: 447,400 sq km
Population: 21,207,000
Capital: Tashkent
Official language: Uzbek
Currencies: Som, rouble

◆ **Tajikstan**
Area: 143,100 sq km
Population: 5,514,000
Capital: Dushanbe
Official language: Tajik
Currency: Rouble

◆ **Kyrgyzstan**
Area: 198,500 sq km
Population: 4,528,000
Capital: Bishkek
Official language: Kyrgyz
Currency: Som

CANADA AND GREENLAND

FACT BOX

◆ **Canada**
Area: 9,922,385 sq km
Population: 30,000,000
Capital: Ottawa
Official languages: French, English

◆ **Greenland**
Area: 2,175,600 sq km
Population: 57,000
Capital: Nuuk (Godthåb)
Official languages: Danish, Inuktitut
Currency: Danish krone

CANADA is the second largest country in the world and yet it is home to only 30 million people. Most Canadians live in the big cities in the south, such as Toronto, Ottawa, Montréal and Vancouver.

The southern provinces take in the St Lawrence River and Seaway, the Great Lakes, the prairies along the United States border and the foggy coasts of the Atlantic and Pacific Oceans.

The severe climate makes it hard for people to live in the northern wilderness, which stretches into the **Arctic Circle**. Here, a broad belt of spruce forest gives way to bare, deep-frozen soil called tundra, and a maze of islands locked in ice.

Canada's wilderness includes rivers, lakes, coasts and forests. It is home to polar bears and seals, caribou, moose, beavers and loons. It also has valuable resources, providing timber, hydroelectric power and minerals, including oil. **Canada** is a wealthy country.

The first Canadians crossed into North America from Asia long ago, when the two continents were joined by land. They were the Native American peoples and they were followed by the Inuit people of the Arctic. Today these two groups make up only four percent of the population. About 40 percent of Canadians are descended from peoples of the British Isles, especially Scots. People of French descent make up 27 percent, and there are also many people of Eastern European and Asian descent.

Canada has two official languages, French and English. In recent years many people in the French-speaking province of Québec have campaigned to become separate from the rest of Canada.

Across the Davis Strait, **Greenland** (or Kallaalit Nunaat) is a self-governing territory of Denmark. Its peoples are descended from both Inuit and Scandinavians.

Map labels:
ARCTIC OCEAN
Melville Island
Banks Island
Prince of Wales Island
Victoria Island
BEAUFORT SEA
ALASKA (U.S.A.)
Dawson
Norman Wells
Great Bear Lake
MACKENZIE MOUNTAINS
Mackenzie
YUKON TERRITORY
Yukon
▲ Mt. Logan 5,951 m
Whitehorse
NORTHWEST TERRITORIE
Dubawnt Lake
HORN MOUNTAINS
Yellowknife
Liard
Great Slave Lake
Fort Resolution
Fort Smith
ROCKY MOUNTAINS
CARIBOU MOUNTAINS
Lake Athabasca
Reindeer Lake
BRITISH COLUMBIA
CANADA
Chu
Ne
Prince Rupert
Peace
Peace River
MANITO
QUEEN CHARLOTTE ISLANDS
Prince George
ALBERTA
Prince Albert
COAST MOUNTAINS
Edmonton
N. Saskatchewan
Lak
Winnipegosis
Lake Winnip
Fraser
Red Deer
Kamloops
Saskatoon
Vancouver Island
Calgary
SASKATCHEWAN
Lake Manitob
Vancouver
Medicine Hat
S. Saskatchewan
Regina
Winnip
Victoria
UNITED STATES OF AMERICA

Wheat Harvest
Large combine harvesters cross the Canadian prairies. These are natural grasslands which are now largely given over to wheat and cattle production. They occupy parts of Manitoba, Saskatchewan and Alberta and stretch across the border into the northern United States.

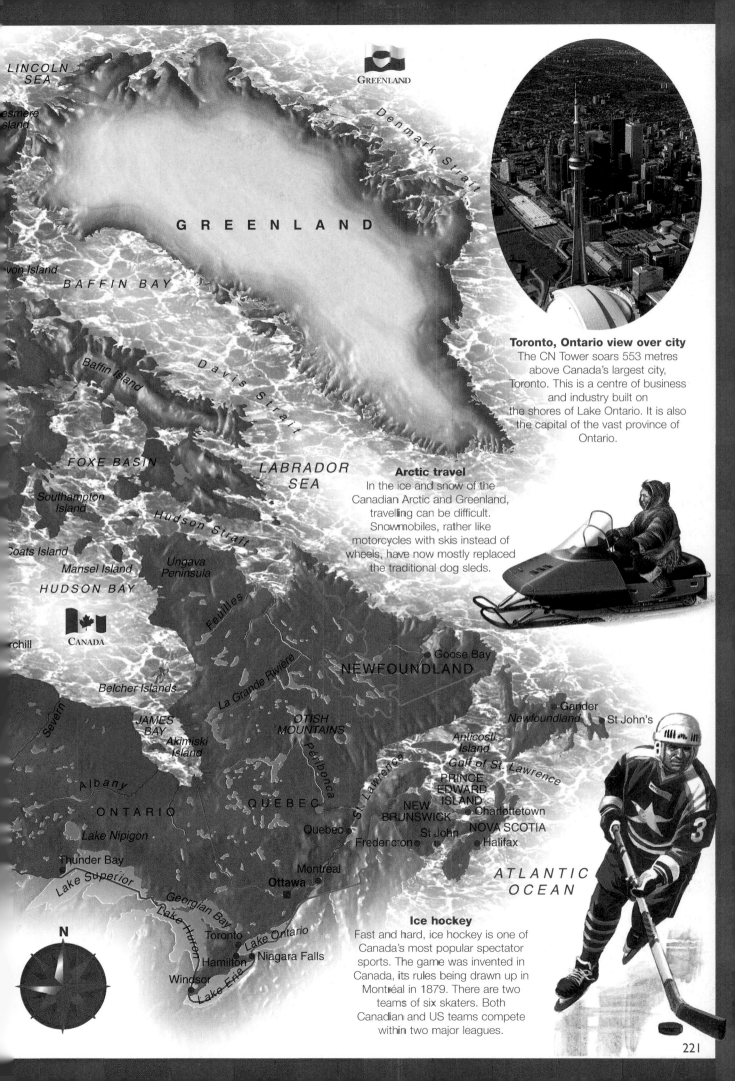

LINCOLN SEA

smere sland

GREENLAND

GREENLAND

Denmark Strait

Toronto, Ontario view over city
The CN Tower soars 553 metres above Canada's largest city, Toronto. This is a centre of business and industry built on the shores of Lake Ontario. It is also the capital of the vast province of Ontario.

von Island

BAFFIN BAY

Baffin Island

Davis Strait

FOXE BASIN

LABRADOR SEA

Southampton Island

Arctic travel
In the ice and snow of the Canadian Arctic and Greenland, travelling can be difficult. Snowmobiles, rather like motorcycles with skis instead of wheels, have now mostly replaced the traditional dog sleds.

oats Island

Hudson Strait

Mansel Island

Ungava Peninsula

HUDSON BAY

CANADA

Feuilles

rchill

Belcher Islands

La Grande Rivière

Goose Bay

NEWFOUNDLAND

Severn

JAMES BAY

Akimiski Island

OTISH MOUNTAINS

Péribonca

Gander

Newfoundland   St John's

Anticosti Island

Gulf of St. Lawrence

Albany

ONTARIO

QUEBEC

St. Lawrence

PRINCE EDWARD ISLAND

NEW BRUNSWICK

Charlottetown

NOVA SCOTIA

Lake Nipigon

Quebec

St John

Fredericton

Halifax

Thunder Bay

Montreal

Ottawa

ATLANTIC OCEAN

Lake Superior

Georgian Bay

Lake Huron

N

Toronto

Lake Ontario

Hamilton   Niagara Falls

Windsor

Lake Erie

Ice hockey
Fast and hard, ice hockey is one of Canada's most popular spectator sports. The game was invented in Canada, its rules being drawn up in Montréal in 1879. There are two teams of six skaters. Both Canadian and US teams compete within two major leagues.

USA

THE UNITED STATES OF AMERICA

make up a huge country, which crosses no less than eight time zones. It extends from the Pacific to the Atlantic Oceans, from Canada south to Mexico.

The modern nation was formed by colonists from Europe, who from the 1500s onwards seized and settled the lands of the Native American peoples. In 1776 the British colonies in the east declared their independence, and the new country grew rapidly during the 1800s as it gained territory from France, Mexico and Russia. Today, in addition to the small Native American population, there are Americans whose ancestors originally came from Britain, Ireland, Italy, France, Germany, the Netherlands and Poland. There are African Americans, whose ancestors were brought to America to work as slaves. There are Armenians, Spanish, Chinese, Cubans, Vietnamese and Koreans. All are citizens of the United States.

The nation today is a federation of 50 states, which have the power to pass many of their own laws. The federal capital is at Washington, a large city on the Potomac River, in the District of Columbia (DC). Here is the Congress, made up of a Senate and a House of Representatives, and the White House, the home of the US presidents.

The American economy is the most powerful in the world. The country is rich in minerals, including oil, coal and iron ore. American companies produce computers and software, aircraft, cars and processed foods. There are also many large banks and finance companies. America leads in space exploration and technology. The films and television programmes produced in America are watched by people in many countries around the world.

FACT BOX

◆ **United States of America**
Area: 9,363,130 sq km
Population: 267,700,000
Capital: Washington DC
Official language: English
Currency: US dollar

The woods of Vermont
Vermont is in New England and nicknamed the Green Mountain State. It is famous for its brilliant foliage in the autumn or fall.

222

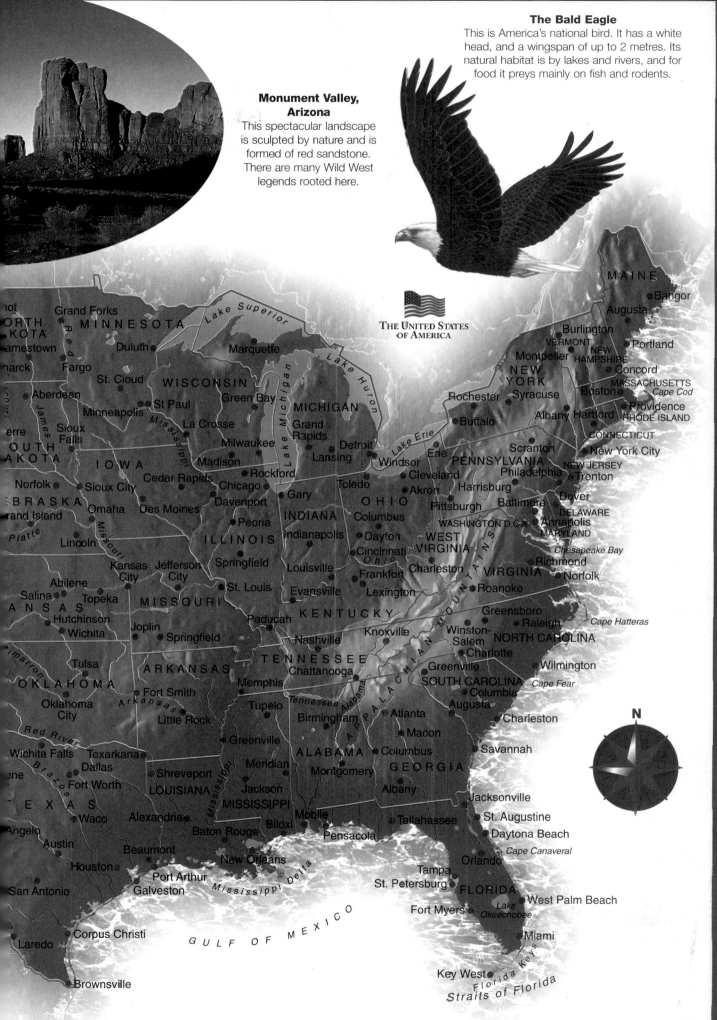

Monument Valley, Arizona
This spectacular landscape is sculpted by nature and is formed of red sandstone. There are many Wild West legends rooted here.

The Bald Eagle
This is America's national bird. It has a white head, and a wingspan of up to 2 metres. Its natural habitat is by lakes and rivers, and for food it preys mainly on fish and rodents.

THE UNITED STATES OF AMERICA

The northeastern United States have a mild climate, although winter snowfall can be heavy and summers can be warm. Inland from the rocks and stormy shores of the Atlantic coast are the woodlands of the New England region, which turn to every shade of red and gold in the autumn. Here there are broad rivers and neat little towns dating back to the days of the early settlers, as well as the historic city of Boston, Massachusetts. In the far north the Great Lakes mark the border with Canada. On this border are the spectacular Niagara Falls, a major tourist attraction which also provides valuable hydroelectric power. The Appalachian mountain ranges run for 2,400 kilometres from north to south, through the eastern United States.

The northeastern United States include centres of industry and mining, and large cities with gleaming skyscrapers, sprawling suburbs, road and rail networks. New York City, centred around the island of Manhattan, is the business capital of the United States and also a lively centre of arts and entertainment. To many people, New York City is a symbol of America – fast-moving and energetic, a melting pot of different peoples and cultures. The northern city of Detroit is a centre of the motor industry, and Chicago, on the windy shores of Lake Michigan, is another bustling city of skyscrapers, and an important centre of business and manufacture.

Travelling south from the Delaware River and the great city of Philadelphia, you come to the federal District of Columbia, the site of Washington, capital city of the United States. Approaching the American South, you pass into warmer country where tobacco and cotton are grown in the red earth. The long peninsula of Florida extends southwards into the Caribbean Sea, fringed by sandy islands called keys. Along the Gulf coast the climate is hot and very humid, with creeks known as bayous and tangled swamps which are home to alligators.

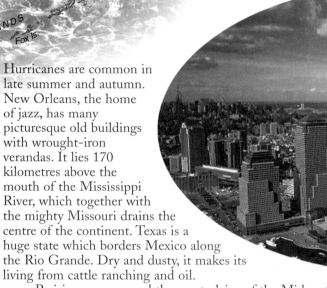

Hurricanes are common in late summer and autumn. New Orleans, the home of jazz, has many picturesque old buildings with wrought-iron verandas. It lies 170 kilometres above the mouth of the Mississippi River, which together with the mighty Missouri drains the centre of the continent. Texas is a huge state which borders Mexico along the Rio Grande. Dry and dusty, it makes its living from cattle ranching and oil.

Prairies once covered the great plains of the Midwest, the home of vast herds of bison or buffalo. Today the grasslands are largely given over to farming vegetable crops and grain, or to cattle ranching. The wheat and maize produced on the Prairies have led to them being called the 'breadbasket of the world'.

Barren, stony 'badlands' rise towards the rugged Rocky Mountain ranges, which form the backbone of the United States as they stretch from the Canadian border south to Mexico. Southwards and westwards again there are large areas of burning desert, salt flats and canyons, where over the ages the rocks have been worn into fantastic shapes by wind and water. In places the Grand Canyon of Arizona is 24 kilometres wide and two kilometres deep, a spectacular gorge cut out by the waters of the Colorado River.

Jambalaya!
Rice, seafood, green peppers and hot spices make up this delicious dish from New Orleans, in Louisiana. The people of this city include many of French and African descent, and this shows in its cooking.

The Statue of Liberty
This huge monument, a gift from the people of France in 1886, was the first sight of America for many immigrants.

224

Badwater, in California's harsh Death Valley, is the lowest point in the United States, 86 metres below sea level.

The Sierra, Cascade and Coast ranges run parallel with the beautiful Pacific coast. The warm beaches, pines and gigantic redwood trees of California stretch northwards to the ferny forests of Oregon and Washington State, which is rainy and cool. Irrigation has made it possible to farm large areas of California, which produce citrus fruits and grape vines. Major cities of the west include Los Angeles, which takes in the world-famous film studios of Hollywood, beautiful San Francisco, set on a wide bay which can be warm and sparkling blue or shrouded in cool sea-fog, and the busy northern port of Seattle.

The United States has a northern outpost in oil-rich Alaska, its largest state. Alaska was purchased from Russia in 1867. Bordered by Canada, the Alaskan wilderness stretches into the remote Arctic, a deep frozen land of mountains and tundra. Its islands are inhabited by large grizzly bears and its waters by schools of migrating whales.

Baseball
Baseball is the the big summer-season game in the USA. It is played with a bat and ball and there are two teams of nine players.

Mount McKinley, at 6,194 metres, is the highest point not just in the United States, but in all of North America.

Far to the west, in the Pacific Ocean, the Hawaiian Islands are also part of the United States. Tourists come here to enjoy the warm climate and the surf and to see the islands' spectacular volcanoes.

The United States also governs or has special links with various other territories, such as American Samoa, the Northern Marianas and the Midway Islands in the Pacific Ocean. Puerto Rico and the US Virgin Islands in the Caribbean are also governed by the United States.

The United States has close economic links with its neighbours, Canada and Mexico, through the North American Free Trade Agreement of 1994. It is also a member of many other international groupings, such as the the North Atlantic Treaty Organization (NATO), a military alliance which links it with Western and Central Europe.

As the world's most powerful country, the influence of the United States is to be seen in many other lands. Films and television programmes have made the American way of life influential around the world. Hamburgers and soft drinks are now bought in many other countries. American blues and jazz has influenced all kinds of popular music and American slang is used by people around the world.

Manhattan
The centre of New York City is built over the island of Manhattan. Unable to build outwards, architects have built upwards. The skyline includes many famous skyscrapers. These twin towers belong to the World Trade Centre.

Cops and crime
American policemen and detectives fight city crime. Their work has been made famous around the world by countless films and television series.

Heart of the nation
The impressive Capitol building is at the centre of Washington, District of Columbia. It is used by the United States Congress and was constructed between 1851 and 1863.

Blast-off!
The space shuttle leaves Earth on another mission. The United States has been a pioneer of space exploration since the 1960s.

MEXICO, CENTRAL AMERICA & THE CARIBBEAN

Ancient stones
Many great civilizations developed in ancient times in Mexico and Central America. Statues like this, called chacmools, were used during human sacrifices.

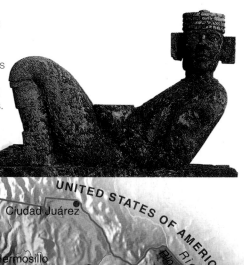

MEXICO is a large, mountainous country with a tropical climate. It stretches southwards from the Rio Grande on the United States border, and meets the Pacific Ocean in the west and the Gulf of Mexico in the east.

Mexico is a land of deserts, forests and volcanoes, dotted with the spectacular ruins of ancient Native American civilizations, such as the Maya, Toltec and Aztec. Mexico City, built on the site of an ancient Aztec city, is a vast, sprawling centre of population.

To the south, **Central America** narrows to a thin strip of land called the isthmus of Panama. Guatemala, Belize, Honduras, El Salvador, Nicaragua, Costa Rica and Panama are all small nations that live mostly by farming tropical crops such as bananas, coffee and sugar-cane. Many Mexicans and Central Americans are of Native American, Spanish or mixed descent.

Tijuana
Mexicali
Ensenada
Ciudad Juárez

UNITED STATES OF AMERICA

Gulf of California
Baja California
Cedros I.
Hermosillo
Chihuahua
Rio Bravo del Norte
Rio Grande

SIERRA MADRE

Torreón
Matamoros
Culiacán
La Paz
Saltillo
Monterrey
Durango
San Luis Potosí
Tampico
Aguascalientes
Guadalajara
León
Cape Corrientes
L. de Chapala
Manzanillo
Mexico City
Puebla
Veracruz
Orizaba 5,700 m

MEXICO

Balsas
Acapulco
Oaxaca
Coatzacoalcos
Villahermosa

GULF OF MEXICO

MEXICO

Havana
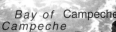
CUBA
CUE
Isla de la Juventad
Cayr
Islands

Mérida
Cancún
Bay of Campeche
Campeche
Yucatán Peninsula
Términos Lagoon
Belize City

BELIZE
Belmopan
BELIZE

Yucatán Channel

Gulf of Tehuantepec

GUATEMALA **HONDURAS**
Tegucigalpa
Guatemala City
San Salvador
EL SALVADOR
NICARAGUA
Managua
Lake Nicaragua
Mosc
G
San José
COSTA RICA

PACIFIC OCEAN

N

GUATEMALA

EL SALVADOR

NICARAGUA

COSTA RICA

Birds of a feather
The quetzal is a brilliantly coloured bird. It lives in rainforests from southern Mexico to Panama, where it feeds on berries and fruits.

Many people in Mexico and Central America are poor and the region has a long history of political strife and civil war.

The **Caribbean Sea** is part of the Atlantic Ocean and is dotted with beautiful islands in warm, blue seas. These were once home to Native American peoples such as the Arawaks and the Caribs, after whom the region is named. Then came European invaders, including the Spanish, Dutch, French and British. Most of today's Caribbeans are descended from West Africans who were brought in as slaves by the early settlers. Caribbean islanders live by fishing, farming, manufacture and tourism. Favourite sports include baseball in Cuba and cricket in Jamaica and Barbados. The region is famous for its range of popular music, from calypso to salsa, from reggae to soca.

Coconut grove
Palms line sandy beaches in the Central American republic of Costa Rica. Coconuts are common around the tropical coasts of Central America and the Caribbean.

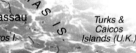
BAHAMAS
BAHAMAS

ANTIGUA AND BARBUDA

H A M A S . I S .

assau
os I.

Turks & Caicos Islands (U.K.)

PUERTO RICO

DOMINICA

Virgin Is. (U.K. & U.S.)

naguey

DOMINICAN REPUBLIC

San Juan
Puerto Rico (U.S.)

ANTIGUA & BARBUDA

tiago
Cuba

HAITI

ST. KITTS & NEVIS

Montserrat (U.K.)
Guadeloupe (FR.)
DOMINICA

Santo Domingo

Port-au-Prince

R E A T E R   A N T I L L E S

Martinique (FR.)
ST. LUCIA

Kingston
MAICA

C A R I B B E A N   S E A

DOMINICAN REPUBLIC

BARBADOS
ST. VINCENT & THE GRENADINES
GRENADA

L E S S E R   A N T I L L E S

TRINIDAD & TOBAGO

JAMAICA
HAITI

Netherlands Antilles

GRENADA

ST VINCENT AND GRENADINES

HONDURAS

TRINIDAD AND TOBAGO

ST LUCIA

BARBADOS

ST KITTS AND NEVIS

PANAMA
JAMA

C O L O M B I A

ama
ty
of
ma

People of Panama
The Kuna are an indigenous people who live on the coasts and islands of Panama and Colombia. They mostly live by fishing and are well known for their craft work, which includes wood carving and the making of molas, the colourful blouses being worn here.

227

NORTHERN ANDEAN COUNTRIES

THE ANDES MOUNTAINS extend down the whole length of South America, from north to south. They rise in Colombia, the country which borders the narrow land link with Central America, the Isthmus of Panama.

Colombia is a beautiful country with three ranges of the Andes running through it. The mountains slope east to grasslands and then to rainforest. The chief cities are on the coast, which is warm and humid, or in the cooler mountain regions. The mountains are mined for gold, emeralds, salt and coal.

The Andes rise to 6,267 metres above sea level at Chimborazo in **Ecuador**. Bananas and sugar-cane are grown here. In the cooler foothills of the Andes coffee is an important crop. To the east of the mountains are rainforests, where oil is drilled. Ecuador is the second largest oil producer in South America after Venezuela.

In the 1400s, **Peru** was the centre of the mighty Inca empire, an advanced Native American civilization which produced beautiful textiles and jewellery in gold and precious stones. Ruined Inca cities such as Machu Picchu still perch high amongst the peaks of the Andes. Terraced hillsides allow crops such as potatoes to be grown in the mountains. Fishing is important along the foggy Pacific coast. In the far east, rivers flow through tropical forests into the river Amazon.

Lake Titicaca lies high in the Andes on the border between Peru and **Bolivia**. Bolivia is an inland country which lies across the high plateau of the Altiplano, where most Bolivians live, and stretches into hot, humid rainforest in the east. The city of La Paz is the world's highest capital city, at 3,660 metres above sea level. Bolivia produces tin, timber, rubber and potatoes.

The lands of the northern Andes are home to many Native Americans, such as the Quechua and Aymara peoples. The whole region was ruled by Spain from the 1500s to the early 1800s, and Spanish is spoken throughout the region as well as a number of Native

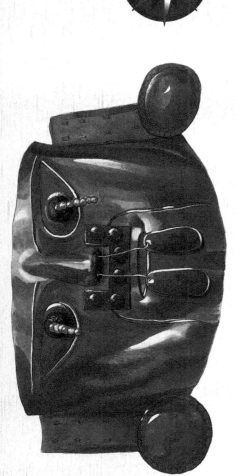

Inca crafts

This mask was made by Inca goldsmiths in Peru. The Incas came to power in the 1400s and were famous for their beautiful work with gold.

N

COLOMBIA

ECUADOR

PERU

Point Gallinas

Barranquilla
Cartagena ●
Cristóbal Colón
5,775 m

VENEZUELA

Cape Corrientes

Medellín ●
Manizales ●
Pereira ●
Ibagué ●
Magdalena
Cauca
Bogotá ■ COLOMBIA

Meta
Guaviare

PANAMA

Buenaventura ●
Cali ●
Nevado del Hula
5,750 m
Pasto ●
Neiva ●

Caquetá
Putumayo

Point Galera

ECUADOR
Quito ●

Chimborazo
6,267 m
Guayaquil ●
Gulf of Guayaquil

Iquitos ●

Amazon

Marañón

● Piura

B R A Z I L

Lake Titicaca

This lake lies on the mountainous border between Bolivia and Peru. At 3810 metres above sea level, this is the world's highest navigable lake.

The incredible llama

The llama is a sure-footed but stubborn member of the camel family. It is used to carry goods over the high passes of the Andes mountains.

Machu Picchu, Inca ruins

High in the Peruvian Andes stand the ruins of this Inca city, Machu Picchu. The city was never found by the Spanish conquerors of Peru and it remained undiscovered until 1911.

Pan pipes

Sounds of the Andes include haunting folk tunes accompanied by panpipes, drums and various types of guitar. They have been influenced by Native American and Spanish music.

BOLIVIA

Guaporé
Mamoré
BOLIVIA
Santa Cruz
Cochabamba
Oruro • Sucre
Nevado • Potosí
Ancohune Lake
▲ 6,550 m Poopó
La Paz
Lake
Titicaca
ALTIPIANO
Volcan
El Misti CHILE
5,842 m ▲
Arequipa ▲
PACIFIC
OCEAN
Cuzco
Huancayo
Nazca
PERU
Nevado Huascarán
6,768 m
Chimbote
Callao
Lima
Paracas
Pen.
PARAGUAY
Pilcomayo

FACT BOX

◆ **Colombia**
Area: 1,138,915 sq km
Population: 37,400,000
Capital: Bogotá
Main language: Spanish
Currency: Colombian peso

◆ **Ecuador**
Area: 461,475 sq km
Population: 12,000,000
Capital: Quito
Main language: Spanish
Currency: Sucre

◆ **Bolivia**
Area: 1,098,580 sq km
Population: 7,800,000
Capitals: La Paz, Sucre
Main language: Spanish
Currency: Boliviano

◆ **Peru**
Area: 1,285,215 sq km
Population: 24,400,000
Capital: Lima
Main language: Spanish
Currency: Nuevo soll

Netherlands
Antilles

Gulf of
Venezuela

Maracaibo

Lake
Maracaibo

Caracas

Barcelona

Port of Spain

**TRINIDAD
& TOBAGO**

GUYANA

Pico Bolívar
5,002 m

ANDES MTS.

LLANOS

Orinoco

Orinoco Delta

VENEZUELA

Angel
Falls

Georgetown

GUYANA

Paramaribo

SURINAM

Cayenne

FRENCH GUIANA

COLOMBIA

G U I A N A   H I G H L A N D S

Orinoco

Branco

SURINAM

VENEZUELA

Pico da Neblina
3014 m

Negro

Japurá

Macapá

Marajó
Bay

Marajó I.

Belèm

São
Marcos
Bay

**FRENCH
GUIANA**

Amazon

Manaus

Santarém

Tocantins

São Lu

S E L V A S

Madeira

Tapajós

Xingu

Teresina

Jurúa

Purus

Aripuanã

Araguaia

Parnaíba

Rio Branco

Jiparana

Arinos

BRAZIL

PERU

SERRA DOS PARECIS

Guaporé

Sobradinho
Reservoir

BOLIVIA

*MATO GROSSO
PLATEAU*

Cuiabá

Brasília

Goiânia

*B R A Z I L I A
H I G H L A N D*

Uberlandia

Coffee beans

Brazil is the world's biggest producer of
coffee. The crop is mostly grown in the south,
on large estates and is exported worldwide.

Campo Grande

Paraná

Belo Horizonte

Campos

São Paulo

Santos

Rio de
Janeiro

Cap
Fric

PARAGUAY

Itaipu Res.

Itguaçu
Falls

SERRA DO MAR

Curitiba

BRAZIL

ARGENTINA

Uruguay

Florianópolis

Santa Maria

Pôrto Alegre

Patos Lagoon

URUGUAY

Mirim Lake

N

Rio panorama

A huge statue of Christ stands high above the
Brazilian port of Rio de Janeiro.

BRAZIL AND ITS NEIGHBOURS

BRAZIL is South America's largest nation. It includes grasslands, fertile plateaus and dry areas of scrub.

About a third of the country is taken up by tropical rainforests. All kinds of rare plants, parrots, snakes and monkeys live in these dense, dripping forests, which are under threat from road-builders, farmers, miners and loggers. The forests are crossed by hundreds of rivers, which drain into the wide, muddy waters of the Amazon, one of the world's two longest rivers. The river basin of the Amazon is the world's largest, covering 7,045,000 square kilometres.

Most Brazilians live in the big cities of the Atlantic coast, such as Rio de Janeiro and São Paolo. The country has rich resources, but many of the population are poor people who live in shacks built on the outskirts of the city. Brasília, with its broad avenues and high-rise buildings, was specially built as the country's new capital city in the 1960s.

To the northeast of Brazil, on the Caribbean coast, is **Venezuela**. This land, crossed by the Orinoco River, includes rainforests, high mountains and the tropical grassy plains of the Llanos. The beautiful Angel Falls (the world's highest at 979 metres) provide hydroelectric power, while Lake Maracaibo, in the northwest, is rich in oil.

The three other countries on the Caribbean coast are **Guyana**, **Surinam** and **French Guiana**. The first was once a British colony, the second was a Dutch colony and the third is still an overseas department governed by France. Most people live in the humid regions of the coast, while the rainforests and mountains of the remote south are more sparsely populated. Crops include sugar-cane, coffee, rice and bananas. An important mineral is bauxite, used in the making of aluminium.

Many different ethnic groups live in the region as a whole, including Native American peoples who have had to struggle to survive ever since Europeans invaded the region in the 1500s. The population of northern South America also includes many people of Asian, African, European and mixed descent, with ancestors from Spain, Portugal, Italy, Germany, France, Netherlands and Britain.

FACT BOX

◆ **Brazil**
Area: 8,511,965 sq km
Population: 160,300,000
Capital: Brasília
Main language: Portuguese
Currency: Cruzeiro real

◆ **Venezuela**
Area: 912,045 sq km
Population: 22,600,000
Capital: Caracas
Main language: Spanish
Currency: Bolívar

◆ **Guyana**
Area: 214,970 sq km
Population: 800,000
Capital: Georgetown
Main language: English
Currency: Guyana dollar

◆ **Surinam**
Area: 163,820 sq km
Population: 446,000
Capital: Paramaribo
Official language: Dutch
Currency: Surinam guilder

◆ **French Guiana**
Area: 91,000 sq km
Population: 300,000
Capital: Cayenne
Main language: French
Currency: French franc

Rainforest creatures
The vast forests which are drained by the River Amazon, support all kinds of wildlife, such as this brightly coloured macaw. Sadly, many species are threatened by the clearance of the forests by farmers and illegal traders in wildlife.

Fishing for a living
A fishing crew check their tackle as children play on the beach. This scene is near Salvador, capital of the tropical Bahía region in northeastern Brazil.

Yanomami hunters
About 13,000 Yanomami people live in Venezuela and another 8000 in Brazil. They live by hunting, fishing and growing food in the rainforest.

ARGENTINA AND ITS NEIGHBOURS

THE SOUTHERN PART of South America stretches from the hot and humid Gran Chaco region to the cold and stormy waters of Tierra del Fuego and Cape Horn.

The largest country of this region is **Argentina**. Its highly populated capital is Buenos Aires on the river Plate. More than eight out of every ten Argentineans are city dwellers. However it was the country's cattle-farming regions – the Pampa grasslands and the northeast – that in the last 150 years brought wealth to the country and attracted large numbers of settlers from Europe. Argentina's western borders follow the high peak of the Andes range, which reach their highest point at Cerro Aconcagua (6,959 metres above sea level). To the south are the windswept plateaus of Patagonia, largely given over to sheep farming. The port of Ushuaia is the southernmost town in the world.

Northwards from Buenos Aires, across the river Plate, lies Montevideo, capital of **Uruguay**. This is another country which raises cattle and sheep, and whose rich grasslands and mild climate attracted European settlers. Neighbouring **Paraguay** is far from the coast. Most of its people farm the hills and plains of the east. Few live in the hot wilderness of the Gran Chaco.

To the west of the Andes is **Chile**, which covers a long and narrow area. Here is one of the driest regions on Earth, the Atacama desert. It also includes fertile orchards and productive vineyards, the big city of Santiago and the spectacular glaciers of the southern Andes. Spanish is spoken throughout the region, and some Native American languages such as Guaraní may also be heard.

Armadillo

The head and body of the armadillo is covered by an armour of plates made of horny and bony material. These usually nocturnal animals, feed mainly on insects and rest in a burrow by day.

Paraná River, Paraguay

Separating Paraguay and Argentina the Parana River flows some 4,500 km. The English explorer Sebastian Cabot was the first to sail up it in 1526.

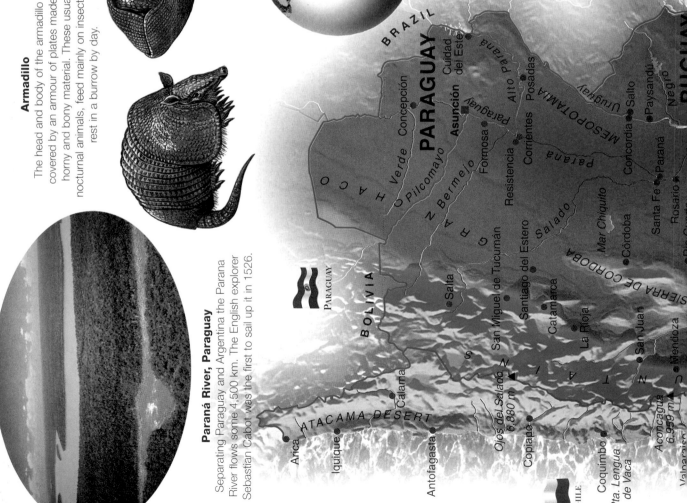

SOUTH GEORGIA (U.K.)

Prickly Pear

The flesh and seeds of the peeled fruit of the prickly pear have a pleasant taste. This cactus is low-growing and has flat oval stem joints and bright yellow flowers and occurs in Central and South America.

URUGUAY

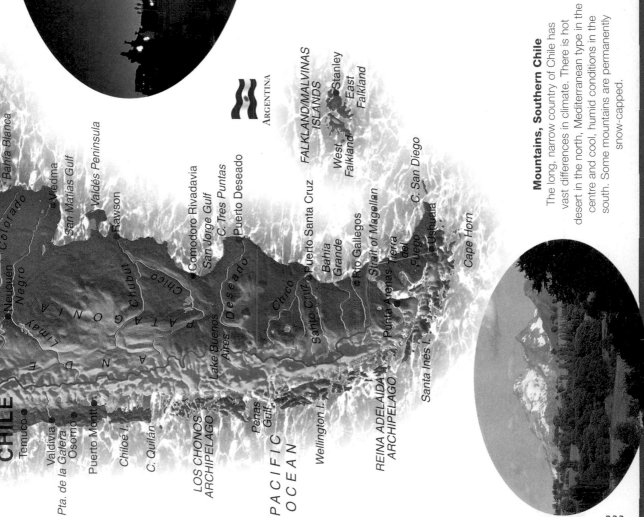

Buenos Aires by night

The Monument of the Two Congresses stands in front of the domed Palace of Congress, built in 1906. The Argentinian capital is a large, lively city.

N

ARGENTINA

Cape San Antonio
Mar del Plata
Cape Corrientes

FALKLAND/MALVINAS ISLANDS
West Falkland
East Falkland
Stanley

Mountains, Southern Chile

The long, narrow country of Chile has vast differences in climate. There is hot desert in the north, Mediterranean type in the centre and cool, humid conditions in the south. Some mountains are permanently snow-capped.

A R G E N T I N A

Bahía Blanca
Bahía Blanca
Viedma
San Matías Gulf
Valdés Peninsula
Rawson
Comodoro Rivadavia
San Jorge Gulf
C. Tres Puntas
Puerto Deseado

Colorado
Negro
Neuquén
Limay
Chubut
Chico
Deseado
Chico
Santa Cruz
Puerto Santa Cruz
Bahía Grande
Río Gallegos
Punta Arenas
Strait of Magellan
Tierra del Fuego
Ushuaia
C. San Diego
Cape Horn

P A T A G O N I A
Lake Buenos Aires

A N D E S

Chillán
Concepción
Pta. Lavapié

CHILE

Temuco
Valdivia
Pta. de la Galera
Osorno
Puerto Montt
Chiloé I.
C. Quilán

LOS CHONOS ARCHIPELAGO

Peñas Gulf.

Wellington I.

REINA ADELAIDA ARCHIPELAGO

Santa Inés I.

P A C I F I C
O C E A N

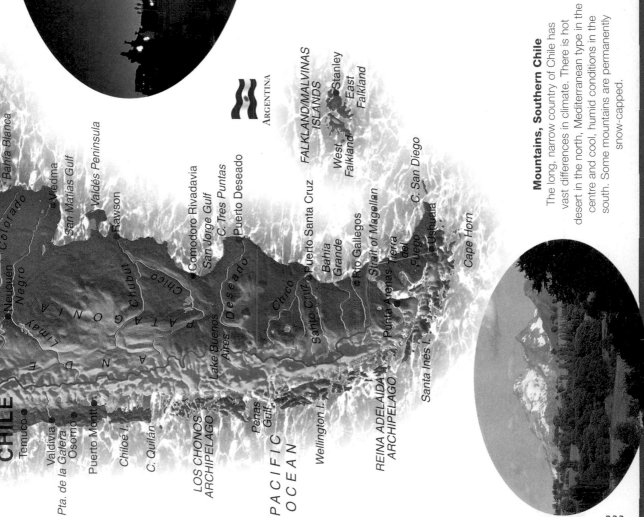

233

Turkish women
These women are from the port of Kas in southern Turkey. They are kneading dough and making pastry. Many Muslim women cover their heads with scarves or full veils.

ASIA

SOUTHWEST ASIA

SOUTHWEST ASIA IS SOMETIMES described as the Near East or the Middle East. Its peoples include Greek Cypriots, Turks, Jews, Arabs, Kurds and Iranians.

The region has seen many political disputes and wars in recent years – between Greeks and Turks on Cyprus, between Palestinian Arabs and Jews in Israel, between Iraqi and Iranians and between Iraqui and Kuwaiti Arabs. The Kurds, whose homeland is occupied by **Iraq**, **Iran** and **Turkey**, have also been at the centre of conflict.

It was in Southwest Asia that the world's first civilizations grew up, between the rivers Tigris and Euphrates, over 6,000 years ago. The region later gave birth to three world faiths – Judaism, Christianity and Islam. In the days of the Roman empire the Jews were scattered from their homeland, and over the centuries their culture spread to Spain, Central and Eastern Europe and the Americas. Arab armies and traders took the Islamic faith into Africa and Spain, and Arab scholars made great advances in mathematics and astronomy. From the 1500s the Turks established a great empire which stretched from Central Europe to the Indian Ocean.

Southwest Asia includes vast deserts, in the Arabian peninsula and in eastern Iran. It also takes in fertile plains, the marshes of southern Iraq and mountain ranges of Turkey and Iran. The north of the region borders the Black Sea and the Caspian Sea, grassy steppes and the Caucasus mountains. To the east lies Afghanistan, Pakistan and the Indian sub-continent.

The region's most valuable resource is oil, which brings wealth to the governments of the lands around the Persian Gulf. However many ordinary people of Southwest Asia remain poor, living by herding goats, sheep or camels. In Israel and some other regions irrigation has made it possible to grow crops in harsh, dry environments. Oranges, dates, grapes and many kinds of nuts are grown in the region.

A summons to prayer
Mosques, like this one in Kuwait, have tall towers called minarets. From here, faithful Muslims are called to prayer. This message is often broadcast from loudspeakers. Muslims are expected to pray five times a day.

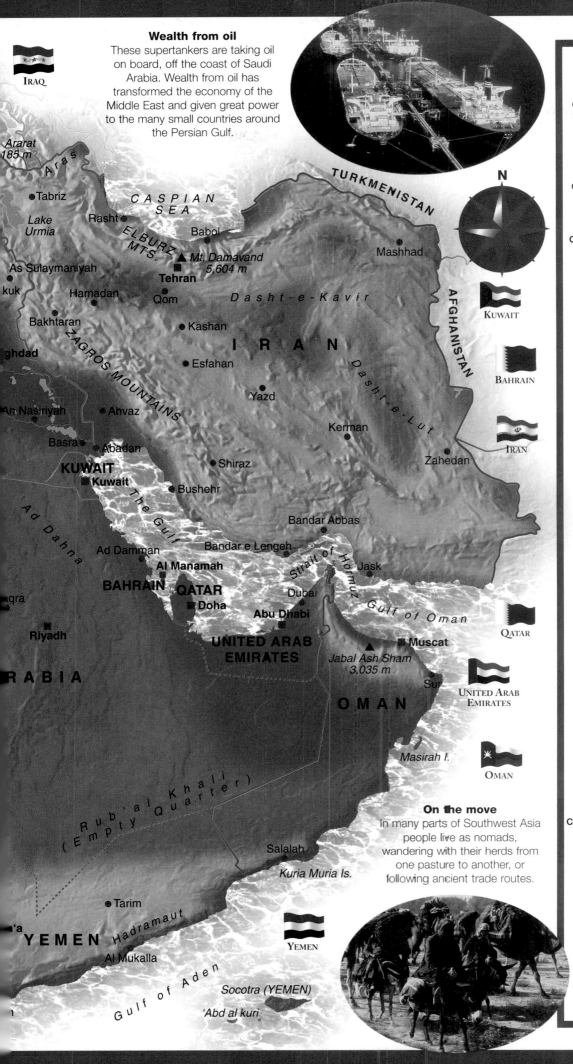

IRAQ

Wealth from oil
These supertankers are taking oil
on board, off the coast of Saudi
Arabia. Wealth from oil has
transformed the economy of the
Middle East and given great power
to the many small countries around
the Persian Gulf.

N

*Ararat
185 m*

Aras

TURKMENISTAN

•Tabriz

*CASPIAN
SEA*

Rasht•

*Lake
Urmia*

Babol•

*ELBURZ
MTS.*

Mashhad•

As Sulaymaniyah•

▲ *Mt. Damavand
5,604 m*

kuk

Tehran

Hamadan•

Qom•

Dasht-e-Kavir

AFGHANISTAN

Bakhtaran•

ZAGROS MOUNTAINS

•Kashan

KUWAIT

I R A N

ghdad

•Esfahan

Dasht-e-Lut

BAHRAIN

Yazd•

An Nasiriyah•

Ahvaz•

Kerman•

IRAN

Basra•

Abadan•

•Shiraz

Zahedan•

KUWAIT
■**Kuwait**

•Bushehr

The Gulf

Bandar Abbas•

Ad Dahna

•Ad Damman

Bandar e Lengeh•

Jask•

Strait of Hormuz

Al Manamah

Gulf of Oman

aqra

BAHRAIN

QATAR

Dubai•

QATAR

■**Doha**

Abu Dhabi

■

Riyadh

**UNITED ARAB
EMIRATES**

▲
*Jabal Ash Sham
3,035 m*

■**Muscat**

UNITED ARAB
EMIRATES

A R A B I A

O M A N

Sur

*(Rub' al Khali
Empty Quarter)*

OMAN

Masirah I.

On the move
In many parts of Southwest Asia
people live as nomads,
wandering with their herds from
one pasture to another, or
following ancient trade routes.

Salalah•

Kuria Muria Is.

•Tarim

Hadramaut

'a

Y E M E N

YEMEN

Al Mukalla•

Gulf of Aden

Socotra (YEMEN)

'Abd al kuri

INDIA AND ITS NEIGHBOURS

SOUTHERN ASIA stretches south into the Indian Ocean, forming a landmass so large that it sometimes called the 'sub-continent'. Its northern limits are marked by the Himalaya and Karakoram mountain ranges. These include many of the world's highest peaks and reach 8,848 metres above sea level at Everest, on Nepal's border with China.

The ranges pass through eastern Afghanistan, the Kashmir region on the border of India and Pakistan, India itself and the small mountain kingdoms of **Nepal** and **Bhutan**. Melting snows flow south from the mountains to form the five great rivers of the Punjab and also the mighty Ganges, which winds across the fertile plains of northern India before crossing Bangladesh into a maze of waterways around the Bay of Bengal. This area suffers from devastating floods.

Central and southern **India** form a triangular plateau called the Deccan, fringed on the east and west by the mountainous Ghats. These slopes are forested, catching the full force of the monsoon winds which bring rains from the Indian Ocean. For most of the year India is extremely hot and dry. Indian Ocean nations include the beautiful, tropical island of **Sri Lanka** and a chain of very low coral islands, the **Maldives**.

Advanced civilizations had developed around the river Indus by about 2500BC, and great religions grew up in India over the ages, including Hinduism, Buddhism and Sikhism. Invaders and traders brought Islam to the region. India today is a fascinating mixture of cultures, with over 800 different languages and dialects. There are many different customs, dress and foods. Spicy dishes from India are now popular everywhere. The Indian sub-continent has a vast population, with many hungry mouths to feed. Many people make their living by farming, growing wheat, rice, millet, sugar-cane, coconut and tea. Most industries are based in the highly populated cities of India and Pakistan.

Himalayan peaks

Breathtaking Mount Makalu, on the border between Nepal and China, rises to 8,470 metres above sea level. Eighty-eight percent of the world's mountains over 7,315 metres rise within the Himalaya-Karakoram ranges, many of them in the kingdom of Nepal.

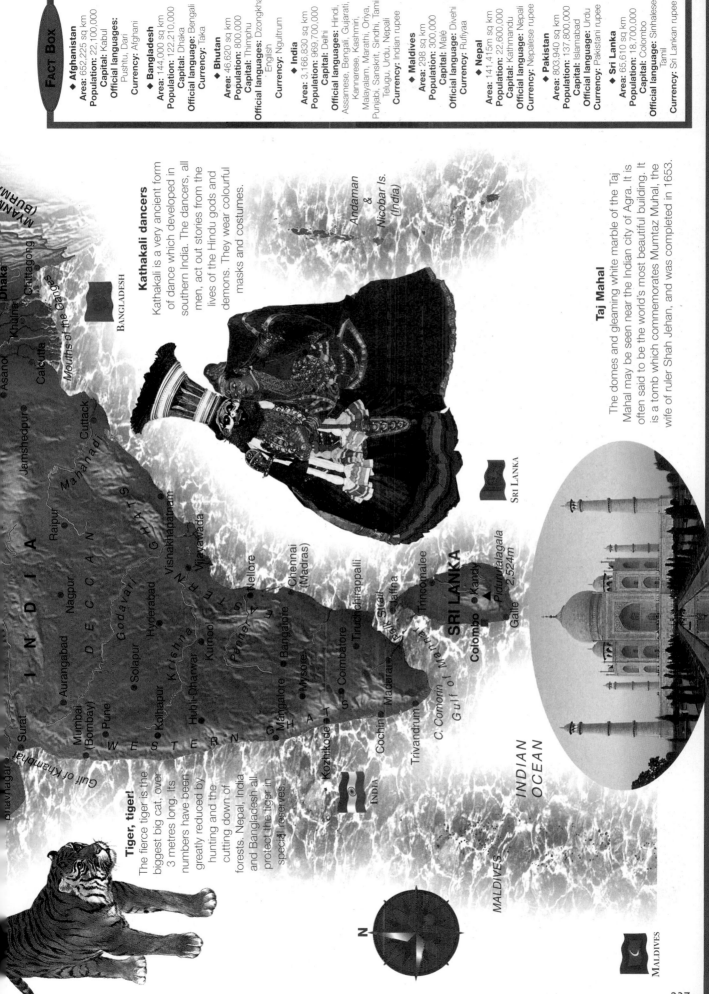

◆ Afghanistan
Area: 652,225 sq km
Population: 22,100,000
Capital: Kabul
Official languages: Pushtu, Dari
Currency: Afghani

◆ Bangladesh
Area: 144,000 sq km
Population: 122,210,000
Capital: Dhaka
Official language: Bengali
Currency: Taka

◆ Bhutan
Area: 46,620 sq km
Population: 800,000
Capital: Thimphu
Official languages: Dzongkha, English
Currency: Ngultrum

◆ India
Area: 3,166,830 sq km
Population: 969,700,000
Capital: Delhi
Official languages: Hindi, Assamese, Bengali, Gujarati, Kannarese, Kashmiri, Malayalam, Marathi, Oriya, Punjabi, Sanskrit, Sindhi, Tamil, Telugu, Urdu, Nepali
Currency: Indian rupee

◆ Maldives
Area: 298 sq km
Population: 300,000
Capital: Malé
Official language: Divehi
Currency: Rufiyaa

◆ Nepal
Area: 141,415m sq km
Population: 22,600,000
Capital: Kathmandu
Official language: Nepali
Currency: Nepalese rupee

◆ Pakistan
Area: 803,940 sq km
Population: 137,800,000
Capital: Islamabad
Official language: Urdu
Currency: Pakistani rupee

◆ Sri Lanka
Area: 65,610 sq km
Population: 18,700,000
Capital: Colombo
Official language: Sinhalese, Tamil
Currency: Sri Lankan rupee

Kathakali dancers

Kathakali is a very ancient form of dance which developed in southern India. The dancers, all men, act out stories from the lives of the Hindu gods and demons. They wear colourful masks and costumes.

Taj Mahal

The domes and gleaming white marble of the Taj Mahal may be seen near the Indian city of Agra. It is often said to be the world's most beautiful building. It is a tomb which commemorates Mumtaz Muhal, the wife of ruler Shah Jehan, and was completed in 1653.

Tiger, tiger!

The fierce tiger is the biggest big cat, over 3 metres long. Its numbers have been greatly reduced by hunting and the cutting down of forests. Nepal, India and Bangladesh all protect the tiger in special reserves.

237

CHINA AND ITS NEIGHBOURS

CHINA is the world's third largest country in area, and has a higher population than any other. It is bordered by the world's highest mountains, by deserts and by tropical seas.

Most people live in the big industrial cities of the south and east and on the fertile plains around two great rivers, the Huang He and the Chiang Jiang. Crops include wheat, maize, tea, sugar-cane and rice. Rice is eaten with almost every meal. Chinese civilization dates back over thousands of years. Chinese inventions included paper and gunpowder and Chinese crafts included the making of fine porcelain and silk. Since 1949 China has been ruled by its Communist Party, but its politics are no longer really socialist. Its economy has become one of the most important in the Pacific region, and in 1997 it took back the territory of Hong Kong, an international centre of business which had been a British colony. China also claims the island of **Taiwan**, which is still governed independently by Chinese nationalists who lost power in 1949.

The **Korean peninsula** saw bitter fighting between 1950 and 1953, when Korea divided into two nations, North and South. These countries remain bitter enemies today. South Korea has become an important industrial power.

Far to the north the Mongol peoples live in the independent republic of **Mongolia**. This includes the barren Gobi desert and remote grasslands.

KAZAKHSTAN

Ulaangom

Fuhai · Hovd

·Karamay

Ebinur Hu

·Yining Kuytun D z u n g a r i a

Ürümqi

·Ham

KYRGYZSTAN

T I A N S H A N

Bosten Lake Turfan Depres

·Aksu

Kashi

TAKLIMAKAN DESERT

Yu

ALTUN SHAN

·Hotan

K U N L U N S H A N

▲Mt. K2

KARAKORAM

PLATEAU OF TIBET

Siling Lake TANGGULA

Tangra Lake

Nam Lake

INDIA

Lhasa

Mt. Everest ·Xigaze
▲ 8,848 m

NEPAL

M

A L A Y A

BHUTAN

The Great Wall
A defensive wall runs across the north of China for about 6,000 kilometres, with many extra twists and turns. It was started in about 246 BC and added to over hundreds of years.

Temple of Heaven
Tiantan, the Temple of Heaven in Beijing, is a beautiful group of buildings first raised in 1420. The Chinese emperors used to come here to pray for a good harvest.

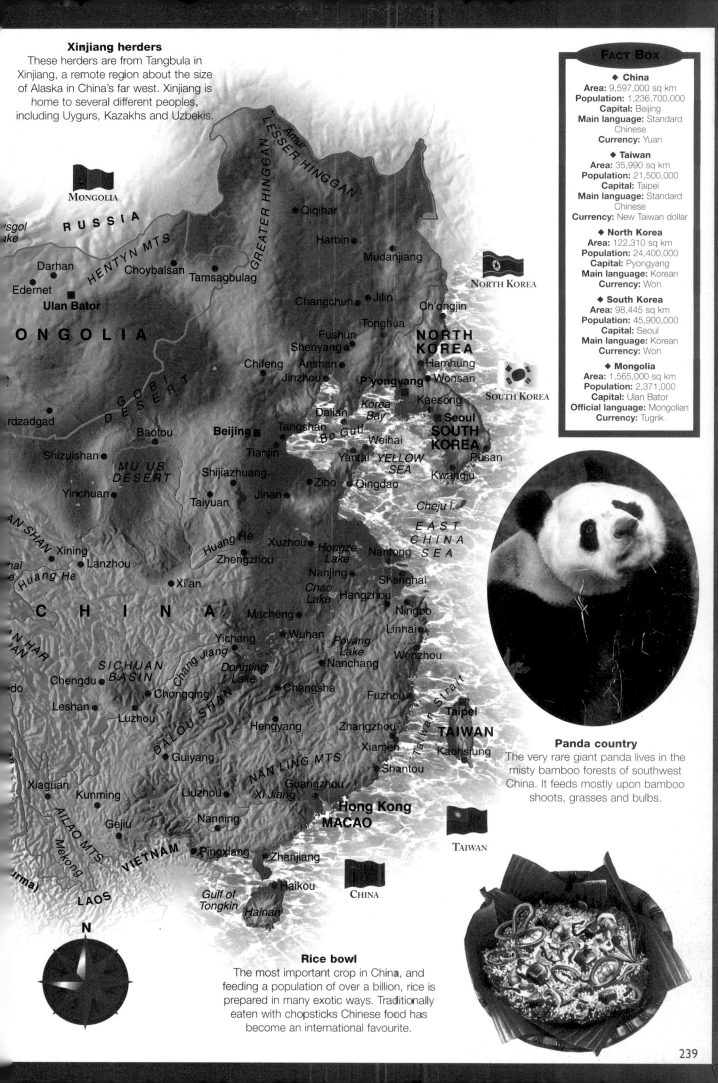

Xinjiang herders
These herders are from Tangbula in Xinjiang, a remote region about the size of Alaska in China's far west. Xinjiang is home to several different peoples, including Uygurs, Kazakhs and Uzbekis.

MONGOLIA

RUSSIA

HENTYN MTS.

Darhan
Edernet
Choybalsan
Tamsagbulag
Ulan Bator

LESSER HINGGAN

GREATER HINGGAN

Amur

Qiqihar

Harbin

Mudanjiang

NORTH KOREA

MONGOLIA

GOBI DESERT

rdzadgad

sgol ake

Changchun
Jilin
Tonghua
Fushun
Shenyang
Chifeng
Anshan
Jinzhou
Ch'ongjin

NORTH KOREA

Hamhung
Wonsan
P'yongyang
Kaesong

SOUTH KOREA

Baotou
Beijing
Tangshan
Dalian
Korea Bay
Bo Gulf
Weihai

Shizuishan
MU US DESERT
Tianjin
Yantai
Seoul
SOUTH KOREA

Yinchuan
Shijiazhuang
Zibo
Qingdao
YELLOW SEA
Pusan
Kwangju

Taiyuan
Jinan

Cheju I.

EAST CHINA SEA

AN SHAN
Xining
Huang He
Lanzhou
Xi'an

hai

Huang He
Xuzhou
Zhengzhou
Hongze Lake
Nantong
Nanjing
Chao Lake
Shanghai
Hangzhou

C H I N A

Macheng
Ningbo
Linhai

N HAR AN

Yichang
Wuhan
Poyang Lake
Wenzhou

SICHUAN BASIN
Chang Jiang
Dongting Lake
Nanchang

Chengdu
Chongqing
Changsha

do
Leshan
Luzhou
DALOU SHAN
Hengyang
Fuzhou
Zhangzhou
Taipei
TAIWAN

Guiyang
NAN LING MTS.
Xiamen
Kaohsiung

Xiaguan
Kunming
Liuzhou
Xi Jiang
Shantou

AILAO MTS.
Gejiu
Nanning
Guangzhou
Hong Kong
MACAO

TAIWAN

Mekong
VIETNAM
Pingxiang
Zhanjiang

CHINA

urma)
LAOS
Haikou
Gulf of Tongkin
Hainan

Panda country
The very rare giant panda lives in the misty bamboo forests of southwest China. It feeds mostly upon bamboo shoots, grasses and bulbs.

N

Rice bowl
The most important crop in China, and feeding a population of over a billion, rice is prepared in many exotic ways. Traditionally eaten with chopsticks Chinese food has become an international favourite.

JAPAN

JAPAN is made up of over 3,000 islands, and these stretch for about 3,000 kilometres from north to south on the northwest rim of the Pacific Ocean.

The chief islands are called Hokkaido, Honshu, Shikoku and Kyushu. The islands extend from the tropical south to the chilly north, where winter snowfalls can be heavy. The region is a danger zone for earthquakes and Japan's highest mountain, Fuji, is a volcano.

The snow-covered slopes of Mount Fuji have been a favourite subject for Japanese artists over the years. Japan has a long history of excellence in art, theatre, poetry, architecture and pottery. Japanese civilization dates back over 2,000 years. The country has been ruled by emperors and, during the Middle Ages, it was fought over by powerful warlords and bands of knights called samurai. Faiths include Buddhism and Shinto, the country's traditional religion.

Japan is very mountainous and so land that is suitable for farming is very precious. Japanese farmers grow rice, tea and fruit and the country also has a large fishing fleet. Many meals are based on rice or fish. Japan has very few natural resources. Even so, over the last 50 years Japan has become a leading world producer of cars, televisions and other electrical goods.

The mountains also limit the spread of housing and so Japan's cities are mostly crowded on to the strip of flat land around the coast. Tokyo has spread out to join up with neighbouring cities, and now has a population of over 25 million.

The Japanese people make up 99 percent of the country's population. The remainder includes Koreans and the Ainu of the far north, who may be descended from the first people to inhabit Japan.

FACT BOX

◆ **Japan**
Area: 369,700 sq km
Population: 126,100,000
Capital: Tokyo
Main language: Japanese
Currency: Yen

Mount Fuji

The beautiful peak of Mount Fuji, to the southwest of Tokyo, is a national symbol and, traditionally, a sacred mountain.

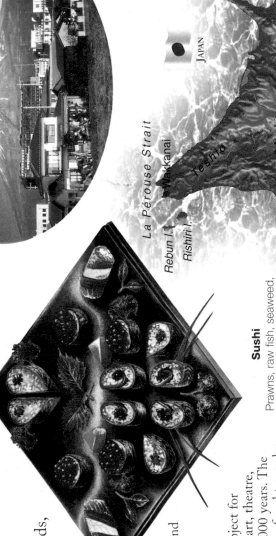

Sushi

Prawns, raw fish, seaweed, pickles and vegetables are used to make these tasty snacks. Like most Japanese dishes, they are served with rice. Japanese food is often beautifully arranged and thoughtfully served.

Tea time

Tea is harvested on the inland slopes. The Japanese are great tea-drinkers and have an ancient ceremony

Kuril Is. (Russia)

JAPAN

H o k k a i d o

La Pérouse Strait

Rebun I.
Rishiri I.
Wakkanai
Teshio
Asahigawa
Asahi/Mt 2,290 m
Obihiro
Kushiro
Ishikari
Ishikari Bay
Otaru
Sapporo
Muroran
Uchiura Bay
Erimo Cape

Tsugaru Strait
Hakodate
Hirosaki
Aomori
Mutsu Bay
Hachinohe
Kita
Morioka
Akita

S E A
O F
J A P A N

Itsukushima, Japan

Japan has many ancient Shinto shrines and Buddhist temples and many of these are set in beautiful scenery or gardens. Japan has always produced very simple and beautiful architecture and design.

Sumo wrestlers

The ancient sport of sumo is still very popular in Japan. Super heavyweight wrestlers aim to ground their opponents or force them out of the ring. There are long ceremonies before each contest.

A Shinto wedding

Dressed in her beautiful silk robe, or kimono, a Japanese bride sits next to her new husband, who also wears traditional costume. The wedding has been a Shinto ceremony. Shinto is an ancient Japanese faith which honours ancestors and the spirits of nature.

Ride the Bullet

Japan's Bullet Train offers one of the world's most famous passenger express services. It speeds across the country, linking the capital, Tokyo, with other large cities.

JAPAN

JAPANESE ALPS

Shinano

Abukuma

PACIFIC OCEAN

Honshu

Shikoku

Kyushu

Inland Sea

Suo Sea

Bungo Channel

Kii Channel

Sagami Bay

Biwa Lake

N

Sendai
Yamagata
Niigata
Fukushima
Koriyama
Iwaki
Hitachi
Mito
Nagaoka
Sado
Toyama
Kanazawa
Ueda
Matsumoto
Utsunomiya
Takasaki
Chiba
Tokyo
Kawasaki
Yokohama
Kofu
Mt. Fuji 3,776 m
Shizuoka
O-shima
Miyake I.
Hachijo I.
Fukui
Gifu
Takefu
Nagoya
Toyota
Hamamatsu
Matsusaka
Kyoto
Kobe
Osaka
Sakai
Wakayama
Oki Is.
Matsue
Okayama
Hiroshima
Takamatsu
Tokushima
Matsuyama
Kochi
Tsushima
Kitakyushu
Fukuoka
Omuta
Kumamoto
Miyazaki
Sasebo
Nagasaki
Amakusa Is.
Sendai
Koshiki Is.
Kagoshima
Tanega
Yaku

241

SOUTHEAST ASIA

MYANMAR is a beautiful land lying between the hill country of India and China. It is crossed by the great Irrawaddy river, which flows south into the Indian Ocean. To the southeast is **Thailand**, a country green with rice fields and teak forests. To the west lie the lands once known as Indo-China – **Laos**, **Cambodia** and, on the long Mekong River, **Vietnam**.

Linked to the Asian mainland by a narrow isthmus, or strip of land, is **Malaysia**. This country also takes up the northern part of the island of Borneo, which it shares with the small oil-rich state of **Brunei**. Malaysia produces rubber, rice, tea and palm oil. Kuala Lumpur is a growing centre of international business with the 452 metre-high Petronas Towers, the world's highest building. **Singapore**, a small independent city state built on the islands across the Johor Strait, is another leader in the business world.

Indonesia makes up the world's largest island chain. It covers over 13,600 islands, which include Sumatra, Java, southern Borneo, Bali and Irian Jaya (the western half of New Guinea). Another large island chain, the **Philippines**, lie between the Pacific and the South China Sea.

All the islands bordering the Pacific Ocean lie in a danger zone for earthquakes and volcanoes. The region as a whole has a warm, often humid, climate, with monsoon winds bringing heavy rains. Southeast Asia's dwindling tropical forests are a last reserve for the region's rich wildlife, such as enormous butterflies and giant apes called orang-utans.

Many different peoples live in Southeast Asia, including Burmese, Thais, Vietnamese and Filippinos. There are also many people of Chinese and Indian descent. Buddhism is a major faith in the region. Most Indonesians are Muslims and the Philippines are largely Roman Catholic. During the last 50 years Southeast Asia has been torn apart by wars. The region now looks forward to a period of peace.

The face of a demon
This fierce-looking demon guards the gate of the Grand Palace in Bangkok, the capital of Thailand. Many tourists come to this kingdom, once known as Siam, to see its ancient temples and enjoy its beautiful scenery and beaches.

A dome of gold
The fantastic roofs of Shwe Dagon pagoda shimmer with gold. This holy site is in Yangon, capital city of Myanmar or Burma. The pagoda honours Gautama Buddha, the founder of the Buddhist faith.

Javanese carving
These beautiful figures, carved from stone, decorate Barobodur, on the island of Java. This 9th-century temple is the most splendid in Indonesia. Its carvings show scenes from the life of the Buddha.

PHILIPPINES

Laoag
Luzon
Mt. Pinatubo ▲
■ Manila
Mindoro
PHILIPPINES
Panay
Iloilo
Tacloban
Palawan
Negros
Cebu City
Bohol
BRUNEI
SULU SEA
Mindanao
Mt. Kinabalu 4,094 m ▲
Zamboanga
Davao
Mt. Apo 2,954 m ▲
Sandakan
SABAH
INDONESIA
ndar eri awan
RUNEI
CELEBES SEA
RWAK
Manado
MOLUCCA SEA
NEO
Halmahera
as
Balikpapan
Palu
Moluccas
Sorong
Jayapura
Barito
Sulawesi
CERAM SEA
IRIAN JAYA
I N D O N E S I A
Seram
Buru
Ambon
Puncak Jaya 5,030m ▲
NEW GUINEA
njarmasin
Ujung Pandang
Aru Is.
PAPUA NEW GUINEA
A
Baubau
BANDA SEA
Digul
FLORES SEA
Wetar
Tanimbar Islands
urabaya
Lombok
Flores
ng Bali
Sumbawa
Ende
Timor
Sumba
Kupang

Floating market
At a Thai market, fruit, vegetables or fish may be sold from small boats. These women traders wear broad-brimmed straw hats to protect them from the tropical sun and the heavy monsoon rains.

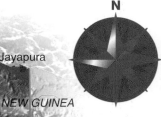

N

Kuala Lumpur
High-rise buildings are influenced by traditional styles in Kuala Lumpur, capital of Malaysia. 'KL' is one of the most important centres of industry, and business in Southeast Asia.

Komodo dragon
Meet the biggest lizard in the world, 3 metres long and weighing in at up to 136 kilograms. It is found on four small islands in Indonesia, called Rintja, Flores, Padar and Komodo.

243

NORTH AND WEST AFRICA

THE SAHARA IS THE WORLD'S LARGEST DESERT, made up of over 9 million square kilometres of baking hot sand, gravel and rock.

Its northern fringes, occupied by **Morocco**, **Algeria**, **Tunisia** and **Libya**, run into the milder, more fertile lands of the Mediterranean coast and the Atlas mountain ranges. They are home to Arabs and Berbers.

Deserts stretch from the Sahara eastwards to **Egypt** and the Red Sea. In ancient times one of the greatest civilizations the world has seen grew up in Egypt. Then as now, the country depended on water from the world's longest

Water for sale

A Berber water seller walks the streets of Marrakech, in Morocco, offering metal cups to passers-by.

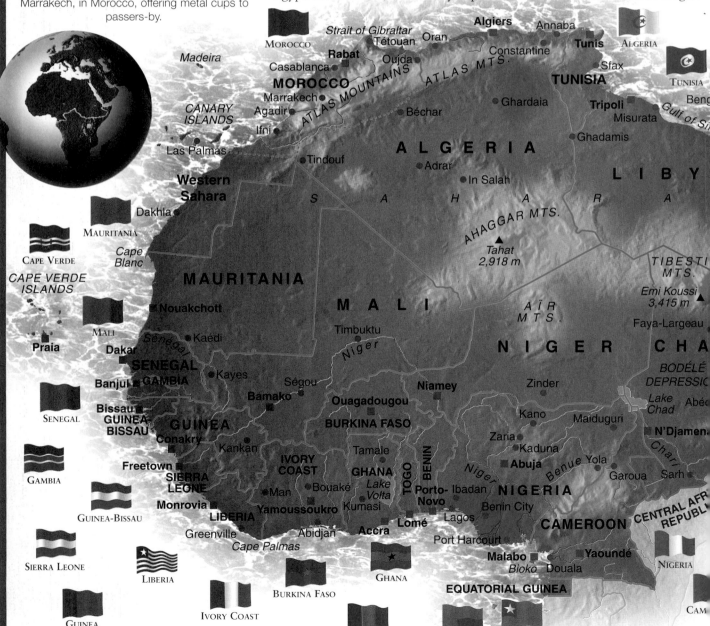

MOROCCO

Madeira

Strait of Gibraltar

Tétouan · Oran

Algiers · Annaba

ALGERIA

Rabat · Oujda

Casablanca

Constantine

Tunis · ALGERIA

MOROCCO

Marrakech · Ghardaia

Sfax

TUNISIA

TUNISIA

CANARY ISLANDS

Agadir

Béchar

Tripoli · Beng

Misurata

Ifni

Las Palmas

Tindouf

A L G E R I A

Ghadamis

Gulf of Sir

Adrar

L I B Y

Western Sahara

In Salah

Dakhla

S A H A R A

MAURITANIA

Cape Blanc

AHAGGAR MTS.

▲ Tahat 2,918 m

TIBESTI MTS.

CAPE VERDE

CAPE VERDE ISLANDS

MAURITANIA

M A L I

AÏR MTS.

Emi Koussi 3,415 m ▲

Faya-Largeau

Nouakchott

Timbuktu

MALI

Senegal · Kaédi

Niger

N I G E R

CHA

Praia

Dakar

SENEGAL

Kayes

Ségou

Niamey

Zinder

BODÉLÉ DEPRESSIC

Lake Chad · Abéc

Banjul · GAMBIA

Bamako

Ouagadougou

Kano

Maiduguri

SENEGAL

GUINEA-BISSAU

Bissau

GUINEA

Conakry

Kankan

BURKINA FASO

Zaria

Kaduna

N'Djamen

GAMBIA

Freetown

SIERRA LEONE

Man

IVORY COAST

Tamale

GHANA

Lake Volta

TOGO

BENIN

Porto-Novo

Abuja

Benue · Yola

NIGERIA

Garoua · Sarh

GUINEA-BISSAU

Monrovia

LIBERIA

Yamoussoukro

Bouaké

Kumasi

Ibadan

Benin City

CAMEROON

CENTRAL AFR REPUBL

SIERRA LEONE

Greenville

Cape Palmas

Abidjan

Accra

Lomé

Lagos

Port Harcourt

LIBERIA

GHANA

BURKINA FASO

Malabo

Bioko · Douala

Yaoundé

NIGERIA

GUINEA

IVORY COAST

EQUATORIAL GUINEA

CAM

CHAD

BENIN

TOGO

river, the Nile. This flows north to the Mediterranean from the mountains of **Ethiopia** and the swamps of southern **Sudan**, Africa's largest country.

The region south of the Sahara is known as the Sahel. It includes **Senegal**, **Mauritania**, **Mali**, **Niger**, **Burkina Faso** and **Chad**. The people include the Fulani, Kanuri and Hausa. The thin grasslands of the Sahel allow cattle herding, but droughts are common and the desert is spreading. Many people are very poor.

Thirteen nations border the great bulge of the West African coast, around the Gulf of Guinea. The coastal strip is made up of lagoons and long sandy beaches fringed with palm trees. Inland there is a belt of forest, which rises to dry, sandy plateaus and semi-desert in the far north. West African history tells of African kingdoms and empires which grew up here long ago, but also of the cruel slave trade across the Atlantic, which lasted from the 1500s to the 1800s. In the 1800s, large areas of West Africa became colonies of Britain and France. Today these lands are independent. The region has rich resources, including oil and diamonds.

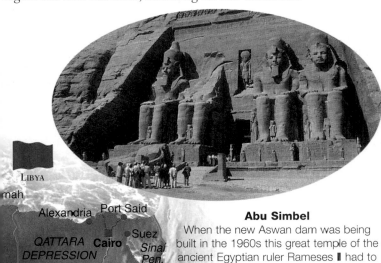

Abu Simbel
When the new Aswan dam was being built in the 1960s this great temple of the ancient Egyptian ruler Rameses II had to be moved stone-by-stone

LIBYA

nah
Alexandria Port Said
QATTARA Cairo Suez
DEPRESSION Sinai Pen.
Asyût
Qena
E G Y P T
EGYPT
Lake Nasser Aswân
N
Nubian Desert Port Sudan
Merowe
S U D A N
Atbara
Kassala ERITREA
Omdurman ERITREA Asmara
Khartoum Aksum DJIBOUTI
El Obeid ETHIOPIAN DJIBOUTI
Jl Marrah Kosti Lake Gonder PLATEAU Djibouti
3,088 Tana Debre Markos
SUDD Addis Ababa
White Nile Gore ETHIOPIA Ogaden
Webe Shebele
RIFT VALLEY
SOMALIA
Nimule
UGANDA KENYA
CHAD
SUDAN

CENTRAL, EASTERN & SOUTHERN AFRICA

CENTRAL AFRICA is dominated by the river Congo, which flows through hot and humid rainforest to the Atlantic Ocean. The great river winds through the **Democratic Republic of the Congo**, and the network of waterways which drain into it provide useful transport routes for riverboats and canoes.

A long crack in the Earth's crust, the Great Rift Valley, runs all the way down **East Africa**. Its route is marked by volcanoes and lakes. Some East African mountains remain snow-capped all year round, even though they are on the Equator. The highest of these is Kilimanjaro, at 5,950 metres. It looks out over savanna, grasslands dotted with trees. Huge herds of wildlife roam these plains. Zebra, giraffe, elephants and lions are protected within national parks. The Indian Ocean coast includes white beaches and coral islands. Mombasa, Dar-es-Salaam and Maputo are major ports.

In southern Africa the Drakensberg mountains descend to grassland known as veld. There are harsh deserts too, the Kalahari and the Namib. The **Republic of South Africa** is one of the most powerful countries in Africa. It has ports at Durban and Capetown.

Central and southern Africa are rich in mineral resources, including gold, diamonds and copper. Eastern and southern Africa are important farming regions, raising cattle and producing coffee, vegetables, tropical fruits, tobacco, and grape vines.

African kingdoms flourished in the Congo region in the Middle Ages and the stone ruins of Great Zimbabwe recall gold traders of long ago. Today the region is home to hundreds of African peoples with many different languages and cultures.

Magnificent Masai
This young Masai girl wears her traditional beaded necklace and headdress. These noble, nomadic people herd cattle and live mainly in Kenya and Tanzania.

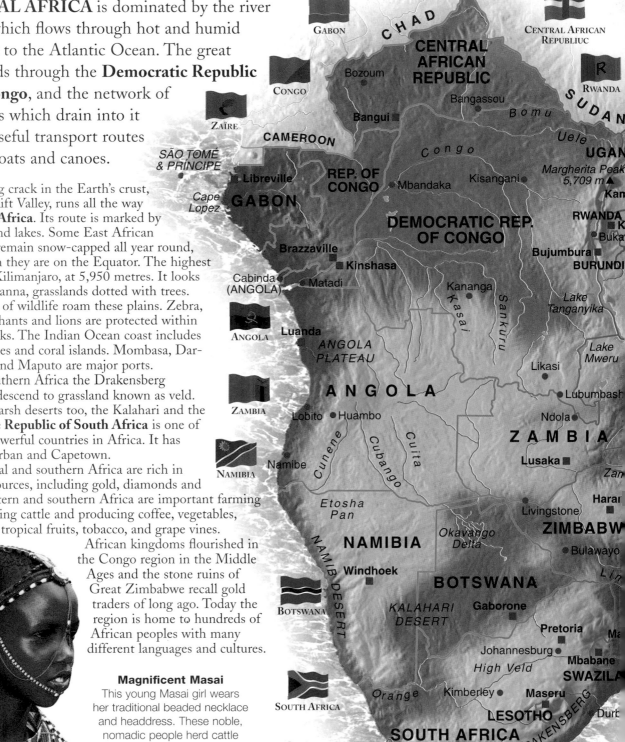

La Digue, Seychelles
Over 100 islands make up the Seychelles. La Digue is only 15 square kilometres in area, but the third most populated.

Sting in the tail
Scorpions always look threatening. The curled-forward tail contains a sting which can be deadly. They eat insects and other animals which they catch with their claws. They are most common in desert areas.

FACT BOX

◆ **Central African Republic**
Area: 624,975 sq km
Population: 3,300,000
Capital: Bangui
Main language: French
Currency: Franc CFA

◆ **Gabon**
Area: 267,665 sq km
Population: 1,200,000
Capital: Libreville
Main language: French
Currency: Franc CFA

◆ **Republic of Congo**
Area: 342,000 sq km
Population: 2,500,000
Capital: Brazzaville
Main language: French
Currency: Franc CFA

◆ **Democratic Republic of Congo (Zaïre)**
Area: 2,345,410 sq km
Population: 46,500,000
Capital: Kinshasa
Main language: French
Currency: Zaïre

◆ **Rwanda**
Area: 26,330 sq km
Population: 6,900,000
Capital: Kigali
Main languages: Kinyarwanda, French
Currency: Rwanda franc

◆ **Burundi**
Area: 27,835 sq km
Population: 5,900,000
Capital: Bujumbura
Main languages: Kirundi, French
Currency: Burundi franc

◆ **Uganda**
Area: 236,580 sq km
Population: 22,000,000
Capital: Kampala
Main language: English
Currency: Uganda shilling

◆ **Kenya**
Area: 582,645 sq km
Population: 28,200,000
Capital: Nairobi
Main languages: Swahili, English
Currency: Kenya shilling

◆ **Somalia**
Area: 630,000 sq km
Population: 9,500,000
Capital: Mogadishu
Main languages: Somali, Arabic
Currency: Somali shilling

◆ **Tanzania**
Area: 939,760 sq km
Population: 29,100,000
Capital: Dodoma
Main languages: Swahili, English
Currency: Tanzanian shilling

◆ **Seychelles**
Area: 404 sq km
Population: 100,000
Capital: Victoria
Official languages: English, French, Creole
Currency: Seychelles rupee

◆ **Comoros**
Area: 1,860 sq km
Population: 600,000
Capital: Moroni
Official languages: Arabic, French
Currency: Comorian franc

◆ **Mauritius**
Area: 1,865 sq km
Population: 1,100,000
Capital: Port Louis
Official language: English

◆ **Madagascar**
Area: 594,180 sq km
Population: 15,200,000
Capital: Antananarivo
Official languages: Malagasy, French
Currency: Malagasy franc

◆ **Mozambique**
Area: 784,755 sq km
Population: 16,500,000
Capital: Maputo
Official language: Portuguese
Currency: Metical

◆ **Malawi**
Area: 94,080 sq km
Population: 9,500,000
Capital: Lilongwe
Official language: Chichewa, English
Currency: Kwacha

◆ **Zambia**
Area: 752,615 sq km
Population: 9,200,000
Capital: Lusaka
Official language: English
Currency: Kwacha

◆ **Zimbabwe**
Area: 390,310 sq km
Population: 11,500,000
Capital: Harare
Official language: English
Currency: Zimbabwe dollar

◆ **Botswana**
Area: 575,000 sq km
Population: 1,500,000
Capital: Gaborone
Official language: English
Currency: Pula

◆ **Lesotho**
Area: 30,345 sq km
Population: 2,100,000
Capital: Maseru
Official languages: Sesotho, English
Currency: Loti

◆ **Swaziland**
Area: 17,365 sq km
Population: 1,000,000
Capital: Mbabane
Official languages: Swazi, English
Currency: Lilangeni

◆ **South Africa**
Area: 1,220,845 sq km
Population: 44,500,000
Capitals: Pretoria, Cape Town
Official languages: Afrikaans, English, Ndebele, Sesotho, Swazi, Tsonga, Tswana, Venda, Xhodsa, Zulu
Currency: Rand

◆ **Namibia**
Area: 824,295 sq km
Population: 1,600,000
Capital: Windhoek
Official language: English
Currency: Namibian dollar

◆ **Angola**
Area: 1,246,700 sq km
Population: 11,500,000
Capital: Luanda
Official language: Portuguese
Currency: Kwanza

AUSTRALIA

THIS COUNTRY is the size of a continent, a huge mass of land surrounded by ocean. The heart of **Australia** is a vast expanse of baking desert, salt pans, shimmering plains and dry scrubland. Ancient, rounded rocks glow in the morning and evening sun.

These barren lands are fringed by grasslands, tropical forests, creeks and fertile farmland. In the far east is the Great Dividing Range, which rises to the high peaks of the Australian Alps. The southeast is crossed by the Murray and Darling rivers. The Great Barrier Reef, the world's largest coral reef, stretches for over 2,000 kilometres off the eastern coast, while the island of Tasmania lies to the south across the Bass Strait.

Most Australians don't live in the 'outback', the dusty back country with its huge sheep and cattle stations and its mines. They live in big coastal cities such as Brisbane, Sydney, Adelaide and Perth. There they enjoy a high standard of living, an outdoor lifestyle, sunshine and surfing.

To the many people who in recent years have come from Europe and Asia to settle in Australia, this seems like a new country. However it is really a very ancient land, cut off from other parts of the world so long that it has many animals seen nowhere else on Earth, such as kangaroos, echidnas and platypuses.

Australia has probably been home to Aboriginal peoples for over 50,000 years. European settlement began in 1788, when the British founded a prison colony at Botany Bay, near today's city of Sydney. Many Australians still like to keep in touch with British relatives and traditions, but the modern country follows its own path as one of the great economic powers of the Pacific region.

Opera on the harbour
Sydney's most famous landmark is its Opera House, built between 1959 and 1973. It rises from the blue waters of the harbour like a great sailing ship. Sydney, the capital of New South Wales, is Australia's biggest city with a population of about 3,700,000.

Christmas beetles
Australia and its surrounding islands are popuated by many weird and wonderful insects and beetles. These beetles are from Christmas Island.

Aboriginal art
An Aboriginal artist from Groote Eylandt, an island in the Gulf of Carpentaria, completes a painting on bark. Paintings by Australia's Aborigines are admired around the world. They often recall the ancient myths and legends of their people, with bold, swirling patterns or pictures of animals.

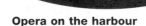

Bonapar'
Archip.
Broome
Fitzroy
Eighty Mile Beach
Port Hedland
De Grey
Barrow I.
Fortescue
Ashburton
Mt. Bruce
GIBSC
DESEF
Lake Macleod
Carnarvon
Murchison
Dirk Hartog I.
WESTERN AUSTRAL
Geraldton
Laverton
Kalgoorlie-Boulder
Perth
Fremantle
C. Naturaliste
Bunbury
Archipelago of Recherche
C. Leeuwin
Albany

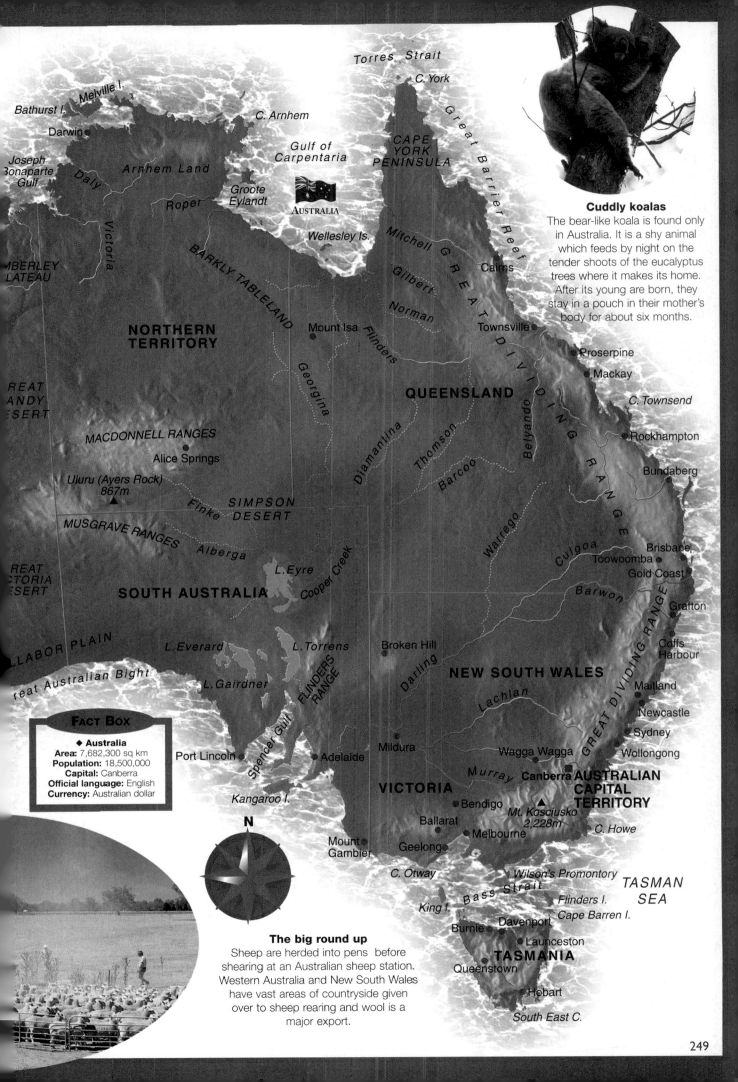

Torres Strait

C. York

Melville I.

Bathurst I.

Darwin

C. Arnhem

Gulf of Carpentaria

CAPE YORK PENINSULA

Great Barrier Reef

Joseph Bonaparte Gulf

Daly

Victoria

Arnhem Land

Roper

Groote Eylandt

AUSTRALIA

KIMBERLEY PLATEAU

Wellesley Is.

Mitchell

Cairns

GREAT

BARKLY TABLELAND

Gilbert

Norman

Mount Isa

Flinders

Townsville

GREAT SANDY DESERT

NORTHERN TERRITORY

Georgina

QUEENSLAND

Proserpine

Mackay

C. Townsend

Thomson

Belyando

Rockhampton

MACDONNELL RANGES

Alice Springs

Diamantina

Barcoo

Bundaberg

Uluru (Ayers Rock) 867m

SIMPSON DESERT

Finke

DIVIDING

MUSGRAVE RANGES

Alberga

L.Eyre

Cooper Creek

Warrego

Culgoa

Brisbane

Toowoomba

Gold Coast

GREAT VICTORIA DESERT

SOUTH AUSTRALIA

Barwon

RANGE

Grafton

L.Everard

L.Torrens

Broken Hill

Darling

NEW SOUTH WALES

Coffs Harbour

NULLABOR PLAIN

L.Gairdner

FLINDERS RANGE

Lachlan

Maitland

GREAT

Newcastle

Great Australian Bight

Spencer Gulf

Port Lincoln

Adelaide

Mildura

Wagga Wagga

Sydney

Wollongong

FACT BOX

◆ **Australia**
Area: 7,682,300 sq km
Population: 18,500,000
Capital: Canberra
Official language: English
Currency: Australian dollar

Murray

Canberra

AUSTRALIAN CAPITAL TERRITORY

Kangaroo I.

VICTORIA

Bendigo

Mt. Kosciusko 2,228m

C. Howe

Ballarat

Melbourne

N

Mount Gambier

Geelong

C. Otway

Wilson's Promontory

TASMAN SEA

Bass Strait

Flinders I.

King I.

Cape Barren I.

Davenport

Burnie

Launceston

The big round up
Sheep are herded into pens before
shearing at an Australian sheep station.
Western Australia and New South Wales
have vast areas of countryside given
over to sheep rearing and wool is a
major export.

TASMANIA

Queenstown

Hobart

South East C.

Cuddly koalas
The bear-like koala is found only
in Australia. It is a shy animal
which feeds by night on the
tender shoots of the eucalyptus
trees where it makes its home.
After its young are born, they
stay in a pouch in their mother's
body for about six months.

NEW ZEALAND AND THE PACIFIC

NEW ZEALAND LIES in the Pacific Ocean, about 1,600 kilometres to the east of Australia. It has a moist, mild climate and many unusual plants, birds and animals may be found there.

Most of its people live on North Island and South Island. These beautiful islands, divided by the Cook Strait, are the largest of several which are included within the country. North Island has volcanoes, hot springs and gushing geysers. South Island is dominated by the peaks and glaciers of the Southern Alps. It also has deep sea inlets called fiords and rolling grassy plains. New Zealand, with its sheep, cattle and fruit farms, has one of the most important economies in the Pacific region.

Papua New Guinea is another island nation, bordering Indonesian territory on the island of New Guinea. It also includes several chains of smaller islands. Many of its mountain regions, blanketed in tropical forests, were only opened up to the outside world in the 20th century. The country is rich in mineral resources and its fertile soils produce coffee, tea and rubber.

Strung out eastwards across the lonely Pacific Ocean are many scattered island chains and reefs. Small coral islands surround peaceful blue lagoons ringed with palm trees. The islanders may make their living by fishing, growing coconuts, mining or tourism. Many of the island groups have banded together to form independent nation states.

Peoples of the Pacific are of varied descent. Some are the descendants of European settlers – for example the British in New Zealand, or the French on New Caledonia or Tahiti. Fiji has a large population of Indian descent. The original peoples of the Pacific fall into three main groups. Melanesians, such as the Solomon Islanders, live in the western Pacific, while Micronesians live in the Caroline and Marshall Islands. The Polynesian peoples, brilliant seafarers, colonized vast areas of the ocean, from New Zealand to the Hawaiian Islands. The Maoris, who make up nine percent of New Zealand's population, are a Polynesian people who have kept and valued many of their ancient traditions.

MICRONESIA

SOLOMON ISLANDS

SEA OF JAPAN

Yellow Sea

East China Sea

SOUTH CHINA SEA

Philippine Sea

Northern Mariana Islands (USA)

Guam (USA)

Federated States of Micronesia

Palau

Celebes Sea

Papua New Guinea

Irian Jaya (Indonesia)

Solomon Islands

Arafura Sea Port Moresby

Coral Sea

AUSTRALIA

TASMAN SEA

New Guinea finery
Feathers and paint are worn by many young warriors at tribal gatherings and feasts in remote areas of Papua New Guinea. The country has a very rich culture with over 860 different languages.

Kiwi fruit
When farmers decided to grow this fruit in New Zealand, they decided to give it a local name to help sales. The kiwi is the national bird, and a nickname for a New Zealander.

BERING SEA

PAPUA NEW
GUINEA

PALAU

NORTH
PACIFIC
OCEAN

Midway Island
(USA)

Wake Island
(USA)

VANUATU

MARSHALL
ISLANDS

Hawaii (USA)

Marshall Island

KIRIBATI

Nauru

NAURU

Kiribati

Tuvalu

TUVALU

Samoa

American
Samoa

SAMOA

Vanuatu

Fiji

New Caledonia
(France)

Cook Islands
(New Zealand)

Tonga

FIJI

French
Polynesia

SOUTH
PACIFIC
OCEAN

Galapagos
(Ecuador)

Pitcairn Island
(UK)

TONGA

NEW
ZEALAND

Easter Island
(Chile)

NEW ZEALAND

FACT BOX

◆ **Papua New Guinea**
Area: 462,840 sq km
Population: 4,400,000
Capital: Port Moresby
Official language: English
Currency: Kina

◆ **New Zealand**
Area: 265,150 sq km
Population: 3,600,000
Capital: Auckland
Official language: English
Currency: New Zealand dollar

◆ **Palau**
Area: 490 sq km
Population: 16,000
Capital: Koror
Official languages: Palauan,
English
Currency: US dollar

◆ **Marshall Islands**
Area: 181 sq km
Population: 52,000
Capital: Majuro
Official language: Marshallese,
English
Currency: US dollar

◆ **Solomon Islands**
Area: 29,790 sq km
Population: 354,000
Capital: Honiara
Official language: English
Currency: Solomon Islands
dollar

◆ **Tuvalu**
Area: 25 sq km
Population: 13,000
Capital: Funafuti
Official languages: Tuvaluan,
English
Currency: Australian dollar

◆ **Kiribati**
Area: 684 sq km
Population: 75,000
Capital: Bairiki
Official language: English
Currency: Australian dollar

◆ **Nauru**
Area: 21 sq km
Population: 10,000
Capital: Yaren
Official language: Nauruan
Currency: Australian dollar

◆ **Fiji**
Area: 18,330 sq km
Population: 758,000
Capital: Suva
Official language: English
Currency: Fiji dollar

◆ **Tonga**
Area: 699 sq km
Population: 103,000
Capital: Nukualofa
Official languages: Tongan,
English
Currency: Pa'anga

◆ **Vanuatu**
Area: 14,765 sq km
Population: 156,000
Capital: Porta-Vila
Official languages: Bislama,
English, French
Currency: Vatu

◆ **Western Samoa**
Area: 2,840 sq km
Population: 170,000
Capital: Apia
Official languages: Samoan,
English
Currency: Tala

◆ **Federated States of
Micronesia**
Area: 702 sq km
Population: 114,000
Capital: Kolonia
Official language: English
Currency: US dollar

Easter Island
Hundreds of huge, mysterious stone heads tower above the hills of Easter Island, in the eastern Pacific. They were erected by Polynesians about 1,000 years ago. Today Easter Island is governed by Chile.

Gusher!
Steam bursts from volcanic rocks near Rotorua on North Island. New Zealand's geysers and hot springs are not just a tourist attraction. They are used to generate electricity.

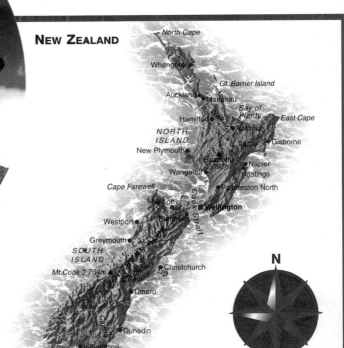

NEW ZEALAND

North Cape
Whangarei
Gt. Barrier Island
Auckland
Manukau
Bay of
Plenty
Hamilton
East Cape
Waikato
NORTH
ISLAND
Rotorua
Gisborne
New Plymouth
L. Taupo
Ruapehu
2,797m
Napier
Wanganui
Hastings
Cape Farewell
Palmerston North
Nelson
Wellington
Cook Strait
Westport
Blenheim
Greymouth
SOUTH
ISLAND
Christchurch
Mt. Cook 3,764m
Timaru
Dunedin
Invercargill
Foveaux Strait
Stewart Island

N

251

POLAR LANDS

THE NORTHERNMOST PART of our globe is called the Arctic. Within this bitterly cold region lie the northern borders of Alaska (part of the United States), Canada, Greenland (a self-governing territory of Denmark), Norway, Sweden, Finland and Russia.

However most of the area is covered by the Arctic Ocean, much of which is frozen solid all year round. At the centre of this great cap of ice is the North Pole. The **Arctic** supports a surprisingly wide selection of wildlife, including seals, walruses and polar bears. Peoples who have learned to live permanently in the far north include the Aleuts, the Inuit, the Saami, the Yakuts and the Chukchi. They have been joined in recent years by workers from the oil industry.

The only people to be found in **Antarctica**, at the other end of the globe, are scientists studying the weather and rocks of the coldest and windiest continent on Earth. The only other living things to survive here are the penguins which breed around the coast and the whales, birds and fishes of the Southern Ocean. The landmass is ringed by a shelf of ice, some of which breaks away to form massive icebergs in the spring. Inland there are mountain ranges and icy plains. The Antarctic winter takes place during the Arctic summer, and the Antarctic summer during the Arctic winter.

Various countries claim territory in Antarctica, and the continent is rich in minerals and fishing. However many scientists argue that this land should never be opened up to mining and industry, but left as the planet's last true wilderness.

Living in the Arctic
The Inuit peoples of northern Canada and Greenland have always lived by hunting and fishing and are experts at surviving in the harsh climate.

Arctic map labels: Yukon, Bering Strait, ALASKA (USA), CHUKCHI SEA, Ambarchik, Kolyma, Barrow, Pt. Barrow, EAST SIBERIAN SEA, Indigirka, RUSSIA, Mackenzie, BEAUFORT SEA, C.Bathurst, New Siberian Islands, Lena, CANADA, Banks Island, McClure Strait, ARCTIC OCEAN, LAPTEV SEA, Victoria Island, Norlvik, Queen Elizabeth Islands, North Magnetic Pole, Severnaya Zemlya, North Pole, Ellesmere Island, LINCOLN SEA, Franz Josef Land, Dikson, Yenl, Foxe Basin, Baffin Island, Novaya Zemlya, KARA SEA, Baffin Bay, Svalbard (Norway), BARENTS SEA, Pechora, GREENLAND (DENMARK), GREENLAND SEA, North Cape, Davis Strait, Murmansk, Godthåb, Denmark Strait, NORWEGIAN SEA, Archangel, ICELAND, Reykjavik

Antarctic map labels: S. Orkney Is, C. Norvegia, Maud Land, Enderby Land, S. Shetland Is, WEDELL SEA, Coats Land, Antarctic Peninsula, Palmer Archipelago, Palmer Land, Mac Robertson Land, Cape Darnley, Alexander I., Berkner I., Ronne Ice Shelf, PENSACOLA MTNS., PR. CHARLES MTNS., AMERICAN HIGHLAND, Charcot I., BELLINGHAUSEN SEA, Vinson Massif ▲5,410m, South Pole, GREATER ANTARCTICA, Queen Mary Land, Ellsworth Land, LESSER ANTARCTICA, TRANSANTARCTIC MTNS., Knox Coast, Thurston I., AMUNDSEN SEA, Mt. Kirkpatrick 4,528m ▲, Wilkes Land, Siple I., Marie Byrd Land, Ross Ice Shelf, Roosevelt I., Mt. Erebus 3,794m ▲, Victoria Land, ROSS SEA, George V Land, C. Adare, South Magnetic Pole

Antarctic melt
Each southern spring, the ice around Antarctica begins to melt, allowing ships to approach the ice shelves around this huge, frozen continent.

FACT BOX

◆ Arctic Circle
Area of ocean:
14,056,000 sq km

◆ Antarctic Circle
Area of land:
13,900,000 sq km

INDEX

motion 144–145
Mozambique 247
Mozart, Wolfgang Amadeus 116
Muhammad 176
muscular system 72, 76–77
music 116–117, 152
Muslim faith 184, 186, 236
    architecture 125
    Empire 176–177
Myanmar 242
myths 108–109

N
nails 74–75
Namibia 247
Native American people 180–181, 190
Nepal 236
nerves 72, 96–97
    senses 74–75, 92–93, 94–95
Netherlands 202–203
New Delhi 236
New York 223
New Zealand 188–189, 250–251
Newton, Isaac 144
Nicaragua 226
Nigeria 245
North America 180–181, 183, 220–226
Northern Ireland 205
Norway 201
nose 94

O
oceans 24–25
Oman 235
orbits 10–11
Ottawa 221

P
Pacific peoples 188–189
painting 122–123
Pakistan 236
Panama 226
Papua New Guinea 250–251
Paraguay 232
Paris 207
Peru 181, 229
Peter the Great 183
Philippines 243
Phoenicians 171
photography 120–121, 138–139
photosynthesis 44–45, 142–143
planets 8, 10–11
plant-eating mammals 62–63
plants 40–41, 42–43, 44–45, 46–47

poetry 111
Poland 214
politics 130–131
pollution 30–31, 69
Portugal 210–211
Prague 215
pyramids 168–169

R
radio 118–119
reflection 150–151
refraction 150–151
religions 113, 114, 126–127
    festivals 128–129
    wars 182
Renaissance 183
reproduction 87, 98–99
    animals 55, 56–57, 59, 61
    plants 44–45
reptiles 58–59
respiratory system 73, 80–81
revolutions 194–195
Reykjavik 200
rockets 14, 15
rocks 18–19, 20–21, 22–23
Roman Empire 106, 172–173
Romania 216–217
Russia 107, 183, 218
    Cold War 197
    Revolution 195
Rwanda 247

S
Sarajevo 216
satellites 14, 15, 164–165, 197
Saudi Arabia 234
Scandinavia 200–201
Scotland 204
screws 146–147
sculpture 122–123
semiconductors 154–155
senses 74–75, 92, 93, 94–95, 96–97
Shakespeare, William 113
sharks 55
shellfish 53
Sicily 213
sight 92–93
Silk Road 133, 179
Singapore 242
skeleton 72, 78–79
skin 74–75
Skopje 216
Slovak Republic 215
Slovenia 216

smell 94
snakes 58–59
Solar System 8, 12–13
solids 136–137
sound 116–117, 152–153
South Africa 247
South America 228–233
    civilizations 181
space exploration 14–15, 197
Spain 210–211
spiders 53
sponges 48, 49, 50–51
Sri Lanka 237
starfish 49, 50–51
stars 8–9, 10–11
Stockholm 201
stomach 82–83, 89
submarines 161
Sudan 245
Sumerians 106, 168–169
Sun, the 10–11, 16
sweat 74–75
Sweden 201
Switzerland 208
Syria 234

T
Tanzania 247
Tasmania 249
taste 94
tectonic plates 18, 21
teeth 82
telephones 165
telescopes 10–11
television 118–119, 151, 154
textiles 140–141
Thailand 242
theatre 112–113
toads 56–57
Tokyo 241
tongue 94
trade 132–133, 184, 186
traditions 128–129
trains 160–161, 191, 192
transport 160–161
Trinidad & Tobago 231
Tunisia 245
Turing, Alan 156
Turkey 234
    Çatal Hüyük 124–125, 168
Turkmenistan 18
turtles 58–59

ACKNOWLEDGEMENTS

The publishers wish to thank the following artists who have contributed to this book:
David Ashby, Mike Atkinson, Julian Baker, Andy Beckett, Martin Camm, Vanessa Card, Andrew Clark, Andrew Farmer, James Field, Wayne Ford, Chris Forsey, Jeremy Gower, Ron Hayward, Gary Hincks, Sally Holmes, Richard Hook, Rob Jakeway, John James, Roger Kent, Kuo Kang Chen, Stuart Lafford, Sally Launder, Alan Male, Janos Marffy, Rob McCaig, Roger Payne, Julie Pickering, Mel Pickering, Gillian Platt, Terry Riley, Martin Salisbury, Peter Sarson, Mike Saunders, Guy Smith, Roger Smith, Roger Stewart, Sue Stitt, Stephen Sweet, Michael Welply, Darrell Warner, Ross Watton, Mike White

The publishers wish to thank the following for supplying photographs for this book:
Page 11 (B/R) NASA; 12 (B/R) NASA; 15 (C,C/R) NASA; 17 (C/R) NASA; 18 (B/L) Frank Spooner Pictures, (B/R) NASA; 21 (C/L) Science Photo Library, (C/R) Science Photo Library; 23 (C/R) Oxford Scientific Films; 28 (C) Oxford Scientific Films; 29 (T/R) Oxford Scientific Films; 36 (T/R) Science Photo Library; 37 (C/R) Science Photo Library; 41 (B/R) Corbis; 51 (C) G.I.Bernard/Oxford Scientific Films; 57 (T/L) R.L.Manuel/Oxford Scientific Films; 66 (T/R) Remi Benali-Stephen Ferry-Life Magazine/Gamma-Liaison/Frank Spooner Pictures; 67 (C/R) Didier Lebrun/Photo News/Gamma/Frank Spooner Pictures; 69 (T) E.T.Archive; 75 (C) Science Photo Library; 77 (B/R) Science Photo Library; 85 (C) The Stock Market; 86 (B/L) The Stock Market; 87 (C/R) Science Photo Library; 89 (B/R) British Diabetics' Association; 92 (B/L) Science Photo Library; 95 (C/R) Science Photo Library; 107 (C/L) The British Museum/AKG; 111 (T/L) The British Library/E.T.Archive, (C) The Kobal Collection/E.T.Archive, (C/R) The Victoria and Albert Museum/E.T.Archive, (B) E.T.Archive; 113 (T/R) Dover Publications; 119 (B/L) Keith Bernstein/Frank Spooner Pictures; 121 (Gamma/Frank Spooner Pictures; 123 (T) Lah Weston, (C/R) Mark Beesley; 124 (B/R) Dover Publications; 126 (T) Cherry Williams; 129 (C) Neil Cooper/Panos Pictures; Page 137 (C) David Parker/Science Photo Library; 143 (T) Alfred Pasieka/Science Photo Library, (C) Novosti Press Agency/Science Photo Library; 154 (B/L) David Parker/Seagate Microelectronics Limited/Science Photo Library; 155 (C) Dixons; 158 (L) Mercedes Benz; 159 (C,T/R) Ford Motor Company; 161 (T,C/R) Brian Morrison; 162 (B) Dover Publications; 163 (B/L) Stansted Airport External Relations Department; 170 (C/L) Dover Publications; 171 (T/L) Mary Evans Picture Library; 177 (T/L) AKG; 178 (B/L) AKG; 179 (C/R) AKG; 191 (T/L) AKG; 194 (T/R) AKG; 197 (C) AKG.
All other photographs from Miles Kelly archives.